DESERTER

DESERTER

THE LAST UNTOLD STORY OF THE SECOND WORLD WAR

CHARLES GLASS

Harper
Press

HarperPress
An imprint of HarperCollins*Publishers*
77–85 Fulham Palace Road
London W6 8JB
www.harpercollins.co.uk

Published by Harper*Press* in 2013

I

A catalogue record for this book is
available from the British Library

ISBN 978-0-00-734592-2

Typeset by G&M Designs Limited,
Raunds, Northamptonshire
Printed in Great Britain by
Clays Ltd, St Ives plc

MIX
Paper from
responsible sources
FSC
www.fsc.org
FSC C007454

To two friends, brave American soldiers,
Private First Class Stephen J. Weiss
and the late Colonel Alfred E. Baker

During the Second World War, the United States awarded Private
Weiss the Bronze Star, three US battle stars, the Second World War
Victory Medal, Southern France D-Day Landing Citation, Combat
Infantry Badge and Good Conduct Medal. France named him *Officier*
of the *Légion d'Honneur* and gave him two *Croix de Guerre*, the
Médaille de la Résistance, the *Croix du Combatant*, the Vosges
Department Citizen of Honour Diploma and French citizenship.

During the Vietnam War, the United States awarded Colonel Baker, as
the Pennsylvania House of Representatives noted in his honour, 'the
Silver Star for gallantry in action, multiple awards of the Defense
Superior Service Medal, multiple awards of the Legion of Merit, three
awards of the Bronze Star, three awards of the Meritorious Service
Medal, four awards of the Purple Heart medal (for wounds received
in battle) and many other service and achievement medals'. At one
time, he was the most highly decorated veteran of the Vietnam War
era.

CONTENTS

I lack the guts to take being thought a coward.

Audie Murphy, *To Hell and Back* (Henry Holt, 1949)

INTRODUCTION

BY HIS OWN ADMISSION, Eddie Slovik was the unluckiest man alive. Nearly 50,000 American and 100,000 British soldiers deserted from the armed forces during the Second World War, but the twenty-five-year-old ex-convict from Detroit, Michigan, was the only one executed for it. Slovik's desertion in northern France on 9 October 1944 was atypical in that, while 80 per cent of deserters were frontline infantrymen escaping after long periods of continuous combat, he never fought a battle. Nor did he go on the run as most other deserters did. His mistake was to make clear that he preferred prison to battle. Rather than grant his wish, a court martial condemned him, in accordance with the Articles of War that then prescribed the forms of military justice, to 'death by musketry'.

Of the forty-nine Americans sentenced to death for desertion during the Second World War, Slovik was the only one whose appeal for commutation was rejected. The timing of his court martial, amid the November fighting in the Hürtgen Forest that caused 6,184 casualties among the 15,000 troops in Slovik's 28th Infantry Division, militated against clemency. So too did the coincidence in January 1945 of his appeal against the death sentence and the German counter-offensive known as the Battle of the Bulge, when the US Army in northern Europe was fighting for its own survival. It was not the moment for the Supreme Allied Commander, General Dwight Eisenhower, to be seen to condone desertion.

Correspondence among senior commanders documents their belief that Slovik's death was necessary to prevent others from following his example. They nonetheless decreed that his execution in the remote French village of Sainte-Marie-aux-Mines be conducted in secrecy. (Slovik, the condemned 'coward', died without pleading for his life or showing anything other than courage before the firing squad.) Even if soldiers at the front had known that the young private was shot for desertion on the morning of 31 January 1945, the Battle of the Bulge had by then ended in an Allied victory. The urgency for lethal deterrence had disappeared, as the Allied armies resumed the offensive that would topple the Third Reich four months later. Concealing the truth about Slovik's execution extended to informing his wife Antoinette only that he had died in the European Theater of Operations.

Journalist and novelist William Bradford Huie uncovered the cause of Slovik's death in 1948, but the issue remained so sensitive that he concealed the condemned man's identity in *Liberty* magazine as 'a twenty-five year old American white man – call him Lewis Simpson – a replacement in the 28th Division'. Huie's article raised fundamental questions about why only one deserter among thousands was put to death. It also cast doubt on the willingness of Americans to fight. Huie, who served in the United States Navy during the war, noted that psychiatrists had permitted 1,750,000 men, one out of every eight they examined, to avoid military service for 'reasons other than physical'. Despite the rigorous screening, soldiers suffered nervous breakdowns, mental trauma and 'battle fatigue' (also called 'battle exhaustion') that rendered them unfit for combat. Huie observed, 'During the Second World War approximately 38,000 officers and men – about 10 per cent were officers – were tried by army general courts-martial for seeking to evade hazardous duty by some dishonorable means.' Their sentences, apart from Slovik's, were less onerous than the hardships suffered by their comrades who fought on. Huie considered this an outrage: 'If a sound-bodied, sound-minded American soldier who deserts his comrades on the eve of battle deserves only comfortable detention, subsequent pardon, and a college education under the G.I. Bill of Rights, then why should any man ever again risk death in combat for this country?'

He added that 'by "abolishing cowardice" the psychiatrists had tended to relieve all Americans of the individual responsibility to fight.' Yet most soldiers did fight. Desertions were almost non-existent in the Pacific, where a man seeking to avoid danger had nowhere to hide. In Europe, the total that fled from the front rarely exceeded 1 per cent of manpower. However, it reached alarming proportions among the 10 per cent of the men in uniform who actually saw combat. Allied commanders debated means to staunch the flow. General George Patton wanted to shoot the 'cowards', and in Sicily he famously slapped a shell-shocked soldier whom he accused of malingering. Senior British commanders in North Africa and Italy pleaded with their government to restore the death penalty for desertion as in the First World War. Other commanders, whose views prevailed, favoured providing psychiatric as well as traditional medical care in forward aid stations. They recognized that the mind – subject to the daily threat of death, the concussion of aerial bombardment and high-velocity artillery, the fear of landmines and booby traps, malnutrition, appalling hygiene and lack of sleep – suffered wounds as real as the body's. Providing shattered men with counselling, hot food, clean clothes and rest was more likely to restore them to duty than threatening them with a firing squad.

Few deserters were cowards. Many broke under the strain of constant battle, having faced the Axis enemy without let-up for months at a time. Owing to the Allies' flawed system of replacing troops at the front, men were pushed beyond their limit. Poor leadership by undertrained junior officers, many of whom stayed back from combat, left young soldiers without inspiration to endure daily artillery barrages along often-static frontlines. High desertion rates in any company, battalion or division pointed to failures of command and logistics for which blame pointed to leaders as much as to the men who deserted. Unit cohesion was poor, as post-war studies demonstrated, because replacement soldiers were distributed individually to assorted companies and divisions rather than as bodies of men who knew and trusted one another. Some soldiers deserted when all the other members of their units had been killed and their own deaths appeared inevitable.

Those who showed the greatest sympathy to deserters were other frontline soldiers. They had, at one time or another, felt the temptation to opt out of the war through desertion, shooting themselves in the foot or lagging behind when ordered forward. It was a rare infantryman who attempted to prevent his comrades from leaving the line. The astounding fact is not that so many men deserted but that the deserters were so few.

Eddie Slovik's identity became public knowledge in 1954, when Huie published his well-researched *The Execution of Private Slovik*. Twenty years later, the actor Martin Sheen played Slovik in a television film of the same title. Sheen recited the actual words that Slovik himself uttered before his execution: 'They're not shooting me for deserting the United States Army, thousands of guys have done that. They just need to make an example out of somebody and I'm it because I'm an ex-con. I used to steal things when I was a kid, and that's what they are shooting me for. They're shooting me for the bread and chewing gum I stole when I was 12 years old.'

Eddie Slovik was the first American soldier executed for desertion since a Union Army firing squad shot one William Smitz of Company F, 90th Pennsylvania Volunteers, in 1865. (More than 300,000 troops deserted from the Union and Confederate Armies in the Civil War. Mark Twain famously deserted from both sides.) Slovik was not the only soldier to desert from the American armed forces between 1865 and 1945. Desertion was common in the post-Civil War Army, when many frontier troops had a cavalier attitude towards military service. Badly paid, miserably fed and maltreated by their officers, they had few qualms about drifting away to the gold fields, silver mines and cattle drives where conditions and pay were better. No one was shot for desertion during the wars against North America's indigenous population or the Spanish-American War. During the First World War, of the twenty-four death sentences imposed for desertion by courts martial, President Woodrow Wilson commuted them all.

If Slovik was the unluckiest deserter in the US Army, Wayne Powers was probably the most fortunate. Private First Class Wayne Powers was a twenty-three-year-old army truck driver when he landed in France three days after D-Day. In November 1944, he met a dark-haired French girl named Yvette Beleuse in the northern French village of Mont d'Origny near the Belgian border. Powers, born in Chillicothe, Missouri, spoke no French, and Yvette did not know English. As the newspaper *France Soir* wrote later, 'She gave him a woman's smile after months of murderous combat.' When Powers was ferrying supplies to the Belgian border a few days before the Bulge counter-offensive, his truck was hijacked (probably by deserters). Alone, on foot and unable to find his unit, he went back to Yvette. Unable to marry without revealing his existence to the police, Powers hid in the Beleuse family house while Yvette worked in a textile factory nearby. The couple had five children, who were forbidden to tell anyone who their father was. In the meantime, the Second World War had ended. The Korean War came and went. Powers's commander, General Eisenhower, became President of the United States. All the while, Powers remained a wanted man. American Military Police and French gendarmes raided the house twice without discovering his hiding place under the stairs.

Four years after Huie's book made Slovik's case a *cause célèbre*, Wayne Powers became front-page news. In March 1958, a car crashed outside the Beleuse house and Powers made the mistake of looking through the curtains. Policemen taking details saw him and turned him over to American MPs. When the story of young lovers Wayne and Yvette hit the newspapers, the American Embassy in Paris received 60,000 letters in three days – all demanding clemency for a young American who had fallen in love with a French girl. A court martial found Powers guilty of desertion and sentenced him to ten years at hard labour, but this was quickly reduced to six months. The Judge Advocate General's office in Washington reviewed his case and released him. Two years later, Powers and Yvette married in Mont d'Origny. By then, their sixth child had been born.

Those who told the stories of Slovik and Powers did not connect them to the wider phenomenon of mass desertion. The vast majority of the 150,000 American and British soldiers who deserted the ranks during the war were unlike both Slovik and Powers. Slovik was the only one shot for his crime, and Powers was one of the few convicted deserters to get off almost scot-free. The real story of Second World War deserters lay elsewhere, and this writer's most important task was to find soldiers whose fates were more emblematic and less publicized.

A serendipitous encounter in London led me in the right direction. It happened in March 2009, when I was promoting my previous book, *Americans in Paris: Life and Death under Nazi Occupation*, at the Frontline Club for war correspondents in London. A courtly and well-dressed American gentleman in the audience asked some pertinent questions. He was that person any speaker fears: someone who knows what he's talking about. It became obvious that his knowledge of the French Resistance was more intimate than mine. A red rosette, discreetly pinned to his lapel, marked him as a member of France's Legion of Honour. It turned out he had been one of the few American regular soldiers to fight with the Resistance in 1944.

We met for coffee later near his house in South Kensington, where he regaled me with tales of life among the *résistants*. Eventually, he asked what I was working on next. I told him it was a book on American and British deserters in the Second World War and asked if he knew anything about it. He answered, '*I* was a deserter.'

We ordered more coffee, and my friendship with Steve Weiss – decorated combat veteran of the US 36th Infantry Division, former *résistant* and deserter – was born.

Until then, my research had led me from archives to libraries, from court martial records to old V-mail letters, from fading documents to myriad academic studies. Steve Weiss infused the war and the dilemmas facing deserters with fresh vitality. His generosity extended to many hours of interviews, as well as access to his cache of memorabilia that included an unpublished memoir, letters, newspaper articles, photographs and books. We went together to the battlefields where he fought in eastern France and found the moss-grown foxholes that he and others like him had dug in the forests. I pestered him often with questions to which he unfailingly and candidly responded. Although born in 1925, he retained the robust health and enthusiasm of the teenager who volunteered in 1942 to take part in Eisenhower's crusade.

As I came to know Weiss better, my respect and admiration increased. His life after the war became a long exploration of the effects on him and others of combat, military conformity and prison. Years in therapy led him to become a psychologist, a profession in which his experience provided the empathy to treat those with traumas similar to and often more disabling than his own. Confronting the anguish that other veteran soldiers preferred to leave dormant, Weiss conducted battlefield tours, revisited the scenes of his triumphs and his shame and sought out old comrades-in-arms. Late in life, he moved from California to London to lecture at King's College's famed Department of War Studies.

'It is always an enriching experience to write about the American soldier in adversity no less than in glittering triumph,' wrote Charles B. MacDonald, an infantry captain in northern Europe in 1944 and 1945, in *The Siegfried Line Campaign*. The Second World War imposed more than enough adversity on the infantry riflemen who did most of the fighting. The majority of those who landed in the first waves on the Italian and French coastlines to fight long campaigns did not survive to see their triumph, and some who lived were in prison for desertion when they heard the news of Germany's surrender. Knowing that they would not be rotated out of the line or receive respite from danger, they had chosen disgrace over the grave. For others, there was no choice. Their bodies simply led them away from danger, and they remembered walking away as if in a dream. Many were afraid, many broke down and many just could not take any more. 'The mystery to me,' wrote Ernie Pyle, the battlefront correspondent known for his sympathetic reports about ordinary GIs, 'is that anybody at all, no matter how strong, can keep his spirit from breaking down in battle.'

A minority deserted to make money, stealing and selling the military supplies that their comrades at the front needed to survive. From 1944 to 1946, Allied deserters ran the black market economies of Naples, Rome and Paris. Their plundering of Allied supply convoys, often at gunpoint, deprived General George Patton of petrol as his tanks were about to breach Germany's Siegfried Line. Rampant thieving left their comrades at the front short of food, blankets, ammunition and other vital supplies. In Italy, deserters drove trucks of looted Allied equipment for Italian-American Mafioso Vito Genovese (who concealed his fascist past and made himself indispensable to Allied commanders in Naples). Military Police chased the notorious Lane

Gang of deserters for most of 1944. The gang's head, who used the pseudonym Robert Lane, was a twenty-three-year-old private from Allentown, Pennsylvania, named Werner Schmeidel. His mob terrorized the military and civilians alike in a crime spree of robbery, extortion and murder. After MPs captured them in November 1944, they made a daring Christmas Eve prison break and hid among the Roman underworld. Recaptured many weeks later, Schmeidel and his top henchman were hanged for murder in June 1945. That did not put an end, however, to other deserter criminal operations that continued well into the post-war era. (Two members of the Lane Gang who remained at large hijacked an army safe with $133,000 in cash on its way from Rome to Florence one week after their accomplices' hangings.) In France, American deserters collaborated with Corsican hoodlums in the theft and sale of cigarettes, whisky, petrol and other contraband. French civilians compared the German troops' supposedly 'correct' behaviour during their four-year occupation to the terror wrought by rampaging American deserters who raped and robbed at will.

In Paris, especially, the lure of pretty women and unearned wealth beckoned to any American GI or British Tommy willing to desert. One of these was Sergeant Alfred T. Whitehead, a Tennessee farm boy who had earned Silver and Bronze Stars for bravery in Normandy. He became a gangster in post-liberation Paris, living with a café waitress and robbing Allied supply depots as well as restaurants and ordinary citizens. His type of deserter, who operated in what the French press called 'Chicago' gangs, caused more worry to the Allied command than the ordinary deserter who simply went into hiding. *New York Times* correspondent Dana Adams Schmidt wrote that 'American Army deserters hijack trucks on the open highway and fight gun battles with the American military police.' Another of his dispatches from Paris added, 'The French police fear to interfere unless accompanied by M.P.'s.' Hunting down deserters became a full-time job for MPs from most Allied countries.

From the beginning of the war, the military in both Britain and the United States understood that some men would collapse mentally under the strain of combat. They had seen it often in the First World

War, when the term 'shell shock' came into common usage. An old school of thought held that 'shell shock', later christened 'battle fatigue', was a newfangled term for cowardice, but psychological research between the wars found that the human mind suffered stress as did the body and acquired its own wounds. Much study was devoted to discovering which men were likely to break down and which were not. Leading psychologists, led by Harvard's Professor Edwin Garrigues Boring, cooperated with the military to produce a book called *Psychology for the Fighting Man*. A kind of guidebook to mental survival in battle, it was intended for every soldier going into combat and quickly sold 380,000 copies. Its insights inform much of this book, especially its dictum about the average soldier who broke down under pressure: 'He is not a coward.'

Just as fear and mental collapse drove Steve Weiss and avarice motivated Al Whitehead, another type of deserter left the armed forces out of pure disgust. *Psychology for the Fighting Man* acknowledged that war and killing were not normal activities for boys raised in peacetime: 'American men have no particular love of killing. For the most part they hate killing – they think it is wrong, sinful, ordinarily punishable by death.' This view of life was not unique to Americans. One British soldier, John Vernon Bain, deserted three times. He never ran during a battle, and he fought well in North Africa and northern France. In Normandy, where the British Army court martialled four officers and 7,018 men for desertion in the field, Bain stayed at the front. He eventually left, not the war, but the army. To him, it was a dehumanizing institution that encouraged actions that in any context but war would be regarded as criminal. He deserted to preserve his humanity. His life story should resonate with those who wonder how much they would have endured before collapsing or fleeing. Fortunately for this writer, Bain's son John provided insights into his father's character, motives and flaws that fleshed out the many writings and interviews Bain left behind when he died.

John Bain wrote a poem in which a deserter told his son:

But son, my spirit, underneath,
Survived it all intact;
They thought they'd crushed me like a bug
But I had won in fact.

The Second World War was not as wonderful as its depiction in some films and adventure tales. It should not be surprising that young men found the experience of it so debilitating that they escaped. John Keegan, who pioneered the writing of war's history through the eyes of its participants, wrote, 'What war can ever be wonderful, least of all one that killed fifty million people, destroyed swathes of Europe's cultural heritage, depraved its politics, devalued the very moral basis of its civilization?'

BOOK I
BOYS TO SOLDIERS

ONE

From the earliest childhood, American boys are taught
that it is wrong – the greatest wrong – to kill.

*Psychology for the Fighting Man, Prepared for the
Fighting Man Himself*, Committee of the National
Research Council with the Collaboration of Science
Service as a Contribution to the War Effort, *The Infantry
Journal*, Washington, DC (and Penguin Books, London),
1943, p. 349

AT THE END OF THE GREAT WAR OF 1914–18, Private First Class
William Weiss was departing France with a leg scarred by German
bullets, lungs choked in poison gas and a plague of memories. While
convalescing in a Catholic hospital near Tours, the Jewish-American
doughboy fell in love with his French nurse. The romance, which
sustained him for four months, ended when his 77th Infantry Division
mustered at Brest for the voyage home to New York City. In April
1919, five months after the Armistice, New York held little promise
for Weiss. The post-war economic recession was beginning, as weapons factories laid off workers and banks pressed for repayment of war
debts. Many 77th Division troops had lost their jobs to civilians when
they entered the United States Army. At least 25 per cent of them had
no hope of work and expected nothing more at home than a grateful
welcome. As they set sail across the Atlantic, even the welcome was
cast into doubt.

To the surprise of the 77th Division's commanders, the
Department of War declared that it would not accord the men a

traditional victory parade. Only one month earlier, the 27th Infantry Division, O'Ryan's Roughnecks, had marched proudly up Fifth Avenue to the acclaim of ecstatic crowds. The 27th and 77th were both New York divisions, about all they had in common. The all-volunteer, mostly Irish 27th were honest-to-God American Christian fighting men. The 77th was comprised of draftees and recent immigrants from Italy, Greece, Russia, Poland, Armenia, Syria and China. Thirty per cent were Jewish. Twelve thousand earned American citizenship while in uniform, making them, to most Washington politicians, not quite Americans.

When New Yorkers insisted on honouring the 77th anyway, the War Department advanced a series of pretexts to block them. It said the doughboys themselves did not want a parade. The men, once asked, were unanimously in favour. War Secretary Newton Baker then cited objections by Fifth Avenue shopkeepers to the erection of grandstands between 97th and 98th Streets. After the courts rejected the shopkeepers' injunction, the department claimed the parade would be too expensive – almost a million dollars, a figure soon lowered to $80,000. Finally, it said that disembarking 30,000 men at the same time would paralyse the docks.

War Department prevarications infuriated New York City. All of the 77th's boys came from the metropolis, whereas the 27th's National Guardsmen hailed from as far as Schenectady and Albany. Meetings assembled throughout Manhattan to lodge protests. The Welcome Committee for the Jewish Boys Returning from the War sent an urgent telegram to Secretary of War Baker: 'The East Side, which has contributed so large a quota to this division, is stirred at being deprived of the opportunity to pay tribute to this division ... We strongly urge you to do everything within your power to make it possible that the parade shall take place. It will be an act of patriotism.' The next day, the Committee cabled President Woodrow Wilson 'as Commander in Chief of the US Army, to rescind the order prohibiting the parade of the 77th Division. The people of the east side have gladly given their sons to do battle in France for their country, and desire to pay loving tribute to the boys who are returning and to the memory of those who sleep on foreign soil.'

Charles Evans Hughes, a former Supreme Court justice and the Republicans' nominee for president in 1916, chaired a gathering of the Selective Service Boards that had conscripted the men of the 77th two years earlier. 'We want to do for the 77th what we did for the 27th,' Hughes declared. 'There should be no desire to discriminate against any of the boys who went to the front, from New York or any other place.'

No one contested the division's achievements: more than two thousand of its men had been killed, and another nine thousand wounded – more than double the casualties sustained by the 27th. They were one of the first American divisions sent into combat and the only one at the front every day of the Meuse-Argonne offensive. The *New York Times* wrote of the mostly immigrant troops: 'The 77th fought continuously from the time it entered the Lorraine sector in June [1918] until it stood at the gates of Sedan when the armistice was signed. It drove the Germans back from the Vesle to the Aisne River. It rooted them out of the very heart of the Argonne Forest. And it ranked seventh among the [twenty-nine] divisions that led in the number of Distinguished Service Crosses awarded for gallantry in action.' When they launched an assault against the Germans along the River Vesle, called by the troops 'the hellhole of the Vesle', General Erich Ludendorff unleashed the phosgene and mustard gas that blinded and crippled thousands of Allied soldiers. William Weiss was one of them, taken out of the front with eyes bandaged from the stinging pain of the poisons and his leg nearly shot off by German rifle fire.

The heroism of New Yorkers like Private Weiss gave the lie to military orthodoxy, as stated in the US Army's official *Manual of Instruction for Medical Advisory Boards* in 1917, that 'the foreign-born, and especially the Jews, are more apt to malinger than the native-born'. Dr William T. Manning, chairman of the Home Auxiliary Association, told a meeting in New York that soldiers' families felt their sons were victims of racial discrimination. Woodrow Wilson, a Southern gentleman whose administration had introduced segregation by race into the federal civil service in 1913, was impervious to accusations of bias. In his State of the Union Address for 1915, the

Democratic president had said, 'There are citizens of the United States, I blush to admit, born under other flags but welcomed under our generous naturalization laws to the full freedom and opportunity of America, who have poured the poison of disloyalty into the very arteries of our national life; who have sought to bring the authority and good name of our Government into contempt ... Such creatures of passion, disloyalty, and anarchy must be crushed out.' Neither the all-black 369th Regiment, known as the Harlem Hellfighters, nor the mostly foreign-born 77th Infantry Division won the president's admiration, although both had earned more decorations than most all-white, 'all-American' units.

Public clamour grew so loud that the War Department backed down. The division's troopships docked at the end of April, and on 6 May the men assembled downtown for one of the biggest parades in New York history. Schools closed, and workers came out of their bakeries, laundries and garment shops to lionize the boys who had won the war to end all wars. With rifles on shoulders and tin hats on heads, the men of the 77th marched five miles up Fifth Avenue from Washington Square to 110th Street past more than a million well-wishers. Usually called the Liberty Division for their Statue of Liberty shoulder patches, and sometimes the Metropolitan Division, they were now 'New York's Own'. 'Every building had its windows full of spectators, waving flags or thrown out [sic] torn paper, candies, fruit, or smokes,' the *New York Times* reported. 'Most of the store windows were tenanted by wounded veterans or their relatives, while park benches were placed at choice sites for men from the convalescent hospitals.' Some of the 5,000 wounded rode in open cars provided by local charities, while others moved on crutches and in wheelchairs. Lest the 2,356 buried in France be forgotten, the procession included a symbolic cortège of Companies of the Dead.

Only the deserters, a mere 21,282 among the whole American Expeditionary Force of more than a million men, went unacknowledged. Most were in army stockades or on the run from the Military Police in France. Of the twenty-four American soldiers condemned to death for desertion, President Wilson commuted all of their sentences. The Great War had a lower rate of desertion, despite its unpopularity in many quarters, than any previous American conflict. More British and French soldiers had run from battle, but their four years in the trenches outdid the Americans' one. Britain shot 304 soldiers for deserting or cowardice and France more than 600. In the 77th Division, only a few men had left their posts in the face of the enemy. Perhaps out of shame, the division referred to most of them as Missing in Action.

When the parade ended at 110th Street, the 77th's commander, Major General Robert Alexander, declared, 'The time has come to beat the swords into plowshares, and these men will now do as well in civil life as they did for their country in France.'

Not all of the men would do as well in civilian life as they had in France. The division's most decorated hero, Medal of Honor winner Lieutenant Colonel Charles Whittlesey, committed suicide in 1921, a belated casualty of the war. Others died of their wounds after they came home, and some would remain crippled or in mental institutions for the rest of their lives. Many enlisted men, unable to find work, drifted west. Among them was William Weiss, who at the age of twenty-seven left home as much to forget the war as to earn a living. The wounded veteran worked as a farmhand in the Kansas wheat fields, then followed the oil boom to Oklahoma and Texas as a roustabout. This led to a stint with the Federal Bureau of Narcotics, which had been subsumed into the Treasury Department's Prohibition Unit in 1920. Among the unit's duties was the interdiction from Mexico of newly illegal drugs like marijuana and alcohol. Something happened in El Paso that compelled Weiss to resign, an episode that he concealed even from his family. He moved back to New York, where he married a young woman named Jean Seidman in 1923. On 3 October 1925, the couple had a son, Stephen James. The family called him Steve, but his mother nicknamed him 'Lucky Jim'. Five years later, the boy was followed by a daughter, Helen Ruth.

Steve and Helen grew up in a redbrick apartment at 275 Ocean Avenue in Brooklyn, opposite Prospect Park. 'The neighborhood was calm and leafy,' Steve Weiss remembered years later. 'The inhabitants were hard-working and white middle class. Most of us

were Dodger fans.' Many, like the Weisses, had moved from tene-
ments in Manhattan's lower east side. William Weiss was an aloof
and undemonstrative father. Every Armistice Day, he would lock
himself away from the family and stay alone in his room for an
hour or so. 'I didn't know who he was,' Steve Weiss said. William
worked at a succession of odd jobs, usually as a watchman. His
unreliability created tension between father and son. 'My father
would not pay the electricity bill,' he recalled. 'He would gamble
with the money.' Yet Steve had good memories of the old man. 'He
was very entertaining, a good story teller. He never grew up.' When
the Depression hit, William Weiss advised other veterans on ways to
obtain pensions and benefits from their years of military service. He
even won some money for himself, which the family used to take its
first summer vacation away from home, in Poughkeepsie.

In June 1942, six months after the Japanese assault on Pearl
Harbor brought the United States into the Second World War, Steve
graduated from Lafayette High School in Brooklyn. He was sixteen,
two years younger than most of his classmates. Tall for his generation
at five foot eleven inches, he weighed a healthy 160 pounds and had
a full head of curly auburn hair. He continued his education at night,
taking college-level courses in psychology, pathology and chemistry.
During the day, the government's new Office of War Information
(OWI) at 221 West 57th Street in Manhattan employed him as a
photolithographer. His task was to make plates from photographs to
print OWI propaganda periodicals and posters. Steve Weiss wanted
to do more by serving overseas in the army's Psychological Warfare
Branch, whose objective in Europe was the same as the OWI's at
home: to engender public support for the Allied cause.

The only way into Psychological Warfare was to enlist in the
United States Army. Aged 17, Steve needed his father's permission.
He brought the enlistment papers home, but William Weiss refused to
sign. The older man stared at his son 'with a combination of shock
and regret,' before telling the boy, 'Real war isn't like the movies.'
Steve's Psychological Warfare aspirations were fading. If he waited
until his eighteenth birthday in October, the Selective Service Board
would draft him. Draftees without college degrees had a good chance

of ending up as infantry riflemen, probably the most dangerous and thankless job in the armed forces.

Steve pleaded with his father, who remained impassive. 'Seems like yesterday,' William explained to him for the first time, 'but in the spring of 1918, I was wounded and gassed near Fismes and those experiences still tick over in my head. I've spent most of my life trying to recover, starting with four months in a French hospital near Tours and at least two years recuperating out West.' William Weiss then revealed the secret he had kept since he left Texas: 'I accidentally shot a man on the streets of El Paso working as a federal narcotics agent. Did you know that? Since then, I've never had any energy left for ambition. Too scared to try.' Seventeen-year-old Steve could only stammer, 'Dad, I ...'

'Forget about the flags, the bands and the parades,' his father said. 'That's seduction! To increase enlistments. War's about killing, terrible suffering and broken spirit.'

'Are you trying to frighten me?' Steve asked.

'No,' his father said. 'I'm just asking you not to make any sudden moves. If the army needs you, it will find you soon enough.' When the youngster wouldn't listen, William appealed to his conscience. 'Look at all your mother and I have done for you. Even during the Depression, you and your sister never went without. I worked at odd jobs, and your mother worked at Macy's day in, day out, as a sales-girl doing everything to keep the family together. On a shoestring! Doesn't that mean something?'

'Dad,' Steve said, 'if you don't sign the papers, I'll forge your name and run away.' Reluctantly, William Weiss signed his teenage son over to the care of the United States Army.

TWO

> But for the foolish and the heroic who ignore all physical limitations, nature may have to provide these peculiar forms of escape from pain or emotion too strong to endure.
>
> *Psychology for the Fighting Man*, p. 320

PRIVATE JOHN VERNON BAIN deserted from the British Army in Scotland long before the British Army sent him into combat. He was no coward. The nineteen-year-old volunteer's record in the boxing ring – finalist at age fourteen in the Schoolboy Championships of Great Britain, Northwest Divisional Junior Champion, Scottish Command Middle Weight Champion in 1941, gold medals and press acclaim – proved as much. Yet, in 1941, he had run away for three weeks from his regimental base at Fort George, which to him was 'that dark and grey promontory that lay in the Moray Firth like a fossilized Leviathan.' At the time, he was a corporal in the 70th Battalion of the Argyll and Sutherland Highland Regiment. Deserting from relatively easy duty in Scotland as PTI, physical training instructor, made little sense, and his rationale was vague even forty-six years later: 'I was supposed to be a corporal, and I was no good at this. I had no idea how to conduct drills and mount guard and all that kind of thing. In a kind of disgust or something, I just sort of cleared off. I wasn't away long, about three weeks.'

Rather than court martial him for desertion, Bain's commanding officer demoted him to private. 'If you did revert to the ranks and had been an NCO,' Bain said, 'you could then claim for a transfer. And I was transferred to the London Scottish, and they were a sister regiment of the Gordons. And that was how I was sent to the Gordon Highlanders.' His new unit was the 5/7th Gordons, a union of the old 5th and 7th Battalions of the distinguished regiment that the Duke of Gordon had established in 1794. Its commanding officer was Lieutenant Colonel H. W. B. Saunders.

Bain had first volunteered in early 1940 to become a pilot in the Royal Air Force, despite his admission that he was 'singularly ignorant of the political realities'. He knew nothing about the Nazis, the German annexation of Austria or Hitler's ambition to conquer most of Europe. A physical examination turned up colour-blindness and one punch-damaged eye that disqualified him from flying, so he and his older brother, Kenneth, decided to become merchant mariners. Neither of the Bain brothers, having grown up in the inland Buckinghamshire town of Aylesbury, was an Able Bodied Seaman or had any shipboard experience. Their attempts to sign on before Christmas 1940 at the docks in London, Cardiff and, finally, Glasgow were met with derision. Staying in a rented room that was reducing the meagre hoard of cash they had brought from home, John and Kenneth chanced on a poster: 'Are you over 18 and under 20? If you are you can join a young soldiers' battalion.'

John asked his brother, 'What about that? At least I'd get some shoes without holes.' Kenneth corrected him, 'Boots.' He added the sticking point that, at two years older than John, he was over twenty.

They had a notion that twin brothers could not be separated. 'The recruiting officer did not show the least disbelief when we gave the same date of birth,' John wrote. 'We were medically examined and passed as A1.' The Army sent them to the 70th Battalion of the Argyll and Sutherlands at the Bay Hotel outside Glasgow. 'The Army was one service I had sworn I would never join,' Bain wrote, 'but, I told myself, a Scottish regiment would be different, more glamorous.' The glamour of the regimental kilt, stylish headgear and bagpipes gave way to recruit training that was disappointingly unglamorous. 'The object is to turn one into a kind of automaton,' he said. 'It works in a way.'

He 'disliked the Army very much,' recalling his time in Scotland as 'nearly two years of boredom, discomfort and misery, relieved by occasional booze ups ...' He resented his 'early days in the army when he had first stood guard at Duff House in Banff in the cruel winter of 1941 ... protecting the old mansion against imaginary German parachutists dressed as nuns'. From the ways that Bain revisited his Army service in letters, books and poems, he appeared to have been pathologically unsuited to soldiering. He wrote, 'By nature I was impractical, unpunctual, and clumsy, attributes that do not endear themselves to military authority.' Thirty years after the war, his thoughts turned

> ... not so much to memories of battle but to the grinding tedium of service in the United Kingdom, training, manoeuvres, guards, courses, discomfort, humiliation, frustration, boredom and – rarely but unforgettably – moments of bizarre comedy, excitement and the joy of extraordinary physical well-being when food, warmth and the rest were not commonplace elements which we had the automatic right to expect in the pattern of our days but pleasure as real intensity, positive blessings.

In common with other British youngsters of the time, Bain had little experience of people from other classes. His own background was what he described as 'working class but with aspirations of an entirely materialistic kind towards stifling gentility'. His mother read books and kept a piano, and his father worked for himself in a photography studio. Officers, some with no leadership qualifications apart from the right accent, irritated him, but the 'other ranks' seemed almost a foreign species. When one of them asked his name, he answered, 'Vernon,' his middle name that he had been called all his life. Bain recalled the squaddies' mocking question: '"Vernon? What's that?" And I'd say, "John", quickly, which they could handle. So, I became "John" in the army.'

'A lot of the chaps in the 70th Argylls were from the Glasgow slums, the Gorbals,' he recalled, 'and had pretty disgusting habits.' In another reflection on his fellow squaddies, he wrote, 'My comrades were mostly sub-literate, embittered children of the general strike, from the slums of Glasgow and Edinburgh.' One of them pilfered Bain's gold boxing medal, indicative of the petty thievery rampant in the ranks. Nevertheless, he wrote, 'They would happily stick by you, and they were generous.' Paid only two shillings a day, the Jocks gave their last pennies to comrades in need or to stand a friend a pint. The only person Bain trusted was his brother Kenneth, who was transferred to the Royal Engineers a year into their enlistment. That was about the time John ran away for three weeks.

To get along, Bain concealed from his squad mates his passion for books, poetry and classical music. In fact, he gave up reading altogether. 'I deliberately suppressed that part of myself that I most valued,' he wrote.

> I became ashamed of my interest in literature, ideas and the arts. I consciously adopted a mask with forehead villainous low. I was already, at eighteen, greedily addicted to beer, so no acting ability was needed to play the part of boozer. My interest in boxing was genuine and my skill was respected, so it was not difficult for me to flex my muscles and roar with the roaring boys. But it was not good for me either. It was shameful and brutalizing.

After the transfer to B Company of 5/7th Gordon Highlanders, Bain made one good friend. Private Hughie Black was a working-class Scotsman of roughly his age and with a more profound contempt for officers. Black's cynicism about the military had a hard class edge to it, and he would have stayed out of the war if it had been possible. The six-foot boxer from Buckinghamshire and the five-foot six-inch Glaswegian made an odd if comradely pair. Like most Scotsmen, Black said 'aye' for 'yes' and expressed himself in a rich vocabulary of profanities including 'Fucky Nell.' He called Bain 'china', as in 'china plate', rhyming slang for 'mate'. If Bain had a friend to replace his brother in B Company, it was streetwise Hughie Black.

The tedium of training and guard duty came to an end on 20 June 1942, when the Gordons with the rest of their Highland Division regiments boarded the *Spirit of Angus* and other ships on the Clyde estuary and at Liverpool and Southampton. Their destination, in common with most other troop embarkations during the war, was withheld from the soldiers. The convoy of twenty-two troopships, escorted by eight destroyers, headed south through the Bay of Biscay towards Africa. For most of the youngsters, it was their first time out of Britain.

The 5/7th Gordons were part of the 51st Highland Division, commanded by forty-three-year-old Major General Douglas 'Tartan Tam' Wimberley. Wimberley stood six-foot-three, usually wore a kilt and waged a futile struggle with the high command to exclude English and Lowland Scots regiments from his division. His predecessor in command of the Highland Division was Major General Victor Morven Fortune. Fortune and the original division were then languishing in German prisoner of war camps, following their surrender to German General Erwin Rommel at Saint-Valéry-en-Caux during the Battle of France in June 1940. The lucky units that managed to escape to Britain formed the core of the reconstituted Highland Division. The glorious histories of the 51st Division and its component regiments, like the Black Watch with its legacy in Egypt dating to the original British conquest of 1882, held no allure for Bain. Then and later, he refused to sentimentalize either war or the army.

Bain and his fellow Gordon Highlanders lived in confined quarters at sea, resenting the privacy and better rations afforded the officers. Bain said later of his comrades, 'They had no respect for their officers.' They amused themselves with cards and boxing. To cheers from his mates in the 5/7th Gordons, Bain defeated a sergeant from the Cameron Highlanders.

On 21 June, the day after the convoy set sail, Britain suffered a major defeat, its fourth of the war after the loss of France, Singapore and Burma. Rommel, who had captured the original 51st Division in France, conquered the Libyan port town of Tobruk and inflicted a casualty toll on British and Commonwealth forces of 35,000. The Australian war correspondent Alan Moorehead, who covered the North African campaign for Britain's *Daily Express*, wrote, 'It was defeat as complete as may be.' Britain's Commander-in-Chief of

Middle East Forces, General Claude John Eyre Auchinleck, pulled his troops back well into Egypt to the coastal railhead at El Alamein. The thinly defended Alamein Line, running between the Mediterranean in the north and the impassable Qattara Depression in the south, lay only sixty miles in front of Alexandria. The Royal Navy had meanwhile evacuated Alexandria's harbour to avoid capture by the advancing Axis forces. This news, hardly a boost to morale, reached the Highland Division while it was far out at sea. Some of the men guessed that they were on their way to reinforce Britain's battered desert defences, but officially they were told nothing.

The ships refuelled at Freetown, Sierra Leone, but the men were not permitted ashore lest they contract malaria. As the convoy cruised further south along the African coast, the soldiers on board remained unaware that in Egypt their comrades had succumbed to panic that the British called 'the flap'.

In Cairo, on 1 July, burning documents at Britain's embassy and military headquarters sent up billows of smoke so thick that the day became known as 'Ash Wednesday'. Trains leaving the Cairo station for British Palestine overflowed with passengers and baggage. British subjects queued outside Barclay's Bank to withdraw their money. A mood of defeat prevailed, as Alan Moorehead, whose wife and baby had taken a train to Palestine, observed on the road between Cairo and Alexandria. It was, he wrote 'a full scale retreat. Guns of all sorts, R.A.F. wagons, recovery vehicles, armoured cars and countless lorries crammed with exhausted and sleeping men, were pouring up the desert road into Cairo … The road on our side – the side that carried vehicles up to the front – was clear …'

Worst of all for the British, about 20,000 soldiers vanished from the ranks. Many took refuge in the Nile Delta, some living through brigandry and others surviving on the charity of the Egyptian peasantry, the *fellahin*. Many hid with girlfriends in Cairo. British Military Police, known as 'redcaps' for the colour of their headgear, established a checkpoint at El Deir on the road between Alamein and Amariya. 'Every vehicle was checked, and personnel travelling eastwards as passengers had to satisfy the military police as to the authority of their journey,' wrote Major S. F. Crozier of the Royal Military

Police (RMP) and Provost Service. 'Written orders had been given to this post to fire on any person failing to halt when called upon to do so.' When some deserters drove off-road to avoid the checkpoint, the MPs placed the desert on both sides of the road under 'continuous observation'.

The Middle East Commander-in-Chief, General Claude Auchinleck, believed the solution was for courts martial to impose exemplary death sentences. As early as April of that year, Auchinleck had written to the War Office requesting 'that His Majesty's Government may be pressed to give urgent consideration to the immediate introduction of legislation necessary to restore into the Army Act the punishment of death for the offences of Desertion in the Field and of Misbehaving in the face of the Enemy in such manner as to show cowardice'. Unlike the United States, Britain had abolished the death penalty for desertion. During the First World War, when the Americans had not executed any deserters, the British had put to death 304 soldiers for desertion, cowardice, disobedience and quitting their posts. Post-war revulsion at the firing squads had led the Labour Government in 1930 to override objections from military chiefs and prohibit the execution of deserters.

'With the increase of number of troops in Egypt and Palestine, following the entry of Italy into the war [in June 1940], crime increased proportionately,' wrote RMP Major Crozier. 'Conscription had brought into the army a percentage of soldiers with criminal antecedents or tendencies. Many of these were drafted to the Middle East.' Major Crozier, who believed there were too few military policemen to deal with criminal soldiers in Egypt, continued:

> On arrival in Egypt they found that a number of soldiers had decided that the delights of Cairo and Alexandria were infinitely preferable to the monotony, discomforts and dangers of the Western Desert and East African campaigns. These deserters combined to form troublesome and dangerous gangs which were to become very familiar to the [Special Investigation] Branch [SIB] under the names of 'The Free British Corps' and 'The Dead End Kids'.

Even before the fall of Tobruk, Major Crozier noted, 'Not a day passed without many arrests being made.' The RMP sent extra officers and men, many of them formerly with Scotland Yard, from Britain and the colonies, to deal with the caseload. It also recruited men locally from regular service battalions. Private Wilf Swales of the Green Howards transferred to the RMP in Egypt on the promise of 'a shilling a day extra'.

Particularly worrying for the MPs were the theft and sale of British arms and ammunition. Zionist settlers in Palestine, planning their own war against the British, were major buyers of the looted Allied weapons. Two leaders in the Jewish Haganah defence force, Abraham Rachlin and Lieb Sirkin, were sentenced to seven and ten years respectively, for purchasing stolen arms. Their accomplices in the Royal Sussex and Royal East Kent Regiments received fifteen years penal servitude. Major Crozier wrote, 'The number of thefts of arms of all types and ammunition was appalling, and the "Dead End Kids" were responsible for many of them.' This deserter band befriended legitimate soldiers to gain access to bases and canteens, where they stole weapons, food, fuel and other supplies. The SIB shot and killed several of them. Another deserter gang calling itself the 'British Free Corps' survived by selling stolen military supplies, until its members too were caught.

Auchinleck argued in his letter of 7 April that nothing less than the death penalty would provide a 'salutary deterrent in a number of cases, in which the worst example was set by men to whom the alternative of prison to the hardships of battle conveyed neither fear nor stigma'. In a memorandum of 14 June to the rest of the War Cabinet, War Secretary Sir Percy James Grigg appeared to support Auchinleck. He wrote:

> My military advisers are unanimous in their opinion that the abolition of the death penalty for desertion in the field and cowardice in the face of the enemy was a major mistake from the military point of view. They hold that the penalty was a powerful deterrent against ill-discipline in the face of the enemy, which might

so easily mean a lost battle and a lost campaign. In this connection it may be noted that the U.S. Army retain the death penalty for practically the whole range of offences to which it applied in the British Army in 1914–18 …

Grigg, a career civil servant whom Churchill had appointed Secretary of State for War the previous February, then turned from the purely military to political factors:

> It is a subject on which there are strong feelings, and to justify a modification of the present law we should have to produce facts and figures as evidence that the British soldiers' morale in the face of the enemy is so uncertain as to make the most drastic steps necessary to prevent it breaking. Any such evidence would come as a profound shock to the British public and our Allies and as a corresponding encouragement to our enemies.

He concluded, 'Nevertheless, if military efficiency were the sole consideration, I should be in favour, as are my military advisers, of the reintroduction of the death penalty for the offences in question. But the political aspects are, at any rate, in present circumstances, as important, if not more important, than the military.' Grigg asked Auchinleck for exact figures on the scale of desertions before the Cabinet could reach a decision.

Neither the 51st Division at sea nor the troops in Egypt knew of Auchinleck's request to reintroduce the death penalty for those among them who might desert. It was kept secret from the public for the same reasons that Grigg opposed the death penalty itself: it would harm military morale, make the public more suspicious of the army command (which was held in low esteem by public and press alike at that time, as Cabinet minutes noted) and give the enemy a propaganda tool. Grigg explained in a memo to Churchill, 'If legislation is necessary, the facts and figures must be serious. But if they are serious, we can't afford to tell them either to our friends or our enemies.' Moreover, Commonwealth troops serving alongside the British were not subject to the death penalty. Changing the law would mean that an Australian and a British soldier deserting together would receive very different punishments: the Australian would receive three to five years in prison, while the Briton would be shot.

The Australian and New Zealand commanders demonstrated more concern for the men's morale than their British counterparts, who in correspondence complained of their soldiers' 'softness in education and living and bad training ...' The first units to establish forward clearing stations for psychiatric cases near the front were the 2nd New Zealand and the 9th Australian Divisions. By allowing the men to sleep and talk over their fears with physicians, the Australian and New Zealand medical staffs helped up to 40 per cent of the psychological casualties back into the field. The British followed suit in August, when the Royal Army Medical Corps' 200 Field Ambulance placed an 'Army Rest Centre' near the Alamein Line. Brigadier General G. W. B. James, the psychiatrist who probably originated the term 'battle exhaustion,' wrote that of the men treated for it 'a fairly constant 30% returned fairly satisfactorily to combatant duty'.

On 18 July, the Highland Division's convoy dropped anchor at Cape Town. For the first time in a month, the men set foot on dry land. White South Africans in English-speaking Cape Province gave them an enthusiastic welcome. On 19 July, while division bagpipers paraded through the city, Auchinleck sent a second entreaty from Cairo to the Cabinet for help in countering the mass desertions after Tobruk: 'Recent desertions show alarming increase even amongst troops of highest category. Present punishments that can be awarded insufficient deterrent. Would stress that cases where deserter takes truck containing food water and means of transport of his comrades are far more serious than similar cases during last war.'

A week later, the Highlanders went ashore again at Durban to the airs of the 7th Black Watch's kilted pipers. From Durban, the ships cruised north up the coast of east Africa to Aden. In the waters off Britain's colony on the Yemeni shore, the convoy divided. Some of the ships went east to Iraq and India, the rest north through the Red Sea towards Egypt.

On 14 August, the 51st Highland Division disembarked at Port Tewfik. Bain's subsequent poem, 'Port of Arrival', recorded the impressions of a foreign soldier landing at the southern gateway to the Suez Canal:

> The place we see
> Is just as we imagined it would be
> Except its furnishings are somehow less
> Spectacular, more drab, and we confess
> To disappointment, something like a sense
> Of loss, of being cheated.

The Highlanders settled into the desert west of the canal city of Ismailia near a village called Qassassin. Their base comprised fifty camps, each a rectangle a thousand yards long and five hundred wide, with identical dug-in tents, latrines and water towers. Here began a period of desert training and acclimatizing men from the highlands of Scotland to the Egyptian summer. The troops learned to navigate the trackless, barren sands with compasses aided at night by the stars and during the day by the sun. For a short period each day, they marched without helmets, caps or shirts for their skins to absorb sunlight without burning.

In his comrades' interaction with local villagers, Bain observed racial hatreds that he had not until then suspected. Men from Scottish slums, themselves subject to abuse by classes above theirs, humiliated the local population. Bain recalled, 'I do remember being very shocked by the attitude to the Egyptians, when we landed in Egypt. This was general all through the army. They were simply called wogs, and they were fair game. They were kicked around, beaten up, reviled.'

Winston Churchill and the Chief of the Imperial General Staff, General Alan Brooke, had flown to Egypt just ahead of the Highland Division. The day after the Highlanders arrived, Churchill dismissed Major General Auchinleck from his dual posts as Commander-in-Chief Middle East and 8th Army commander. He and Brooke appointed General Sir Harold Alexander C-in-C Mideast and placed

General William Gott in command of the 8th Army. General Gott, however, was killed when two German Messerschmitts attacked a transport plane taking him to Cairo. The officer chosen to replace him was a wiry general with a distinctly unmilitary falsetto voice named Bernard Law Montgomery.

'Monty', who assumed command on 13 August, made immediate changes to the 8th Army characterized by his declaration, 'There will be no more belly-aching and no more retreats.' Morale improved thanks to Montgomery's contagious confidence, the delivery of new American tanks and the failure of the Axis to exploit its victory at Tobruk by pushing through Alamein to Alexandria and Cairo.

Many of the post-Tobruk deserters were returning to the army, amid signs that Britain was not losing Egypt after all. There were too many of them to punish at mass court martials, which would attract publicity and undermine the myth of the universally brave British Tommy. Moreover, the 8th Army needed them. Experienced soldiers were more useful at the front than in prison. Privates were taken back without penalty, beyond the abuse their sergeants meted out. Non-commissioned officers were reduced to privates and put back into their units. Some of the more resourceful deserters, who had lived off the land in the Delta, went into the newly created Special Air Service (SAS) and Long Range Desert Group, where their survival skills and ingenuity were put to good use. Some deserters held out, as Major Douglas H. Tobler discovered while gathering intelligence in the desert. In September, he met a band of men 'who for their own reasons had deserted their units or perhaps made no effort to get back to their own lines after getting lost during an engagement with the enemy'. Tobler, who had not come to arrest them, noted that they were 'glad to be out of the fighting, content to live by their wits knowing it was unlikely anyone would check their credentials'.

While Bain was training at the camp near Qassassin, the division received an unexpected visit from Winston Churchill. The prime minister reviewed the troops and wrote afterwards, 'The 51st Highland Division was not yet regarded as "desert worthy", but these magnificent troops were now ordered to the Nile front.'

The 'Nile front' was, for the 5/7th Gordons and the rest of the division's 153rd Brigade, the desert south of the road between Cairo and the pyramids. Bain recalled taking the train there from Alexandria: 'An Arab was selling hard boiled eggs and bread, and they simply took his entire stock and threw him off the train.' Near the Mena House, Egyptian Khedive Ismail's nineteenth-century country lodge that had become a fashionable pyramid-side hotel, the 153rd Brigade dug trenches and constructed other defences to protect Cairo. Their exertions were wasted, because Monty was no longer planning to defend Cairo. The time had come to commit soldiers like John Bain to an all-out offensive.

THREE

On the average the men from the northwestern part of the
United States get the highest scores [on the Army General
Classification Test], the men from the southeast the
lowest.

Psychology for the Fighting Man, p.189

STEVE WEISS BLACKMAILED HIS FATHER for permission to join the
Army, but Alfred T. Whitehead of Tennessee claimed that he deceived
his widowed mother to achieve the same end. Whitehead asked her to
sign papers for his entry into the Civilian Conservation Corps (CCC),
a New Deal programme for the Depression's unemployed to plant
forests and establish state parks. For a penniless youngster like
Whitehead, the CCC's monthly pay of $30 ($25 of which went direct
to the parents) made it an attractive option. Or so his mother, who
was raising six children in a backwoods cabin, imagined. Whitehead
related in his privately printed memoir, *Diary of a Soldier*, that he
waited until she had signed the document before telling her the truth:
he was becoming a soldier.

Whitehead had left home before, when he was fourteen. Beatings
by his 'heavy handed stepfather' forced him to run away. In the town
of Lebanon, in Tennessee's Wilson County, a family of moonshiners
took him in and put him to work driving a truck. He learned dice and
poker at their gambling den. 'Once in a while, they cut a guy's throat,'
Whitehead wrote, 'just to keep their reputation for being tough.'
Being tough appealed to the young Whitehead, whose upbringing
required a thick hide.

His coal miner father, Artie Whitehead, had been crushed to death in an underground accident. Alfred wrote that he shed tears at his father's funeral, which he remembered as taking place when he was four years old. In fact, he was older. His Social Security and service records give his date of birth as 31 January 1922, which made him four in 1926. Artie Whitehead had a daughter in 1927, when Alfred was five. And the US Census reported him as living with his family in Putnam County, Tennessee, in 1930. Alfred T. Whitehead was at least eight, if not older, when his father died. This was the first of many inconsistencies between Whitehead's memory and the historical record.

Artie Whitehead was interred in 'the family cemetery' at Silver Point, Tennessee, 'with generations of relatives: Whitehead, Hatfield, Sadler, and Presley.' Alfred's mother returned by train to Buffalo Valley with her children to live near 'the one room, stone chimney, log house where I was born'. Young Whitehead's rural upbringing was typical for the impoverished Southern hills of the time. His family sent him to school only a few weeks a year, 'just enough to keep the authorities off their backs'. Even by the standards of the Depression-era South, his was a brutal childhood. Alfred's great-grandfather, Wily Whitehead, who was 'as old as the hills and senile', lived in a henhouse with a rope tied around his waist to keep him in. Their stepfather treated the six Whitehead children still living at home so harshly that the county assumed custody of them for a time. Young Alfred enjoyed rare moments of freedom, usually alone fishing or shooting in the woods. For the most part, he wrote, his mother and stepfather robbed him of his youth:

> They had me working in the fields from sunup to sundown: plowing, clearing land, and helping to make moonshine whiskey by the time I was nine. Other times, my stepfather would hire me out as a laborer to other farmers for fifty cents a day. Then he'd take all the money I made and drink it up, gamble it away, or spend it whoring around South Carthage, depending on the mood he was in.

The wartime army offered an escape from backwoods poverty and abuse. It was unlikely Whitehead needed his mother's permission, though, to join it. His service records put his enlistment date at 11 April 1942. At that time, he was twenty. Parental consent was required only for volunteers younger than eighteen. Just as he must have been older than four at his father's funeral, he was more than eighteen in 1942. Yet depicting himself as underage stressed his role as victim in the saga he was making of his life. He portrayed his departure from his mother in poignant terms: 'She followed me all the way out to the front gate by the road, crying, and telling me that I had better get a good insurance policy in the Army. I couldn't help remembering how she and my stepfather had squandered my dead father's insurance money and property.'

For many relatively well-off young Americans, like Steve Weiss, the army was pure hardship. To Alfred T. Whitehead, it was liberation. The training and discipline were light compared to farm labour. The army supplied three meals a day, regular rations of meat, hot showers, clean clothes, medical care, a bed to himself and, above all, travel beyond the hills where he was born. Such luxuries were unobtainable for a poor rural Southerner, white or black, in civilian life.

Whitehead and other young recruits reported early one warm April morning to a restaurant in Carthage, Tennessee. Carthage, originally a trading port where the Cumberland and Caney Fork Rivers met, was known to Whitehead and the other recruits as the town from which the state's most famous First World War veteran had embarked on his military career. Alvin Cullum York, having conquered alcoholism before the war to become a devout Christian and pacifist, was drafted into the Army in 1917 at the age of twenty-nine. Trained at Fort Gordon, Georgia, he served in France with the 82nd Division. On 8 October 1918, York earned the Medal of Honor. His citation, presented to him personally by General John J. Pershing, read:

After his platoon suffered heavy casualties and three other non-commissioned officers had become casualties, Corporal York assumed command. Fearlessly leading seven men, he charged with

25

great daring a machine gun nest which was pouring deadly and incessant fire upon his platoon. In this heroic feat the machine gun nest was taken, together with four officers and 128 men and several guns.

York, about whom a Hollywood movie starring Gary Cooper had been released the year before, set a high standard for the young Tennesseans. Whitehead was proud to set out from the same town York had.

The recruits ate a hot breakfast at the little restaurant and boarded a bus. Driving along the ramshackle road past Whitehead's family's cabin at Sulphur Springs, Alfred wondered if he would ever see it again. It did not matter to him either way. While the driver filled the bus with petrol in Lebanon, he slipped away to buy 'a jug of moonshine'. He and his companions drank the illegal alcohol before nightfall, when the bus entered the gates of Fort Oglethorpe, Georgia.

After a few weeks of kitchen duty and barracks cleaning at Fort Oglethorpe, Whitehead was shipped to Camp Wolters, Texas, for Basic Training. The Infantry Replacement Training Center, where Texan Audie Murphy trained with Company D of the 59th Training Battalion, was then the country's largest. The nearest town was Mineral Wells, which some of the GIs called 'Venereal Wells' for obvious reasons. Whitehead became a buck private with about sixty other youngsters in the 4th Platoon, Company D, 63rd Infantry Training Battalion. His boyhood proficiency with a rifle qualified him as 'sharpshooter' and then 'expert'. Despite his success and easy adaptation to military life, he hated the Texas heat and burning winds. 'At night,' he recalled, 'I had to sleep with my blanket over my head just to breathe and keep the sand from stinging my face.' Training lasted seventeen weeks. This short time, reduced from the previously standard fifty-two weeks, was necessitated by the urgent need for troops overseas. On completion of the course, Whitehead took a train to Camp Polk, Louisiana.

At Camp Polk, Whitehead was assigned to an 'antitank platoon with Headquarters Company, 2nd Battalion, 38th Infantry Regiment of the 2nd Infantry Division'. On his shoulder was the divisional

patch with an American Indian's head for which the 2nd was called
the Indian Head Division. The assignment gave him many advantages
over men who would be sent overseas as replacements for regiments
that had lost soldiers in combat. He would train with the men who
were going to fight beside him, and his officers would know him.

Both the regiment and the division had honourable records of
service. The 38th Regiment was called the 'Rock of the Marne' for its
stiff resistance during the German offensive of 1918. The 'Second to
None' Division's bravery during the Meuse-Argonne offensive had
earned it three Croix de Guerre from the French government. By
1942, the division's main components were the 2nd, 9th and 38th
Regiments, together with the 2nd Engineers Battalion, four field artillery battalions and support units.

The 2nd Infantry Division was at Camp Polk to take part in war
games. The Louisiana Maneuvers had begun the year before as the
largest ever on American soil, and they would be staged with new
units each year of the war. Their objective was as much to find and
correct flaws in American battle strategy, tactics, equipment and
organization as to train the inexperienced troops. To Private
Whitehead, the 1942 summer manoeuvres seemed 'like a great game,
much like my childhood games of hide-and-seek, where one would
surprise the "enemy"'. Without enough weapons to equip all the
troops, Whitehead and some of his comrades carried broomsticks
instead of rifles and used empty mortar rounds as anti-tank guns. In
some places, wooden signs saying 'foxhole' and 'machine gun' substi-
tuted for the real thing. The war games pitted 'Reds' against 'Blues'
over 3,400 square miles of rugged swampland, hills and rivers. In the
previous year's exercises, General George Patton's 2nd Armored had
swept across the River Sabine into Texas to come back into Louisiana
and trap the 'Reds' in Shreveport. The exercises included cavalry
charges, relics of an earlier era that would not amount to much
against the Wehrmacht.

Whitehead and the rest of his platoon lived rough in the Louisiana
woods to hone survival skills, like foraging for food, hiding from the
enemy and washing in streams. Some of the men paid local families to
cook them fried chicken with biscuits and gravy. Whitehead lit out

after a Cajun girl, who responded to his advances by pelting him with stones. Louisiana had two types of weather, as far as Whitehead could judge, 'hot and then hotter'. Mosquitoes and snakes proved more menacing than the Blue Army.

On 22 September 1942, the 2nd Division returned to Fort Sam Houston. Whitehead's days revolved around close order drill, twenty-five-mile hikes with fifty-pound packs, kitchen police (KP), training films, field inspections and rifle practice. Despite the resilience his hard-labouring childhood gave him, he came into conflict with authority more than once. Officers told him to use his free time to catch up on sleep, but he left the base as often as he could to drink, gamble and chase women. 'I had numerous girlfriends,' he wrote, 'but figured anyone could have a girlfriend. What I really wanted was to get married.' His attention focused on a girl with red hair, whom he dated and to whom he proposed. The engagement would be prolonged, because the girl's mother 'wanted her to finish school first'.

FOUR

When he has his first encounter with the immediate threat
of death, when he must kill and see men killed, when he
must steel himself to hear the unheeded cries of the
mortally wounded and endure the stench of battle, a man
may become sick to his very vitals.

Psychology for the Fighting Man, p. 295

IN LATE SEPTEMBER 1942, John Bain moved west from the bivouac
where Winston Churchill had addressed the men to the Alamein Line.
His job was to shoulder B Company's light automatic Bren gun. Yet,
despite Monty's rigorous training, he and most of the other squaddies
had little idea what to expect when fighting began. The Allied and
Axis armies had reinforced their opposing positions from the
Mediterranean shore forty miles south to the Qattara Depression.
Almost as if recreating the French battlefields of the First World War,
the two sides had laid down miles of landmines, barbed wire, concrete
gun emplacements, tank traps and trenches. Montgomery placed the
51st Highland Division between the veteran 9th Australian and 2nd
New Zealand Divisions, reasoning that the novice Scots would benefit
from the Dominion soldiers' battlefield experience. He added that 'the
Scottish soldier quickly makes friends with the Dominion soldier. It
may be because both of them are slightly uncivilized.' Montgomery
set the offensive for 23 October, when he had nearly twice as many
troops as his adversary – 220,000 to Rommel's 115,000. For an
assault on entrenched positions, however, the minimum recommended
was three-to-one.

The Highlanders received General 'Tartan Tam' Wimberley's Order of the Day as they prepared to set out from their starting positions: 'There will be no surrender for unwounded men. Any troops of the Highland Division cut off will continue to fight.' Young troops like John Bain moved forward. General Wimberley recalled, 'I watched my Jocks filing past in the moonlight. Platoon by platoon they filed past, heavily laden with pick and shovel, sandbags and grenades – the officer at the head, his piper by his side. There was nothing more I could do now to prepare for the battle.'

Just before ten o'clock, the 8th Army unleashed the full force of its artillery batteries. Shells from more than a thousand British guns lashed the German positions with what two leading historians of Alamein called 'the biggest artillery barrage the British army had laid on since the First World War'. The heaviest artillery pieces fired more than twenty-five rounds a minute, aiming their first salvos at the enemy's artillery. 'For all the manoeuvres you'd done, there is no preparation for an artillery barrage,' Bain recalled. 'The barrage itself is enough to send you mad with terror. Our own barrage, I'm talking about, the twenty-five pounders, a deafening, terrible noise.' In the poem 'Baptism of Fire', Bain would later write about the initiation of a young soldier ('He is no kid. He's nineteen and he's tough …'):

> And, with the flashes, swollen thunder roars
> as, from behind, the barrage of big guns
> begins to batter credence with its din
> and, overhead, death whinnies for its feed
> while countering artillery shakes and stuns
> with slamming of a million massive doors.

It did not take long for the Germans to match the British fire. Exploding shells crashed into the earth around him, but explosions were less terrifying to Bain than the sounds made by human beings: 'One of the most memorable and nightmarish things is hearing the voices of the wounded, who have been badly wounded, the voices raised in terror and pain.' Shrapnel hit the company sergeant, 'a kind of father figure' ten years older than Bain. 'Hearing his voice sobbing

and in fact calling for his mother was so, I don't know, demeaning,'
Bain said. 'I felt a kind of shock that I cannot fully understand even
now, because he had been reduced to a baby.' He would later write in
'Remembering Alamein':

> And the worst sound in a battle
> The noise that I still hear
> The voices of comrades raised
> In agony and fear.

After the artillery came the infantry offensive, when the soldiers of the
8th Army emerged from their underground lairs to charge into the
enemy guns. The Highland Division marched forward, many falling
to German machine gun and mortar fire when they were barely out of
their trenches, while the bagpipes played. 'When you're in action, you
have no idea what's happening,' Bain said. 'You haven't the foggiest
idea of where you are, where the enemy is, what's happening or
anything else.'

Six days into the battle, one young officer deserted from the 10th
Armoured Division's headquarters well behind the lines. Twenty-
three-year-old Lieutenant Keith Douglas was not avoiding combat. He
was running straight to it. 'I enlisted in September 1939,' he wrote,
'and during two years or so of hanging about I never lost the certainty
that the experience of battle was something I must have.' He was a
tank commander in the Sherwood Rangers, which arrived in the
Middle East a year before the Gordon Highlanders in August 1941.
He was also a poet, who as an undergraduate had edited Oxford's
literary magazine *Cherwell*. To his distaste, the regiment assigned him
to division as a camouflage trainer. The army neglected to include
camouflage equipment in its exercises, leaving Douglas in Cairo with
nothing to do. It demoralized a young soldier yearning to be atop a
tank with his men.

When Douglas told his batman, Private Lockett, they were leaving
to find their regiment somewhere on the Alamein battlefield, Lockett
replied, 'I like you, sir. You're shit or bust, you are.' Lockett drove at

speed across the desert until they found a rear echelon of the regiment four miles before the lines, just north of John Bain and the Highlanders. A captain Douglas knew asked, 'Have you come back to us?' Douglas said that depended on the colonel of the regiment. 'Oh, he'll be glad to see you. I don't think "A" Squadron's got many officers left.' At that, Douglas and Lockett rushed forward. They found the colonel, whom Douglas called 'Piccadilly Jim', sitting in a truck.

'Good evening, sir,' Douglas said. 'I've escaped from Division for the moment, so I wondered if I'd be any use to you up here.' Piccadilly Jim, who could send him for court martial on a desertion charge, pondered the enthusiastic officer's fate. Because A Squadron had only one officer left alive and unwounded, the colonel gave Douglas command of two tanks. Douglas reflected, 'Best of all, I had never realized how ashamed of myself I had been in my safe job at Division until with my departure this feeling was suddenly gone.'

Soon, Douglas was facing German tanks in his Mark II Crusader: 'Every gun was now blazing away into the twilight, the regiment somewhat massed together, firing with every available weapon.' As his gunner took aim at the Germans, Douglas 'tossed out empty cases, too hot to touch with a bare hand.' The tank filled with smoke, but Douglas did not care: 'I coughed and sweated; fear had given place to exhilaration.' His impression of the battlefield contrasted with infantry Private John Bain's. He liked the action, while Bain detested the suffering.

'My first day in action had been eventful enough,' Douglas wrote. 'I felt as if I had been fighting for months.' The tanks, which needed repair and servicing, withdrew for the next four days. Douglas looked forward to getting back into the battle.

The Alamein fighting raged relentlessly for nine days and nights, while the British made steady if unclear gains against an enemy that was unafraid to retake positions it lost. John Bain's appreciation of objective, strategy and tactics – the lifeblood of the soldier – took second place to comradeship, pain and fear. On 2 November, Rommel cracked and retreated into the desert. Out of what Bain saw as 'almighty confusion and shambles', came Britain's first significant land victory of the war.

The achievement was nothing short of extraordinary for a nation that had been defeated in France and Libya by the Germans and in the Far East by Japan. 'Before Alamein we never had a victory,' Churchill would say with characteristic hyperbole. 'After Alamein we never had a defeat.' Credit went to the commanders as well as to infantrymen like John Bain and tankers like Keith Douglas. Soldiers in the field and hard-pressed civilians throughout the British Empire sensed that the Axis was not, after all, invincible.

The 8th Army lost 13,500 soldiers killed, wounded or missing in action, almost 10 per cent of the number who started. The toll was particularly high among the Highland Division's bagpipers. Until El Alamein, pipers played the Scottish regiments into battle. Bain recalled,

After Alamein they didn't, because they virtually all got killed. The pipers actually played you into battle. They were there at the entrance to minefields, playing the pipes as the Highland Division went in. There was something mad and heroic, I suppose, about it, but something terribly sad too. After that, they became stretcher bearers.

In Bain's poem 'Remembering Alamein', a Kiplingesque 'old sweat' recalled,

And at the gap one piper
Played *Highland Laddie* for
Our comfort and encouragement,
Like a ghost from another war.

Of course that brave young piper
Did not stand there long;
Shrapnel or a Spandau-burst
Ended that brief song.

From Alamein, the 8th Army pursued the Germans and Italians along the Mediterranean shore towards Italian Libya. The New Zealand Division, which correspondent Alan Moorehead wrote was 'by common consent the finest infantry formation in the Middle East', drove the Germans out of the small Egyptian port of Mersa Matruh on 8 November. That morning, on the other side of North Africa in Vichy-controlled Morocco and Algeria, the United States armed forces entered the war against Germany at the head of an Anglo-American invasion. The Americans provided some relief to Montgomery by diverting German resources to the west.

After the conquest of Mersa Matruh, when the 10th Armoured Division moved its headquarters closer to the front, Keith Douglas had to face his commanding officer. The colonel, who was playing poker in the officers' mess tent, made Douglas wait for a break in the game. When he put his cards down, he said to the young lieutenant, 'Just step outside with me awhile.'

While the colonel smoked his pipe under the African stars, Douglas feared immediate arrest. 'This business of your running away,' his commander asked Douglas. 'Why did you do it?' Douglas noticed that the old officer seemed more hurt than angry, and he answered that he did not know why he left. He thought that it may have been that he had nothing to do in the rear. 'That's absurd, of course,' the colonel said. 'If you'd asked me, I should have given you permission to go back while the battle was on, willingly.' Douglas had the tact not to remind him he had made a request and was refused. Instead, he said, 'Well, I'm very sorry, sir.' The colonel told him not to be unmilitary again. He would not court martial him. In fact, he let him remain with his regiment at the front where he saw more combat.

A short time later, Douglas wrote the poem 'Dead Men', which included the stanza,

> Then leave the dead in the earth, an organism
> not capable of resurrection, like mines,
> less durable than the metal of a gun,
> a casual meal for a dog, nothing but the bone
> so soon. But tonight no lovers see the lines
> of the moon's face as the lines of cynicism.

Like John Bain, Douglas interpreted his experience through poetry in which the dead emerged as more important actors than the living. Their deaths reminded both soldiers that, at any moment, they too might become the object of others' reflections on mortality.

On 11 November, the 8th Army expelled the last Germans and Italians from Egypt. Two days later, it recaptured Tobruk, whose fall the previous June had demoralized the British with a humiliating retreat and mass desertions. A week later, Benghazi fell. Three more weeks of marching, fierce fighting, armour battles and artillery exchanges brought the 8th Army back to El Agheila. Finally, after the loss of thousands of lives and many battles, the British were back in the Roman fortress they had captured in February 1941. Of that first British conquest of El Agheila in the Libyan province of Cyrenaica, Alan Moorehead had written,

> The ancient law of the desert was, in fact, coming into play. Once more the British had proved you can conquer Cyrenaica. Now unwillingly they began to prove that you cannot go on. It had been the same for both sides. Tripoli and Cairo were equidistant from Cyrenaica ... The trouble was that the farther you got away from your base the nearer the retreating enemy got to his. Consequently as you got weaker, the enemy got stronger.

This time, though, the British did not weaken. They solved some of the supply problems by rebuilding the shore ports that Rommel's sappers had destroyed. The British assaulted El Agheila on 11 December and battled for a week to expel the Germans. The chase continued from Libya's Cyrenaica province into Tripolitania. On 23

January, the 8th Army captured the Libyan capital, Tripoli. It was John Bain's twenty-first birthday. At the victory parade, Montgomery praised his soldiers for advancing 1,300 miles in three months. Their achievement, he said, was 'probably without parallel in history'. Winston Churchill, in Libya to share the glory, declared, 'Let me then assure you, soldiers and airmen, that your fellow-countrymen regard your joint work with admiration and gratitude, and that after the war when a man is asked what he did it will be quite sufficient for him to say, "I marched and fought with the Desert Army."'

The desert war moved to Tunisia, where the Axis received fresh reinforcements from Germany to block the Americans in the west and the British from the east. Taking advantage of the Mareth Line defences the French had built years earlier against a potential Italian thrust from Libya, the German and Italian forces dug in again to meet the British onslaught.

The 5/7th Gordons had endured searing daylight heat, freezing nights, rainstorms and long spells without cooked food or rest. Many had won battle honours, more lost their lives. Replacement troops were sent to the front to fill the missing men's places. One was a Scotsman from Banffshire named Bill Grey, who had volunteered from 'a cushy pen pushing job in Palestine' to go into combat. Bain thought he was brave, having been seen to stand up to a tough, drunken sailor and to play football well. Yet, when he and Bain became friends, Grey admitted having made 'a colossal blunder' in joining a frontline unit. Battle terrified him.

The deaths and wounding of the men around him affected John Bain more than the valour and the medals. Although he claimed not to be brave, he did not run from combat. He recalled that a captain in his company did, during a 'a mock attack on the Mareth Line'. The feint involved walking through a minefield to draw German fire that would allow the 2nd New Zealand Division to make 'a flanking movement called a left hook'. Bain, at that time the company runner, stayed beside the captain ready to transmit his orders.

We were going through this minefield. Our artillery was what they call a creeping barrage, so the range is gradually increased as the infantry goes in. Somehow it went wrong. Either the creeping barrage wasn't creeping fast enough, or we were advancing too quickly. We were under our own twenty-five pounders, and the German 88s were coming the other way. In the middle of this minefield, somehow we had wandered off the track, and the German machine guns, Spandaus, seemed to have a fixed line on the gap, everything seemed to be coming at us. I remember crouching down, because all this stuff was coming over. Without warning to us, the artillery centre put down smoke as well. Someone thought it was gas. I was crouching down with my head down, and the company commander on my right, not looking at anything. All you're doing is your teeth are chattering. And you're praying and you're swearing. I looked to see how he was getting on, and he wasn't there. He deserted. He'd gone back. He ran away in the middle of an attack. I never knew what happened to him. That was the last time I saw him.

The Tunisian fighting became so fierce that an officer in the Scots Guards Regiment wrote, 'I have seen strong men crying like children.'

General George Patton's II Corps drew the German 10th Panzer Division away from the Mareth Line, and Montgomery's offensive dislodged the rest of the German forces on 27 March. The Germans established their next line of resistance about twenty miles to the north in Wadi Akarit, a deep sand gulley four miles long and normally impossible for vehicles to cross. However, the winter rains had stopped and the ground was drying. To its left, away from the sea, was high ground along the Roumana Ridge. While waiting for the British to arrive, German engineers reinforced the wadi and the ridge with entrenchments, observation posts, mines and barbed wire.

The assault at Wadi Akarit began on the night of 5/6 April. Bain, whose recollection of earlier battles was sketchy, recorded with a poet's eye almost every detail of the brutal but relatively minor engagement. 'The ridge of hills was a dull grey dusty shade like the hide of an elephant,' he wrote.

After the sun had set, the surface darkened to a smoky blue which gradually melted into the gathering darkness. But, although the ridge was not physically discernible, there was not a man in the battalion who was not aware of its menacing bulk as they moved as quietly as they could to the area at the foot of the hill where they were to dig in and wait for the dawn when the other battalions in the brigade would pass through their positions and attack the enemy in the hills.

Just before daybreak, Bain and his Scottish friend Hughie Black were sheltering in a slit trench. Black looked behind and said, 'They're coming Johnny. Here they come. Poor bastards!' As a battalion of Seaforth Highlanders came close, Black said, 'All the best mate!' One of them answered, 'It's all right for you Jimmy ... Lucky bastard!' Bain recalled the Seaforth's 'tone of voice did not carry true resentment: it was rueful, resigned.'

Although John Bain absorbed every sound and smell of the battle, he was so remote from the experience that he wrote of himself in the third person. Watching the Seaforths pass his trench, 'John felt immense relief that he was not one of them but the relief was tainted with guilt.' He told Black that he feared that the Seaforths would reach the ridge at daylight and be 'sitting ducks'. 'Hughie nodded. "Sooner them than me. But let's hope they chase the bastards out. 'Cos you know what'll happen if they don't? It'll be us in there with the bayonet. And I don't fancy that one little bit."'

Gunfire erupted along the ridge. 'They [the Seaforths] were easy targets for the German machine gun fire,' Bain told an interviewer later. Major G. L. W. Andrews of the 5th Battalion of the Seaforths remembered, 'Once daylight came, I lay with my glasses fixed on Roumana, but not a man could I see amongst the clouds of slate grey smoke and chestnut dust which cloaked the entire ridge as the German guns and mortars hit back.'

In his memoirs, Bain continued the story: 'Twilight was sharpening into the metallic, clearer greyness of early morning but you could not see much of what was happening in the hills. Human figures moved insectile and anonymous in little clusters, forming irregular patterns that kept breaking and coming together again.' A battle was taking place, but B Company's orders were to stay in the trenches. The commander of D Company of the 5/7th Gordons, Major Ian Glennie, recalled that the advancing battalion fought at the base of cliffs a mile ahead. 'We then could do nothing but watch, but couldn't see very much at all.'

While the Gordons waited, Hughie Black bewailed the army's failure to provide breakfast or even a cup of tea. He drank some water from his flask, but spat out the 'camel's piss'.

A lieutenant from Headquarters Company brought orders for B Company's Corporal Jamieson to take the platoon up to the ridge. The men stepped in single file towards the sound of firing. John Bain's rhythmic plodding along the sand, combined with six months of unrelieved anxiety, induced in him 'an almost trance-like indifference to, or unawareness of, his immediate circumstances. It was not that he was mentally elsewhere; rather that his mind was nowhere at all. He had become a kind of automaton.' In that state, he climbed the ridge. When he reached the summit, the battle was over.

General Montgomery noted in his diary, 'We had on this day the heaviest and most savage fighting we had had since I commanded the 8th Army. Certain localities changed hands several times, my troops fought magnificently.' Neither Monty nor his senior officers referred in their written recollections to the events that followed the battle's conclusion. John Bain did, but only years afterwards.

At the top of the ridge, Bain saw the first corpses from the Seaforth unit that had passed him a few hours earlier. Hughie Black, indicating one dead soldier, said, 'There's one poor bastard's finished with fuckin'-an-fightin'.' Bain saw no wound, as if the man were asleep. B Company moved forward to the Germans' slit trenches. More dead lay over most of the ground. The Seaforths had lost more than one hundred men killed and wounded, as one of its officers, Major G. L. W. Andrews recalled. Black noticed that there were no wounded on the ground, concluding that the 'meat wagons' must have removed them. What happened next was unexpected. Bain recorded his impressions, again in the third person,

Then he saw that the other men in his section and from the other platoons must have been given the order to fall out because they were moving among the dead bodies, the Seaforths' corpses as well as the German, and they were bending over them, sometimes turning them up with an indifferent boot, before they removed watches, rings, and what valuables they could find. They seemed to be moving with unnatural slowness, proceeding from one body to another, stooping, reaching out, methodical and absorbed. Hughie had gone. He must have joined the scavengers.

In a post-war interview, Bain elaborated, 'My own friends went around looting the corpses, taking watches and wallets and that sort of thing. Off their own people. Why that is so much worse than taking it off the Germans, I don't know, but it was somehow.' He stopped thinking, transfixed in a state of 'almost trance-like indifference'. A poem he would write at century's end, 'Remembering the Dead at Wadi Akarit', made no reference to the looting of the dead:

> He sees the shapes of rock, the sand and rubble
> on which, at unshaven dawn, the bodies sprawl
> or lie with unpurposed and tidy decorum,
> all neat in battle-order and KD uniform.

His reaction to the desecration and pillaging of the corpses would change the course of his life.

FIVE

They are longing for those upon whose presence and affection they have long depended. They want their wives or mothers.

Psychology for the Fighting Man, p. 334

PRIVATE ALFRED WHITEHEAD had not married the girl who needed to finish school by the time the 2nd Infantry Division left Texas for Camp McCoy, Wisconsin, in late November 1942. A troop train carried them over a thousand miles north, 'as the land changed from sagebrush, then flat barren wheat land, to empty rolling farm country.' It reached Wisconsin, where many of the Southern boys saw snow for the first time. An excited soldier from Florida rolled around in the ice, stopping only when he realized how cold it was. Camp McCoy, carved out of 14,000 acres of Monroe Country in 1909, was the army's winter warfare training base. In February 1943, the division took part in warfare exercises in northern Michigan. Whitehead remembered, 'We learned there what cold weather really was – the thermometer stayed at a steady forty degrees below zero.' Whitehead coped with the cold by trudging on snowshoes to find alcohol and bring it back to the squad. Although he skirted the rules, he had no objection to discipline. 'Both as individuals and units,' he wrote, 'we were put through specific types of combat instruction designed to prepare us for the kinds of fighting we might be expected to run into overseas, until we believed we were the toughest outfit in the whole U.S. Army.'

Whitehead saw himself as one of the toughest in a tough outfit. His readiness to settle arguments with his fists got him into fights, and his weakness for alcohol added to his belligerency. In photographs, he looked brash, small in stature yet full of bravado, with curly chestnut hair parted in the middle and a boyish smile. One snapshot of him at Camp McCoy showed the young GI defiantly astride the hood of his commanding officer's jeep. His combat helmet's raffish angle seemed to say that this youngster was not afraid of anyone.

The nearest village to Camp McCoy was Sparta, in Kent County, where Whitehead spent as many off hours as he could getting drunk, shooting craps and courting. 'Taverns were plentiful, but money and women were on a strict war-time ration basis, so we had plenty of fights over both,' he remembered. He rented a room in Sparta, 'a place I could call my own on my time off', where he slept off his drinking bouts. Weekends found him spending days in a bar, nights in his room. He was a loner, who assumed the only remedy to his loneliness was a bride.

He spotted three young women one afternoon in a Sparta pool hall, and he offered to buy them some Coca-Cola. They turned him down. He asked another GI who the 'stuck up girls' were. The soldier said they were his sisters. Whitehead brought three bottles of Coke to the girls, but they still didn't want them from the cocky Southerner. A moment later, Whitehead noticed his wallet was missing and declared that no one could leave the pool hall until he had it back. This led to a brawl that ended with the arrival of MPs. When the other soldier saw that Whitehead had no money left, he invited him home for dinner.

This led to Whitehead's acquaintance with the soldier's three sisters and, soon, Whitehead's proposal of marriage to the oldest. A photograph of Selma Sherpe taken at about this time showed a young woman with buoyant blonde hair, tied back like Betty Grable's, and full lips that would have attracted almost any young man. She resisted his advances and his proposal, but she eventually dated him when he was out on liberty. 'Many happy evenings and weekends followed, and I found I was growing very fond of the Sherpe family, who gave a sense of belonging I never had at home.' There were dinners at the Sherpe farm, Pleasant Valley, as well as movies and carnivals. 'My Southern accent also provided some amusing moments,' he recalled.

'One Sunday, while assisting Mrs. Sherpe with Sunday dinner, I asked where she kept the "flare" (flour), and had the house in an uproar trying to figure out and find whatever "flare" was.' The Sherpes were incredulous when he told them about his childhood diet of 'wild onions, poke salad, wild mustard greens' and his career as a moonshiner. They enjoyed his visits, but Selma evaded Alfred's questions about a date for a wedding she had not agreed to.

'Many of the boys were getting married and had someone to come home to and live for,' Whitehead wrote. As the day for shipping out approached, he asked his sergeant for a pass to get married. The army gave him three days off, on the understanding he would return with a marriage certificate. Whitehead bought a ring and hitchhiked to the Sherpes' house, twelve miles from town. He gave the ring to Selma. The next morning, 9 August 1943, Mr and Mrs Sherpe drove the couple to a justice of the peace in Caledonia, Minnesota, where there was no waiting period for marriages. Their honeymoon was spent at the Sherpes' farm. The idyll did not last long.

At the end of September, Whitehead told his bride the division was going overseas. He reassured her he would win the war quickly and be home soon, but she responded gravely, 'It will be very hard for you, and it will be many years before you return.' On their last morning together, Selma wept. On 3 October, the newly minted troops of the 2nd Infantry Division boarded a train bound for New York. There, on 8 October, the USS *Florence Nightingale* was waiting to take the young soldiers in convoy across the Atlantic. As Whitehead approached the gangplank, he noticed a squad of MPs armed with rifles, bayonets and machine guns. They were there to ensure no one tried to desert.

SIX

Such a sufferer from war shock is not a weakling, he is
not a coward. He is a battle casualty.

Psychology for the Fighting Man, p. 353

A FEW MILES INTO THE EGYPTIAN DESERT east of Alexandria, the
prison at Britain's Mustafa Barracks was the final destination for
soldiers convicted of crimes from desertion and disobedience to rape
and murder. The base had stood, since the British occupation of Egypt
in 1882, beside the Roman camp that Octavian erected after his
victory over Mark Antony and Cleopatra in 24 BC. For the British, it
had additional resonance: in 1801, they had defeated Napoleon's
forces there; and the barracks was an assembly point for many of the
regiments sent on the disastrous Gallipoli campaign against Turkey in
1915. Like Rome, Britain used the base primarily to cow the natives
in Alexandria. The prison to punish wayward troops was a later
addition.

The military detention centre at Mustafa was notorious. Allan
Campbell McLean based a novel, *The Glasshouse,* on his fifty-six
days confined within its walls. A character in his book recalled that
the 'old sweats' who had done time in many prisons reserved a special
hatred for Mustafa Barracks:

Their talk always came round to the one in the desert near
Alexandria. The Alex one was the worst of the lot, they said, the
screws there egged on by a mad bastard of a commandant, who
would have stuck the boys in front of a firing squad if he hadn't

reckoned on Rommel doing the job for him when they had done their time and got back to their units.

One blazing afternoon in the early summer of 1943, an army truck dumped John Bain and five other prisoners at, in Bain's words, 'the great iron-studded door that looked almost jet-black against the high white walls'. The door to 55 Military and Detention Barracks opened, and the shackled convicts marched into a square formed by two-storey detention barracks and rows of solid steel cell doors. While the men stood at attention, a Military Policeman named Staff Sergeant Hardy informed them of their new status: 'From now on, you are S.U.S's – Soldiers Under Sentence. You will do everything at the double. You understand? Everything. You do not move unless it's at the double.' So confident were the guards that escape was impossible that they removed the men's chains. Staff Sergeant Hardy then marched them double-time into the middle of the square, where he turned them over to Staff Sergeant Henderson.

Hardy and Henderson dressed in identical starched khaki drill clothes, peaked caps and shining boots. In common with the other MPs guarding prisoners behind the lines, they had not been to the battlefront or faced the enemy in combat. This did not, however, deter them from playing tough with men who had. Henderson ordered each SUS to answer to his name and serial number. When the first, Private Morris, answered, 'Sarnt', the sergeant's face seemed to Bain to contort into 'a mixture of snarl and smile'. Henderson went into a rage: 'Not Sarnt, you dozy man! Staff! You call us Staff ... Understand? Staff's what you call us. All except the RSM [Regimental Sergeant Major] and the commandant. You call them Sir.'

> Reading out Bain's name and number, he said, 'I see you're in the Gordon Highlanders. What's your regimental motto?'
> Bain answered, 'Bydand.'
> 'Staff!'
> 'Bydand, Staff.'
> 'Bydand. Aye. And what does that mean, Private Bain?'
> 'Stand fast, Staff.'

'Stand fast. That's the motto of the Gordon Highlanders and they've always lived up to it. Till now. They never retreated. Not in the whole history of the regiment. But you didn't stand fast, Private Bain, did you! You horrible man. You took a powder. You got off your mark. You're a disgrace to a great regiment. My father fought with the Gordon Highlanders in the Great War. He stood fast, Bain. He didna take a powder. So I'm going to keep a special eye on you, Bain.'

Henderson detailed the daily regimen: reveille at zero six hundred hours, inspection, daily assignment of tasks, back into the cells at seventeen hundred, lights out at twenty-one thirty. Speaking was forbidden. 'If you're caught talking at any time you'll be on a charge and you'll get punished,' he said. 'Three days solitary on PD One. That's Punishment Diet Number One. Bread and water.' Bain noticed Henderson's lips curl to expose a 'mad, ferocious grin' as he ordered the new SUSs to strip and throw their clothes and belongings onto blankets. Henderson made a demonstration of examining item after item, then instructed them to wrap everything in the blankets and raise them over their heads.

When Henderson barked the order for the naked and sweating men to run back and forth across the square, humiliation gave way to physical pain. The weight pressing on Bain's arms was almost impossible to bear, although he was a physically strong twenty-one-year-old with a prizefighter's physique. For those with less stamina, it was worse. Henderson shouted, 'Get them knees up! Straighten them arms! Left-right, left-right, left … Right … wheel!' This went on relentlessly until the sun had nearly set, when Henderson ordered a halt and marched them to their cell.

Three other prisoners were already inside, squatting against the far wall and scouring a rusty bucket. The airless space, fifty feet long and only eight feet wide, reeked of urine. Henderson told the men to dress and take two blankets each from a pile in the corner. A diagram on the wall explained how the blankets were to be folded for inspection. Each man was issued a 'chocolate pot' for body waste. When Henderson locked them inside, each convict claimed a portion of the floor as his bed. Bain and two others, 'Chalky' White of the Middlesex Regiment and Bill Farrell from the Durham Light Infantry, whispered to one another in violation of the rules. Bain was afraid that someone was watching through a small hole in the door, although he did not hear anything. 'Of course you didn't,' Chalky whispered. 'The bastards wear gym shoes at night.' Farrell said their guards were worse than those in civilian prisons.

Chalky asked him, 'You been in civvy nick then?'

'Aye. Armley in Leeds. Six months.'

'What was that for?'

'Minding my own business.'

The first lesson of prison, Farrell explained, was never to ask a man his crime. He admitted, though, that his offence was stealing lead from a church roof. Chalky said he had served fifty-six days in the military 'glasshouse' at Aldershot, but he did not say what he had done. Suddenly, the door opened and a new voice shouted, 'SUS's … stand by your beds!' This was Staff Sergeant Pickering, who introduced himself as 'a proper bastard'. Lights out was in three minutes, Pickering shouted, after which he would be listening at the door. 'If I hear as much as a whisper I'll put the whole lot of you on the peg. That understood?'

Bain lay on one blanket and pulled the other two over his aching body. From a corner of the cell, a man with diarrhoea squatted noisily over his 'chocolate pot'. All Bain could do was wait for 'the brief mercy of sleep'.

Bain had not had a peaceful sleep since he witnessed his friends' looting their comrades' corpses at Wadi Akarit. In his mind, he had not run away, because he was no longer there. 'I seemed to float away,' he recalled. A psychiatrist later told him he had suffered a 'fugue'. From the Latin for flight, it meant a sudden escape from reality.

No one noticed his departure from the Roumana Ridge, until some minutes later a jeep stopped him. Still dazed, Bain stared at a lieutenant. The lieutenant asked him, 'Are you going back to rear echelon?' It was as simple as that. Bain got in, and the lieutenant took him to a camp in the rear.

From camp, he walked without a word into the desert, still carrying his Lee Enfield rifle. 'All he cared about was moving back, away from the front, away from where the dead Seaforths were disposed on the sand and rocks in their last abandonment, in their terrible cancellations, their sad mockery of the living.' Along the route he had traversed as a fighting soldier, he wandered in the opposite direction as a deserter. Trucks carrying men and supplies to the front ignored him, and in his 'trance-like state' he paid them little attention. He found cans of meat that had been abandoned by Italian troops, and he chanced upon a Gurkha private who invited him to share his tea and chapatis. Later, as he walked east along the desert road, an RAF supply truck stopped.

The driver introduced himself as Frank Jarvis and offered to take him to Tripoli. It did not take long for Frank to realize Bain was not a straggler: 'You're on the run, John? You can trust me, mate. I wouldn't shop you.' He would have to leave Bain outside Tripoli, before the RMP checkpoints where Bain would be arrested. 'You might be able to scrounge some grub at the Transit Camp but you'll get picked up sooner or later,' Frank warned. 'Unless you dress up as a wog or something. Kip up with an Arab bint.' John fell asleep for a few hours, until Frank stopped to brew tea. While they drank, Frank took some English cigarettes from a can he had picked up at the docks. 'You scared?' he asked Bain, as they lit up. 'I'd be fucking scared I don't mind telling you. They reckon the glasshouses out here are fucking terrible. Worse than in Blighty. And that's saying something.' John said he had not thought about it, adding, 'Nothing could be worse than action.'

Several miles before Tripoli, Bain got out of the truck to walk into town. Frank handed the young deserter three tins of corned beef and some hard-tack. As he was about to drive off, he said, 'You'd better take these, mate.' 'These' were the precious English cigarettes.

Walking alone with rifle and pack on his back, he reached Tripoli after dark. It occurred to him that the city had a port, from which he could stow away on a ship. He imagined that friendly sailors would hide and feed him on the voyage to Britain. There, all would be well. 'His reverie was abruptly smashed by the squeal of tyres as a fifteen-hundredweight truck skidded to a halt in the gutter at his side,' he wrote. The truck was driven by the Military Police. He was under arrest.

The army appointed a lieutenant to represent him at his court martial. At a brief meeting before the trial, the lieutenant prompted Bain for excuses, 'troubles at home perhaps', that he could use on his behalf. The defendant was no help, saying only that he was sick of the business of war. The court martial convened a few days later in Tripoli and convicted him of desertion 'in a forward area'. The crime was not as serious as deserting 'in the face of the enemy', but it was enough to earn him three years at hard labour in the harshest prison in North Africa.

Mustafa Barracks provided Bain with long hours to reflect on the life that had brought him to his desertion and imprisonment. He remembered the town where he spent much of his childhood, Aylesbury in Buckinghamshire, 'as a kind of amulet against despair, a dream of rural sweetness and light, an arcadian landscape in which music and poetry and the possibility of romantic love were ubiquitous presences'. Like all childhood fables, Bain's was inhabited by an ogre. His was his father, a tough veteran of the Great War and a brutal disciplinarian who did not permit his sons to wear underwear because it was 'sissy'. Also 'sissy', in the old man's view, were books, poems and classical music.

James Bain had married Elsie Mabel, a woman three years older than he was and a few notches up the social ladder, just after the Great War. While Bain had left his Scottish regiment as a private, Elsie's uncle had been an officer. The couple had three children, Kenneth, John Vernon and Sylvia. John was born in Spilsby, Lincolnshire, on 23 January 1922, while his father earned a livelihood photographing visitors on the beach at Skegness. When John was three, his father in a chimerical bid to break out of poverty moved the family to Ballaghaderreen in the Irish Free State and opened a photography studio. On the ship to Ireland from Liverpool, James played 'one of his little jokes' on three-year-old John, lifting him 'over the rail with only the black waves below me, leaping and foaming like enormous wolves, hungry for the proffered titbit'. The boy's cries for help earned only his father's 'wild laughter'.

The staff sergeants at the Mustafa Barracks resembled so many omnipotent fathers. Bain's description of his father's 'peculiar half-grin, half-snarl' came close to the 'mixture of snarl and smile' he spotted in Staff Sergeant Henderson. Although he made no direct comparison between his father and the MPs, Bain's appraisal of his father might have applied to Staff Sergeants Hardy, Henderson and Pickering: 'I now understood and have understood for many years that he was a sadist. I remember many instances of his grim pleasure derived from inflicting physical or mental pain on my brother or me ...' In Ireland, Kenneth and John survived on a diet of potatoes, porridge and soda bread. Meat appeared rarely. Sweets were unknown. Once, their father called the boys into the kitchen to give them a half-pound chocolate bar. With childish delight, Kenneth unwrapped it. Inside was a block of wood.

Their father kept a leather strop for sharpening straight razors on a hook beside the fireplace; but, Bain reminisced, 'I do not recall this one being used for any other purpose than flagellation.' The flagellated, of course, were Kenneth and John. When his business failed in Ireland, James Bain took the family back to England. They settled in Beeston, Nottinghamshire, where James opened another photography shop. When John was seven, he watched his father challenge a Sunday teatime guest, an unassuming man named Bob Linacre, to a fight. While the men's wives and children squirmed, James forced Bob to don boxing gloves, reduced him to a state of terror and bloodied his nose. 'What I felt was disgust and shame and hatred,' Bain wrote. 'Until then I think that I had known nothing but a simple fear of him. Now I hated him.'

For reasons left unexplained, John went to live with his father's parents in Eccles, Lancashire, for two years. Then, in 1931, when John was nine, the family moved together to that 'dream of rural sweetness and light', Aylesbury. Living in a dingy flat above the photo studio in Market Square was, in Bain's own account, anything but sweet. Their father continued to beat the boys, once knocking twelve-year-old John flat with a punch to the head. Their mother, whose hard-drinking husband was brazenly unfaithful to her, took refuge in her conversion to what John called 'that quasi-religion called Christian Science'.

While life with their father in Aylesbury was hardly 'sweetness and light', the Bain brothers retreated into a world of books and music that was. Kenneth taught himself to play his mother's piano, and John borrowed a wide range of books from the library – Dickens, T. S. Eliot, John Buchan and the lowbrow crime novels of Edgar Wallace. The boys wandered together into the meadows with armfuls of works by their favourite poets. Literature gave Bain his 'only distraction from the fairly grim present'. From the age of fourteen, he wrote poems that he did not show to anyone. The boys bought a gramophone, but they waited until their father was out of the house before playing Liszt, Debussy, Schubert and the great mezzo-soprano Marian Anderson. James Bain, detesting his sons' 'sissy' interest in music and books, enrolled them in the Aylesbury and District Boxing Club. Within two years, John made the final round of the British Schoolboy Championship.

James Bain told his sons he had enlisted in the army at fourteen and been wounded at Mons. His endless stories of Great War escapades, in which he invariably played a heroic role, made John suspicious: 'I began to wonder about their historical veracity, until his boasting became something of a secret joke between Kenneth and me.' To avoid a thrashing, they kept that joke to themselves. Yet his childhood was awash with reverence for a war he knew only through hearsay. John later told an interviewer, 'I also remember very vividly Armistice Days when I was a child, because I actually wore my father's medals. He got his medals out, and I would have them on my jersey, my jacket, whatever I was wearing.' He would turn out in the town square, while old soldiers observed silence for comrades who had died in France. 'It was a very militaristic occasion, in fact. I still feel uneasy. There was a kind of glorification of war itself.'

While their father made them wary of the army, the boys shared a fascination with the Great War's poetry, novels and films. To John, the conflict in the trenches was a 'tragic and mythopoeic event'. He became 'haunted by its imagery, its pathos, the waste, the heroism and futility' via the writings of Robert Graves, Siegfried Sassoon and Ernest Hemingway.

The 1938 Munich Crisis, when the British and French ceded western Czechoslovakia to Hitler's Germany, affected him less than 'two momentous discoveries: D. H. Lawrence and beer'. Having left school at the age of fourteen in 1936, he was working as a junior clerk in an accountant's office. In his free time, he read James Joyce, courted young women and drank Younger's Scotch Ale at the pub. He and Kenneth were not above getting into trouble, once drunkenly climbing the roof of a hotel to break into it. After their arrest and trial, the local newspaper called them 'the boxing Bain brothers'. Their two-year probation was less notable than the newspaper's disclosure that John was eighteen. Until then, his twenty-six-year-old girlfriend, Sally, thought they were the same age. She accepted the age difference, but John's father disapproved of the girl. He ordered John to leave her, backing up the command by throwing a punch. For the first time, John fought back and gave his father a black eye. It was the last time his father would strike him, but they stopped speaking to each other.

John's response to the declaration of war in September 1939 was 'one mainly of puerile excitement'. He did not, however, rush to the colours. When the German bombing raids known as the Blitz began in September 1940, Bain's mother and sister were evacuated to the Cotswolds for safety. The three men of the family stayed on in uncomfortable silence in Aylesbury. Having lost his job with the accountants after his arrest, John went to work selling spare parts for the Aylesbury Motor Company at thirty-five shillings a week. His attempted enlistment in the Royal Air Force faltered over the medical exam that discovered his bad eye. He wrote later in 'The Unknown War Poet',

> He enlisted among the very first
> Though not from patriotic motives, nor
> To satisfy the spirit of adventure …

In December, he and Kenneth decided to enlist in the Merchant Marine. While their motives were unclear, merchant service offered two advantages: a way out of an intolerable life at home and the opportunity, provided the Luftwaffe or Kriegsmarine did not sink their ship, to cruise around the world. With £400 that they stole from a hidden store of cash their father kept to avoid income tax, they fled to London. They spent lavishly, taking a room at the Regent Palace Hotel and buying tickets for Donald Wolfit's production of *King Lear* and Myra Hess's lunchtime recitals. They got drunk in one Soho pub after another. Finally, they went to the Shipping Federation to sign on as merchant seamen. 'Our interview with the uniformed officer at the Federation was brief and humiliating,' Bain wrote. They tried the docks in Cardiff and Glasgow, where the recruiting poster drew them into the infantry that Christmas.

The journey from Scotland to El Alamein to Wadi Akarit to the Mustafa Detention Barracks seemed to follow a grim logic. The conflict between his contempt for his father and his love of war litera-ture led to his flight from home and enlistment in the army. That Bain ended up, however much by chance, in a Scottish regiment as his father had in the First World War seemed more than coincidental. He had, after all, followed his father into boxing, boozing and woman-izing. Having escaped paternal cruelty by standing up to it, he took the one action – desertion – that would imprison him even more surely than he had been at home under his father's oppressive control. A system of gratuitous bullying confronted him now.

His poem 'Love and Courage', though written years later, captured his predicament:

> ... He could conceal
> his terror till his Company was called
> to face real battle's homicidal storm.
> He chose desertion, ignominy and jail.

That is, if any choice existed, which I doubt.

SEVEN

On him – the average, free soldier – victory depends.

Psychology for the Fighting Man, p. 365

IN LOWER MANHATTAN on Thanksgiving Day 1943, Stephen J. Weiss took the oath to 'support and defend the Constitution of the United States against all enemies, foreign and domestic.' At the end of the induction ceremony, similar to his own only twenty-five years before, William Weiss told his son, 'If you need me, just say the word.' The older man's reserve, an effect of wartime trauma, had denied Steve a functioning father since childhood. Neither father nor son knew the full psychological toll of America's previous war in Europe. *Fortune* magazine reported at the time of Steve's induction, 'Today, twenty-five years after the end of the last war, nearly half of the 67,000 beds in Veterans Administration hospitals are still occupied by the neuro-psychiatric casualties of World War I.' Steve was going where his father had been, to unlock secrets long concealed from him. He did not plan to 'say the word'. It was his time to experience war, and paternal guidance would have to come from the army.

Steve and the other recruits boarded a train bound for the army's transit camp at Fort Dix, New Jersey. The army issued him a serial number, 12228033, and ordered him to commit it to memory. If he were captured, that number, his name and his rank were all that he was permitted to tell the enemy. Fort Dix began the transformation of youngsters into soldiers. The previous year's hit song by Irving Berlin might have been written there:

This is the Army, Mister Green,
We like the barracks nice and clean,
You had a housemaid to clean your floor,
But she won't help you out any more.

While Fort Dix's officers and non-commissioned officers feasted on Thanksgiving turkey, a freshly sheared Steve Weiss spent all of that Thursday, as well as Friday, on his hands and knees scrubbing barracks floors. One week later, the army shipped him south to the Infantry Replacement Training Center (IRTC) at Fort Blanding, Florida. Weiss's General Classification Test score qualified him for Officer Candidate School and a shot at the Psychological Warfare Branch. But the army, he quickly realized, 'needed infantry replacements, not junior officers, in late 1943'.

The army posted Weiss to Combat Intelligence (CI), which a second lieutenant defined for him as 'specialized C.I. infantry probing beyond the front line, patrolling and observing either on foot or by jeep ...' Weiss wrote, 'Although seemingly glamorous, I felt that C.I. missions would be more dangerous than those assigned to the regular infantry.' Whether glamorous or dangerous, it was still the infantry. Weiss applied for transfer to Psychological Warfare. In the meantime, the army put him through seventeen weeks of Basic Training, 'map reading, aerial photographic interpretation, enemy identification, prisoner interrogation, infantry tactics, use of weapons, and small group cohesion'. Propaganda films screened at Fort Blanding, like director Frank Capra's *Why We Fight* series, did not impress him. He thought the documentaries 'gave a false impression of modern war' and 'added little to my reasons for enlisting'. Many aspects of life at Fort Blanding grated on the trainees, especially the swamps, the chow and what the GIs called 'chickenshit', rigid enforcement of petty rules. Incompetence was rife in an army that had expanded from its 1939 level of 227,000 regular soldiers (with another 235,000 National Guardsmen) to a total of 7,482,434 personnel by the end of 1943. Health care suffered along with everything else in the military's rapid growth. One medic gave Weiss stomach tablets for his athlete's foot, and another injected him with so many vaccines at the same time that he spent five days in the base hospital with a dangerously high fever.

Weiss experienced no anti-Semitic bullying or slurs at Fort Blanding, but the only other Jewish recruit he knew there did. This youngster, nicknamed Philly, was short and as religious as Weiss was secular. When a Southern redneck insulted Philly in anti-Semitic terms, Weiss warned the Southerner to lay off his friend or he would 'stomp his ass'. One day in the kitchen, Philly and the Southerner had a punch-up. The sergeant broke it up and ordered them to settle it in the boxing ring. The other trainees watched as Philly took punch after punch, but the Jewish kid did not go down. Philly was losing on points, until he smashed his opponent's jaw and knocked him out. The sergeant told the loser, 'If you don't change your attitude, I'll have you court-martialed.' To Weiss, 'this was an object lesson in human rights connected to the war itself.'

While Weiss underwent Basic Training at Fort Blanding, other recruits were deserting or suffering severe psychological problems. *Time* magazine reported that 300 trainees each week were succumbing to nervous breakdowns. Dr Edward Strecker, chair of the University of Pennsylvania's Psychiatry Department and an adviser to the Secretary of War, bemoaned 'the cold hard facts that 1,825,000 men were rejected for military service because of psychiatric disorders, that almost another 600,000 had been discharged from the Army alone for neuropsychiatric reasons or their equivalent, and that fully 500,000 more attempted to evade the draft ...'

The army Adjutant General alerted commanding generals in his letter of 3 February 1943, 'Absences without leave and desertion especially from units which have been alerted for movement overseas, have reached serious proportions.' Secretary of War Henry L. Stimson proposed a more punitive solution to the desertion problem. On 22 October 1943, he wrote to the Director of the Bureau of the Budget, Harold D. Smith, 'Absence without leave in time of war is under any circumstances a serious offense ... sufficiently grave to warrant serious punishment which cannot be imposed under the present limitations.' Stimson recommended that President Franklin D. Roosevelt issue an Executive Order suspending the limits on punishments in the Table of Maximum Punishments of the *Manual for Courts-Martial* of 1928. Roosevelt duly signed Executive Order 9367 on 9 November 1943, 'Suspending until further orders the maximum limitations of punishment for violations of Article of War 61.'

A letter from Brigadier General M. G. White, the army's Assistant Chief of Staff, informed army Chief of Staff General George C. Marshall that 'in May, 1942, there were 2,822 desertions ...' The overall number of deserters grew as the Army expanded, but the percentage remained low at less than 1 per cent of the total number of personnel in uniform. However, most of the desertions were coming from the small percentage of soldiers serving or about to serve as combat infantry troops.

General Marshall established a committee to study desertions and their relationship to nervous disorders. Among those he appointed to the committee was a First World War veteran, Brigadier General Elliot D. Cooke. Cooke assumed he was selected because 'if a guy like me could understand such a subject, anybody could'. Cooke had no fixed view of the problem, its causes or its solution. He noted in early 1943 that 'nearly as many men were being discharged from the Army as were entering through induction stations'. This was before most of them had been shipped overseas. General Cooke, a bluff and self-effacing soldier, wrote that he had not heard the word 'psychoneurosis' before this time and had no idea how to spell it. He also admitted to sharing a common military suspicion of 'psychiatricks'.

Cooke visited Fort Blanding during Weiss's training period. The camp commandant gave him access to one 'locked' and three 'open' wards for psychoneurosis patients. In an open ward, not all of the patients seemed genuine.

> A hundred or more patients were loafing around in hospital suits, talking, reading, or playing games. They didn't act any sicker than I did. As a group, they seemed just about like any other collection of soldiers. I spoke to one of the more intelligent looking ones.
> 'What's wrong with you, soldier?'

He stared at me defiantly.

'I'm queer,' he stated flatly, meaning he was homosexual.

Another patient complained of back pain, and a black soldier said simply, 'I'se got the misery.'

At the Officers' Club, Cooke had a drink with the camp psychiatrist to discuss the malingerers he had met. The psychiatrist told him,

> Whether you believe it or not, I can assure you those men suffer with the pains they complain about. You say they are malingerers and merely pretend to be sick. But, after ten years of practicing psychiatry, I am confident I can tell the difference between a person who is suffering from pain and one who isn't.

Pain with a psychological cause was still pain. Cooke said he did not understand, but he resolved to continue his investigation with an open mind.

At Fort Blanding, Steve Weiss gravitated to older soldiers, as if seeking a reliable father or older brother. Sheldon Wohlwerth, a twenty-eight-year-old trainee from Cleveland Heights, Ohio, became a friend. Wohlwerth was 'ungainly, artistic and bright' and had 'sound common sense'. Weiss said, 'I liked him a lot.' On completion of their seventeen weeks' Basic Training, Weiss and Wohlwerth went to Fort Meade, Maryland, for rifle training. To his surprise, Weiss qualified as a marksman. At Fort Meade, a recruit named Hal Sedloff befriended him. In civilian life, Sedloff had been a butcher. Weiss looked up to Sedloff, who like Wohlwerth was ten years his senior. The older man's extreme yearning for his wife and baby daughter, however, left him miserable. In April 1944, the army shipped Sedloff overseas from Newport News, Virginia. A week later, it was Steve Weiss's turn.

Not every soldier assigned to overseas duty made it as far as the ships. General Cooke interviewed doctors and recruits at induction stations, hospitals and army stockades to discover why so many were refusing to serve. Some of his discoveries undermined his faith in the young generation's patriotism. Special treatment by civilian Selective Service Boards had created resentment among draftees. 'When, in 1943, it was found that fourteen members of the Rice University football team had been rejected for military service, the public was somewhat surprised,' he wrote. They were not the only athletes whose talents spared them military service early in the war, and General Cooke sympathized with those who believed that local Selective Service Boards were unfair.

So urgent had the problem of desertion within the United States become that the Adjutant General's Office circulated a memo on 3 February 1943 to 'Commanding Generals, Army Ground Forces, Amy Air Forces, Services of Supply, the commanders of all ports of embarkation, all officers exercising general court martial jurisdiction in the United States' and commanders of most continental bases. The memo began, 'Absences without leave and desertion, especially from units which have been alerted for movement overseas, have reached serious proportions.' So many men had deserted it was impossible to put them on trial, 'except in aggravated circumstances'. Because many deserters preferred prison to overseas duty, the Adjutant General's Office wrote, 'The intent of the new regulations is that the shirker's purpose will be frustrated instead of assisted ... He must find that after early apprehension, a vigorous administration expedites his return to duty with his unit if it is still in the United States, or to an active overseas theater if his unit has gone.'

The memo painted a gloomy picture of draftees' willingness to take part in the war. Because the stockades were overflowing with captured deserters and others Absent Without Leave (AWOL), 'it has been necessary to encroach upon the barracks area for staging in order to house, feed and detain deserters and AWOL's [sic] apprehended'. The Adjutant General advised commanders to beware of the 'various tricks and ruses used to avoid being assigned to a task force or placed in a group for overseas shipment ...' The deserters' 'tricks' were:

a. They maim themselves, necessitating hospitalization.
b. They feign physical and mental illness.

c. They hide out for days to avoid being placed on an overseas shipment list.
d. They go AWOL in order to stand trial and be confined.
e. They dispose of clothing and equipment.
f. They throw away their identification tags.
g. They answer for absentees on roll call.
h. When an officer approaches the area, the word is passed along and they dash for the woods through windows and doors, even jumping from upstairs screened windows, taking the screens with them.

General Cooke extended his mission to Camp Edwards on Cape Cod, where 2,800 soldiers who had deserted in the eastern United States were imprisoned. (Deserters west of the Mississippi went to a similar prison in California.) Cooke asked the camp's commandant how long the men remained behind bars. 'As long as it takes to find out who they are and what outfit they belong to,' he said. 'Then we take them under guard and put them on a ship.' When trainees broke their spectacles or false teeth to avoid shipping out, the army changed the regulations so they could be sent to battle without them. Many went into hiding. The commandant said, 'We've dug them out of bins under the coal and rooted them out of caves and tunnels dug underneath their barracks.' Camp guards resorted to confining deserters in special compounds without explanation a few hours before putting them on trains for embarkation ports. Cooke asked whether any men tried to bolt outside the camp. 'Only when they're being taken to the port. Then they'll jump out of windows, off of moving trucks and even over the sides of harbor boats.' The army name for it was 'gangplank fever'.

Cooke spoke to the prisoners. Some had family worries that they had to deal with before they could leave the United States. One soldier said he could not abandon his wife, who was pregnant and sick. Others told him: 'I can't fire a gun or go under fire.' 'I can't kill anyone, I don't believe in killing people.' 'I was afraid, I guess, so I went home.' 'I wanted to see my girl; I don't like the Army and I'm scared of water.'

* * *

From Fort Meade, Steve Weiss, Sheldon Wohlwerth and the other graduate trainees went to Newport News to board ships. None of them knew their destination or their future divisions and regiments. As infantry 'replacements', they would fill positions left in the ranks by men who had been killed, captured, disabled physically or mentally or were missing in action. Some of the battlefield missing, about whom no one spoke, had gone 'over the hill', deserting the army with no intention of returning. As the replacements neared the Straits of Gibraltar aboard troop transports that were prey to German U-boats, a rumour circulated that they were bound for a place they had never heard of, Oran. The French Algerian port town, occupied by the Americans and British since November 1942, had become the US Mediterranean Base Section and theatre supply depot. A few of the replacements were so sure Oran was Iran that they lost a month's pay betting on it.

Brigadier General Elliot D. Cooke had beaten Weiss to North Africa, where he continued his research into the high rate of desertions and nervous breakdowns. He asked a nineteen-year-old corporal, Robert Green, if he had been afraid when the patrol he was leading ran into the Germans. 'Yes, sir, I was scared all right! Anybody tells you he isn't scared up front is just a plain liar.' Cooke probed the young soldier about men who 'cracked up'. He answered, 'Some of them do. But you can see it comin' on, and sometimes the other guys help out.' Cooke asked how he could see it 'coming on'. Green said they became 'trigger happy':

> They go running all over the place lookin' for something to shoot at. Then, the next thing you know they got the battle jitters. They jump if you light a match and go diving for cover if someone bounces a tin hat off a rock. Any kind of a sudden noise and you can just about see them let out a mental scream to themselves. When they get that way, you might just as well cross them off the roster because they aren't going to be any more use to the outfit.

Cooke wondered how to help such men, and Green answered,

Aw, you can cover up for a guy like that before he's completely gone. He can be sent back to get ammo or something. You know and he knows he's gonna stay out of sight for a while, but you don't let on, see? Then he can pretend to himself he's got a reason for being back there and he still has his pride. Maybe he even gets his nerve back for the next time. But if he ever admits openly that he's runnin' away, he's through!

In Algiers, a senior officer told Cooke, 'If a soldier contracts a severe case of dysentery from drinking impure water, his commander feels sorry for him and is glad to see the man sent to a hospital. But if the soldier becomes afflicted with an equivalent ailment from stress and strain, that same commander becomes incensed and wants the soldier court-martialed.'

General Cooke wryly proposed a cure, 'Then the only remedy is to eliminate fear.'

After two weeks in a camp near Oran, Steve Weiss and eighty-nine other replacements from Fort Meade boarded a converted British passenger liner, the *Strathnaver*, for the four-day cruise to Naples. The Allies had conquered Naples on 1 October 1943. By May 1944, when Weiss arrived, the Allied armies, the Mafia and the Allied deserters who controlled the black market in military supplies jointly ran the city. Thousands of soldiers were enriching themselves at army expense, stealing and selling Allied supplies. Some Italian-Americans had deserted to drive trucks of contraband for American Mafia boss Vito Genovese. Other deserters had joined armed bands in the hills, robbing both the Allies and Italian civilians. Reynolds Packard, the United Press correspondent who had lived in Italy before the war and returned on the first day of the invasion, wrote,

Within a few weeks Naples became the crime center of liberated Italy. And the word 'liberated' became a dirty joke. It meant to both the Italians and the invaders that an Allied military government got something for nothing: such as an Italian's wife or a bottle of brandy he took from an intimidated bartender without paying for it.

Prostitution, black marketing, racketeering, and confidence games were rampant ... It was a mixed-up circle. The GIs were selling cigarettes to the Italians, who in turn would sell them back to the Americans who had run out of them. But the main trade was trafficking in women.

Norman Lewis, an Italian-speaking British intelligence officer in Naples, noted the same phenomenon: 'Complaints are coming in about looting by Allied troops. The officers in this war have shown themselves to be much abler at this kind of thing than the other ranks.' The officers were both American and British, some of whom had sent looted artworks back to England on Royal Navy ships. When Lewis investigated corruption in Naples, the black marketeers' influential friends blocked him. He wrote,

> One soon finds that however many underlings are arrested – and sent away these days for long terms of imprisonment – those who employ them are beyond the reach of the law. At the head of the AMG [American Military Government] is Colonel Charles Poletti, and working with him is Vito Genovese, once head of the American Mafia, now become his adviser. Genovese was born in a village near Naples, and has remained in close contact with its underworld, and it is clear that many of the Mafia-Camorra sindacos [mayors] who have been appointed in the surrounding towns are his nominees ... Yet nothing is done.

Army gossip about these activities circulated among the troops, some of whom believed that the officers' behaviour justified their own acts of theft or extortion. Steve Weiss, as yet unaware of the war's seamier side, saw the Italian campaign in terms of his father's experiences of the First World War. The cargo wagons on the train he took from Naples to Caserta were just like the 'previous war's forty men and eight horses'.

At Caserta, the new GIs were stationed at the Replacement Depot (which they called the 'repple depot' or 'repple depple'), near the palatial headquarters of the 5th Army Group under British Field

Marshal Sir Harold Alexander. The former royal palace was also home to Allied press correspondents. One of the best, Australian Alan Moorehead of the British *Daily Express*, thought the headquarters 'a vast and ugly palace', even if it was more commodious than the GIs' tents. 'Unlike the field marshal,' Weiss wrote, 'we at the "repple depot" were herded together like cattle, waiting for assignment to any one of a number of infantry divisions fighting across the Italian peninsula. I was adrift, alone and friendless, as usual, in a sea of olive drab, feeling more like a living spare part.' For two weeks in May, the young soldiers had nothing to do while the army decided where to put them. At the end of the month, a sergeant called out the names of ninety soldiers for posting to the 36th Infantry Division at Anzio. Among them were two trainees from Fort Blanding, Privates Second Class Sheldon Wohlwerth and Stephen J. Weiss.

The 36th was a Texas National Guard division that had come under federal control in November 1940, whose men wore the Texas T, like a cattle brand, on their left shoulders. The commanding officer of the 'T-Patchers' was Major General Fred Livingood Walker, a First World War veteran with a Distinguished Service Cross for exceptional gallantry and a strong supporter of his troops. Ohio-born Walker had assumed command of the Texas division in 1941.

War for the 36th began with the first American landing on the European continent at the Bay of Salerno in southern Italy on 9 September 1943. German artillery dug into the Roman ruins at Paestum hit the invaders hard, pinning down one battalion of the 36th Division's 141st Regiment on the beach for twelve hours. The Texans pushed inland to launch a frontal assault on Wehrmacht units in the village of Altavilla. Misdirected American artillery, however, halted their advance and forced the men to scramble for shelter in the brush. When they eventually conquered the village, a German detachment moved onto a summit above to batter Altavilla with artillery. The 36th withdrew, momentarily exposing its divisional headquarters to a German onslaught. Assisted by hastily armed rear echelon cooks, typists and orderlies, the 36th retook Altavilla and secured the southern portion of the beachhead. The Salerno invasion cost the 15,000-man division more than 1,900 dead, wounded and missing.

As murderous as their first few days in Italy proved, the Texans soon suffered worse. When the Wehrmacht poured in reinforcements from the north, the counter-offensive hit the 36th head-on. The division suffered another 1,400 casualties while taking San Pietro, a key village in the Liri Valley on the route to Rome, in December. In January, Fifth Army commander General Mark Clark ordered General Walker to send his division across the Rapido River as part of an operation to break out of the Salerno beachhead. It was nothing less than a suicide mission. The fast flowing river at that time of year measured between twenty-five and fifty feet wide and around twelve feet deep, not an insurmountable obstacle. However, other factors militated against a successful crossing. Winter rain made the current both fast and powerful. The river's wide, muddy flood plain was impassable to trucks, forcing the men to carry boats to the bank. The Germans had planted a dense field of landmines, and they positioned heavy artillery on the heights beyond the river's west bank. General Walker opposed the operation, but he obeyed Clark's orders. His men, as he feared, were slaughtered during three attempted crossings. Those who made it to the other side fought without air or armour support. Lacking communication with the friendly shore, they ran out of ammunition and were driven back by German artillery. The two-day 'battle of guts' ended on 22 January with 2,019 officers and men lost – 934 wounded, the rest killed or missing in action. Some of the missing had drowned, and their bodies were swept downstream. General Walker wrote in his diary after the Rapido failure, 'My fine division is wrecked.' Raleigh Trevelyan, a twenty-year-old British platoon commander in Italy, summed up the 36th's resulting reputation, 'The 36th had, frankly, come to be looked down on by the other divisions of the Fifth Army. It was considered not only to be a "hard luck outfit", but trigger happy.'

In eleven months of Italian fighting, the division lost 11,000 men. Only 4,000 thousand of the original cadre remained, the rest having been replaced by inexperienced young recruits like Steve Weiss. When Weiss arrived in Italy in May 1944, there were few less hospitable divisions than the war-drained 36th and no more dangerous place than the Anzio beachhead. In his memoirs, General Clark called Anzio a 'flat and barren little strip of Hell'. British platoon commander Trevelyan wrote that 'nowhere in the Beachhead was safe from bombs or shells'. Even the naval shore craft, the only means of supplying the troops from the rear area at Naples, were subject to German fire.

Only thirty miles from Rome, the beaches had been peacetime resorts with first class hotels, restaurants, cafés and ice-cream shops. Allied bombardment of Anzio and Nettuno before the landing, intended as an end run north of Salerno that would ease the advance to Rome, emptied both towns of most of their inhabitants. The Anzio invasion began at two o'clock on the morning of 22 January 1944, when the US 3rd Infantry Division hit the undefended beach and British commandos and American Ranger units took control of the surrounding area. As with the landing at Salerno, early success was undermined by the Allies' failure to take advantage of weak German defences by pushing quickly inland. The Germans thus had time to regroup and counter-attack. By May 1944, when Private Steve Weiss and the other replacements arrived to fill the ranks of the badly depleted 36th Division, the Allies were still dug in on the exposed beachhead.

The first soldiers Weiss encountered were barricaded in a make-shift stockade of wood and barbed wire. The fifty dishevelled troops were not German prisoners of war, but, to Weiss's astonishment, Americans. 'Under armed military police guard, some of the prisoners seemed very weary and disoriented, like vagrants down on their heels and luck,' Weiss wrote. 'Others, more aggressive than the others, threatened and hurled obscenities at us, warning, with pointed finger or clenched fist, we'd end up like them, misunderstood and deserted by the army.' The army, though, had not deserted these men. They had deserted the army.

Raleigh Trevelyan, the British platoon commander who spent months at Anzio, wrote that not all deserters were in the stockade: 'There were said to be three hundred deserters, both British and American, at large on the Beachhead. At first nobody made out where they could hide themselves in such a small area.' Another British officer, Lord John Hope of the Scots Guards, was bird-watching in some deserted gardens east of Nettuno, when he uncovered a cache of canned food under a pile of wood. He told Trevelyan:

> I turned a corner and was confronted by two unshaven GIs, one with a red beard, with rifles. I knew it was touch and go. 'What are you doing here?' one of them asked. I showed him my British badges, and when I said I was bird-watching they burst out laughing. They pretended they were just back from the front.

Hope reported the deserters to the American Provost Marshal, who sent MPs in a jeep with Hope on the hood to show the way. They found the deserters, who, in Hope's words, 'jumped up and ran like hell into a tobacco field; the men in the jeep belted off into the crops ... No expedition was organized to go into the bushes to find out who was there. Men just couldn't be spared.'

United Press correspondent Reynolds Packard came across another deserter near Anzio. The American soldier had no rifle, a court martial offence. Packard asked where it was. 'Fuck it,' the GI said. 'I threw it away. I've quit fighting this goddamn war.' Packard told his jeep driver to hold the deserter while he searched for the missing weapon. He found it and gave it to the soldier, who threw it away again. 'Fuck this war,' he said. 'I'm not fighting anymore.' Packard decided to take him to division headquarters:

> Just before we got there, I hauled off and hit him, knocking him unconscious.
> 'What the hell are you doing?' my driver, Sergeant Delmar Richardson, asked. 'Gone nuts?'
> 'I don't want to take him into a hospital while he's talking about not fighting this fucking war anymore. That's all.'

The deserters in the Anzio beach stockade, like sentries at the inferno's gates, persisted in their warnings to Weiss and the other arrivals. The replacements endured the abuse, until trucks pulled up to take them away. They drove through Anzio town, most of it destroyed by Allied and then German bombardment, to a hill above the beach. There they made camp for the night.

In the morning, Steve Weiss attended the Catholic chaplain's outdoor Mass. He then went to find his friend from Fort Meade, Hal Sedloff. Sedloff had been posted to the 45th 'Thunderbird' Infantry Division, composed of National Guard units from Oklahoma, Colorado, Arizona and New Mexico. The 45th had fought as part of General George Patton's Seventh Army in Sicily the previous July, took the beach at Salerno in September and landed at Anzio in January 1944. Although Sedloff went into the line with the 45th as it fought its way north to Rome, Weiss discovered he was still near Anzio in a field hospital. A nurse there told Weiss that Sedloff had taken part in two battles, but he had been incapable of fighting due to 'night blindness'. His wounds were not physical. Weiss did not understand. The nurse explained that he had 'battle fatigue', a term Weiss heard for the first time. In his father's war in 1918, they called it 'shell shock'. Army psychiatrists had begun using the term 'psychoneurosis', while the British preferred 'battle exhaustion' with its implication that rest could cure it. The nurse whispered to Weiss, 'No one is immune.' Weiss was unaware that, by this stage of the war, a quarter of all combat casualties were psychiatric.

Deciding that Sedloff's trauma made him a risk to a combat unit, medical staff recommended him for rear echelon duty. This was a discreet and humane way to retain the services of men rendered unfit for combat. One battalion officer, after relieving a veteran from further frontline duty, explained, 'It is my opinion, through observation, that he has reached the end of endurance as a combat soldier. Therefore, in recognition of a job well done I recommend that this soldier be released from combat duty and be reclassified in another capacity.' Weiss, who guessed that Hal Sedloff cracked because he still missed his wife and daughter, left the hospital without being allowed to see his friend.

'I thought Hal, at twenty-eight, was someone to depend on, because of his age and experience,' Weiss wrote. 'I was chilled by the prospect of carrying on, alone, without the support of and belief in some kind of father figure.'

Weiss's initiation into the war zone had been a beach stockade filled with men who ran from battle and an older friend comatose with fear. Neither increased his confidence in himself or the army. Aged 18 without someone to trust, he questioned his capacity to measure up under fire. A study of American combatants had found that 36 per cent of men facing battle for the first time were more afraid of 'being a coward' than of being wounded. Weiss needed an experienced commander to show the way, but officers and non-commissioned officers did not survive much longer on the line than enlisted men. Many were replacements themselves, without time to become acquainted with soldiers under their command. The replacement system, as the army was beginning to realize, undermined morale. Weiss did not know that, not yet.

The system in earlier conflicts withdrew whole regiments or divisions from battle to absorb replacements during re-training. This permitted new soldiers to know their officers and their squad-mates. General George C. Marshall, the US Army Chief of Staff, had initiated a policy of replacing individual soldiers within each division without pulling them back from the front. Marshall explained, 'In past wars it had been the accepted practice to organize as many divisions as manpower resources would permit, fight those divisions until casualties had reduced them to bare skeletons, then withdraw them from the line and rebuild them in a rear area ... The system we adopted for this war involved a flow of individual replacements from training centers to the divisions so they would be constantly at full strength.' The First World War's 30,000-man divisions had been cut in half for the Second, and divisional losses in combat left many with a majority of troops who did not know one another. Marshall concluded, 'If his [an army commander's] divisions are fewer in number but maintained at full strength, the power for attack continues while the logistical problems are greatly simplified.' Logistics were simpler, but group loyalty evaporated.

In the evening after Weiss's attempt to visit Hal Sedloff, Luftwaffe planes breached the Anzio defences and bombed the beachhead. Steve Weiss watched five German HE-111 medium bombers soar only 500 feet above him. Ground fire, he wrote, was 'erratic, no spirited defense here'. Why weren't the anti-aircraft batteries doing their job? The planes hit several targets, including an American ammunition depot, and flew away untouched. Weiss felt that American soldiers were unsafe everywhere, even on a beachhead that had been established four months before. How much worse would it be in the hills where the 36th Division was face to face with the Germans? Ordnance from the ammo dump exploded and burned all night, its unnatural light reminding Weiss of the war his father never told him about.

EIGHT

They enlisted in a condition almost like drunkenness and some woke up to find themselves under arms and with a headache.

Psychology for the Fighting Man, p. 306

A CACOPHONY OF TIN WHISTLES and shouts from the prison yard woke SUS John Bain from the refuge of sleep. His eyes adjusted gradually to dawn trickling through three small windows set high in the wall opposite his cell door. On this first morning at the Mustafa Barracks, he experienced a double awakening: to the curses and groans of his eight fellow prisoners and to 'a drench of pure horror as the full knowledge of his circumstances drove like a bayonet to the gut'. Sight and sound disturbed him less than the smell of 'unclean bodies and bodies' waste, the reek of disgrace and captivity'.

Staff Sergeant Pickering unbolted the door. The nine prisoners snapped to attention, grasping their 'chocolate pots'. Pickering ordered them to the latrines to 'slop out' the pots, back to the cell to fetch their wash bags and double-time outside again. Pressing their faces to a wall, they waited for Pickering to bring a tray of razors. The used blades were so blunt that Bain cut his cheek. A staff sergeant whom Bain had not seen the day before relieved Pickering: 'The NCO advancing towards them across the square was short, not a great deal over five and a half feet, but he looked powerful, his shoulders wide and the exposed forearms thick and muscular. He had a neat dark moustache and his eyes were small and very bright, like berries.' He was Staff Sergeant Brown.

71

Under the barking of Brown's commands, the SUSs marched, double-time, to the storehouse for buckets and brushes. For an hour on hands and knees, they scrubbed the barrack square. With that completed, they carried their mess tins to the cookhouse. Kitchen workers filled half of each tin with congealed porridge and bread, the other half with tea. The SUSs rushed back to their cell, inevitably spilling tea, to eat. Next came Physical Training, which veteran inmates called Physical Torture.

Under a cloudless African sky, Staff Sergeant Henderson directed standard military calisthenics: jumps, bends, push-ups and sit-ups. Wearing full combat uniform, including heavy boots, in heat over 100 degrees Fahrenheit, the men tired more rapidly than during the toughest training in Britain.

Sweat flowed within seconds. In minutes, the men were winded. When one collapsed onto the sand, Henderson kicked his ribs to get him back up. The men were 'gasping for air like stranded fish and trying desperately and ineffectually to press their bodies clear of the ground'. Then, along with another two hundred or so inmates in the square, they halted.

Into the sandy square sauntered Regimental Sergeant Major Grant. Dressed more smartly than the already punctilious staff sergeants, he wore a tailored uniform with a hat and Sam Browne belt normally reserved for officers. A leather band with a shiny RSM insignia was tied around one wrist. Bain saw in Grant's face 'the bitter, clenched and potentially vicious expression that seemed to be part of the uniform of the corps'. His apparent lack of physical strength lent him 'a powerful sense of menace'. RSM Grant strolled among the ranks without a word, reeking disdain.

'You will march at the double,' Grant instructed the six new arrivals. 'I give the commands mark time, then halt and then right-turn. You will then be facing Captain Babbage.' Babbage was camp commandant. 'He'll have your documents in front of him. He'll read out your sentences, which you already know. Then he'll read out the official rules and regulations of Number Fifty-Five Military Prison and Detention Barracks. He'll ask if you've got anything to say. My advice is to keep your mouths shut.'

Bain, a meticulous observer, was harsh in his unspoken assessment of prison staff. It astounded Bain that Babbage, slouched at his desk, was 'quite as repulsive as he was':

> He was very fat and the sparseness of the colourless hair that was spread in ineffectual thin strands across the pale and lumpy baldness of his head made it difficult to guess his age. The open collar of his KD [khaki drill] shirt showed his almost imperceptible chin disappearing into folds of flesh and his mouth was half open and sagged slightly to one side. The rest of his features were smudged and blurred; his eyes were ill-tempered and bilious looking and the pudgy hands on the desk were noticeably tremulous.

Captain Babbage dealt with each man in turn, reading out name, sentence and offence. To Bain, he said, 'Three years penal servitude. Desertion in a forward area.' Bain was not expected to respond, and he didn't. Babbage, whose appearance did little to detract from his pomposity, launched into a speech he must have given before:

> You're here because you committed crimes. In your case – all of you – it's the crime of desertion. You're all cowards. You're all yellow. You think you're tough guys and you're not. You're soft and you're yellow. If you weren't you wouldn't be here. You'd be with your comrades, soldiering, fighting. Well, you listen to me. You thought you'd leave the dirty work to your comrades. You'd have it nice and easy here. In fact I wouldn't be surprised if you don't wish to God you were back with your units. Wherever they are. We're going to punish you. Make no mistake about it …

Babbage continued in this vein, berating them for cowardice and threatening additional punishments. He warned, 'You get funny with us and we'll smash you.' He recited the regulations, which included: no photographs to be kept; no smoking, ever; no speaking except on Communication Parade, which was ten minutes per day, under the eyes of the staff sergeants; one censored letter to be written home every other Sunday; complaints to be made only to the commandant;

frivolous complaints to be punished by solitary confinement on Punishment Diet Number One (eight ounces of dry bread twice a day and a bucket of drinking water); and violence or threats of violence to earn constraint in body-belts and straitjackets. 'Any questions?'

There were no questions. RSM Grant returned them to the square and Staff Sergeant Brown. Brown ordered them to the cell and into full Service Marching Order, which mean fastening on large and small packs, (empty) ammunition pouches, gas cape and ground sheet. Brown drilled them for an hour outdoors, marching them forward and back, wheeling and turning. Bain remembered struggling for breath and being unable to see for sweat over his eyes. At drill's end, they marched back into the cell to clean it. The time was eleven in the morning.

Tiffin, or lunch, was at noon: the same as breakfast, except that jam was added to the bread. The afternoon consisted in pack-drill, during which Bain experienced 'a dark numbness' that defused some of his anger. Standing motionless, the SUSs were ordered to talk to one another for ten minutes. This was Communication Parade. The staff sergeants walked up and down the lines, directing men who were not talking to speak to the man opposite, telling those who were speaking to watch what they said. Bain did not know the man he was facing, but, to avoid a reprimand from Staff Sergeant Brown, asked him his civilian job. He had worked at Watney's Brewery. Brown ordered Bain to continue talking, and he asked, 'Read any good books lately?' This made the man smile, prompting a rebuke from Staff Sergeant Brown: 'I catch you two grinning again I'll have your dinners.' At Mustafa Barracks, 'Smiling on Parade' was a punishable offence.

Late afternoon brought the last meal of the day: watery mutton stew with rice. The SUSs ate silently in their cells, and the lights went out on schedule at 9.30 p.m. 'John had completed a full day,' Bain wrote, 'one which, with perhaps minor changes, would be the model for every other week-day he would spend as a prisoner in this place.' Some days were different in one respect: they were worse.

Six weeks into Bain's confinement, the administration introduced a novel punishment: the hill. One afternoon, a truck delivered three loads of sand that the SUSs piled onto a corner of the square. They returned to their cells that night wondering what new torment the sand portended.

Ray Rigby, a British writer who as a soldier served two spells in a British military prison in North Africa, wrote about another sand pile in his novel *The Hill*. As at the Mustafa Barracks, his fictionalized prison received truckloads of sand without explanation one day: 'All day long trucks roared into the prison grounds and deposited the sand, and slowly the hill began to take shape. The prisoners, bare to the waist and sweating in the intense heat, shovelled away in silent fury.

The hill grew, reinforced with large rocks, until the men had built it up to a height of sixty feet. Rigby wrote that 'every man-Jack of them hated the sight of it'. They were ordered to scale its summit and race down the far side, again and again, until they could no longer walk, let alone run. A staff sergeant forced one prisoner over the hill so many times that it killed him. The hill of the novel symbolized everything the inmates, and even a few guards, despised about British military justice.

At Mustafa Barracks, on the morning after the SUSs had piled the sand up at one corner of the square, the staff sergeants ordered them to collect two buckets each. Columns of inmates ran double-time with a bucket in each hand, filled them with sand, ran to the diagonal corner of the square and poured it out. The morning's labour succeeded in moving the entire hill from one corner to the other. When they had finished, their lungs gasping for the dry desert air, the men were ordered to move the sand back again. This would be repeated, along with drills and Physical Training, every day. The sand hill at Mustafa Barracks epitomized the Sisyphean absurdity of their daily 'tasks'. Bain called it 'the sheer lunacy of the regimen.'

Joseph Heller, who served as a bombardier in the US Army Air Forces in Italy, observed a similar madness in his army's punishment system. It led him to conceive the character of a habitual deserter, Ex-Private First Class Wintergreen, in his comic masterpiece *Catch-22*:

Each time he went AWOL, he was caught and sentenced to dig and fill up holes six feet deep, wide and long for a specified length of time. Each time he finished his sentence, he went AWOL again. Ex-P.F.C. Wintergreen accepted his role of digging and filling up holes with all the uncomplaining dedication of a true patriot.

'It's not a bad life,' he would observe philosophically. 'And I guess somebody has to do it.'

On alternate Sundays, the men at Mustafa Barracks wrote letters. Bain wanted to write to his brother, but he did not know where Kenneth's unit of the Royal Engineers was stationed. He had no desire to communicate with his parents, so he fabricated a family as remote from his own as his imagination could contrive. This Bain family's exalted address was Radcliffe Hall, Long Willerton, Hampshire. His letters referred to his younger brother at Eton and their fox-hunting sister. Knowing that Captain Babbage censored inmates' letters, Bain employed as many difficult words as he could to force the lazy officer to consult a dictionary.

Commandant Babbage, RSM Grant and the staff sergeants held absolute power over Bain and the other prisoners. They could insult them, humiliate them and batter them. Any man who allowed himself to be provoked into striking back was restrained in a bodybelt, and, out of sight of other prisoners, beaten senseless. In Rigby's *The Hill*, based on the author's experience, the camp medical officer accepted the staff sergeants' explanations that prisoners with broken noses and ribs had fallen down. Bain did not mention similar cover-ups by the MO at Mustafa Barracks, but he noticed that no staff sergeant was reprimanded for mistreatment.

Every night in their cells, some of the men whispered among themselves. They did it softly to avoid detection by staff sergeants listening at their doors. But Chalky White, cocky as ever, sometimes raised his voice. One on occasion, Staff Sergeant Hardy flew into the cell and shouted at White, 'You've been communicating, haven't you?'

'No, Staff.'

'I saw you! I heard you! You were communicating, you horrible little man, weren't you?'

'Yes, Staff.'

Hardy imposed Punishment Diet Number One, bread and 'desert soup', in a solitary cell for three days. Stating that it took two to communicate, he charged Bill Farrell with listening and gave him the same sentence. Three days later, the two prisoners returned to the communal cell chastened and starving.

In the parade square one afternoon, harsh sunlight glowing off the white walls made Bain squint. Suddenly, Staff Sergeant Pickering called out, 'You there! What do you think you're grinning at?' Bain thought Pickering was speaking to someone else, until he closed on Bain's ear: 'You horrible man! Answer when I ask you a question. What do you find so funny? Why were you grinning?'

'I wasn't grinning, Staff.'

'Are you calling me a liar?'

'I was frowning. The sun was in my eyes. I've got fuck all to laugh at.'

'You're right! You've got fuck-all to laugh at. And you'll have a bit less tomorrow when you're on jockey's diet.'

The next morning in Captain Babbage's office, RSM Grant read out the charge: 'Smiling on Parade', Bain pleaded to Babbage, 'I wasn't smiling, Sir. The sun was in my eyes. I was frowning.'

'If the Staff Sergeant says you were smiling,' Babbage replied, 'that's what you were doing.' He sentenced him to three days on Punishment Diet Number One in solitary confinement.

The isolation cell, on the upstairs floor in one of the barracks, measured six by eight feet. Three blankets, a piss-pot and a bucket of water lay on the stone floor. When Staff Sergeant Hardy locked him in, Bain thought, 'I've got to stay here for three days, seventy-two hours, with nothing to do, nothing to read, nothing to look at. I shall go mad.'

Bain squatted on the ground and thought back to the first book of poems he had ever read, Algernon Methuen's *Anthology of Modern Verse*. With the fond recollection of a first love, he saw his teenaged self opening the book at Thomas Hardy's 'Afterwards'. ('When the present has latched its postern behind my tremulous stay ...') Reading a sequence of Hardy poems had afforded a kind of pleasure he had not known before. The next poem he had read was Walter de la Mare's 'Farewell', which he whispered to himself in the cell:

> When I lie where shades of darkness
> Shall no more assail mine eyes,
> Nor the rain make lamentation
> When the wind sighs;
> How will fare the world whose wonder
> Was the very proof of me?
> Memory fades, must the remembered
> Perishing be?

Reciting verse eased the first hours of idleness and solitude. He was soon recalling when and where he had discovered various poets. T. S. Eliot and A. E. Housman came in the winter of 1938, during the Junior Amateur Boxing Association Championship at the Holborn Stadium Club. His thoughts wandered forward to 'that long and golden summer of 1940 ... a lyrical interlude of sheer pagan bliss' in the arms of a girl named Barbara. Where, he wondered, was she? He feared she 'was probably bringing comfort and joy to some well-hung G.I.'. Putting her out of his mind, he paced the cell. There were four more hours until the evening slice of dry bread.

Bain had until then resisted the temptation to hate the guards, keeping at bay emotions that he believed self-destructive. But hunger for food and books was forcing him to despise Pickering. Even if 'Smiling on Parade' had been a legitimate cause for a penalty, Bain had not been smiling. He had not done anything. Childlike rage consumed him, and he sought an outlet in imagined acts of revenge.

He saw himself after the war, walking up to Pickering in a pub. He would ask the former staff sergeant whether he recognized him. Pickering would say no. Bain would answer, 'Does Mustafa, Alexandria mean anything to you?' As Pickering made for the exit, Bain would grab him by the arm. At the moment of retribution, reality intervened in the form of commands barked by the staff sergeants outside.

Bain was suddenly 'embarrassed, even a little ashamed, as if his fantasizing had been observed.' As the hours passed, filling time challenged his imagination. He tried to name a novelist for each letter of the alphabet, 'then a composer, then a boxer, a poet, a cricketer, a politician and so on …' Hardy opened the door, threw him his evening slice of bread and said, 'Try not to make a pig of yourself.' The guard taunted Bain with that night's menu at the sergeants' mess: steak, fried potatoes, salad, fruit, cheese and, afterwards, drinks in the bar. 'How's that sound?'

'It sounds very nice, Staff.'

'You fancy yourself, don't you? You think you're a fly man. Well, you're not. You're nothing. You're nobody. And let me tell you this. There's a few of us got our eyes on you … So, watch your step, my lad, or you're going to get a lot worse than PD One.'

That evening, an unexpected act of near-kindness by Staff Sergeant Brown plunged Bain into confusion. Brown came into the cell just before lights out and told him to get his blankets ready for the night. 'I'd use one of them for a pillow if I was you,' he said, 'and keep your clothes on. Gets cold in the night.' Brown's words, so unexpected, hinted at something 'approaching humanity'. When the cell went dark, Bain regretted Brown's solicitude. Clinging to the purity of his hatred, he curled into a foetal position with his head on a folded blanket and thought, 'Fuck 'em all, including Brown.'

Staff Sergeant Henderson woke him in the morning with another piece of bread. Bain kept half of it to eat later. When Henderson returned to the cell, he seized the leftover bread. 'You've been hoarding food. You expecting a siege or something?' Bain's fists clenched, but he kept them at his sides. 'Don't you look at me like that, lad!' Henderson exited the cell before Bain could move.

Alone without the food he had saved, Bain was more outraged with himself than with Henderson. His inaction made him feel cowardly:

All right, he thought, they were right, the commandant and the rest of them. He was a coward. If he hadn't been a coward he would have knocked Henderson's dirty teeth down his throat. He hadn't done it because he was afraid. He was afraid of the consequences: the body-belt, that wide leather waist-band with a steel cuff on either side to pin the prisoner's hands down so that he was a man without arms, defenceless against the time they crept, silent at night on plimsolled feet, to burst into the cell and use him as a punch-bag and a football ... He was afraid.

Bain was closer to despair than at any other time since his arrest. But it struck him that Henderson's eyes had betrayed fear. The staff sergeant had left the cell quickly, much faster than usual. If Henderson taunted him again, 'He'd smash the bastard.' Henderson did not taunt him again.

The treatment meted out to him earned a mention in his poem 'Compulsory Mourning':

> You'll be confined in darkness and we'll not
> Allow you more than two hours' light each day.
> You'll be on bread and water. There you'll stay
> For three full days and nights and we shall find,
> I think, that this will concentrate the mind ...

Bain returned to the communal cell after his three days' isolation, secure in the knowledge that he had survived PD One and could do it again.

No news reached the inmates, apart from what little seeped through in censored letters from their families. Bain did not know that his friend Hughie Black and the rest of the 5/7th Gordon Highlanders were fighting that summer in Sicily. After Bain left them at Wadi Akarit, the Gordons had advanced north up the Tunisian coast. Tunis fell on 12 May 1943, ending the North African campaign. The 51st Highland Infantry Division disembarked for Malta on 5 July, spent three days near Valletta and landed unopposed on the Sicilian beaches on 10 July. The British and Americans achieved victory in Sicily on 17

August. But, as in North Africa, they failed to prevent the bulk of the Axis forces from escaping to fight again.

Chalky White, who seemed privy to every rumour circulating in the barracks, told Bain that a second front was about to open in Europe. The army had begun recruiting men for the invasion even from military prisons. Soldiers willing to fight again would have their sentences remitted for the duration. Bain had doubts.

The steady cruelty of the regime persisted. 'More days passed, each an ugly replica of the one that had gone before,' Bain wrote. Bain's friend from the Durham Light Infantry, Bill Farrell, collapsed during drill. The sergeants took him away, and Chalky White told Bain later, 'Bill's kicked the bucket, the bastards killed him. I'll get one of them fuckers for this, I swear to God.' White and the other SUSs, however, were powerless.

Bain, whose hatred of the guards was growing 'like a malignant flower,' wrote,

> It was outrageous that the mean, stupid and sadistic staff, not one of whom had ever been within range of any missile more dangerous than a flying cork, should be able to abase, mock and abuse men who were, in many cases, their physical, moral and intellectual superiors or at least had been tested in circumstances of pain and terror beyond the imaginings of their present captors and whose failures surely merited something other than this kind of punishment.

At the daily ten-minute Communication Parades, the men could not speak about Farrell's death within earshot of the staff sergeants. Instead, they rehearsed the formulaic exchanges of a suburban cock-tail party. 'Where do you come from?' Bain asked a man facing him.

'The Midlands. Near Coventry. What's left of it.'

The man said he had read that American privates in Britain were paid more than British officers. 'No wonder they're fucking all our women.'

Bain asked, 'How'd you get anything to read? Who gave it to you?'

The man from Coventry explained that the regulations, 'the bit that Babbage never reads out', allowed any prisoner with more than fifty-six days inside to request a book or magazine. All Bain had to do was ask one of the 'screws'. Bain considered which staff sergeant to approach, settling on Brown. Brown, the short sergeant who had advised him how best to use his blankets in solitary, 'was probably the least overtly hostile and sadistic.' Bain found a chance two days later, when Brown took charge of the cell. 'Excuse me, Staff,' he said. Brown, startled that an inmate would 'speak before spoken to', said, 'Well?'

'I wondered if I could get something to read,' Bain dared, with the innocence of Oliver Twist asking, 'More.'

'And what put that into your head?' Bain answered that the regulations allowed him books and magazines. Brown demanded to know who had told him that. Bain protected his source, saying only that it was someone he did not know on Communication Parade. Peeved, Brown left to find something for Bain to read. He returned a few minutes later and threw a magazine in Bain's direction. Bain looked at it in the near-darkness of the cell, suddenly seeing that the letters were in Arabic. Brown grinned. 'Satisfied?'

Bain lunged, but Chalky White grabbed him before he got close to Brown in the doorway. Another prisoner, Ron Lewis, held him down. Brown slammed the door behind him, and Bain yelled, 'You little shit! I'll kill you!'

Lewis and White let him up. Lewis warned him that the screws would 'have you strapped in a body-belt before your fucking eyes are open. Then they'll kick the shit out of you.' He said it had happened to a friend of his in the Black Watch. Bain realized he should have kept his temper to avoid more time in solitary and a savage beating. Pondering what awaited him made him so ill that he could not eat the next morning's breakfast. At the first muster, he waited for his name to be called. Nothing happened. He assumed Brown had not yet had time to submit a charge sheet, so they would come for him later.

Chalky White said, 'You scared the shit out of the little bugger. He's not put you on a fizzer 'cos he's so bloody scared'. Lewis reminded him that, while Brown might be afraid to go against Bain one to one, he had 'the whole fucking army behind him'. Whether White was right or wrong, he had saved Bain from a beating. In his poem 'Compulsory Mourning', Bain wrote,

But I'll get out and then I'll drink to you
Chalky and Jim – and this I hope is true:
As long as I am able to survive,
While I still breathe, I'll keep you two alive.

A few days passed without John being placed on a charge. When Staff Sergeant Brown took the rotation over Bain's cell one evening, he came in and gave him a book. Before Bain could speak, he left and bolted the door. The book was in English: George Moore's *Esther Waters*, which Bain told Chalky was a novel. Chalky said it proved Brown was 'shit-scared'. Bain did not believe it. Thinking that Brown was making amends for his cruelty with the Arabic magazine, he wrote, 'He was capable of remorse and of compassion.'

Some of the prisoners noticed 'three strange officers' coming out of Captain Babbage's office one day, further igniting the rumour that the army was preparing to reprieve those who would fight in Europe. A few weeks later, Bain was called in to meet the Sentence Review Board. A colonel and two majors interrogated him in Captain Babbage's office, without Babbage. The colonel explained that a Second Front was about to open 'somewhere in Europe'. Many soldiers lacked combat experience, and 'battle-hardened' troops were needed. Bain's division, then training in Britain for the invasion, was understrength. The colonel said. 'We need every battle-experienced man we can find, and so we've been taking a look around various punishment establishments to see if we can find chaps who've learnt their lesson and are prepared to soldier on.'

With Bain's file in front of him, the colonel said he deserved his punishment: 'It was a damned bad show. Your let your comrades down.' Then he asked the important question: would Bain return to his battalion and fight?

'Yessir.'

Later, Bain would say, 'I'd have promised to be a human torpedo or anything to get out.' Having served only six months of his three-year sentence, Bain left the Mustafa Barracks that afternoon.

After Bain's release, Scottish Labour Member of Parliament Thomas Hubbard asked the Secretary of War in the House of Commons whether he was 'satisfied with the living conditions obtaining at Mustafa Detention Barracks, Alexandria'. The War Secretary, Sir Percy Grigg, responded, 'I am not aware of any grounds for complaint.'

NINE

Although most of the mentally and emotionally unfit men are weeded out before they get into the Army or in their early days at training camp, severe advanced training conditions and combat itself can put new strains upon any man.

Psychology for the Fighting Man, pp. 294–5

STORMS MADE MANY OF THE US 2ND INFANTRY'S TROOPS, including Alfred T. Whitehead, seasick on the USS *Florence Nightingale* as she made her way from New York to Ireland. The 2nd Infantry Division had been fortunate in one respect: German U-boats that patrolled the North Atlantic to sink Allied shipping had not attacked their convoy. At midnight on 21 October 1943 in Belfast, Northern Ireland, the 38th Infantry Regiment disembarked and took a train to their new bivouac in the County Down town of Newry.

Whitehead, whose ancestors had come from Ulster, discovered an affinity with the Irish. He made friends easily, and he enjoyed drinking with local men in the pubs. Accommodation was primitive, straw mattresses on wooden planks for beds and chamber pots for body waste. A diet of cabbage, turnips and sprouts disappointed most of the men, but it satisfied Whitehead. He enjoyed dark beer in Ireland's pubs, and he happily ate fish and chips. As self-appointed barber and tailor to his Headquarters Company, he earned extra cash to spend on drink and women.

While most GIs got on well with the Irish, the Americans were not universally cordial to one another. Fights broke out between men of the 2nd and 5th Divisions. After some 5th Division soldiers attacked a youngster from the 2nd, Whitehead went as part of a forty-eight man platoon to clear the 5th Division troops out of town. Marching from one pub to another, they told the men of the 5th, 'We've had enough of your bullshit, and if we catch any more of you assholes in this town, we'll kill you.'

Training included aircraft identification, map reading, hand-to-hand fighting and the construction of booby traps. Whitehead took some of his leaves in Belfast, where he tried and failed to pick up Irish girls. Among the few diversions from the interminable Irish rain were touring United Services Organizations (USO) troupes with singers the soldiers recognized from radio shows at home.

On 1 April 1944, the 2nd Division assembled in the Mall at Armagh for a major address. The speaker turned out to be the Third US Army commander, General George S. Patton. 'Old Blood and Guts' (or, in the troops' words, 'Our blood, his guts') gave a rousing speech: 'Remember this. If you can't stick the son of a bitch in the ass, shoot him in the ass as he runs away.' Whitehead liked Patton's 'colorful command of four letter words'. The general's admonitions about the hazards ahead, though, hinted to Whitehead that he might be killed.

From Northern Ireland on 17 May, Whitehead was shipped along with the rest of his division to a marshalling camp in Wales, where his company lived in wooden huts beside a cheese factory whose fumes sickened the Americans. Mornings were for calisthenics, afternoons for combat instruction. British-trained American commandos taught raiding skills, including use of the garrotte for slicing off heads. The lessons were nothing if not realistic. One young soldier was killed in a not-so-mock bayonet charge. 'As rough as we were,' Whitehead wrote, 'and as dangerous as the training was, I could see that we would need it all in the days ahead.'

Whitehead began an affair with a Welsh redhead whose husband was fighting the Japanese in Asia. 'I never knew what tomorrow would hold,' he wrote, 'so I took every day as it came. War does strange things to people, especially their morality.' For Whitehead, though, the war had yet to begin.

On 3 June 1944, the training and the waiting came to an end. The 2nd Infantry Division boarded invasion craft and cruised from ports in Wales into the English Channel. While they hovered with thousands of other ships in the waters between England and France, rough weather postponed the invasion. Naval commanders stood ready for the order to shell the coast and deliver the young warriors to the edge of Adolf Hitler's Fortress Europe.

Every Allied soldier who survived the D-Day landings in Normandy on 6 June 1944 took home unique memories of the 'longest day'. Many recorded their impressions in diaries, letters, audiotapes and books. Alfred T. Whitehead would write his recollections thirty-seven years later in 1981. Although his 2nd Division landed at Omaha Beach on 7 June, D-Day-plus-one, his memoir stated that he took part in the D-Day invasion itself. He wrote that he and eleven other soldiers from the 2nd Division 'wound up joining the 116th Regimental Combat Team of the Big Red One.' The 116th Regimental Combat Team, part of the 29th Infantry Division, had been loaned to the 1st Division to give it extra strength on D-Day and to provide fire cover for engineers clearing the beaches and roads inland for troops and equipment.

The Big Red One had already fought in North Africa and Sicily, making its men who were not replacements America's most experienced fighters. Many 1st Division troops were resentful at being selected to fight again, when men who had never fired a shot were kept in reserve. The 1st and the inexperienced 29th would spearhead the American assault on Omaha Beach on 6 June.

Whitehead wrote a lengthy account of his participation in the invasion. At 2.30 on the morning of 6 June, he claimed, he was on board a troopship in the English Channel, when a loudspeaker announced the invasion. The men assembled their packs, each of which contained 'a raincoat, gas mask, K-rations and a few other odds and ends'. Whitehead equipped himself with an arsenal: five hand grenades, a trench knife, a .45 calibre pistol and a Thompson sub-machine gun. 'We were instructed to rip off all patches and military insignia of rank,' he wrote. 'Non-coms could be recognized only be [sic] a

87

horizontal strip of white across the back of their helmet, while the officers' mark was vertical. Other then [sic] that, we all looked the same – just one long wave of drab olive green fatigues.'

Whitehead hoped that the B-17 Flying Fortresses overhead would destroy German defences before he landed. They didn't. German shore batteries unleashed the fury of their guns on the first wave of Americans. Whitehead, part of the second wave aboard a wooden-decked Landing Craft Assault (LCA), saw his comrades slaughtered in the water and on the beach. Company A of the 116th Regiment lost more than 90 per cent of its men, killed or wounded, within ten minutes. That was at 6.30 in the morning. An hour later, Whitehead's LCA cruised towards the beach. 'Onward our wave rushed past rows of wrecked and burning landing craft, with underwater obstacles and mines jutting out above the water all over,' he wrote. German 88-millimetre shells exploded along the beach and on the LCA's line of approach. As the navy crew manoeuvred as close as it dared, a sergeant ordered the men off. The bow ramp descended and the men jumped.

Heavy surf dragged Whitehead, burdened with pack and ammunition, down. His feet could not find bottom. Bobbing to the surface, he gasped for air. 'Bodies and pieces of bodies were floating in the water and flying through the air,' he wrote. 'Mines were exploding, men screamed and yelled, and those who couldn't swim sank in that bloody sea.' He scrambled ashore, but land was no safer than water. American dead and wounded lay everywhere. One soldier's body 'had been shot in the back by our own troops who were so scared they were shooting wildly at the enemy and hitting each other'. Whitehead became convinced he too would die.

The irreligious Tennessean found himself praying. Amid the relentless explosions, prayer gave him 'a strange feeling of calm'. Something inside, 'an unseen presence,' told him, 'Wait … wait … I'll tell you when to move.' But he did not see anywhere safe. 'It looked like the end of the world,' he wrote. 'There were knocked out German bunkers and pillboxes, cast-off life preservers and lost gas masks, plus piles of all kinds of equipment …' He thought the Americans were losing the battle and would be driven off the beach.

One German 88 artillery piece in a bunker above the beach was 'slaughtering our men'. Everyone coming near it was cut down. A Sherman amphibious tank appeared. Firing from the crest of a small rise in the sand, it missed the bunker twice. The third round went straight through the gun slit in the concrete and exploded inside, silencing the 88. The battle raged for the rest of the day, although Whitehead's memoir omitted the assault at 8.30 that morning by the 116th Regiment, with a detachment of Army Rangers, on the heights of Les Moulins. The Rangers went on to destroy German gun emplacements beyond the cliffs at Pointe du Hoc. Whitehead wrote that, of the twelve men from his division attached to the 116th, only he and two others survived. His memoir did not state their names.

After nightfall, German planes strafed Allied ships. Whitehead recalled, 'Big naval barrage balloons burst into flaming pillars as flak fell like hail on the ship decks. German bombs and American ack-ack fire turned night to day on every explosion, while creating a constant deafening thunder.' Whitehead tried to sleep in the bunker the Sherman had taken out, but the dead German gun crew, one of whom had been decapitated, spooked him. He lay down outside and waited for dawn.

The 2nd Infantry Division landed in Normandy the next afternoon, when Whitehead claimed to have rejoined his company outside the town of Trévières. The official history of the 38th Regiment stated the 2nd Division was in the English Channel when it received its invasion orders early on 6 June. It continued,

> The following afternoon, June 7, 1944 – D-Day-plus-one – leading elements of the 38th Infantry Regiment rode landing barges to Omaha Beach, near St. Laurent-sur-Mer. Some barges hung up on reefs and obstacles and men from the 3rd Battalion, 2nd Battalion, and the regimental command group waded and swam ashore to the debris-strewn beach still under enemy fire. The first Command Post of 'Impressive' – tactical code name of the regiment – was in a sunken road. For two days the regiment probed forward between the 1st and 29th Divisions.

Whitehead somehow detached himself from the 116th and moved off the beach. 'I was waiting beside an old, shot up farmhouse when I caught sight of Indianhead-patched soldiers moving along the road,' he wrote. 'I was worn out and sat there until my own company came by, and I joined them.' He added, 'They asked how the landing had been. All I could say was that it was just like what it looked like, and they didn't ask anymore.' The 2nd Division troops would have had little reason to ask him about the D-Day landing, because they saw its carnage and met its survivors the next day when they struggled ashore near Saint Laurent-sur-Mer under German fire. Four of 2nd Division's lieutenant colonels were killed in the initial stages of the Normandy invasion, hardly an indication of an easy arrival. Moreover, Whitehead's 38th Regiment was not before Trévières, its initial objective in Normandy, until 9 June. If he landed on 6 June, as he wrote, three days would have been unaccounted for. He may have been AWOL, as many men were, and chose not to mention the fact to either his comrades or the readers of his memoir.

Whitehead's account of the war from the time he rejoined the 38th Regiment coincided more closely with divisional and regimental histories than his version of D-Day did. Records indicated that he was in combat with the 38th Regiment throughout the war in France. His memoir and the official history agree that, for lack of transport, the 2nd Battalion of the 38th Regiment marched four miles inland to Trévières on 9 June. Whitehead wrote, 'Moving ahead through the green, flowered countryside, I was in a big field when someone opened fire on me – a low rifle crack sounded in the distance.' The shot came from one of many German snipers, who stayed behind American lines, hidden in trees or behind hedges, to harass the advancing GIs.

The 2nd Battalion attacked Trévières, a town with a German headquarters ten miles south of the beachhead, from the north. The 3rd Battalion forded the River Aure to penetrate the town from the south and west. One platoon inside Trévières engaged in hand-to-hand fighting with the Germans. The divisional history described the contest for the division's first objective on the road south to the Forêt de Cerisy:

Only a limited number of hand grenades was available. Not until the closing stages of the battle were machine guns brought up from the beach area. To replenish the meager supply of ammunition, a French two-wheel cart was commandeered. But the ammunition still had to be hand-carried across the river. Wounded were hand-carried on the return trip across the stream.

The 38th fought without rest all night. Whitehead wrote of his German opponents,

> They doggedly defended the town, house by house, yard by yard, and we literally had to dig them out with a savage bayonet assault before they would surrender. I saw one soldier ahead of me empty a carbine clip in the chest of a charging German, until finally knocking him down with the butt of his gun.

The contest for Trévières cost the 2nd Battalion of the 38th Regiment nine men killed and three officers and thirty-five enlisted men wounded. The Battalion's official history noted, 'The attack had taken twelve and one half hours; made without benefit of any substantial heavy weapons and featured tough bayonet fighting and extensive use of grenades which were available only in the latter part of the fighting ...' When the fighting ended, the 38th Regiment, together with the 9th, left on trucks heading south towards Saint-Georges-d'Elle. 'Then,' Whitehead wrote as the convoy approached the Forêt de Cerisy, 'all hell broke loose. We'd driven head-long into a waiting ambush!' Soldiers ran from the trucks to dig in against a mortar barrage, which set some of the vehicles alight. Whitehead sprinted to a house and leapt under a bed. The two 2nd Division regiments dug in for the night, and the men watched US bombers hit German ammunition dumps in the forest. When the Luftwaffe bombed later in the night, Whitehead jumped over a wall into a cemetery. He whispered to himself amid the graves of generations of French dead, 'Damned if I'm not going to end up in one of these places before my time.'

TEN

There is, first, the fear of death.

Psychology for the Fighting Man, p. 347

On the morning of 3 June 1944, Rain lashed the tents of the 5/7th Gordon Highlanders' camp at the town of Grays, Essex, beside the River Thames east of London. Reveille woke the men, at least those who could sleep through the storm, a half hour earlier than usual at 0530 hours. Breakfast was at 0600. Forty-five minutes later, the men assembled outdoors in full battle order: seventy pounds of rations, ammunition and other equipment, with an extra twenty pounds for those, like Private John Bain, carrying their sections' Bren guns. To make matters worse, Bain and most of the others were hungover from a final night's drinking. Trucks collected them at their tent camp. The men rode sombrely in the back through dawn's drizzle to Tilbury a few miles away. 'The machinery had been set in motion and there was nothing much to be done about it,' Bain wrote. 'Cigarettes were lit but nobody said much.' At the docks, the Gordons and the other regiments of the 51st Highland Infantry Division reassembled. Eventually, they boarded a Landing Craft Infantry (LCI), a vessel that had dropped many of them on the shore of Sicily almost a year before. Veterans were familiar with the spartan accommodation, while young replacements and former deserters, like John Bain, were experiencing its discomfort for the first time. Once the men were below deck, they threw off their packs and lit cigarettes.

Bain and Private Hughie Black, his five-foot six-inch Glaswegian mate from the North African campaign, inhaled and waited for the flotilla to cruise through the Thames estuary. Bain and Black, as their platoon's two-man Bren gun team, shared the twenty-two pound automatic rifle and its .303 calibre ammunition. At 0800 the next morning, when the 51st Division was due to embark, Captain Forbes, commander of B Company, called the men up to the deck to tell them they were to wait a few more hours for better weather. As rough as conditions were on board, the news was not unwelcome. No one was in a hurry to meet death on a French beach.

Bain was back in his old platoon, his old company, his old regiment, among friends like Bill Grey and Hughie Black. Black introduced him to a new man named Alec Stevenson. Mustafa Barracks was forgotten. Captain Forbes had told Bain on his return to the regiment five months earlier, 'I want you to know that nothing is going to be held against you. You know what I mean, what? It's a completely fresh start. So carry on and good luck to you.' Gordon Rennie, another friend from North Africa, grabbed his hand the moment he saw him. 'Johnny Bain!' he said. 'How are you man? It's great to see you.' In one poem, Bain would refer to 'Gordon Rennie, the world's pet uncle'. Rennie, who had been promoted to corporal, arranged for Bain to serve with him in 1st Section of the 2nd Platoon and to shoulder the Bren gun with Hughie Black. Neither the platoon commander, Lieutenant Mitchell, nor his platoon sergeant, Sergeant Thom, referred to Bain's desertion or made him feel different from anyone else. This institution that Bain detested had become more of a home than his family's house in Aylesbury, which he had not bothered to visit between his arrival from Egypt and reporting to the regiment.

The only man in B Company to withhold an unqualified welcome was his closest friend, Hughie Black. Noticing his old friend's reserve, Bain asked whether he was angry with him for deserting. 'Jesus Christ, no!' Black said. 'I was just mad you'd gone off without me.' If Bain had taken him along, he said, he would not have been caught.

In March, the Highland Division transferred from Vache Camp in Buckinghamshire to Halstead near Sevenoaks, Kent. Intensive training began then. The Scottish regiments practised urban street fighting in the bomb-devastated streets of east London. In Harlington, Bedfordshire, the 5/7th Gordons learned to deploy the new 'Wasp' flame-throwers, with a 100-yard range, against simulated German pillboxes. The Highland Division conducted exercises on Salisbury Plain, Larkhill and the Thetford battle area. These were followed by river crossings, reconnaissance patrols and night fighting on the featureless rural plains of East Anglia. The Suffolk Broads coastal town of Lowestoft was the scene of their final and crucial manoeuvre, a dress rehearsal called Operation Fabius, on 10 and 11 May: unloading men and supplies on a beach under fire.

The Scottish regiments of the Highland Division moved in mid-May to a string of purpose-constructed bases along the Thames between Southend and London. When the 5/7th Gordons reached a tent encampment near Grays on 17 May, Hughie Black was ready to 'fuck off' and pleaded with Bain to desert with him. They could go to Glasgow, where Black had friends. Bain refused, saying he would rather go back into battle than return to prison. 'It's no' a straight choice between the two,' Black argued. 'We don't have to get caught. I know some that's been on the run for bloody years.'

Glasgow had by then become Scotland's primary deserters' refuge, as the 'L-Triangle' of London, Leeds and Liverpool had in England. British troops on the run were joined by thousands of Americans, Canadians and other Allies. In the spring of 1944, the US Army Provost Marshal noted that 'there were thousands [of] soldiers running around without passes or furloughs'.

Inevitably, the large number of men without identification papers or food ration coupons gravitated towards the criminal underworld for sustenance and false papers. Many deserters stole military supplies that gangsters sold for them on the black market, while others lived by armed robbery. One teenage deserter, a small-time criminal named 'Mad' Frankie Fraser, later recalled, 'The war was a criminal's paradise. The most exciting and profitable time ever. It broke my heart when Hitler surrendered.'

To track down deserters, the police made regular raids on pubs, gambling houses, brothels and cheap hotels. Men at railway stations, dog tracks and horse races regularly had their papers checked. A police trawl through the pubs in Soho usually turned up at least a few deserters. In April 1944, the *New York Times* quoted the American Provost Marshal of Greater London, Colonel Ernest Buhrmaster, that tracking down deserters was his office's main preoccupation. Eleven days later, *Time* magazine wrote,

> The Provost Marshal's white-helmeted, white-gaitered MPs ('Ike's Snowballs') make periodic sweeps of London looking for AWOLs. They sift Red Cross clubs, dance halls, pubs, hotels and railway stations, check dog tags and furlough papers. In one recent six hour sweep, they caught 104 soldiers absent without leave, three of whom were wearing civilian clothes.

One of the deserters had so convincingly impersonated an officer, in full uniform with medals including the Distinguished Flying Cross, that, in *Time*'s words, 'he made the MPs who questioned him stand at attention'.

In May 1944, the British and American Military Police conducted joint mass raids on London's West End. On 16 May, MPs fixed bayonets to their rifles for a round-up of Soho's seamier night spots. The *Chicago Daily Tribune* reported that police apprehended forty-two suspected deserters. 'They also trapped a one-star general, but his papers were in order,' the paper added. Five nights later, on 21 May, the MPs together with the Metropolitan Police targeted restaurants, hotels and the Astoria Cinema and Ballroom on Charing Cross Road in their drive to return deserters to their units in time for the invasion of France.

In Liverpool, Military Police Lieutenant Timothy Sharland recalled that the city's military court was in permanent session during the war. Most defendants were charged with desertion. 'An awful lot of soldiers just didn't like the idea of the war and they'd just push off,' he said. 'Or they'd use the excuse that their wife was playing around with someone else. But in a place like Liverpool, there were some pretty rough people about the place. Around Bootle and Seaforth and Riverland and places like that, not exactly places I'd choose to go and live. A lot of chaps [were] deserting and hiding out in places like that.'

Something more than fear of prison kept John Bain from deserting a third time. He could not bear to prove Captain Babbage right. Babbage's words, spoken on his first day at Mustafa Barracks, haunted him: 'You're all cowards! You're all yellow!' Hughie Black, having seen Bain in the boxing ring and beside him at Alamein and Wadi Akarit, protested, 'For crying out loud, Johnny, you're no fucking coward!' Black tried again to persuade Bain to desert. As they smoked during a break in training, Bain repeated, 'I'm not going to take a powder. I've got to have another go. And I don't mind telling you, I'm shit scared. But if I fucked off now, I'd never know, would I? And I don't know why, but somehow I've got to know. I've got to find out if those bastards in the nick were right or wrong.'

Three days later, on 25 May 1944, desertion became impossible. MPs encircled the Gordons' camp near Grays with a triple ring of Dannert barbed wire and mounted round-the-clock patrols. 'Unlike conventional security measures these were aimed not at frustrating penetration from outside but at preventing the escape of those within the camp,' Bain wrote. Throughout southern England, military encampments with British, Canadian, American and other Allied soldiers were 'sealed' from the outside world. On the perimeter of the 5th Cameron Highlanders' camp at Snaresbrook, east London, bemused Italian prisoners of war noticed that they had more freedom to roam than their captors.

The 21st Army Group, primarily the 2nd British and 1st Canadian Armies, was under the command of Bernard Law Montgomery. Promoted the previous September to field marshal, Monty worked furiously to bring to full strength divisions and regiments that had lost men in battles from Dunkirk to Anzio. The 2nd Army had gone so far as to recruit convicted deserters like John Bain, as well as to overlook the civilian crimes of men willing to take the King's shilling as an alternative to prison. Britain was running out of good men. After the RAF, the Royal Navy, military intelligence and other branches of the armed forces, as well as vital civilian sectors like arms production and coal mining, claimed their shares, the infantry received the rest. Some infantry commanders doubted the quality of their recruits. Major General Harold Freeman-Attwood, commanding the British 46th Infantry Division, summed up the view of many senior infantry officers in May 1943: 'The men we get in the infantry are to a great extent those not required by the RAF or with insufficient brains for technical employment.'

While the infantry was taking all the men it could find, it was weeding others out. 'The resistance to be expected by our landing forces at the beaches is far greater than anything we have yet encountered in the European War,' General Eisenhower had written to Chief of Staff George Marshall in February 1944. That meant not sending men the army believed were likely to break down or desert. In preparation for the French invasion, unfit men in the infantry were sent to support units. Overweight troops were the first to go. Those whose psychological profile disposed them, in the opinion of psychiatrists, to mental collapse were also reassigned. A May 1943 British Army pamphlet, 'Casualty Report', explained, 'We can do very little in an actual battle area to limit the stresses and strains or to alter the adverse environment; and, given sufficient stress and sufficient strain, any person may break down. We can, however, sift out those who are likely to break down early ...'

Because most of Monty's formations lacked combat experience, 'battle-hardened' divisions like the 51st Highland Infantry and the 7th Armoured Division were expected to set examples for units that had yet to be 'blooded'. John Bain was sceptical that there was such a thing as 'battle-hardened'. He compared veterans like himself to eighteen-year-old boys who had yet to see action: 'But the truth was that we were little better prepared than they were for the coming assault on the beaches of Normandy.'

General Montgomery's dictum, 'THE MORALE OF THE SOLDIER IS THE MOST IMPORTANT SINGLE FACTOR IN WAR', applied, if not necessarily to all wars, certainly to the one Allied commanders were contemplating in 1944. In March 1944, Monty wrote, 'We have got to try and do this business with the smallest possible casualties.' Believing the war would be won by the autumn of 1944, the government decided in late 1943 to limit the number of recruits to 150,000 men. That left too few men in Britain's armed forces for commanders to squander their lives as they had in the First World War. The loss of large numbers of men to enemy fire, ill-health, mental breakdown, self-wounding, desertion and surrender would doom the enterprise.

To avoid the levels of desertion that had plagued Allied operations in North Africa and Italy, each corps in the British 2nd Army was assigned a military psychiatrist. Every field dressing station included a Combat Exhaustion Centre, recognition that mental wounds were as inevitable as physical. The centres' function, as with treatment for bullet and shrapnel injuries, was to return men to their units as soon as they could fight again. Efficiency, not compassion, was the prime consideration.

At noon on 4 June, the LCI carrying John Bain and Hughie Black cruised out of Tilbury a few hours behind schedule. Secrecy surrounding each unit's objectives did not permit commanders to unseal their orders until they were out at sea. When the flotilla passed Dover's white cliffs that afternoon, Captain Forbes read that his company would land at Courseulles-sur-Mer with the objective of seizing Caen, the capital of Lower Normandy, on D-Day. A ferocious downpour was still lashing the ships. Bain recalled that 'the LCI circled around in the Channel waiting for the weather to improve. It was a good 48 hours of brutal discomfort and stress before the storm abated.' It was hardship they shared with more than 200,000 other men on the invasion fleet of 5,000 vessels. Not knowing their destination, biding their time in the rough waters, they waited for something they dreaded.

By the morning of 6 June, the Highland Division had used most of its army-issue vomit bags as their landing craft bobbed up and down on the waves. Bain remembered that time as 'two whole days of wretched discomfort and strain, with no easing of wind and high seas and a large proportion of all ranks repeatedly sick'. Bain, one of the few to avoid throwing up, was nevertheless so ill he could not eat. Captain Forbes addressed his haggard and unshaven company under a cloudy sky to give them their orders. He added that, while the 3rd

Canadian Infantry Division would go before them, they had the honour of being 'the first battalion of the Highland Division to land on French soil'. Bain would write later,

> What I with many others that day shared
> was *pre*-traumatic stress disorder, or,
> as specialists might say, we were 'shit-scared'.

The LCI had trouble finding Juno Beach, the 51st Division's designated landing area near Courseulles. (The British landing beaches, on the east of the invasion zone, were designated 'G', 'J' and 'S' for Gold, Juno and Sword. To the west were the American beaches, 'O' for Omaha and 'U' for Utah.) When the LCI came to within a hundred yards of shore, B Company's sergeant major ordered, 'Stand by for landing!'

So much debris littered the shallows that the landing crafts could not reach dry land. Sailors lowered ramps, dropping the Highlanders into the rolling surf. The waves beat the chests of taller men like John Bain but swamped Hughie Black and others of average height. The regiment took its first casualty, when a Glaswegian soldier's heavy equipment dragged him under one of the landing craft. Hughie Black clung onto Bain's backpack to stay afloat as they waded to the sand. Once ashore, they sheltered from German shellfire and moved inland. A regimental history recorded,

> There was only one exit from the beach, for mines had yet to be cleared from the dunes and from the marshland beyond; and the defile was congested by vehicles of the 3rd Canadian Division, one of the leading formations in the assault landing. However, by 8 p.m. the Gordons were all ashore and moving in detachments to Banville, four miles inland, where they concentrated for the night.

The Germans had only just abandoned the hamlet of Banville, where uneaten rations in a farmhouse tempted the hungry men of B Company. Lieutenant Mitchell ordered the men not to touch food and wine that might have been poisoned or open drawers and cupboards that were potentially booby-trapped. Bain would later write a poem with traces of the warning:

> We seized the city like a promised toy,
> The most inviting doors were booby-trapped,
> The wine was sour, they'd burned all the gold;
> The dogs and children snarled and cursed and snapped,
> And every woman was gun-hard and cold.

The difference was that Banville's women and children, along with all the other civilians, had abandoned the village. During the night, the Gordons dug trenches in a field to sleep. They resumed their advance early the next morning, D-Day-plus-one, towards the objective the 2nd Army had failed to seize on D-Day, Caen. They established defensive positions at Bénouville, moved to Ranville and dug in again along the Caen Canal. Mortars hit them all night. In the morning, Bain was surprised the heavy barrage had not cause more casualties than three men killed and five wounded. One of the dead was a young soldier from Aberdeen named Robbie, who had only recently joined the regiment and received only twelve weeks' training. Mortars did not kill him. 'He had managed to get the muzzle of his own rifle into his mouth and had blown away most of his head.'

Robbie's death would stay with Bain for years, as his poem 'Robbie' made clear:

> It seemed impossible that anyone would live
> But when the morning came things weren't too bad.
> They checked their losses – only three were dead,
> Among them, Robbie. Clever for once, he had
> Sucked on his rifle-muzzle like a straw
> And somehow blown away most of his head.

A pattern was emerging. The Gordons stopped to dig in, chased the retreating Germans before they could rest and dug in again. Bain wearied of digging, marching and digging without sleep. On the third day, Caen seemed as distant as when they landed.

The Germans hit the Highlanders day and night. From the tree-tops, snipers took out men one at a time. On the ground, landmines and trip wires killed and mangled. The feared multiple mortar launcher, the Nebelwerfer, whose projectiles the men called Moaning Minnies for the screech they made before they hit, caused a large share of casualties. Among them was Captain Forbes, B Company's young commander. Shrapnel lacerated his throat, forcing his evacuation to the beach for emergency surgery. Forbes, although he had what Bain called a 'plummy accent' and was part of a class he despised, had been one of the few officers to earn his praise. Forbes's deputy, Captain Urquhart, assumed command.

Their first week in Normandy left the 5/7th Battalion of Gordon Highlanders with 98 dead and 209 wounded from their original contingent of about 850 men. At first, the wounds were physical. Medical clearing stations reported no cases of battle exhaustion on D-Day and D-Day-plus-one. As Allied soldiers slogged through hedgerows, orchards and minefields, some of them broke down. The percentage of British casualties from mental causes was only 3 per cent in the first week of the invasion, rising to 13 per cent the next. Within a month, almost a quarter of all injuries were battlefield trauma. Doctors put them to sleep with injections of Nembutal, hoping to return them to the line when they woke.

As casualties, physical and mental, mounted, Hughie Black told his trench-mate, 'I'd fuck off if there was anywhere to run to.' Bain, suppressing his fear, refused to consider running away. There were moments, however, when the storm of German artillery and machine guns made Mustafa Barracks look inviting.

ELEVEN

It takes more than brains to make a good soldier; it takes guts.

Psychology for the Fighting Man, p. 295

ON 6 JUNE, MOMENTOUS NEWS circulated among Allied troops in Italy. Their comrades had just invaded France on the beaches of Normandy, opening up a new front against the Wehrmacht. Moreover, the American Fifth Army had liberated Rome, 'just half an hour's jeep drive away', the day before. Credit for the breakout went to the 36th Infantry Division, one of whose reconnaissance units had found a gap in the German lines near Velletri. General Walker, despite General Clark's misgivings, quickly exploited the opportunity. The mission was a complete success, opening the road to Rome. 'Maybe the war will end soon, after all,' Private Steve Weiss thought.

Italy was being relegated to a sideshow. The Normandy campaign moved to top priority for both matériel and attention at home. Even Ernie Pyle, the Scripps Howard newspaper chain correspondent known as the GIs' friend, had left Italy for France. That was where the war in the west would be won or lost, and everyone knew it. Troops in Italy, no matter how many battles they fought or how many men they lost, would soon be called 'D-Day Dodgers' for missing D-Day in Normandy. This would be no help to morale, already low in Italy owing to poor strategy, command mistakes and tenacious German resistance.

The replacements from Fort Meade packed their gear and climbed into open trucks on 6 June to rendezvous with the 36th

Division north of Rome. At nightfall, they reached a battlefront of barren earth where the sight of bodies wrapped in canvas made Weiss 'physically ill'. A sergeant counted in the ninety replacements, who jumped from the trucks and got into sleeping bags for the night. Morning came and with it a shock: the corpses of the night before crawled out of their canvas covers. Weiss realized they were not 'goblins, but ordinary GIs', who had been sleeping. Awake, though, they were no friendlier to the arrivals than when they appeared to be dead.

A sergeant about his own age ordered Weiss into a twelve-man rifle squad in the 2nd platoon of Company C (Charlie Company), 1st Battalion, 143rd Regimental Combat Team of the 36th Texas Infantry Division. Weiss soon learned that the regiment had been wiped out twice before he joined it – 'the first time at the battle of San Pietro in December 1943 and at the Rapido River, one month later. Only in the relative safety of the division's rear did some of the original cadre remain.' Sheldon Wohlwerth, the twenty-eight-year-old Ohioan whom Weiss had befriended at Blanding, was posted to the same rifle squad. The two became foxhole buddies. The other eighty-eight replacements were distributed among the rest of the division's rifle companies. The sergeant offered Weiss a choice of assignment. He could join a three-man team to lug the Browning Automatic Rifle (BAR), a First World War vintage light machine gun that weighed sixteen pounds and fired at half the speed of its German equivalent. Or he could be first scout. Weiss chose first scout. Although the Germans would spot him before they saw the rest of the squad, he could move faster without a BAR.

Weiss crouched in the dirt with his M1 rifle and awaited orders. Charlie Company's commanding officer, Captain Allan Simmons, came up to the line. Simmons, a native of Belfast, Maine, did not acknowledge the replacements. Nor did he greet the veterans, signalling an absence of rapport with the men. The captain, aged about thirty, looked to Weiss like an old man. Weiss thought that, with his soiled fatigues and three-day beard, he was 'locked within himself, his own emotional executioner', not unlike Weiss's father.

The platoon sergeant, a tough but friendly Texan named Lawrence Kuhn, sent Weiss on his first mission with a corporal named Robert Reigle. They were ordered to find Company A (Able Company) somewhere forward out of radio contact. Bob Reigle was a five-foot, seven-inch non-com from Hershey, Pennsylvania, who had fought with the Texas Division throughout the Italian campaign, at Salerno, the River Rapido and Monte Cassino. Reigle took Weiss in hand. The younger soldier immediately sensed in the corporal competence and solicitude he could trust. 'The two of us headed out,' he wrote, 'hacking our way noisily through a jungle of heavy underbrush. Skirting the side of a hill towards the canal, we walked in single file.' As they neared the edge of the natural cover, Reigle motioned to Weiss to stop. The two went dead quiet. Reigle listened carefully. Someone was coming their way. A lone German soldier with a sniper's rifle called, '*Kamerad.*' He was trying to surrender.

'Damn!' Reigle whispered to Weiss. 'We're as exposed as hell, and it could be a trap. Might be more Krauts around.' Reigle patted Weiss's arm to reassure him. The German could come to them. When he did, they shoved him against a tree. Reigle searched him and told Weiss to check his papers. These showed that he was a Nazi Party member and part of the Fallschirm-Panzer Division 1, the elite Hermann Goering 1st Paratroop Panzer Division. Reigle knew the division by reputation. After the Allies invaded Sicily, it had escaped intact across the Straits of Messina to mainland Italy. At the end of the previous January, two US Ranger battalions had fought a pitched battle with it in the village of Cisterna. As the Rangers ran out of ammunition, some of them were captured. The Germans threatened to murder the prisoners if the rest of the Rangers did not surrender – a blatant violation of the laws of war.

'Let's shoot the sonofabitch' Reigle said. Weiss said that was illegal. Reigle conceded, 'I'd do it, but his pals are bound to hear the shot.' They brought the prisoner to 1st Battalion intelligence, which assigned his interrogation to a Jewish corporal who had immigrated to the United States from Germany. The corporal thanked Reigle for delivering the prisoner, whom he planned to question for many hours, 'before I throw him in the cage'. Weiss, recounting his first patrol, noted, 'We never found Able Company.' But he had found someone in his new division to rely on, Corporal Bob Reigle.

The 36th Division advanced north, methodically pushing the Germans up the Italian peninsula. The Germans were retreating, but they were not running. They regrouped, established defences and launched counter-attacks against their pursuers. The steep and rocky terrain was a godsend to the defenders, hell to an attacking army. Allied troops in Italy paid a high price in lives for every acre they took. Shortages of trucks and jeeps meant the Americans had to walk and climb most of the way, although they occasionally hitched rides on the sides of tanks.

On the way to Grosseto, a coastal town in southern Tuscany, a staff sergeant ordered First Scout Weiss to cross a field alone in heavy rain. 'The Germans are out there somewhere',' he said. Weiss realized he was a 'clay-pigeon, a fall guy', set up to make the Germans expose their position by firing at him. He marched through the mud, afraid but determined to make it across. Rain hit him in the face and dripped inside his shirt. He did not let his fear show. He wrote later, 'I discover that the battlefield is a lonely place, increasing fear to a higher, unexpected level, and alienating soldiers rather than bringing them together.' The rain increased its tempo the rest of the day, pouring mud into the squad's hillside foxholes. For a moment, Weiss could not take any more. 'Feeling wet, cold, and depressed, my eyes fill with tears. Cradling my head in my arms, I cry. My tears merge with the rain. I think of my mother. I call out to her, in need of her comfort and protection.' Weiss did not understand why he broke down, unaware that many other soldiers had the same experience.

For the next twenty-four hours, the 36th Infantry Division marched through brush, pastures, olive groves and swamps towards Grosseto. Sparsely inhabited owing to malarial mosquitoes in its marshes, the Maremma region with its *butteri*, cowboys and long-horned *chianina* cattle resembled the ranges of Texas. Trudging through mud, up and down hills, the only opposition Charlie Company met that day came from the harsh landscape and miserable weather. Slipping in mud, Weiss grabbed a branch that turned out to be a dead German's hand. The company reached the periphery of Grosseto, where the troops took a cigarette break. Using helmets for pillows, they slept beside the road. When Weiss woke up, the rest of the company was gone.

Alone and lost, he went into the seaside town to search for his comrades. Two armies were battling for control of Grosseto, while Weiss rushed from street to street. In urban fighting, soldiers had to be wary of rooftops, windows, doorways and piles of rubble concealing snipers and booby traps. Dodging through the city, Weiss sought a moment's shelter in the basement of an abandoned house. It turned out to be the temporary Command Post of another American unit. An officer cast a suspicious eye at Weiss, who stammered that he was lost. 'Lost?' the officer shouted. 'Cut the crap. You probably took off like a jack rabbit.' Weiss insisted he had not run away, but was merely cut off from his company. The officer told him, 'I ought to have you court-martialed for desertion.' Not wanting to end up caged in the stockade back at Anzio, Weiss took advantage of gunfire that distracted the officer to run outside. Searching for Charlie Company in Grosseto's whitewashed streets and alleys, he crossed from one side of town to the other. Bob Reigle spotted him approaching and said nonchalantly, 'I thought you were either killed or captured.'

Grosseto fell to the 36th Division on the evening of 15 June. The old hands donned Stetsons and played guitars for a Texas-style jamboree. Replacements from New York, Pennsylvania, Ohio and the rest of America joined them in singing, 'The Rose of Ole San Antone'. The T-Patchers had become a Texas division in name only, most of the original volunteers having been killed, wounded or captured. Weiss, listening to Texan ballads in every sort of American accent, thought that 'most divisions took on the same coloration, regardless of attempted mythology'. Myth was strong in the 36th, whose origins stretched back indirectly to the Alamo. The division carried a Lone Star flag to hoist over Germany, if it ever got there.

From Grosseto, the 36th advanced north, again on foot, and crossed the River Ombrone that night. They marched towards Siena through foothills of the wine country around Monte Amiata and Montalcino. If the Americans were short of modern transport, so were the retreating Germans. When Charlie Company spotted them, horses were pulling the Wehrmacht's heavy artillery up rugged Tuscan hillsides. American artillery opened with a barrage of 105-millimetre howitzer shells, and Panzers returned fire. Shells from both sides flew over Charlie Company's freshly dug foxholes. When the Germans extricated themselves and escaped north, Charlie Company moved towards their position. Weiss came face to face with a German soldier. He aimed his rifle, but the German, sitting upright on a tree stump, did not react. He was dead. The ground was an undug graveyard of men and horses, their flesh shredded and bleeding. Weiss recalled, 'The stench of decomposition pervaded the air.'

Although the army sometimes failed to send food and ammunition to men at the front, the Army Post Office delivered their mail. Weiss received a letter that night from a friend in the Office of War Information, where he had worked in New York. He read it by candlelight in an abandoned house. The roof let in the rain, and stucco walls provided scant protection from German artillery. His friend had written that, despite her efforts, his request for a transfer to Psychological Warfare had been rejected again. This was the last time they would consider it. Listening to the mingling of thunder and 155-millimetre Long Tom artillery, he knew he was stuck in the infantry for the rest of the war. How much longer would that be? At the rate the Allies were moving through Italy, it might take years. He wrote, 'I was nothing more than a dog-face slogging infantry soldier.' For troops who were not killed or injured, the only way out was surrender, a self-inflicted wound, insanity or desertion. Weiss stuck with it.

Proceeding on foot the next day, Weiss's rifle squad came to a farm. Its two-storey *casa colonica* (peasant house) might have been empty. Or Germans may have been waiting inside to attack the squad after it passed. The sergeant ordered Weiss, as first scout, to check. Weiss went cautiously to the door and kicked it open, ready to fire at any Germans inside. The only inhabitants were a peasant family, all four of them terrified at the intrusion of an American warrior. Weiss held the life of the farmer, his wife and two teenage children in his almighty hands, and he felt a surge of power that he immediately despised in himself. The father, shielding his family, spoke to him in Italian. Weiss, who did not understand, used one of the few Italian words he knew, '*Tedeschi?*' (Germans?) The man indicated there were none in the house, but Weiss made a fruitless search anyway. The absurdity of the scene weighed on him as he went back to the squad. It did not seem right that, owing to his armed presence, 'the son had displaced the father'.

First Scout Weiss marched uphill ahead of the squad through heavy brush. Two soldiers in German uniforms suddenly stopped him. Rather than shoot, they put their hands up and spoke to him in what sounded like gibberish. Their Oriental features marked them out as Turcoman tribesmen, recruited by the Wehrmacht as a partial solution to its manpower shortages. Behind the Asians, Weiss saw five more enemy troops with a light machine gun. He knew they could easily kill him and eliminate the rest of the rifle squad, but they too surrendered. To Turcoman conscripts, a US Army prison camp was preferable to a German graveyard.

Charlie Company's commander, Captain Allan Simmons, arrived and ordered the men to fix bayonets. Company A, the same Able Company that had gone missing south of Grosseto, was under German attack on the high ground to Charlie Company's left. Simmons wanted Charlie Company to charge the hill. 'Lying in a fold in the ground, I fixed my bayonet and noticed my hands were shaking,' Weiss wrote. The troops had trained with bayonets on straw-stuffed dummies, but they had yet to rip a man's guts open in face-to-face combat. Weiss waited for Simmons to order the attack, but no order came. Company A beat back the German force – without bayonets.

The squad went ahead to reconnoitre the woods up to the nearest hilltop. First Scout Weiss led the way. An American Piper Cub overhead was spotting artillery targets. As it circled, one of the more experienced veterans said the pilot probably took them for Germans and would direct artillery to their position. The platoon sergeant picked up the walkie-talkie to ask Captain Simmons to call off the barrage, but the walkie-talkie wasn't working. 'Of all the lousy fuckin' luck,' the sergeant said. 'All right, let's get off this hill right now and fast!' The squad ran down at top speed. Shells exploded behind them, spreading shrapnel and earth in their wake. A minute longer, and their war would have been over.

The next few days saw a tedious slog north towards Siena through what Weiss called 'Italy's interminable hills'. Australian war correspondent Alan Moorehead described the Italian campaign's frustrations, 'All advanced – a thousand, two thousand miles – there was always the enemy in front, always another thousand miles to go.' Weiss and Sheldon Wohlwerth dug a foxhole in a valley, where the Germans lobbed an artillery shell each time either of them moved. Weiss feared the Germans were targeting them, but Wohlwerth was pleased to see Germans wasting precious ammunition on two infantrymen. 'If they keep this up,' he said, 'there will be an earlier end to the war.'

In the field, the squad's most dependable member was Corporal Bob Reigle. Weiss recalled, 'He was in every major operation the 36th was in, and the only thing that I remember was that eventually he didn't want to share a hole with anybody. It was, why get to know somebody when they are going to get killed soon?' Although kept out of Reigle's foxhole, Weiss stayed close to him.

Charlie Company fought more skirmishes, took more prisoners and conquered more territory. In three weeks, they moved 240 miles from their launch point near Rome. The 36th Division's three regiments – the 141st, 142nd and Weiss's 143rd – slowly converged on the walls of Siena, when orders came to pull back. On 29 June, nine months after the 36th Division landed in Italy and twenty-three days after Steve Weiss became one of them, the Texans were relieved at Piombino by the 34th Iowa Division. The Italian campaign had cost the 36th about 75 per cent of its men and officers dead, wounded, captured or missing. It had earned some time off.

Deloused in showers of DDT and dressed in fresh uniforms, Weiss, Wohlwerth and some of the Charlie Company GIs headed into Rome on a one-day pass. Their mission: to eat and drink well.

Rome lay in a shambles from months of German occupation and Allied assault. Many inhabitants had fled to the provinces for safety and food. Most of the city's businesses, including its restaurants, were closed even a month after liberation. Weiss asked some children in pidgin Italian where they could have lunch. The kids led them to a shuttered trattoria, whose owners opened immediately for the GIs and their youthful followers. The conquering heroes sat down to lashings of the first real food they had tasted since they arrived in Italy. Having been reduced to army K-rations (Norman Lewis thought K-rations were 'so despised by the Americans, and so adored by everyone else'), they gorged on pasta, meat, fruit and cheese. They also bought lunch for the children, who were hungrier than the soldiers. The Americans finished five courses at one restaurant and proceeded to repeat the experience in another. 'Liter after liter of ordinary vino from the nearby slopes, although red and raw, trickled down our throats,' Weiss recalled. He was in a soldier's paradise, having survived three weeks of combat against a formidable enemy. A song came to him that Italian-Americans in Greenpoint, near his neighbourhood in Brooklyn, used to sing.

> Oh Marie! Oh Marie!
> In your arms I'm longin' to be
> Uhm, baby
> Tell me you love me
> Kiss me once, while the stars shine above me ...

The children accompanied him in Italian: '*Uhe Marie! Uhe Marie! Quanta suonno aggio perzo per te ...*' Hearing the familiar tune, the cook rushed from the kitchen to dance with the proprietor's wife. The Romans, despite shortages, were generous to the young men who had expelled the Germans.

'Our tastes were basic,' Weiss wrote. 'We roamed about on full stomachs and waved at the local girls, who only smiled and playfully thwarted our seductive advances with Roman sophistication, knowing we were harmless as butterflies.' In common with many teenage Americans before they went overseas during the war, Steve Weiss was a sexual innocent. His passionate fumbling with a girlfriend named Jeannie in Brooklyn in the weeks before his induction, despite the

(*Above*) William Johnson, an African-American soldier in the Union Army, hanged for desertion and 'an attempt to outrage the person of a young lady' in June 1864. A little over a year later, in October 1865, William Smitz became the last US soldier to be executed for desertion until Private Eddie Slovik (*right*) was shot by firing squad on 31 January 1945. Of the 150,000 British and US soldiers who deserted during the Second World War, Slovik was the only one executed for it.

A young Private Steve Weiss (on the left in both photographs) at the Infantry Replacement Training Center at Fort Blanding, Florida, in late 1943.

US Navy and Marine Shore Patrolmen (*right*) at a railway station near a US naval operations base in the United Kingdom to prevent US servicemen going AWOL. (*Below*) In the run-up to D-Day, military and civilian police rounded up US soldiers in London whose papers were not in order.

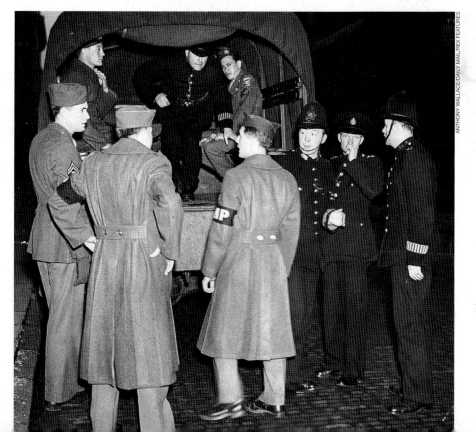

Official US Army photograph, taken at Pozzuoli near Naples in August 1944, that happened to capture Private First Class Steve Weiss boarding a British landing craft. He is climbing the gangplank on the right-hand side of the photograph.

Telegram received by William Weiss on 25 September 1944: 'The Secretary of War desires me to express his deep regret that your son Private Stephen J. Weiss has been reported missing in action …'.

Steve Weiss's rifle squad in the Vosges, October 1944. Weiss is standing, second from left, and to his left are, in turn, Dickson, Reigle and Gualandi; kneeling left is Fawcett.

In Alboussière, Steve Weiss refused to join the firing squad that executed a Vichy *milicien*. This photograph (*below*) is of the execution of six members of the Milice that was witnessed by CBS correspondent Eric Sevareid in Grenoble. The *épuration* (purification) of collaborators also saw young women accused of having had sexual relations with German soldiers suffer ritual humiliation (*right*). An accusation was enough to establish guilt in the eyes of the mob.

(*Above*) Steve Weiss in Paris on Armistice Day, 11 November 1945. And (*right*) receiving the Croix de Guerre from Commander Francois Binoche – to Weiss the father figure who fought in the *maquis* under the *nom de guerre* 'Auger' – in Paris, July 1946.

RÉPUBLIQUE   FRANÇAISE

ORDRE NATIONAL DE LA LÉGION D'HONNEUR

HONNEUR   PATRIE

LE PRÉSIDENT DE LA RÉPUBLIQUE FRANÇAISE
GRAND MAÎTRE DE L'ORDRE NATIONAL DE LA LÉGION D'HONNEUR

nomme, par décret de ce jour   Monsieur Stephen   W E I S S
Ancien combattant ayant participé aux opérations de Provence. Parachutiste du 2671 ème bataillon de reconnaissance

de nationalité américaine

OFFICIER DE LA LÉGION D'HONNEUR

Fait à PARIS, le 31 mai 2005

Scellé du sceau de l'Ordre sous le n° 506 LHE 99
Le Secrétaire Général Adjoint,

Par le Président de la République :
LE GRAND CHANCELIER DE LA LÉGION D'HONNEUR,

Général KELCHE

(*Above*) The certificate appointing Steve Weiss an officer of the Légion d'Honneur. (*Right*) Weiss wearing some of his awards, which include the Bronze Star, three US battle stars, the Second World War Victory Medal, Combat Infantry Badge and Good Conduct Medal, two Croix de Guerre, the Médaille de la Résistance and the Croix du Combatant.

earnest intentions of them both, had come to nothing. His twenty-four-hour Roman holiday in June 1944 was so taken up with his stomach that he left himself no time for romance. In this, he was in a minority of the GIs in liberated Rome.

TWELVE

Sometimes the soldier's troubles cannot be attributed to any one person.

Psychology for the Fighting Man, p. 329

DURING HIS FIRST WEEK with the Gordon Highland Regiment in Normandy, John Bain 'felt himself becoming absorbed and obliterated as an individual by the familiar process of combat'. Normandy was another North Africa, apart from the 'superficial': hedgerows rather than sand dunes, orchards in place of palm trees. 'The smell of war,' he wrote, 'was the same everywhere: that sweet yet pungent odour of cordite and fear and putrescence.' Both war theatres engendered

> the sense of being dehumanised, reduced to little more than an extension of your equipment and weaponry, the constant feeling of being used as an object, manipulated by blind, invisible hands, controlled by a force that was either malignant or stupid, the sense of being exhausted in a metaphorical and quite often literal darkness, of being exhausted, frightened, sick, sometimes so weary that you slept while on your feet like a horse. And ignorance, stupefying, brutalising ignorance.

After their landing on D-Day, the 5/7th Gordon Highland Regiment moved into a bridgehead that the British 6th Airborne Division had captured. It consisted of the area around two bridges (one dubbed 'Pegasus' for the airborne unit's winged horse insignia) spanning the Caen Canal and River Orne. Bain's battalion, part of the 153rd

Brigade as it had been in Egypt, moved into the bridgehead on 10 June, four days after its D-Day landing. The brigade crossed to the east bank of the Orne and advanced towards a triangle of rural villages northeast of Caen: Ranville, Touffréville and Bréville. Part of the brigade, the Black Watch, went to Bréville with the 6th Airborne. On the evening of 11 June, Captain Urquhart commanded the 5/7th Gordons in their first large assault of the campaign. The objective was Touffréville, which first received a battering from division artillery. The Germans responded with Nebelwerfers and Spandau MG42 machine guns. While Bain and Hughie Black crouched low with the Bren gun, Sergeant Thom called out, 'Right lads! Up you get! We're moving in!'

Bain threw the Bren gun over his shoulder and went straight towards the enemy's Spandau fire. Hundreds of other men were risking their lives with him, but Bain felt a terrifying loneliness. Multiple mortar rockets exploded nearby, followed by the cries of the wounded that had sickened him in North Africa. Yet he went forward, part of the military machine, while Hughie Black uttered endless profanities.

A green flare shot up, the signal that Corporal Gordon Rennie interpreted for his mates: 'Jerry must be pulling out!' Hughie Black answered, 'Who's firing them fucking guns then?' Rennie led the platoon into the village, where Bain and Black saw he was right. Jerry had pulled out. So had the inhabitants, who had already endured a failed D-Day attack by paratroopers of the 6th Airborne against the German 125th Panzer Grenadiers. While the 1st Gordons moved into a brick factory on the outskirts of Touffréville, the 5/7th Battalion approached the village square. Bain recalled,

> In the middle of the place was a small public garden with trees and from many of these hung dead British paratroopers, suspended by their harnesses, who had evidently been picked off by small arms fire as they hung helplessly there. On the lawns and flower beds of the garden, too, were more dead soldiers wearing flashes of the Sixth Airborne Division, and others lay on the cobbled stones outside the little park. None was alive.

The Germans had pulled their lines back to the forest, where their artillery kept the British troops within range.

Captain Urquhart commandeered an empty farmhouse to use its cellar as B Company's headquarters and kitchen. The troops dug bivouacs in the ground outside, where they sheltered all night from the incessant shelling. Just before dawn, German patrols infiltrated their lines. 'B and C Companies, in front and on the left, were drawn back to better defensive positions, but no one knew where the Germans would appear next,' wrote a regimental historian. Squads of Spandau machine gunners shot up Urquhart's headquarters, while German riflemen attacked the British defenders in their trenches. By the time the Germans pulled back at noon, they had inflicted twenty-eight casualties on the Gordons. They also took prisoners, including B Company's Sergeant Aitkenhead. Aitkenhead used a hidden knife to stab his guard and escape, but his own side's artillery nearly hit him on his run back to base.

The next day, 13 June, RAF planes accidentally bombed the Gordons, wounding ten of them. This was followed by another German infantry assault. When the Germans pulled back, they resumed their shelling of the Gordon trenches. Venturing above ground even to defecate could have been fatal. Hughie Black complained to Bain, 'It's no' right to keep us here. It's all right for Urquhart in his fucking cellar.' Around noon, the cooks were ready with a hot lunch of stew and potatoes. To ferry food to the trenches, one man from each two-man team fetched it from the kitchen and brought it back to his comrade. They usually took turns, and this lunchtime Bain made the run to the farmhouse.

In the cellar, cooks stirred the stew in one corner and Captain Urquhart attempted to radio battalion headquarters in another. The company bagpiper, who was also a medic, was in between ministering to a 'huddled figure whose sobbing and choking voice was unrecognisable'. It took Bain a moment to realize the soldier had no wounds. 'The neatly-shaped, alert features had melted and blurred,' Bain wrote, 'the mouth was sagging and the whole face, dirty and stubbled, seemed swollen and was smeared with tears and snot.' The boy was crying like a baby for his mother. The cook, filling Bain's mess tins with stew, looked at the babbling soldier with disgust and said, 'I know what I'd do with the fucker, and it wouldn't be send him back to Blighty.'

Bain crawled back into the trench to eat, but he did not tell Hughie about the sobbing soldier. The young man was Private Victor Denham, a replacement whom Black already detested. Denham had joined the battalion in England a few months earlier. He obeyed all the rules, kept his uniform pristine and exhibited a naïve enthusiasm for combat. Black had physically attacked him before embarkation and persuaded Gordon Rennie to transfer him to another section. Denham's breakdown had shaken Bain 'in a way that was more difficult to contend with than anything else that had happened in Normandy'. The trembling boy haunted him for hours, because he shared the cook's contempt and felt 'even a stab of sadistic hatred'. A more frightening thought was the 'intolerable suspicion that he was witnessing something of himself'.

Shelling persisted most of the afternoon, and Bain huddled with Hughie in the soft earth. During a lull, Black offered to wash out his and Bain's mess tins at a pump near the farmhouse. Bain said they could scrub them clean with grass, but Hughie reminded him that they needed water anyway. He would also bring back some 'Callow doss'. 'Calvados,' Bain corrected him, handing over his mess tin and water bottle.

Black ran to the pump, and Bain lit a cigarette. He had no idea why they were at Touffréville, how long they would stay there or where they were going next. Life was little more than a series of freshly dug pits with the ever-present fear of ending up in one for ever. A few weeks earlier, Hughie had complained that the sealing of their transit camp on the Thames robbed them of their last chance of running to Glasgow. Bain pointed out to Hughie that he could have deserted on his own. 'I told you,' Black replied. 'I wasna going without you.'

'That puts a big responsibility on me, doesn't it?' Bain answered. Hughie absolved his friend, 'It's my decision. I'm a big lad. It's what I decided. If anything happens to me, it's no' your fault. I could've gone but I decided to stay. Me. I decided. Not you or anyone else. Okay?' He added, 'Any case, nothing's going to happen to me, son.'

To commanders, decisive moments came with the capture or loss of high ground, offensives, retreats and massive battles. To infantry soldiers like John Bain, significant events were personal: surviving a mortar barrage, finding shelter in a building or a ditch, eating hot food and losing a friend. The war itself meant nothing to Bain, who did not hate the Germans. Friends like Gordon Rennie, Alec Stevenson, Bill Grey and especially Hughie Black had come to mean everything.

A close bond formed between two-men trench teams. 'They would live, eat, work and sleep together,' one infantry platoon commander wrote. 'If one of them was killed or wounded the other was quite lost.'

Bain's cigarette smoke floated upwards into the strangely tranquil Norman sky, when all of a sudden cluster after cluster of Moaning Minnies screeched to the earth. The Gordons cowered in their trenches, until, as abruptly as it began, the mortaring stopped. Bain took the risk of putting his head up to look around. Hughie Black lay on the ground halfway to the farmhouse. Bain ran from his trench. He and Gordon Rennie reached their friend at the same moment. Rennie put his hand on Hughie's shoulder, gently rubbing as if to wake him. When Hughie did not respond, he slowly rolled him onto his back and blurted, 'Jesus Christ.'

Hughie Black's chest was gone, leaving 'a great dark cave of blood and slivers of bone'. Bain tried not to look, but he had already seen Hughie's face, 'like the face of all the dead. The eyelids were not shut but the pupils had swivelled up beneath them so that the eyes looked like those of a blind man.'

Bain staggered back to the hole he had dug with Hughie three days before. He sat in the mud and 'stared across at the space where Hughie should have been'. Gordon Rennie dived into Bain's trench, saving him from his thoughts. 'It was quick, Johnny,' he said. 'He wouldna felt a thing. If you got to go that's the best way.' Gordon arranged for two of their friends to dig Hughie's grave in a row with five other Highlanders, and he assigned Alec Stevenson to replace Hughie on the Bren gun. Stevenson was next into the trench. He offered to wash the blood from Black's ammunition bags, but Bain insisted on doing it himself. As the sun was setting, they buried Hughie. Bain could not watch. He felt almost as he had at Wadi Akarit, when he fled a reality he refused to accept. This time, though, he fled only in his mind. It was not grief, but a departure from 'hope or love, anger or sadness'.

Stretcher bearers soon transported sixteen seriously wounded men to the Casualty Clearing Station near the beachhead. 'The lucky bastards,' Stevenson told Bain. 'It's a funny old world where you call somebody lucky because they've had their foot blown off.'

The surviving Gordons left Touffréville that night. A regimental history noted, 'They were confident they could hold on to Touffréville, and felt disgusted when ordered to withdraw later in the day.' Bain, in his memoir, evinced no regret at leaving the village where his friend Hughie Black died.

By this time, Bain was 'floating' as in North Africa, his mind elsewhere in another 'fugue'. But he was not the only demoralized soldier in the 51st Division. The Highlanders had been divided into elements under Airborne or Canadian command. They occupied and abandoned a series of villages around Caen to no identifiable object and were not driving forward in a coherent manner. Commanders sent companies or regiments to dislodge fortified positions that needed ten times the number of men. 'The fact must be faced that at this period the normal very high morale of the Division fell temporarily to a low ebb,' wrote a division historian. 'A kind of claustrophobia affected the troops, and the continual shelling and mortaring from an unseen enemy in relatively great strength was certainly very trying.'

Diaries kept by Highland Division officers noted a loss of energy at all levels. Major David F. O. Russell of the 7th Black Watch, who had earned a Military Cross at El Alamein, wrote that 'during the whole of this period, the morale of the battalion was at its lowest ebb which made the task of competing with day to day troubles and worries even more difficult'. The 5th Cameron Highlanders' Captain Fraser Burrows echoed Russell's conclusion:

The private soldier had nothing to think about except where the next hostile bullet or shell was coming from. Nothing was easier in a night attack, but to stop, tie a bootlace and disappear. In Normandy this became more and more prevalent ... I had one Jock in Normandy who was marched into battle with a bayonet up his backside.

Lieutenant Hugh Temple Bone noted, in a letter from Normandy to his mother, an increase in desertions as the campaign progressed: 'People get lost all over the place in battle, some deliberately, most quite by accident.'

Bain was not thinking about desertion. He was not thinking at all. The march from Touffréville took all night. At sun-up, they halted. Bain and Stevenson dug a slit trench for themselves and the Bren gun. As soon as Bain tried to sleep, they were on the march again. For three hours that morning, they proceeded in single file on either side of a country road towards Escoville. When they stopped beside a hedgerow, Bain lit a cigarette and fell immediately to sleep. Alec woke him a few minutes later to say they had to dig new trenches beside a field of summer corn. Night came and with it German artillery fire that somehow missed the Gordons. In the morning, they moved into the deserted town of Escoville.

B Company dug in behind a church that had become its headquarters. It was so quiet that day, 14 June, that the Gordons shaved and washed themselves and their clothes for the first time since they left England. While they braced for a German counter-attack, there was little more than desultory artillery fire. On the evening of 16 June, the Germans escalated the bombardment, showering B Company with Moaning Minnies and artillery. Alec Stevenson, who was outside taking a piss when it began, ran back to the trench. His foot bashed Bain's chin as he fell beside him, and both men hunkered down. As many as thirty mortars exploded at the same instant, gashing and tearing at the earth around the church. Bain wrote, 'The fury of artillery is a cold, mechanical fury, but the intent is personal.'

The trenches afforded little protection from the relentless downpour. As in past engagements, Bain heard the wounded screaming in agony and begging for help. During a pause in the onslaught, Gordon Rennie dived into Bain and Stevenson's trench. 'We're pulling out,' he said. The platoon commander, Lieutenant Mitchell, was dead. Stevenson asked whether Mitchell had been the man they heard screaming. 'Aye,' Rennie said. 'He was hit bad. Thom had to finish him off.'

Bain said, 'Fucky Nell.'

'You sound like Hughie,' Rennie told him.

Captain Urquhart called the company into the church, where wounded men lay everywhere. He told them to regroup within the church's graveyard and use its wall for cover in case the Germans advanced. He ordered all the Bren guns onto the west wall facing the forest. Bain kept watch with the Bren gun, while Alec Stevenson shovelled deep to make another trench. When Bain heard a Spandau burst, he fired back with the Bren gun. 'You hit anything?' Stevenson asked.

'I hope not.'

German tanks approached Escoville at 1930 hours that evening. An hour later, infantry units attacked battalion headquarters. The opposing forces clashed in and around the hedgerows and the church-yard until almost midnight. The Gordons pushed the Germans back, but they lost thirty-eight men killed, wounded and missing. German mortar and artillery fire resumed at 0425 hours.

At first light, Sergeant Thom, who had replaced Lieutenant Mitchell in command of the platoon, led Bain, Stevenson, Rennie and another man on patrol through the Norman hedgerows. Thom slashed through the foliage of a hedge with wire cutters and squeezed through. The other four followed him into a field enclosed on all sides by tall, thick hedgerows. As Thom cut into another hedge at the far corner, a German patrol spotted him and opened fire. Thom, with his Sten gun on full automatic, shot back.

In the ensuing skirmish, Bain suddenly found himself staring over the hedge into the eyes of a German soldier. Alec Stevenson urged, 'For fuck's sake Johnny shoot! Shoot the fucker!' The German raised his Schmeisser machine pistol. Bain snapped out of his daze and pulled the Bren gun's trigger. Nothing happened. He knew then he was dead. His legs gave way, as if a sledgehammer had smashed into them. Stevenson jumped on top of him. Taking the Bren gun out of his hands, Stevenson unleashed an automatic burst that felled the German. The battle ground went silent, and Alec called out, 'Hey Gordon! Johnny's been hit! Gie's a hand.'

Bain's mates carried him through the brush, while he writhed in agony. Both legs were bleeding from the Schmeisser's 9-millimetre parabellum cartridges, fired at 500 rounds a minute. 'By now he had become the wound itself,' Bain wrote of himself. 'It was not a part of his body that was suffering pain. It was all of it.'

A medical orderly at battalion headquarters injected him with morphine and dressed his wounds. Bain recovered sufficiently to thank Alec Stevenson for saving his life, but he could not understand why his Bren gun would not fire. Stevenson told him the truth, 'Of course it wouldn't. You had the bloody safety catch on.'

His incompetence, the technical maladroitness for which he often chastised himself, had taken him out of the war. From France, doctors sent him back to Britain for a series of operations and a long recuperation. He would have many months to reflect on soldiering, violence and death, while his comrades fought on towards Germany. This would lead to some of the finest poetry of the war.

THIRTEEN

The second great issue of the flesh is sex.

Psychology for the Fighting Man, p. 365

BY THE TIME THE 36TH INFANTRY DIVISION came off the line at Piombino on 29 June, six of its members had won the Medal of Honor. It retired from the line with a record second to none among the Allied forces in Italy, although the 'hard luck' reputation from its early reverses persisted. When the army posted the 36th, alongside the 45th, to the Invasion Training Center on the Bay of Salerno, the T-Patchers found themselves back on the beach beside the Roman ruins at Paestum, where they had begun the Italian invasion on 9 September 1943.

They pitched their pup tents and were issued boxes of twenty-four Clark Bars. Steve Weiss finished off the chocolate and peanut butter confections in a few minutes. Hunger still gnawed at him, as it did in Rome before his five-course lunches. He walked off the base, climbed a fence into an orchard, picked four large peaches – as many as he could fit into his helmet – and devoured them. All that food, he reflected, must have been 'a prize for surviving combat'. What he needed, though, was a woman.

Many of the Italian women around Paestum had already attached themselves to rear echelon soldiers, who had been there for months and were likely to linger. The 'pencil pushers', as the infantrymen called them, had access to regular supplies that they dispensed to their girlfriends. Rivalry between frontline troops and those in the rear led to fights, and the two sides shouted insults at one another whenever

Charlie Company drove through town in open trucks. The sight of clerks and quartermasters in fresh, summer-weight khaki uniforms roused a sense of injustice in frontline troops sweating out the July heat in winter olive drab.

Combat troops turned to prostitutes, whose numbers in southern Italy had grown in proportion to the level of starvation. Weiss got his chance one day when a roving brothel stopped near his bivouac. From a small group of unkempt, unattractive girls, he paired off with a short, black-haired ingénue. She warned him it was her time of the month, but the eighteen-year-old soldier had waited too long to be deterred. Unbuckling his belt and dropping his trousers, he began an impromptu coupling. 'Stop that!' shouted the battalion's medical officer, whose unexpected appearance was as welcome as the chaplain's. Medical officers had frequently lectured the men on the dangers of venereal disease. 'Stay where you are,' came the officer's command. Weiss fled, pulling up his trousers as he ran.

The military's efforts to separate soldiers from prostitutes had no effect. Films and lectures on hygiene did not impress young men whose normal impulses were intensified by the prospect of imminent death. A British soldier in Italy at this time prayed as he came under German machine gun fire, 'Dear God! Please don't let me die until I've had a woman!' Syphilis and gonorrhoea were no deterrents, when all they brought were a few days in a hospital bed. One self-defeating measure was a leaflet in Italian for soldiers to give to pimps saying, 'I am not interested in your syphilitic sister.' Norman Lewis, the British intelligence officer, wrote in his diary, 'Whoever dreamed this one up clearly had no idea of some of the implications or the possible consequences. Remarks about sisters are strictly taboo to Southern Italians ... there are bound to be casualties.'

Weiss did not give up. He went to Naples, about fifty miles up the coast, on leave. A long line of troops 'that seemed to include everyone serving in the Mediterranean' had beaten him to one backstreet bordello. Waiting his turn, he asked the soldier in front of him, 'What's the babe like?'

'Never seen her. S'posed to be a beaut' though.'

When Weiss went in, the girl behind the door was no beaut', but 'a skinny urchin, as Mediterranean as a flannel cake, wearing a faded cotton dress'. He could not go through with it.

The Psychological Warfare Branch that Weiss longed to join was operating out of an office in Naples on the Via Roma. A billboard advertised Franklin Roosevelt's Four Freedoms – 'freedom of speech, freedom to worship, freedom from want and freedom from fear' – in Italian. Vincent Sheean, a prominent author and journalist in Italy as an Army Air Forces lieutenant colonel, commented, 'The sheer irony of the display can seldom have been equaled in recent times, for none of the four – except the freedom of religion, which is the least difficult and least valued in this era – existed in our part of Italy.' By this time, Weiss was siding with his frontline comrades against the 'pencil pushers', including the bureaucrats in Psychological Warfare. Like most of the other guys in his squad, he was becoming too cynical to sell the Italians ideals in which his faith was diminishing.

General Mark Clark relieved General Fred Walker, whom he blamed for the 36th Division's bad luck, of command at the end of June. Walker's soldiers believed their misfortunes were Clark's fault for consistently assigning them impossible missions like the River Rapido crossing. Walker reluctantly accepted the post of camp commandant of Fort Benning, Georgia. The men requested a division parade to honour the old man. Weiss recalled watching General Walker from the ranks on 7 July:

> His face was furrowed, his expression, grim, sad. He loved the 36th. Fifteen thousand men stood in the bright sunshine and listened to the general's closing remarks; quoting from a letter he had received from the widow of a captain killed on the Rapido River, he read, 'The next time you meet the Germans, give it to them.'

The new divisional commander was Major General John Ernest Dahlquist, a forty-eight-year-old son of Swedish immigrants from Minneapolis, Minnesota. The career officer had served in the occupation of Germany after the First World War. His previous posts during the Second World War had been as Eisenhower's deputy chief of staff and commander of the 70th Infantry Division in the United States. He had never commanded troops in combat, and his appointment was unwelcome to the troops who admired General Walker.

Whenever Weiss was on liberty, he pursued his quest for erotic consummation. In Naples, he and a buddy picked up two prostitutes and took them to a squalid hotel. The women were neither young nor pretty. The encounter, although technically successful, was anything but satisfactory. In the morning, Weiss went to a bar near the port for a coffee. The barmaid flirted with him. As he recalled it later, she asked, 'Would you like to go upstairs?' The girl was kind and warm, and she treated him with as much tenderness as lust. Despite the temptation to remain with her, he went back to the base before his twenty-four-hour pass expired. At this time in Naples, many troops did not go back. Reynolds Packard, the United Press correspondent who had saved one soldier from deserting, wrote:

> Desertions became wholesale: US soldiers would shack up with Italian girls and not return to their regiments. Groups of these soldiers banded together and became dangerous outlaws. Scores of amphibious ducks [land-water cargo transports], laden with flour, sugar, and coffee, just disappeared into the underground.

Back at the Paestum base, the troops were put on alert. All leaves were cancelled. Amphibious training took on greater urgency. The Americans went through intensive British battle drills. Weiss endured

> twenty-five mile hikes, the usual close order drill and calisthenics, bayonet and rifle practice, and map reading. Rumor had it that we would participate in an invasion somewhere in the Mediterranean. For the next four weeks, during night and day exercises, some lasting up to forty-eight hours, we trained in every type of landing craft.

The 36th Division practised for fifteen hours a day between 8 and 22 July. The 141st Regiment climbed steep rock faces, while Weiss's 143rd worked on assault tactics. British ships took them to Mondragone to rehearse amphibious landings. A Royal Navy crew dropped Weiss's squad in the water, drenching them to their bellies, on every practice run. 'Don't worry, mate,' one of the British sailors said. 'When we do this for real, you won't even get your feet wet.' The training seemed inadequate to Weiss, with vessels crashing into one another in the surf, chaos on the beach as troops herded together when they should have spread out to avoid being targeted in clusters and a colonel shouting, 'You'll never get off the beach alive. This is an absolute disaster.' Weiss's new squad leader, Sergeant Harry Shanklin, requested a transfer to the paratroops. When the army approved it, Weiss feared going into combat with a replacement sergeant he had never met. The army gave the men no briefings on the mission, no maps and no instructions on what they were to achieve. They did not know where they might lose their lives. Northern Italy, Greece, Yugoslavia and southern France were all possibilities.

During a break in the rigorous training, Weiss went over to Company B (Baker Company) of his 143rd Regiment, to visit a friend. 'I immediately sensed a change in morale and mood between Charlie and Baker's officers and enlisted men,' he wrote. Troops spoke naturally with officers, something that he could not imagine with Captain Simmons. The grunts of Baker Company remembered with affection the commanding officer they had lost the previous January, Captain Henry T. Waskow. Weiss did not know about Waskow, although most of America, thanks to Ernie Pyle, did. Pyle had written, 'In this war I have known a lot of officers who were loved and respected by the soldiers under them. But never have I crossed the trail of any man as beloved as Capt. Henry T. Waskow of Belton, Texas.' Pyle was with Baker Company when its soldiers retrieved the bodies of five fallen comrades, including Captain Waskow, from the mountains on mule-back. Pyle's dispatch appeared in almost every newspaper and magazine in America, one of the finest reports of a peerless journalist:

One soldier came and looked down, and he said out loud, 'God damn it.' That's all he said, and then he walked away. Another one came. He said, 'God damn it to hell anyway.' He looked down for a few last moments, and then he turned and left.

Another man came; I think he was an officer. It was hard to tell officers from men in the half light, for all were bearded and grimy dirty. The man looked down into the dead captain's face, and then he spoke directly to him, as though he were alive. He said: 'I'm sorry, old man.'

Then a soldier came and stood beside the officer, and bent over, and he too spoke to his dead captain, not in a whisper but awfully tenderly, and he said:

'I sure am sorry, sir.'

Then the first man squatted down, and he reached down and took the dead hand, and he sat there for a full five minutes, holding the dead hand in his own and looking intently into the dead face, and he never uttered a sound all the time he sat there.

One sergeant told Pyle, 'After my own father, he came next.' Henry Waskow was twenty-five years old. Weiss, who had never met an officer like Waskow, decided that 'this was the kind of team I wanted to be part of'.

On 12 August, with the rest of Charlie Company, he set sail from Pozzuoli in a British landing craft. On the journey over, Captain Simmons did not address a word to him.

FOURTEEN

You have to kill the enemy or make him surrender. There isn't any other kind of victory.

Psychology for the Fighting Man, p. 17

EARLY SUMMER NIGHTS IN NORTHERN FRANCE were so cold that Private Alfred T. Whitehead had to strip a bloody blanket from a dead GI to keep warm. As well as the chill, nights harboured dangers as varied as artillery barrages, German patrols and, for any soldier leaving his foxhole to relieve himself, landmines and snipers. Another hazard had not been anticipated. Near the Forêt de Cerisy, Whitehead was told, two men left their bivouac for a rendezvous with French girls. The romantic encounter turned out to be fatal: the next morning, the soldiers were found decapitated. Whitehead's commanders then issued an unenforceable order prohibiting fraternization with French women.

Allied units advancing through France captured more and more prisoners. Whitehead distinguished two types of captives: 'One was a group of strange, dejected men, speaking weird dialects and groveling before our soldiers. They were Turks, Poles, Russians and Georgians.' They contrasted with 'the finest spit-and-polish soldiers of the Wehrmacht: German paratroopers ... These Germans were elite, arrogant, highly trained tough fighters, and their morale was high.' The laws of war demanded that troops protect and feed captured enemies until they turned them over to MPs. Whitehead wrote that this was standard practice, until his platoon entered a town where American paratroopers lay barefoot and dead in the town square.

The Germans had made the Americans dance on the hard ground 'until their feet bled, then they shot them down like dogs'. Although he did not provide details, Whitehead wrote that from then on his division 'made it rough on the enemy'. He did not admit killing prisoners, as American troops had in Sicily, but the implication was clear. Another private in the same battalion, Harold G. Barkley, later said that German snipers in Normandy were killed 'without mercy'. His son, Cleve C. Barkley, wrote in his book *In Death's Dark Shadow: A Soldier's Story*, 'Snipers were seldom taken prisoner.'

Whitehead became more superstitious the longer he was in combat. He thought the 'voice' or 'presence' told him how to stay safe on several occasions. A squad mate, Private Paul S. Turner, gave him a 'cold feeling' by saying, 'Yeah, Whitehead, you'll make it to Paris, but I'll never live to see it.' Turner was a fellow Tennessean, from Roach Creek, and went by the nickname 'Timmiehaw'. Whitehead feared that Turner, one of the few soldiers he regarded as a friend, was invoking an early death.

Whitehead never lost a chance to get drunk. When ordered to destroy a cache of wine and hard cider to prevent the men from drinking on duty, Whitehead consumed all he could before completing the task. On another occasion, bottles of wine hidden under a fence caught his eye. 'I sat right down and proceeded to get drunk,' he wrote. 'In fact – higher than a Georgia pine.' He grabbed as many bottles as he could carry, so the rest of the squad could get drunk too.

The division met more German opposition on its march to the River Elle. Of the terrain, Whitehead wrote:

This was hedgerow country, and the going was slow and rough. No matter where you were, it was an isolated, miniature battlefield measuring no more than a few hundred yards in all directions. The enemy positions were well camouflaged, and they made few mistakes. Even aerial photographs scarcely showed any signs of where their guns were dug in. They had their 88's and heavy machine guns placed in boxed-in apertures in the hedgerows at ground level. They could also flood rivers in their favour, and they had ceaseless, tireless patrols and numerous snipers.

From the air, Normandy looked like a crazy quilt of patches held together by long seams that turned out, on the ground, to be ancient earth walls up to six feet thick and ten feet high. Some sprouted trees that added another thirty feet. The *bocages*, hedgerows, enclosed orchards, fields and pastures of varying sizes and shapes. 'The hedgerows themselves provided an excellent natural advantage which the Germans were quick to seize in building their fortifications,' wrote Major General Walter Melville Robertson, commander of the 2nd Division. When troops managed to penetrate a hedgerow, they had to face interlocking German machine gun positions that covered the entire enclosure.

The 2nd Division's troops dug in wherever they stopped. 'It seemed like I was forever digging,' Whitehead wrote. 'Foxholes and slit trenches, foxholes and slit trenches.' The German and Allied armies fought at such close quarters, sometimes only a hedgerow apart, that they could eavesdrop on one another.

A replacement from the 5th Division, the 2nd's hated rivals in Northern Ireland, was assigned to the 2nd. The man was afraid and made loud complaints about his transfer. Whitehead had no patience with a whiner, and he assigned him to guard duty. A shot rang out. Assuming the man had been killed by a German, he thought, 'Problem solved.' Then the man called out, 'Medic! Med-ic! I'm hit!' He had shot himself in the foot.

Whitehead's 2nd squad under Staff Sergeant Kenny Koonz reconnoitred enemy positions at night, while division artillery kept the Germans in their trenches. The patrols bagged German prisoners for interrogation. 'I'd get an enemy soldier by the collar, stick my trench knife in his back, and if he let out a yell, I had to kill him,' he wrote. 'It was a terrible feeling.'

German snipers, some of whom stayed behind in trees or other hidden positions when their units withdrew, took a daily toll of American lives. Whitehead remembered, 'They used every pile of debris, hedge corner, and bush to hide in, under, or in back of.' He wrote that Sergeant 'Hardtack', who had trained him at Camp McCoy, killed twenty-one snipers before being killed himself. 'I still miss that old man,' he lamented. This was undoubtedly Staff Sergeant Frank Kviatek, at age 47 the oldest enlisted man in the division. Two of Kviatek's brothers had died in Italy, and he had sworn to kill twenty-five Germans for each one. Up to this date, his bolt-action Springfield rifle had taken out twenty-one snipers. Despite Whitehead's impression that Kviatek died in Normandy, the division's official history recorded that he was wounded and survived this encounter to fight again.

Whitehead wrote of young men losing limbs to landmines and being trapped by artillery fire in no man's land. No medics could reach them, and their comrades listened to their cries without being able to help. Whitehead confessed to thinking, 'I wish the hell he'd hurry up and die and get it over with.' One rainy night, his squad tried to end one victim's suffering by shooting him with light machine guns. They missed, and the man did not die until dawn.

German artillery in the hedgerow fighting was so relentless that Whitehead would 'curl up in a ball like a cat, to avoid getting an outstretched arm or leg blown off'. American shelling of the Germans was just as ferocious. Towards the end of June, he recalled, American artillery 'started serenading the enemy with T.O.T.s, or Time-On-Target fire. At times, we used T.O.T. firepower to drive the enemy underground so that our patrols could operate.' Paul Fussell, then a twenty-year-old second lieutenant in the 103rd Infantry Division, described time-on-target as 'a showy mathematical technique of firing many guns from various places so that regardless of their varying distances from the target, the shells arrive all at the same time. The surprise is devastating, and the destruction immediate and unimaginable.'

It was less the artillery than an engineer's innovation that broke through the hedgerows. 'A second division sergeant in the engineers,' Whitehead wrote, 'devised "bulldozer" blades salvaged out of the German beach defenses. With those blades, our tanks plowed through instead of over the hedgerows.' Troops called the blades 'Rhinos'. A subsequent army study of the improvised device explained, 'The

"Rhino" was run into the hedgerow by the tank, thus loosening the dirt and roots, and permitting the tank to crash through to the next field with the minimum reduction of speed.'

Whitehead, who took rough conditions in his stride, detected inequalities between frontline and rear echelon troops: 'I "lived" in a hole dug into the side of a hedgerow. I ate cold, packaged rations, and had no change of clothes ... To the rear there were Red Cross dugouts with coffee and doughnuts, but I never saw them.' The system that kept a small percentage of troops constantly at the front, while the majority of the men in uniform were out of danger in the rear, did not cause him any further reflection. He was disgruntled rather than rebellious, like the dogface GIs, Willie and Joe, in Bill Mauldin's cartoons for *Stars and Stripes*. He killed Germans, without regret, because that was his job. Many men in his unit died in battle, but he was not close enough to most of them to feel any loss. When a young Jewish soldier eating rations beside him was suddenly shot dead, Whitehead's only impression was, 'He was dead – killed by a stray bullet. Another soldier's life passed – one of the nearly 800 casualties lost by our regiment so far.'

The exception to his indifference was Private Paul Turner, the Tennessee friend whom he called 'Timmiehaw'. On the evening of 10 July, 'Timmiehaw' and some of the other men played cards to pass the time. When Turner won, he tried to repay Whitehead some money he owed him. Whitehead told him not to bother. Timmiehaw insisted. 'You'll make it through the war,' he said, 'but I haven't got long left.' Whitehead hated to hear his friend speak that way.

The next day, the 2nd Division was given the objective of conquering Hill 192, so called because it was 192 metres above sea level, overlooking the town of Saint-Lô. Hill 192 presented a formidable obstacle, ringed with German gun emplacements, strongpoints and deep, reinforced trenches. At six o'clock on the morning of 11 July, the US assault on Hill 192 erupted, as bombs from the 9th Tactical Air Force and thousands of artillery shells decimated the enemy positions. The 9th Regiment made a feint along one side of the hill to distract German attention from the main assault by the 23rd and

38th. Whitehead's platoon went forward in trucks. When they stopped on the road, his friend Timmiehaw jumped off to piss. A moment later, Whitehead heard the explosion of a 'bouncing Betsy' mine, so called because it sprang up to chest height spreading more than a hundred ball bearings over fifty yards in all directions. Suddenly, Turner grabbed his bleeding chest, staggered over to Whitehead, and gasped, 'Oh my Lordie.' Then he died. As he predicted, he would not see Paris. Whitehead wrote,

> I don't believe I ever felt as bad in my life as I did just then … There was an old abandoned barn near the road, and I carried Timmiehaw into it where I broke down and wept bitterly. Death closed the door on our friendship, and it was hard to accept the sudden shock that my closest friend was gone forever. Tears were running down my face as I said a short prayer, then took all his ammunition and his map, covered him with a blanket, and as I ran out of there, I swore, 'Those sons of bitches are going to pay for this today!'

The mine that killed Turner took two other lives and left three wounded. The other dead were Privates Roy L. Schwerdfeger and Pedro S. Sanchez. Sanchez had turned 18 that day. Among the wounded was Sergeant Hawks, which left Whitehead as acting platoon leader in his place. The squad rushed up Hill 192. Whitehead saw a German and was ready to take revenge, but the man was already dead. Another 'Kraut' lying wounded on the slope motioned to Whitehead to stay back. It took Whitehead a moment to understand the man was warning him he had been booby-trapped. An American medic went to the German's aid, leaving Whitehead no time to shout. The booby trap killed both the medic and the German.

By the time Whitehead reached the summit, he had yet to keep his promise to avenge Turner. A German shell exploding in the treetops sent Whitehead flying. When he hit the ground, he thought he had lost a leg. The leg was bleeding, but intact. He scrambled for safety under a large cooking pot. Soon a bayonet propped up the pot, and a voice said, 'Oh, it's you, Whitehead.' Both GIs ran to a farmhouse, where a German soldier coming down the stairs put his hands up.

Whitehead shot him dead. Another German, Whitehead wrote, lunged at him from the corridor and tried to stab him with his bayonet. The blade cut Whitehead's hand, and he shot the German with his Thompson sub-machine gun. He claimed that he grabbed a German 30-calibre machine gun and ran outside, firing blind as he went. When Germans attempted to surrender, 'I mowed them down and didn't stop until I reached the third hedgerow, where I sat down.'

The 38th Infantry Regiment captured Hill 192 later that day, with Whitehead's 2nd Battalion losing 22 killed and 158 wounded. One of the eighty-three German prisoners told interrogators that he had been told the division's Indianhead patch signified that the soldiers were American Indians intent on taking German scalps. Whitehead claimed the army awarded him both a Silver Star and a Purple Heart for his actions on Hill 192. His service record confirmed that he earned one Silver Star, three Bronze Stars, the Combat Infantry Badge and the Presidential Unit Citation award, but no Purple Heart. Many 2nd Division veterans later doubted Whitehead's heroism, despite his awards and the fact that he was promoted to corporal. On Hill 192, however, he lost more than he gained:

I went a little crazy with the rest of the world that day ... I know that I left a part of me back there on Hill 192. Part of me died along with my friend Timmiehaw, and my comrades Sanchez, Schwerdfeger, and others. Just as surely as they had died, part of my being died with them, and a cold, merciless killer emerged.

FIFTEEN

As a unit gets nearer to combat new worries develop.
Actual battle is likely to increase them.

Psychology for the Fighting Man, p. 347

ON 13 AUGUST 1944, a cryptic message went to the USS *Bayfield*, a troop transport that had served at Utah Beach in June and was now carrying the 36th Infantry Division's new commander, Major General John E. Dahlquist. The decoded transmission informed the general: 'D-day, 15 August 1944, H-hour, 0800 hours.' With barely forty hours to go, the men were informed their mission was to invade France via its southern beaches. All that most of them knew about the French Riviera was what they had seen in movies or read in F. Scott Fitzgerald. Soon, provided they drove the German Army back, they would see the famed resorts of St Tropez, Cannes and Nice.

At almost the same time, the BBC broadcast a message to France, 'Nancy has a stiff neck.' This was the signal for the French Resistance to mobilize and hit the Germans in the rear. A few hundred American, British and Free French paratroopers had already landed in France to support the local *résistants*.

A fabulous armada of 885 ships, with more than a thousand smaller landing vessels stowed on deck, steamed along the Mediterranean past the islands of Sardinia and Corsica towards the French coast. Looking at the ships from the deck of a Royal Navy Landing Craft Infantry (LCI), Private Steve Weiss 'experienced the magnitude of American power'. His worry, in common with most of the other 151,000 American and Free French soldiers, was more personal than military. While generals needed beachheads to push men and equipment deep into enemy-held territory, a mere private like Steve Weiss wondered whether he would shoot straight without breaking down or running away. More than that, he wanted to stay alive. Many of the troops carried lucky charms or wrote letters home that they suspected might be their last. Weiss did neither. His world revolved around 'a persistent ache in my stomach', a common sensation in anticipation of danger.

A British sailor, who had put Americans ashore at Normandy two months before, told Weiss what had gone wrong during the 6 June invasion: tanks dropped in deep water sank to the bottom, men drowned, others ended up on the wrong beaches and more were cut down before they reached the shore line. Weiss asked Bob Reigle if he thought they would survive. Reigle kept his thoughts to himself. He may have worried for his own life, but the twenty-eight-year-old veteran bore an added responsibility for teenage privates to whom he was the old man, the corporal of the squad, the guy they would look to when they didn't know what to do. He had no answer to Weiss's question. No one did. The answer was on the beach.

Weiss and the other two hundred American infantrymen aboard the LCI did not know, because military secrecy did not permit them to, that Winston Churchill was watching them from the bridge of the British destroyer HMS *Kimberley*. The US Army's official war history said the British prime minister enjoyed 'a ringside seat at what many believed was one of the gravest Allied strategic mistakes of the war'. As the most fervent opponent of the southern French invasion, Churchill had employed his usually effective powers of persuasion on both President Roosevelt and General Dwight Eisenhower to thwart Operation Dragoon. The Allies, he argued, should have concentrated their Mediterranean forces in Italy and, possibly, the Balkans to expel Hitler's legions before the Soviets did. Only ten days before this D-Day, Churchill had urged Eisenhower to divert the Seventh Army from the Riviera to Brittany. Vindication of his strategy would come only if the Germans drove the 36th Division, along with the rest of Seventh Army, back into the sea. If Weiss had known how Churchill felt, his stomach might have ached more than it did.

Weiss had reasons to be hopeful about the landing. He had been with the division long enough to have friends, including Pennsylvanian Bob Reigle, Sheldon Wohlwerth of Ohio and James Dickson from Watertown, New York. He had combat experience, and the other guys in the squad respected him as a good first scout. His squad's sergeant, Harry Shanklin, whose transfer to the paratroops had been delayed, was with them after all. And the summer weather was ideal for an invasion.

Dawn broke dry but hazy at 0638 hours on 15 August, the Catholic Feast of the Assumption of the Blessed Virgin Mary. On this holy day in France, businesses and schools were closed. As the natural mist lifted, a darker cloud blotted the horizon. Naval Western Task Force, with the battleship USS *Texas* firing 2,000-pound shells, slammed German defences on the ridges above the shoreline. Light naval craft went in close to take out the coastal batteries and clear underwater mines. Allied bombers from Corsica dropped tons of explosives. Smoke and dust made the first American troops on the beaches at eight o'clock nearly invisible to the Germans. Many of the men were, as Private Don Nelson of the 36th Division admitted, 'absolutely petrified' at the sight of the 'dizzy heights of the vertical walls that were coming closer to us and looked as if they went on for miles'. The 3rd US Infantry Division went ashore first, taking what the Allies called the Alpha Beaches at the left of the invasion zone. The chic resort of St Tropez became a battlefield, where Staff Sergeant Audie Murphy, the most decorated American soldier of the war, took a German strongpoint and captured forty prisoners. For this feat, he earned the Distinguished Service Cross.

The 45th 'Thunderbird' Infantry Division, which had participated in assaults on Sicily, Salerno and Anzio, made its fourth D-Day amphibious landing in the centre, along the Delta Beaches. Resistance was as light as it had been for the 3rd Division, because German defences were concentrated further up the coast, near the town of Saint-Raphaël. These 'Camel' Beaches – Green, Red and Blue – were assigned to the 'hard luck' 36th.

Observing the invasion from HMS *Kimberley*, Churchill noted, 'Here we saw the long rows of boats filled with American storm troopers steaming in continuously to the Bay of St. Tropez.'

The 141st Regiment of the 36th Division led the assault on Camel Green, engaging German machine gunners and the four strongpoints of *Stützpunkt Gruppe Saint-Raphaël*. Weiss's 143rd Regiment came ashore behind them. Private Sam Kibbey of the 143rd recalled that, although he had not yet learned to swear properly, he would have to 'prove myself a man'. 'The LCI's hull grated on the rocky beach between St. Raphaël and Agay, at 09:45,' Steve Weiss recalled of his landing near Le Dramont. 'As soon as the craft's two parallel ramps tilted toward the surf, we moved along their length and onto the beach.' The British mariner who promised they would not get their feet wet had been as good as his word.

Heading towards the town of Saint-Raphaël, Charlie Company met heavy fire from entrenched German machine guns and artillery. Weiss manoeuvred up the beach, carrying the infantryman's standard load of 'webbing and leather straps supporting bandoliers of thirty caliber ammunition, a canteen, medical kit, and two hand grenades, all of which clinked, rocked, and bumped against me in the increasing sunlight'. Everyone carried extra weight: *A Pocket Guide to France*, five days' rations, two packs of cigarettes and an American flag brassard. One GI, who complained of a bad back, persuaded Weiss to lug his flame-thrower ashore. The weapon added seventy-eight pounds to an already heavy load. It also threatened Weiss's immolation if a German bullet hit either of its napalm tanks. Weiss, who had not been trained to use a flame-thrower, stumbled up the beach with the useless equipment. The soldier who lumbered him with it was, in Weiss's irritated view, a shirker. (The army soon discovered the boy with the bad back was too young for combat and shipped him home.) Weiss left the flame-thrower on the beach.

German light bombers strafed the landing zone and the ships delivering troops to the shore. Weiss saw a guided bomb hit one Landing Ship Tank (LST), detonating its store of ammunition. Although the LST floundered in the water, forty sailors on board died. The beachhead became a scene of as much confusion as valour. The crew of a

Sherman tank lost control and crashed on a road above the beach. Weiss's squad rushed to provide first aid. Nearby, a truck carrying a light howitzer turned over and blocked the road off the beach. An African soldier, somehow separated from Free French units to the right of the 36th, turned up in Charlie Company's ranks. Brandishing a curved dagger, he joined the company as it moved up the ridge.

The 143rd Regiment raced through a fierce battle between the 141st Regiment and the German 765th Grenadier Regiment en route to its primary objective, the town of Saint-Raphaël. The 36th Division's war history recorded, 'The 143rd Infantry ran into more opposition in the west. After assembling at Camel Green, its 1st [Weiss's] and 3rd Battalions advanced west and northwest to secure the high ground along the slopes of the Esterel and a mile or two inland.' They soon eliminated the German garrison in Saint-Raphaël, affording the 143rd a commanding position to protect Camel Red Beach for the landing of the 142nd Regiment. In Saint-Raphaël, Shanklin's squad rested near a pillbox at one end of an old iron bridge. As Weiss sipped from his canteen, a German shell crashed into the pillbox. Burning shrapnel and shards of concrete hit eighteen-year-old Private Truman Ropos in his right leg. The bleeding was severe, and medics wrapped the boy in blankets against shock. Two of them carried him away on a stretcher, while a third ran alongside with a plasma bottle connected to his vein. Doctors amputated his leg later in the day.

Reigle, Wohlwerth, Dickson, Weiss and the rest of the squad joined the fight to take the airstrip west of Saint-Raphaël. They blew up grounded German planes and cut a railway line. Along the way, dozens of German prisoners, many from the unenthusiastic *Ost* units recruited in German-occupied eastern Europe, surrendered to the Americans. Weiss's squad moved north from Saint-Raphaël towards Fréjus. The squad heard that their two-man bazooka team was surrounded in a ravine, and they raced there to rescue them. The two soldiers had vanished, either killed or captured, to be reported as Missing in Action.

Ten hours after the first wave of American attackers hit the beaches, more than 20,000 troops were ashore. The Allies lost 95 men killed and 385 wounded, but had captured 2,300 Germans. Most of the prisoners were old men or from *Ost* units. Elite Wehrmacht and SS forces might not have surrendered as easily. The Seventh Army had taken the area between Toulon and Saint-Raphaël, securing the beachhead from German counter-attack and preparing the way for advances north up the Rhône Valley and west to the vital ports of Marseilles and Toulon. Operation Dragoon was anything but the disaster Churchill predicted. The official US Navy historian, Samuel Eliot Morison, called it 'an example of an almost perfect amphibious operation from the point of view of training, timing, Army-Navy-Air Force cooperation, performance and result'.

Allied commanders made the most of German weakness in the south to drive speedily into France, the momentum affording no rest to the GIs. The German Nineteenth Army retreated more or less intact with the Americans and Free French in hot pursuit. On the second day of the campaign, 16 August, Weiss's squad continued probing north of Saint-Raphaël and paused near some trees. As Sheldon Wohlwerth put down his rifle, it accidentally launched a grenade that slammed into the mouth of a private named Taylor. The grenade did not explode, but it mangled the boy's flesh and teeth. Taylor fell in agony, and Weiss, Reigle and Wohlwerth held the young soldier until medics carried him to a field hospital.

The deputy commander of the 36th Division, General Robert I. Stack, led most of the division ninety miles north over the following fourteen hours. 'This was a dangerous, gambling attack,' the 36th Division's newspaper, *T-Patch*, wrote. Stack stretched the 36th's lines of communications to 100 miles, forcing drivers to work twenty-four hours a day carrying supplies from the beachhead to the front. Town after town fell to the Allied advance, which slowed only to accept the thanks, kisses and wine of the inhabitants. 'I was hugged and kissed until my mouth and ribs ached,' Weiss wrote.

Eric Sevareid, the CBS radio correspondent who accompanied the soldiers, wrote:

For the first time in the war, the troops themselves, like the optimistic people at home, began to wager on a quick end to the war. And for the first time in my observation of them they began to enjoy the war. The sun was warm and the air like crystal. The fruits were ripening, and the girls were lovely. In every village the welcome was from the heart, and for once civilians were a help instead of a hindrance.

On 17 August, Weiss took part in liberating the capital of the Var department, Draguignan. The GIs called the town, about fifteen miles inland from their landing beaches, 'Dragoon'. Most of its 20,000 inhabitants came out to submerge the soldiers in gratitude and presents. Men, women and children kissed the American boys and decked them in wildflowers. Weiss thought it was 'more like a Broadway musical than war'. The mood changed when the mayor invited the commander of Weiss's regiment, Colonel Paul D. Adams, through a stone wall into a tranquil garden shaded by tall cypress trees. It was the quietest spot in Draguignan. 'All the people of my town have contributed to give you this land,' the mayor said. The land was a cemetery.

Trucks collected Shanklin's squad the next morning, 18 August, and drove them along highway N-85, the old Route Napoléon, in an armoured convoy. For the first time, Weiss saw the *résistants* of the FFI (*Forces Françaises de l'Intérieur*), tough fighters who guarded roads and mountain passes for the Allies. They wore 'baggy trousers and ill-fitting, mismatched suit jackets' and wielded obsolete but serviceable rifles. Most had cigarettes fixed tight between mustachioed lips. Called *maquisards* and sometimes simply the *maquis*, names taken from the Corsican word *macchia* which meant a type of bush, Resistance members in the south of France numbered about 75,000. Although roughly two-thirds of them lacked even rifles, they contributed significantly to the Allied advance. Their sabotage destroyed bridges, train tracks and telephone lines, forcing the Germans to divert troops from defence to chase the 'terrorists' in the mountains both before and during the invasion. 'Many of them carried on the fight for three or four years, operating as individuals or in small bands,' a US Army study noted during the campaign in the south.

'They made the occupation of FRANCE a continual hell for the Germans.' The Resistance gave the American boys confidence, and grateful civilians made the war seem worth fighting.

'If we paused for a moment's respite, our shirts bathed in sweat and covered with dust, our mouths parched with thirst, they would run to greet us, arms outstretched, with tears of joy streaming down their cheeks,' Weiss wrote of the Provençal population. In four days, the 36th Division liberated Castellane, Digne, Sisteron and Gap. It pushed north of the main German forces in line with Seventh Army commander General Alexander Patch's strategy to entrap the German Nineteenth Army between Allied forces to the north and south. On 22 August, the 36th drove into Grenoble, an Alpine ski resort and university town. The crowd, the largest the Americans had seen, wielded flags and wine that were by now familiar tributes to the boys who had come far to liberate France from foreign occupation.

The 143rd Regiment's officers installed themselves at the Hôtel Napoléon, where Colonel Adams made his headquarters. The GIs were billeted behind the walls of an old French Army barracks. The noise of celebration tempted some of the soldiers outside. Weiss wrote, '[Jim] Dickson and I found an old, possibly forgotten, rusty iron door, falling off its hinges, embedded in the stone wall that gave way to our touch.' Leaving the barracks, they walked past a bakery where women waiting for bread applauded them. Another woman leaned out of a window and invited the two soldiers upstairs. Assuming she wanted to demonstrate her gratitude in the most basic manner, the boys ran to her door. The scene was not what they expected. An exhausted, sickly man was standing beside an old cupboard, almost the only furniture in the room. Weiss's high school French and the woman's few words of English helped them to communicate. Pouring out her only bottle of cognac, she said her husband had waited four years for this moment. Her husband wept, raised his glass and said he had never doubted that the Americans would come. Weiss and Dickson drank the cognac and went out to find the festivities.

The two young Americans tried to buy bicycles from a shop, whose owner insisted they borrow them free of charge. After all, the man said, the Germans took bikes without paying or returning them. The GIs cycled from café to café, where people gave them wine and thanks. At sunset, they dropped off the bicycles and walked through a city alight with bonfires and fireworks. 'Hordes of men and women strode arm in arm singing *La Marseillaise* and drinking champagne,' Weiss recalled. He and Dickson drank wine and they exchanged kisses with exuberant and not always young women. Their new French friends kept them up until dawn, when the two liberators fell asleep on the ground beside a petrol station.

SIXTEEN

There are a few men in every army who know no fear –
just a few. But these men are not normal.

Psychology for the Fighting Man, p. 304

A YOUNG REPLACEMENT LIEUTENANT in Headquarters Company of
the 2nd Battalion, 38th Infantry Regiment, had a nervous breakdown
in the aftermath of the battle for Hill 192. Alfred T. Whitehead, now
promoted to corporal, had no sympathy. Taking the trembling officer,
a high school teacher in civilian life, to the company commander, he
said, 'I've been doing this man's job all day, and here he is crying and
carrying on like a baby. I'm scared too, but I'm still fighting.' The
lieutenant was reassigned, undoubtedly to a psychiatric centre behind
the lines. Already tough when he entered the army, Whitehead was
becoming merciless.

The conquest of Hill 192 left the just-promoted corporal with
two wounds, one in his left thigh, the other in his left hand.
Although he stated in his memoir that the injury to his hand was
from a German bayonet, medical records indicated that he sought
treatment for both at an aid station. The medical tent was filled
with casualties that made his shrapnel wounds look slight, and
seeing limbless soldiers made him decide to rub sulpha powder on
his cuts and leave. His hand sometimes bled through the bandages,
and he changed the dressing daily. For the next few days, during the
battle that destroyed the ancient Norman town of Saint-Lô, his unit
was in reserve. This gave him time to recuperate physically, if not
mentally.

The 38th Regiment's next objective was the village of Saint-Jean-des-Baisants. This meant more fighting through hedgerows and across pastures defended by German machine guns. One night on guard duty, Whitehead admitted, he fell asleep. This was a serious offence, punishable in military law by death but usually by long imprisonment. Sentries who fell asleep could easily be killed by German patrols. More than that, they endangered all the men of the unit. Whitehead's squad leader woke him, but did not report him. Whitehead claimed he later chanced upon a sleeping German sentry and severed his throat with a wire garrotte.

Whitehead's memoir described his squad's existence at this time: foraging, occasionally shooting cattle for food, stealing eggs from farmers and picking apples. Some unripe apples upset his stomach. He recalled the smell of 'dead bodies lying along the sunken roads – bloated, blackened, rotting bodies of Americans and Germans, with maggots working through them'. While he occasionally exaggerated his martial feats, his was anything but a heroic war. There was no mention of patriotism, of struggling against Nazi tyranny or of the unit cohesion that made men risk their lives for one another. Whitehead's war was a steady slog through minefields, up and down hills and over fields littered with the human and mechanical debris of war.

Germans often surrendered by raising their hands and calling out, '*Kamerad*.' Whitehead's response was, 'Kom-a-rod, hell! After all you put me through, and then you come out with your hands up. Shame-on-you.' Acknowledging his duty to turn prisoners over to MPs, Whitehead added, 'A combat soldier is a lot different from anyone else: he's not eager to live-and-let-live or forgive-and-forget. He'll shoot the hell out of you, damn quick, and he won't bat an eye when he does it.' When two Germans surrendered to him near a bombed-out bridge, he gave each of them a cigarette. This turned out to Whitehead's advantage. He released them to persuade the rest of their company to surrender. They returned with forty more soldiers.

Germans were not the only ones ready to surrender. Whitehead carried a clean, white handkerchief to wave at the enemy if his time came.

* * *

At nine in the morning on 15 August, the 2nd Division moved on the town of Tinchebray. Whitehead had his first encounter with Free French partisans, who provided his unit with intelligence on German positions. The destructive battle for Tinchebray lasted most of the day. Many civilians were sheltering in their houses. Whitehead recalled,

> We sometimes accidentally killed whole families while clearing out buildings: you didn't have time to ask who was in the cellars when you tossed hand grenades in them. It was a terrible experience. Sometimes, too, a little girl or boy would come running out with one or both arms blown off, crying hysterically and wild with fear.

The German defence of Tinchebray had been, in the estimation of 2nd Division commander Major General Walter M. Robertson, 'half-hearted and ragged ...' The Germans surrendered at 4.30 that afternoon. The 2nd Battalion quickly secured Hill 248 above the town, where they heard on their radio that Allied forces had invaded southern France earlier that day. The men were grateful that the Germans would be forced to divert resources from them to another front. A British battalion soon arrived to relieve them. General Robertson wrote, 'The last objective of the 2nd Division in Normandy was secure.'

The next morning, the 2nd Division was given two days off the line. It was their first break from combat for seventy days, a respite that should have been welcome. However, because their rest area was beside the division's heavy artillery, they did not get much sleep.

The 2nd Division moved on 18 August by truck from Normandy to Brittany. Driving through the Breton countryside, Corporal Whitehead admired the way General George S. Patton's armoured columns had conquered the terrain: 'bomb damage had been limited to small patches around key road junctions and railroad stations, hardly disturbing anything else.' At a crossroads, Corporal Whitehead saw the general himself. He remembered his rousing speech to the 2nd Division in Northern Ireland. The general was standing up in his jeep and shouting at an American tank commander.

'What are you coming back for?' Patton demanded.

'We're out of ammo, sir,' the tanker answered.

'God damn it,' the general bellowed. 'Get the hell back up there and run over the sonsabitches. They don't know you're out of ammunition.'

As the trucks carried the 2nd Division west across Brittany towards the Atlantic port of Brest, citizens of towns and villages along the way surged outside to thank their liberators. Whitehead recalled that 'the French people swarmed over our jeeps, trucks, and tanks, embracing us with much shouting, tears, and kisses, while showering us with gifts of wine, fruit, and eggs.' He went into a farmhouse, where its peasant owners wore wooden shoes that reminded him of his own barefoot childhood. They accepted his offer of K-rations, which they fashioned into an edible cooked dinner with cider. When he left, he thought that 'here among strangers in a foreign land, I was more welcome than in my own home back in the South.'

On 21 August, the 2nd Division moved to an assembly area on the Daoulas Peninsula, *résistants* from the French Forces of the Interior joining them to provide intelligence on enemy positions. The 2nd Division assaulted Hill 154 southeast of Brest on the Daoulas Peninsula the next day. The division history recorded, 'The tactic was to creep Indian-fashion through low-lying bushes which the enemy had failed to cut down around the hill, to encircle and surprise.' To avoid alerting the Germans, no artillery or mortars prepared the way. The 3rd Battalion assaulted defences on the lower hill, forcing the enemy into the waiting fire of Whitehead's 2nd Battalion. Whitehead, who despised rather than feared junior officers, claimed that one replacement lieutenant aimed at a fleeing German but forgot to take the safety off his M1 carbine. The German was killed anyway by Whitehead's .45 pistol, one among many unlikely feats of arms trumpeted in his memoir. He said he and his 'gun crew' then fastened a captured German 88 field gun to a tree and fired it at German pillboxes. 'Afterward, I was severely called down by our company commander and almost got court-martialed for it, but I gave the Germans a hell of a time before I was discovered,' he wrote. Normally, a field gun anchored to a tree would recoil and kill the men using it.

When the Americans seized Hill 154 late that night, the Germans counter-attacked and nearly took the regimental Command Post. The regiment's three battalions pushed them back. Possession of Hill 154 gave the Americans a commanding position above their next major objective, the ancient fortress of Brest.

Brest, where William Weiss had embarked with the 77th Division in 1919 for New York City, was home to German submarine pens and a naval squadron. The Allies needed the port to offload troops and equipment. On 23 August, the Germans destroyed their only exit route from Brest to the Daoulas Peninsula. As Adolf Hitler had ordered, 50,000 German soldiers girded themselves to defend Fortress Brest to the last man.

BOOK II
SOLDIERS TO DESERTERS

SEVENTEEN

It is one of the first duties of a company officer to make
clear to his men that he knows each of them.

Psychology for the Fighting Man, pp. 376–7

LATE ON THE MORNING OF 24 AUGUST, Steve Weiss and Jim Dickson
woke up near the petrol station where they had fallen asleep after the
night's revelry in Grenoble. They decided to eat breakfast in town and
sneak back into the barracks before anyone noticed they were missing.
Some GIs gave Weiss and Dickson a lift in their jeep to the town centre.

Bob Reigle and two other soldiers, who had also slipped out of the
barracks, were sitting with three girls at a pavement café. Weiss and
Dickson joined their breakfast, an appropriate postscript to the
night's carousing. Souring the mood, one of the soldiers with Reigle
mentioned that had he heard their regiment had left Grenoble early
that morning – about twelve hours later than the time that it had
actually pulled out. (The 143rd had been ordered to leave Grenoble
at 1730 hours the previous day. Colonel Paul D. Adams, the regiment's commanding officer, had objected to the abrupt departure. 'We
captured the town,' he said, 'and we ought to be able to enjoy it!'
Overruled, he reluctantly took his regiment south. The division's
newspaper, *T-Patch*, noted that 'the 36th Division left Grenoble as
rapidly as it had come' with no time to search for absentees.) Weiss
and the other four troops were now Absent Without Leave (AWOL),
liable to court martial for that offence and for leaving their weapons
in the barracks along with their ammunition, packs, sleeping bags
and rations.

One of the five AWOLs in the café proposed leaving immediately to catch up with the regiment. Weiss, with unconvincing bravado, said, 'Sure, but let's finish our coffee and pastry first. It might be a long time before we eat this well again and in such company.' Jim Dickson took the girls' addresses, and the five soldiers left to face the wrath of Captain Simmons.

Luckily for the young GIs, a half-track driver from Alabama stopped to let them jump aboard. The GIs held tight, Weiss hugging a .50 calibre machine gun fixed to the truck bed, as the Alabaman drove like a moonshiner through Grenoble down towards the Rhône Valley. Sharp curves and steep climbs had the passengers fearing for their lives. About forty-five miles down the road, the five hitchhikers took advantage of a momentary stop to jump out and look for Charlie Company.

Two young Frenchwomen in light summer frocks bicycled up the road. Weiss, who since Naples had become more confident with the opposite sex, asked if they had seen any other American soldiers. One girl answered that *les américains* had come through her village, Romans, during the night. They caused such a stir that she went out and kissed all of them. (Weiss was unaware that the regiment that liberated Romans without a fight was his own.) 'I'm a day late,' Weiss said, 'but I'm here to collect my kiss.' Leaning over the handlebars, she kissed him on both cheeks. 'That did it!' Weiss wrote. 'For me the war was over. I wanted this woman.' Forgetting about Charlie Company, he invited the girls to a picnic. They accepted and cycled into town to bring back bread, sausages and cheese. Reigle called after them, 'Don't forget the wine.' While the five soldiers lounged on the grass awaiting their idyll in the woods, a column of six US Army jeeps broke the magic. At the head of the convoy was their regimental commanding officer, Colonel Paul Adams. The AWOLs had nowhere to hide. Adams went on without stopping. He had more a pressing concern: a rendezvous with the regional chief of the French Resistance, Colonel Jean-Pierre de Lassus Saint-Geniès, to plan joint operations.

The next four jeeps sped along the highway in Colonel Adams's wake. The AWOLs thought they were safe, until the last jeep

stopped. Without leaving the passenger seat, a young second lieutenant barked, 'Who's in charge here?' Corporal Reigle got up and
brushed himself off. 'Hell, soldier,' the junior officer said. 'Move
when I say so.' The lieutenant asked what outfit they belonged to.
Seeing they had no rifles and no helmets, he accused them of desertion and ordered them into the back of his jeep. Reigle asked where
he was taking them, and the lieutenant snapped, 'Smarten up, soldier,
or I'll have you charged with insubordination and court martialed.'
Weiss wondered where this hard-ass came from. They drove to the
143rd's Regimental Command Post, where the lieutenant put in a
call to Captain Simmons.

A Charlie Company jeep arrived to collect the five offenders.
Reigle asked the driver, 'How's the captain today?' The answer
boded ill: 'Hard to know, really. He holds his cards pretty close to
his vest.' They went to Charlie Company's Command Post in a
farmhouse between Chabeuil and Valence. The soldiers saluted
Captain Simmons, who did not salute back. He said, 'Gather around,
guys.' Weiss, hearing what he took to be a 'non-threatening voice',
thought the captain was not angry after all. Then Simmons let rip, 'If
one of my men had been killed while you were playing heroes with
all those French babes, I'd have you up before General Court Martial
and charged with Article of War 107, desertion before the enemy.
Get it right and get it straight, desertion is punishable by death by
firing squad.' Weiss and the others did not realize that Simmons was
giving them a break. Article of War 107 called for soldiers who had
deserted merely 'to make good time lost'. The death penalty for
desertion fell under Articles of War 58 (Desertion) and 75
(Misbehavior before the enemy). Simmons kept up the bluff. 'No
half measures, see,' he said. 'To hell with a dishonorable discharge
and a long prison sentence. It's nothing but the best for screw-ups
like you. You're in contempt. You've lowered the morale of my
company, failed the other men and in your absence put them under
additional pressure.' He docked their pay for the cost of the
equipment left in the Grenoble barracks. Although Weiss had yet to
learn which article of war was which, he accepted that 'Simmons had
saved face and let us off the hook.'

Weiss reported to his squad leader, Sergeant Harry Shanklin, who was hunkered down in a ditch with his men. While American artillery pummelled the town of Valence, Shanklin declared, 'The lover boys return. Damn! Why didn't you tell me you wanted to take off?' The sergeant called them 'dumb shits', but he did not mete out any punishment. Despite their teenage prank, they had been good soldiers until now. The army still needed good soldiers.

While the 143rd Regiment awaited orders, its commander was having dinner at the headquarters of French Colonel Jean-Pierre de Lassus Saint-Geniès. Colonel Adams and the Free French were planning the liberation of Valence, where a strong German garrison was holding American and French prisoners. With the approval of 36th Division commander General Dahlquist, Adams assumed command of a joint Franco-American force to take Valence and continue south to the main front at Montélimar. Adams and Lassus Saint-Geniès set the time of the attack, H-Hour, for 2200 hours that night, to be preceded by an artillery barrage. After dinner, Adams returned to his Regimental Command Post on the newly captured airfield at Chabeuil-La Trésorerie to begin operations.

Valence was a diversion from the Seventh Army's main objective, which was to block the German Nineteenth Army's retreat via Montélimar. Disagreement among American commanders over Valence, even after they had promised to assist their French allies in the town's conquest, portended a half-hearted effort. The official war history noted, '[General] Dahlquist dispatched no less than four contradictory directives – three by radio, one by liaison officer – to the 143rd Infantry still above Valence. The regiment started to receive them at 1600 in the wrong sequence. Not until 1900 did the regiment, reinforced by FFI units, get underway towards Valence ...' This was three hours before Colonel Adams and French Colonel Lassus had planned to attack.

A Free French intelligence officer who had surveyed German defences in Valence, Lieutenant Armand, argued that available forces were insufficient to take the town. He sent a message to Resistance Commandant Paul Pons: 'I do not understand why, with the Intelligence I have given, one is going to attempt such an attack, for no artillery piece which I have identified and marked on the map has been moved. I am sure we won't succeed, but I am going with the American tanks.' Dahlquist's order to Adams confirmed the attack for that evening: 'Seize Valence today. Seek assistance from Maquis.' Dahlquist further ordered Adams to bring his regiment to Crest by dawn next morning. Crest, a small town already in American control about twenty miles south of Valence, was on the road to Montélimar. An impending operation to destroy the German Nineteenth Army there meant Colonel Adams had only a few hours to seize and pacify Valence.

Charlie Company made ready to fight its way into Valence from the southeast along the Route de Chabeuil. Just before dark, four M10 tank destroyers (TDs) came forward to transport Charlie Company. The M10s, although they resembled tanks, were defensive weapons. The 143rd was using them instead for offensive operations and as troop carriers. (The M10 TD was mounted on a tank chassis with an open, pulpit-like turret, a converted naval three-inch gun and a .50-calibre machine gun. Like America's Shermans, the M10 was no match for German Panther and Tiger tanks.) Weiss found a spot on the left side of the lead TD. While they waited to depart, the company runner ordered Weiss's squad onto another TD. Weiss moved onto the second TD, and another squad climbed onto the first. Charlie Company rode out in the fading summer sun. When the TDs squeezed through concrete posts on either side of the narrow mountain highway, one unlucky GI's foot was crushed. A moment later, German machine guns, rifles and grenades opened up.

Bullets tore into the soldier who had taken Weiss's spot on the lead TD, propelling him headlong onto the earth below, dead. The other men took cover in ditches beside the road. They shot at German-held buildings that caught fire, forcing three German soldiers to run for cover. Weiss leapt back onto the TD to stop them with its .50-calibre machine gun, raking the ground with rapid bursts. The Germans' luck held, and they made it to nearby farmland. The squad regrouped and pushed again towards Valence. This time, they walked while the TDs rumbled along their flanks. Their advance had not proceeded far

when Germans on Valence's outer defences opened fire, killing two
more Americans, Privates Longo and Taylor. Both had trained with
Weiss at Fort Blanding. Weiss led the squad's survivors through the
darkness. A German shouted, 'Halt!' and fired twice. Weiss threw
himself into the soft earth. He remembered the scene vividly:

> Lying there, I waited for the men behind me to fan out to form a
> skirmish line, but no one came. Alone and exposed, I decided to
> make a break for it; as I got up to run, the German tossed a grenade.
> Fortunately, my timing was excellent … [The German threw three
> grenades at him.] Each grenade disintegrated beside me, as I hit the
> ground; otherwise, I would have taken the full force of any one of
> the explosions in an upright position. After the last grenade
> exploded, its fragments showering over me, I landed safely in a ditch
> beside my company commander, Captain Allan E. Simmons …

The thirty-year-old captain looked sixty in the middle of battle that
night. He said nothing to Weiss about his dance with death. 'As the
C.O., he's not fatherly or protective,' Weiss wrote. 'At eighteen, I need
all the understanding and guidance I can get, but none is forthcom-
ing.' Simmons seemed 'dazed, lacking in will power and self-confi-
dence'. Considering what to do next, the captain looked at Weiss and
ordered, 'Take your squad back out to that field. Keep moving toward
Valence.' Captain Simmons did not move forward with the squad. If
no man could be a hero to his valet, no officer could hide his character
from his men. Weiss grew more resentful of Simmons's leadership.
However, Simmons was no martinet. He could be fair, as Weiss admitted when he did not punish him for going AWOL in Grenoble. His
main flaws for Weiss, and undoubtedly for some of the other men,
were his aloofness and his frequent absences from the frontlines.
Watching the captain lean against a tree with his back to the enemy,
Weiss thought bitterly, 'What the hell can he see that way, except to
take it in the ass?'

Sergeant Harry Shanklin and three others went missing, reducing
the squad from twelve to eight – Weiss, his friends Corporal Bob
Reigle, Privates Sheldon Wohlwerth and Settimo Gualandi, and four

others, Sergeant William Scruby and Privates Caesar, Fawcett and Garland. Weiss knew little about Scruby, a farmer from Chillicothe, Missouri, and Gualandi, who had been a bartender in Peoria, Illinois. Caesar, Fawcett and Garland were completely unknown to him. He doubted he could trust any of them, after their failure to cover him while under fire only a few minutes earlier. Nevertheless, he resumed first scout position ahead of the squad and behind the three TDs. The TDs, though, made so much noise that he was certain the Germans would hear them. He was right. As the squad neared the Berthet quarter at the edge of Valence, anti-tank guns blasted the TDs. Two TDs and a half-track went up in flames. German 88s pounded the tree line, pelting the Americans with sharp wood fragments and shrapnel. The GIs dived for cover. 'Within seconds, men die,' Weiss wrote, 'piercing the night, the wounded scream and shout for medics.' German flares lit up the battlefield for their mortar crews, and the Americans fell back.

Weiss's squad raced fifty yards to an irrigation canal of the River Bourne. They tried to observe the battlefield beyond the canal banks, but smoke from the burning tank destroyers obscured their vision. Wounded American and German soldiers screamed for help. The rifle fire died down, while the artillery impacts and machine gun bursts came more rapidly. The eight men crawled from one side of the muddy cover to another, tearing their uniforms at the knees and elbows in their search for a way forward or back to the company. 'We stopped and waited, slowly sinking to the ground,' Weiss wrote. 'Machine guns blazed at us, pinning us down but hitting no one. We knew we could go no further.'

While the men waited, the commotion of battle surrendered to an ominous silence. The ground around the ditch was no longer a battlefield. It was German territory. The squad was on the wrong side of the American lines, trapped. Where the hell were Captain Simmons and the rest of Charlie Company?

EIGHTEEN

If the war and the safety of the world didn't demand their
services, most American soldiers would rather be home
than where they are.

Psychology for the Fighting Man, p. 344

EARLY ON THE MORNING OF 25 AUGUST 1944, while the Allies were
liberating Paris, American and Free French forces in the south of
France lost a small piece of ground to the Germans. The offensive to
expel the Wehrmacht from Valence, begun by Lieutenant Colonel
David M. Frazior's 1st Battalion of the 143rd Regiment, failed. Under
ferocious German fire, medics could not reach the wounded. Valence
proved more costly in time and lives than the town was worth to Allied
objectives. 'Then at about five in the morning,' wrote Colonel Paul
Adams, the 143rd's commander, 'I got orders to disengage and bring
myself and the rest of the outfit to Crest.' In what would soon be called
the 'Montélimar Battle Square', the US Seventh Army was massing to
block the German Nineteenth Army's retreat up the Rhône Valley.

The aborted battle for Valence on the night of 24–5 August,
according to the official after-action report, left sixty-eight Americans
dead. Steve Weiss's Charlie Company lost one man killed, twenty
wounded and another twenty-eight Missing in Action (MIA). Two of
the MIAs were later confirmed dead. The other missing were assumed
captured or killed. At least eight, however, were alive and holding out
in a muddy irrigation canal on German-held terrain between Valence
and Chabeuil. No one had told Steve Weiss and the seven other men
of the squad that the 143rd Regiment had retreated.

'Morning came, clear and bright,' Steve Weiss recalled, 'and we were sure we were surrounded by the Germans.' A German soldier, seated casually on top of a stone wall, watched the Americans without bothering to shoot or call in machine gun fire. When he dropped down and walked away, the eight Americans were puzzled but relieved. Other Germans, though, were bound to see them and report their presence. 'We knew if we stayed where we were, we would be killed or captured,' Weiss recalled. Morning grew late without any prospect of rescue. 'We were angry at Charlie Company for abandoning us,' Weiss wrote. The squad could neither engage the superior German forces nor escape to the American lines.

In Valence, the population woke to discover the Free French and the Americans had abandoned them. German units still patrolled the streets, which US artillery had shelled overnight, while American and Free French prisoners were marched into captivity. At nine o'clock, Valence police began investigating the night's events. Unlike most other police departments in occupied France, Valence's force had a hard core of *résistants*. Chief of Police Gérard called for a volunteer to inspect the scene of the all-night battle and find Allied survivors before the Germans did. Reports of desperate Germans shooting unarmed prisoners added to the urgency of his appeal. A young police officer named Louis Salomon, whose house at 296 avenue de Chabeuil was on the route of the American attack, took the assignment.

Armed with a police *laisser passer* to clear the German checkpoints, Salomon set off by bicycle for a farm at Les Martins. The property, which belonged to his friend Gaston Reynaud, offered an unobstructed view of the field of battle. German sentries at two roadblocks examined Salomon's papers and let him pass. Further along the road towards Les Martins, Salomon pedalled past the burning American tank destroyers as well as the German artillery that had taken them out. When he came to a third checkpoint, a German soldier ordered him off his bicycle and took him to an officer. Salomon explained that he was under orders to bring farmer Gaston Reynaud to police headquarters for questioning. Relaxing with a Frenchman he took for an ally, the German officer said, 'During the night, those dirty beasts of invaders have tried to enter Valence. Fortunately, thanks to the courage of German soldiers, the attempt failed.' The officer boasted that at least ten Americans had died to the loss of only one German. After this exchange, Salomon was allowed to proceed.

Back in the irrigation canal, Weiss and the others were waiting to be captured or overrun. Sergeant William Scruby reconnoitred the area and spotted a farmhouse several hundred yards away. Concluding that it would provide more secure shelter than the ditch, he huddled the men together to go over their alternatives. All agreed they could not remain where they were. Sooner rather than later, the Germans would find them. The time was 1130 hours.

'Tell you what,' Scruby said. 'I'll go first. If I make it, look for my signal from that second story window.' If there were no signal, the Germans had killed or captured him. If he made it, the men were to follow his route, one by one, every two minutes. Weiss gained respect for Scruby, whom he barely knew: 'I had a lot of admiration for him, in terms of his realism and his bravery. He was able to consider the situation and then take into account what options he had and then made his decision.' Scruby crawled to the edge of the ditch, surveyed the ground ahead and lunged forward. As he made a bee-line over an exposed pasture to a peach orchard, Weiss and the others rooted for him in excited whispers, 'Come on, Scruby! Come on, Scruby!' A minute later, the sergeant was out of view in the trees. More minutes passed without another sighting. No signal came from the farmhouse. Another minute went by. Was Scruby dead? A prisoner? Suddenly, from a window on the upper floor, the shutters opened. That was the signal.

Every two minutes, one more man from the squad leapt out of the ditch and ran for his life. When Weiss's turn came, he rushed over the bare field and crossed a road he had not noticed from the ditch. He sprinted through the trees towards the farm, his backpack feeling heavier than ever. When all eight soldiers had made it to the farmyard, they saw the farm's owner. Gaston Reynaud, his wife, Madeleine, and their nine-year-old daughter, Claudette, thanked the Americans for liberating them. The GIs responded with the disappointing news that they were seeking rather than offering deliverance. Reynaud immediately took the Americans into his barn, led them upstairs and gave them shelter in the loft. Seven men settled into the sweltering and dusty barn, while First Scout Weiss kept watch outside.

Weiss spotted a bicyclist in a policeman's blue uniform coming towards the farmhouse. He crouched in the bushes and took aim. All soldiers knew that the French police worked for the Vichy government in collaboration with the German Army. In many parts of France, they had arrested Jews for the Germans and tortured *résistants*. With the policeman's head in his sights, Weiss prepared to fire. The policeman got off the bike and approached the farmer, all the while under the rifleman's gaze. Weiss had a second thought. If he killed the policeman, the Germans would hear the shot. 'There's something else,' Weiss wrote. 'I can't kill a man in cold blood.'

When Gaston Reynaud greeted the gendarme, '*Bonjour, Louis,*' Weiss lowered his rifle.

'*Comment ça va, Gaston?*' Louis Salomon asked. The farmer and the policeman held a short discussion that Weiss could barely hear and would not have understood. Speaking softly in French, Reynaud said, 'I've got a terrible problem that needs to be solved.'

'What problem?' Salomon asked.

'Eight Americans hiding my hayloft.'

That was all Salomon needed to know. He picked up the bicycle and rode away at speed. Gaston Reynaud walked over to Weiss and took him inside so the Germans would not see him. Weiss described the scene upstairs: 'The hayloft, partially full of hay, is about twenty by forty feet square. Scruby is in shadow, keeping watch near the window, looking through a crack in the shutters onto the field we have just left; the others are resting on the hay, their weapons beside them; the farmer insists that we move as little as possible and remain silent. The loft is old and the floor boards creak.' All they could do was to keep watch and wait.

In Valence, Louis Salomon told the police chief and the commissioner about the Americans. An emergency Resistance meeting convened in the basement of the Cristal Bar, owned by *résistant*

Georges Valette. Although most of those attending were policemen, a Free French intelligence officer named Ferdinand Lévy, who used the *nom de guerre* Michel Ferdinand, took charge. Lévy belonged to three different Resistance networks and was the liaison between the local *maquis* and the newly arrived Free French Army. His plan to rescue the Americans required Louis Salomon, Maurice Guyon, Richard Maton and driver Marcel Volle to take him in a black Citroën *traction-avant*, front-wheel drive, police car over back roads to Les Martins.

At the farm, Scruby was keeping watch through the shutters. The Reynauds' labourer, René Crespy, brought the GIs a bucket of water. The men thanked him, but they felt as uncertain of surviving there as they had in the ditch. The farm and the surrounding land were quiet. Boredom increased their apprehension, as the Americans' imaginations conceived disastrous outcomes to their predicament. The silence broke when farm animals outside made a commotion. Machine gun fire erupted nearby, and the GIs grabbed their rifles.

'Automobile tires grate on the gravel below,' Weiss wrote. 'Strangers race up the stairs, taking two steps at a time, shouting in French, "*Allons, allons!*" Standing, we point our rifles at the entrance.' Before the Americans could shoot, they saw that the men were not German. Their blue uniforms were identical to the one worn by the man who had cycled to the farm a few hours earlier. The cyclist himself was with them, urging, 'Hurry! You must leave the hayloft! The Germans are coming. They've killed many of the wounded and are setting fire to farmhouses nearby. You'll be trapped.'

Free French intelligence officer Ferdinand Lévy unwrapped a brown-paper bundle. From it, he took four blue uniforms for the Americans to wear over their fatigues. Disguised as French policemen, the GIs were instructed to leave the farm in two shifts of four. Weiss volunteered to wait and go with the second group. Louis Salomon noticed that the uniforms – 'the kepi was too large, the helmet too small, the pants too short' – did not fit the well-fed American boys. When Bob Reigle squeezed into the clothes, he complained, 'This isn't going to work. We're too big.' Private Settimo Gualandi demanded, 'Got a better idea?' They could not button the trousers. Arms and legs protruded beyond the cuffs. But they managed. The first four pounded down the stairs.

When the police car departed, the waiting began for Weiss, Reigle, Gualandi and Wohlwerth. The GIs took turns at the window and listened for the Citroën's return. Weiss was tense with foreboding. Would the car come back? Were Scruby and the rest on their way to safety or a German prison? If the gendarmes failed to return, his survival was in doubt. Four lightly armed infantrymen could not fight their way out, and the farmer could not hide them for ever. Everything depended on the Valence policemen. Could they be trusted?

About an hour later, the Citroën raced into the farmyard. Ferdinand Lévy came up the stairs with the uniforms the four other Americans had worn. The GIs struggled into the undersize police clothing, then stowed their weapons, equipment and rations out of sight under bundles of hay. The last thing they wanted was for the Germans to find their belongings and punish farmer Reynaud and his family.

The four Americans hurried into the back seat of the police car with the three Frenchmen in front. The only place for Weiss to sit in the four-door Citroën was on Wohlwerth's lap. As they pulled out of the farm, Weiss said goodbye to the family who had helped them. It was then that he remembered he had not even asked their names. Gaston Reynaud bid the Americans farewell and went to the barn to remove their weapons from the hay. Trudging to the fields, he buried them in a water-conduit in the muddy bank of an irrigation canal.

The police car drove up to the highway and turned right. That route led northwest. American lines were due southeast. Instead of taking the GIs to the safety of the US Army, the policemen were driving them straight into German-occupied Valence.

NINETEEN

A dim outline of a better world to be achieved by supreme effort has
the power to call forth the last resources of the fighting man.

Psychology for the Fighting Man, p. 312

AS THE BLACK POLICE *traction-avant* drove through the German
defences that the 143rd Regiment had failed to penetrate during the
night, Steve Weiss wondered why the Frenchmen were not taking him
to the American lines. From his backseat perch on Sheldon Wohlwerth's
lap, he observed a formidable array of trenches, barricades, barbed
wire barriers, pillboxes and armoured cars. The Citroën was waved
through a checkpoint by German sentries and rattled over cobblestones towards the ancient town centre. German soldiers, armed with
machine guns, patrolled in pairs amid resentful French civilians. The
Americans had no weapons. 'Passing slowly through the town,
Germans peered into the car, close enough for me to touch them,'
Weiss remembered. Despite their disguise as French gendarmes, the
GIs would not have survived a moment's scrutiny from an inquisitive
German.

The Germans were understandably wary. Valence had suffered
massive Allied air bombardment and artillery shelling for days. Only
a few hours earlier, at 1.15 p.m., a nitroglycerine-filled goods van
blew up on the track near the main railway station. The resulting fires
and explosions destroyed 280 train wagons. Saboteurs also wrecked
eight steam locomotives, denying their use to the German Army. This
caused panic among the occupiers, who worried more about sabotage
than treachery from their supposed collaborators in the police.

The car passed American prisoners, some standing with hands behind their heads and others sitting dejectedly on the ground. Weiss watched the Germans push the POWs through the portal of a ten-foot wall into an old barracks. Further along the street, German officers with binoculars and side-arms were so intent on studying their maps that they ignored the Citroën.

The *traction-avant* dropped intelligence officer Ferdinand Lévy near a café. Weiss was so grateful to the Frenchman for saving his life that he reached out of the window to press a pack of American cigarettes into his hand. The Camel label, however, was visible. Lévy stuffed the cigarettes into his pocket and melded with the crowd. Wohlwerth cursed Weiss for risking their lives by exposing an American cigarette brand that was not available in occupied France. Dressed in police tunics rather than American uniforms, they could be executed as spies. 'Fortunately,' Weiss wrote, 'there were no Germans passing by.' Nor, apparently, were any French collaborators. Weiss, regretting his impulse, recalled, 'I felt like an amateur.' The eighteen-year-old, who had been trained as a soldier rather than a spy, was entering 'a world of signs and counter-signs, of cover stories and cover names, of agents and stratagems'.

The four Americans were soon on a road out of Valence, following the River Rhône south into the countryside. Weiss looked out at rolling vineyards and isolated farmhouses, which seemed strangely tranquil in the midst of a great war. He did not know where they were going. The car slowed for a flock of sheep grazing beside the road near a place called Maubole. Marcel Volle hooted the car's horn in order, Weiss thought, to clear the sheep out of the way. An old shepherd appeared, took out a red handkerchief and made a display of blowing his nose. Weiss guessed the shepherd was signalling that the route ahead was safe. The police car turned onto a dirt track towards an abandoned house.

Sergeant Scruby and the three other GIs were waiting inside. Their own journey, they told Weiss, nearly ended in disaster when German soldiers stopped the Citroën and demanded the policemen's documents. The real policemen bluffed, saving the Americans from questions that would expose their ignorance of French. The encounter had been so tense that one of the gendarmes went home rather than return to collect Weiss's group. The new arrivals removed their blue uniforms, and the policemen gave each American a Beretta 7.65-millimetre automatic pistol. Fifteen minutes after their arrival, a Resistance lookout ran in and shouted, 'Gestapo!'

Another black Citroën, this one containing Gestapo officers, drove up the dirt road. As its headlights illuminated the house, the Resistance men rushed the Americans out the back towards the river. Sliding down the sheer bank, they ran to two old, wooden boats. One of the boatmen, Augustin Bouvier, nicknamed Tin Tin, looked like the archetypal *résistant*. Sporting a black beret and buff coloured duffel coat, Tin Tin held an unfiltered cigarette in one hand and a vintage barrel-magazine sub-machine gun in the other. As the Frenchmen and the Americans crowded into the primitive vessels, the two river rats rowed for their lives against a strong current. The boats passed a bridge that had recently been destroyed by the US Army Air Forces, 'twisted and broken in the water, starkly framed by its concrete pillars standing in mute testimony on either shore'. They needed to reach the west bank three-quarters of a mile distant, and the fast-flowing Rhône was not helping. The Germans' headlights appeared at the river's edge. Gestapo men ran to the shore and shot at the boats. Bullets peppered the water. The boatmen rowed faster, pulling with all their strength to get out of range. When the boats at last reached the other side, the Germans walked back to their car.

The Americans followed their French guides up the bank onto level ground and ran across a road. One of the Frenchmen broke the lock on a metal gate outside a three-storey house. They went inside, and each of the Americans was assigned to a room. Steve Weiss, too tired to remove his uniform and mud-caked boots, lay on a red brocade bedspread and tried to sleep.

That morning at Les Martins, farmer Gaston Reynaud received a visit from SS troops. Having unearthed American weapons and equipment from an irrigation canal on his land, they searched his house and barn. Although they found nothing suspicious, one soldier pressed a rifle to Reynaud's head. What did he know about the weapons? Where were the Americans? The rigorous interrogation included threats to burn Reynaud's farm. The SS had already torched the farms of the neighbouring Vernet and Chovet families. Despite that and a threat to arrest his wife and daughter, Reynaud did not give away the Americans or their Resistance rescuers. To his surprise, the Germans departed without doing any damage.

Weiss, although thick curtains kept sunlight out of his room, could not sleep all that day. His adrenaline was up from the hours of tension and danger. At dusk, a Resistance guide took the Americans outdoors. They marched through the night, along country paths into the village of Soyons. Dogs barked, but the people seemed to be asleep. Leaving Soyons, the men went through fields and vineyards for about three miles. The next place they came to was Saint-Péray. Its 2,000 inhabitants must have been sleeping, because the streets were deserted. In the central square, Weiss saw a stone monument to the dead of the 1914–18 war, his father's war.

The men filed into the Hôtel du Nord opposite the memorial. The Frenchmen took them to a dingy back room barely furnished with a wooden table, a few chairs and a wall map of the region. Five men with British Lee Enfield rifles filed into the room, and one of them addressed the Americans in French. Weiss, who assumed they had come to welcome the Allies whose lives their organization had just saved, found himself subjected to fierce questioning. Where had they come from? What unit were they with? Why had they left their division? In the limited French he remembered from high school, Weiss struggled to defend himself. He pointed at the map to show where the squad had been cut off from the 143rd Regiment on Highway D-68 during the battle for Valence. His 'short, hesitant answers' to their questions seemed to leave the *résistants* dissatisfied. 'The French were surly,' Weiss wrote. 'I despaired.' If the Resistance concluded they were Germans disguised as Americans, they were dead. The interrogation went on for forty-five minutes. Then, for no reason Weiss could detect, the Frenchmen relaxed. They set glasses before the GIs and filled them with the local Côtes du Rhône red wine. The French and the Americans, comrades in arms, drank toasts to one another.

French scouts reported that elements of the German Nineteenth Army probing for routes of retreat across the Rhône were approaching Saint-Péray. Local commanders assembled a convoy of trucks and cars in the town square to drive the eight Americans and the *résistants* north to safety in the higher mountains. Because of petrol shortages, the vehicles ran on *gazogène* – charcoal made from wood chips that smelled to Weiss like a warm fireplace. For thirteen miles, under-powered engines struggled up steep roads to an elevation of 1,800 feet.

The convoy stopped in the barely lit streets of an Alpine village called Alboussière. Weiss retained a clear memory of that night: 'Standing next to a side door of a country hotel, illuminated by a raw electric bulb, a man dressed in jodhpurs and black riding boots, wearing an open shirt, awaits our arrival.' The Frenchman threw down his cigarette. Extending his left hand for the Americans to shake, he introduced himself, 'I am Auger.'

TWENTY

There is also the civilian's natural horror of the
unaccustomed sight and smell of death and bloodshed.

Psychology for the Fighting Man, p. 348

ON THE MORNING OF 27 AUGUST at the Hôtel Serre in Alboussière,
the eight Americans from Charlie Company feasted on a warming
breakfast of milky coffee in china bowls with hot bread, fresh butter
and jams. The other guests in the hotel's cosy dining room welcomed
the GIs to the communal table. Most of them, including French Jews
who had escaped Paris and deportation to the death camps in Poland,
were themselves hiding from the Nazis. The hotel's owners, Maurice
and Odette Serre, went to great lengths to provide for their guests,
combing the countryside for vegetables and chickens, overseeing the
preparation of food in the kitchen and extending credit to those whose
bank accounts in Paris had been frozen. The staff included two cham-
bermaids, Élise and Simone, girls not much older than Steve Weiss.
From that first morning in the hotel, Weiss appreciated the risks the
Serre family took for everyone in the hotel: 'The Serres are protective
and considerate of their charges, who, thus far, have been fortunate to
avoid capture and death.'

The guests at the remote inn, as dotty as the cast of an Agatha
Christie mystery, fascinated the young Weiss. One was a
Frenchwoman in her late thirties, who knitted quietly in a corner and
reminded Weiss of Dickens's Madame Defarge. He took a more
personal interest in a girl in her early twenties, who was 'slim with
red-dyed hair and rarely speaks'. He found her 'theatrical' and

169

appealing, but he was slow to find the pluck to approach her. An impeccably dressed older gentleman, Monsieur Haas, like Weiss's father, had fought for the Allied cause in the First World War. When the German occupiers sequestered Jewish property and forced Jews out of the professions in 1940, he lost his job in Paris as a merchant banker. Weiss also met M. Haas's two sisters, 'tall, slender figures', who had escaped with him from Paris, and the son of one of them, a fellow eighteen-year-old named Jean-Claude. M. Haas had pasted a Michelin touring map of France on his bedroom wall. A maze of pins and strings marked Allied progress against the Germans, based on reports from the BBC's French-language broadcasts. Valence was still held by the Wehrmacht. Further south, the Americans and Germans were engaged in fierce combat for the road and river junction at Montélimar. Weiss guessed that was where the rest of his 36th Division had gone.

At Montélimar on 27 August, while Weiss became acquainted with Auger and the other *maquisards* in the Hôtel Serre, the 36th was fighting a life and death battle. Division losses were so high that a battalion commander of the 141st Regiment ordered Lieutenant Albert C. Homcy to lead a hastily assembled squad of cooks, bakers and orderlies to find a German position that was thought to conceal tanks, tank destroyers or machine guns. Homcy was a career soldier, who had enlisted in 1938, earned his commission in November 1942 and been awarded a commendation for 'exceptionally meritorious conduct' under sustained enemy artillery fire in Italy. This time, though, he disobeyed orders. His objection to taking the inexperienced rear echelon troops into battle was that they would all be killed without achieving their objective. He stated later, 'I didn't think those men could do any good on that patrol and if I took them out they would get killed doing something they knew nothing about.' Two of the cooks had already run back to Homcy's Command Post after coming under German shells. One said, 'Lieutenant, we can't go on patrol. We don't know anything about firing bazookas or anything like that.' At the time, the Germans were taking a toll of the most experienced riflemen. Although Homcy's refusal probably saved the men's lives, battalion commander

Lieutenant Colonel William A. Bird immediately relieved him of command and arrested him under Article of War 75 for 'misbehavior before the enemy'. The charge, a term applied to both insubordination in combat and desertion, carried a penalty of death by firing squad.

Weiss was far from the 36th and its problems of command, supply and discipline. His life had taken a new turn. The GI was now a *résistant* with dozens of French hill fighters under the command of the mysterious, one-armed Auger. 'Auger', a word meaning 'drill bit' for boring into wood or earth, was the code name of Captain François Binoche. Thirty-three-year-old Binoche was a legendary figure in the French war against German occupation. The Germans had captured the then Lieutenant Binoche of the French Foreign Legion in June 1940, when France fell. Escaping from a prisoner of war camp near Nancy at the end of July, he reached French Morocco a month later and was assigned to the Foreign Legion at Casablanca. His Gaullist sympathies earned him arrest by Vichy officers, who imprisoned him first in North Africa and then at Clermont-Ferrand in France's Vichy zone. A court martial exonerated him of charges of conspiring with the enemy, Great Britain, for lack of evidence. He then joined the Gaullist underground. On 5 July 1944, almost two months before he welcomed the Americans to Alboussière, Binoche lost his right arm in a battle near the village of Désaignes. The *nom de guerre* 'Auger' did little to conceal the unmistakable identity of the handsome regular officer with a missing right arm.

Steve Weiss, whose unconscious need for a surrogate father had not been met by Captain Simmons or any of the other American officers in his battalion, fell under the spell of Captain Binoche. Binoche confided in him more than in the other Americans, and he invited Weiss to sit at his table for meals. Weiss learned about France from the veteran officer, and the two trusted each other. 'I really admired Binoche,' Weiss said. 'Making a connection with a father figure, although at the time I couldn't have put it into words [meant] I wanted to stay with him.' Weiss had little choice. He and the seven other Americans could not reach their division sixty miles away. By default, they joined the French Resistance.

A *maquis* patrol brought intelligence to Binoche that German troops nearby were scouting for escape routes over the River Rhône. Binoche decided to impede the German retreat by destroying a bridge two miles from Alboussière, and he asked the Americans to help. A truck loaded with the eight GIs and a dozen *résistants* set out after dark for the river crossing. At the bridge, Sergeant Scruby and Corporal Reigle guarded the French sappers as they dug explosives deep under the foundations. Weiss and the rest of the squad, armed with old bolt-action Lee Enfields, took a position south of the bridge to prevent German infiltration.

When the sappers had buried the charges, the men regrouped a safe distance away. The detonator was prepared, and Captain Binoche had the honour of pushing the handle with his only hand. 'The explosion shattered the still August night and reverberated against the steeply sloped mountains and across the valley,' Weiss wrote. 'Pieces of the concrete bridge, ripped from its moorings, rose then fell into the chasm below with a whooshing sound.' Another route of German retreat had been severed.

Steve Weiss embraced clandestine warfare more than he had the life of an infantryman. Resistance fighting allowed him his independence, and it usually let him sleep in a bed at night. Such luxuries were denied the ordinary infantryman, who obeyed orders and spent nights outdoors under enemy fire. Weiss trusted his commanding officer, Binoche, as he had never relied on Captain Simmons. Binoche knew all of his men, their names and their families. Their lives were never put at risk needlessly, and he was usually beside them on operations.

On one occasion, though, Binoche was conspicuously absent. Alboussière was one of the villages liberated by the Resistance. With *libération* came *épuration*, the purging of French people believed to have collaborated with the Nazis. These included young women, so-called *collabos horizontales*, accused of having had sexual relations with Germans. The ritual humiliation of these girls took the same form throughout liberated France, much to the country's shame: their heads were shaved, they were stripped naked, whipped in public and paraded through the streets by members of their own communities.

An accusation, even from a thwarted suitor, was usually enough to merit mob justice. Many of those taking part in these near-lynchings had themselves collaborated to varying degrees. (Under the German occupation, some Frenchmen had denounced their countrymen to the Nazis for supposed Resistance activity, being Jewish or Roma, belonging to the Freemasons or trading on the black market. When liberation came, some of the denouncers claimed to have been with the Resistance all along.) There were few trials worthy of the appellation.

The *épuration* was an aspect of newly reacquired French liberty that Steve Weiss had yet to experience, because the 36th Infantry Division had passed through the towns it liberated so quickly that it missed the kangaroo courts. A few days after Weiss left Grenoble, CBS correspondent Eric Sevareid witnessed the execution of six French members of Vichy's version of the Gestapo, the *Milice*. The *Milice* had earned a reputation for ruthlessness that outdid its German model, and many French men and women died in its torture chambers. Hundreds of Grenoble's citizens, who turned up for the execution of several *miliciens*, screamed for the youngsters' blood. When the firing squad had done its duty, boys spat on the corpses and adults laughed. 'A mob?' Sevareid wrote. 'The people were citizens of Grenoble, who had always raised families, gone to church, taken pride in their excellent university of higher culture and done no general hurt to humanity before. Was the important thing the way they had behaved or *why* they had so behaved?' Sevareid did not provide an answer to his question, and many American commanders looked the other way when French mobs meted out instant justice.

Alboussière's turn came one day, when two *maquisards* led a young man into the village. Weiss, standing outside a café with some of his Resistance comrades, observed the prisoner: 'Of medium height and build, he wore a short-sleeved khaki shirt, open at the throat, khaki shorts with large military pockets, a black belt, white socks and black shoes. His hands and legs were bound in chains.' An old *résistant* invited Weiss to join him on the firing squad that would take the boy's life. 'What's the fella done?' Weiss asked. The old man said that he was a traitor.

Weiss wanted to explain his American faith in 'trial by jury, justice for all, due process and equality before the law'. Unfortunately, his French vocabulary was inadequate. He asked whether there had been a real trial. The aged Resistance fighter believed *miliciens* did not deserve trials, and he repeated more forcefully his invitation for the American to participate in the execution. 'If Binoche wants me on the firing squad,' Weiss said, 'he can ask me himself.' He walked away, but he did not seek out Binoche to plead for a fair trial. He regretted this lapse, writing, 'I rationalized that, as [I was] an American, the man's fate was none of my concern.'

The townspeople and *résistants* waited outside the café in the main square for the ritual to begin at two o'clock. Captain Binoche, who blew up bridges and fought Germans with gusto, did not appear in the square. Ferdinand Mathey, a major in the national gendarmerie, assumed command of the firing squad. 'Stocky, with square features, a Belgian .45-caliber pistol strapped to the side of his blue gendarme uniform, he reminded me of the French movie idol, Jean Gabin,' Weiss wrote. Mathey called out the firing squad's members, who 'disengaged from the crowd and shuffled into line, but not before placing their glasses, some half-filled with wine, into the hands of eager spectators.' Like the rest of the mob, the executioners had drunk too much.

The square went abruptly still, the only sound that of the *milicien*'s shoes shuffling over cobblestones beside the boots of two guards. The guards left him standing alone with his back to a high stone wall. Major Mathey offered the condemned prisoner a blindfold that he declined with a contemptuous gesture. When Mathey asked for his final words, the youth flicked his head to indicate he had nothing to say to people he despised. Mathey marched back to the executioners and ordered them to prepare their rifles. The crowd watched intently from behind the riflemen. The death detail raised their weapons, took aim and, when Mathey gave the command, fired. Some of the bullets found the boy's chest, and others ricocheted off the wall behind him. The boy collapsed, knelt for a few seconds and fell to his side. As he writhed on the ground, it was obvious the fusillade had not killed him. Mathey rushed over, looked down at the bleeding form and unholstered his .45-calibre. Weiss described the scene: 'He stood over the man, aimed at his head and pulled the trigger. No explosion followed, only a click; he aimed again and pulled the trigger, another click, one surely heard for miles around.' The boy was still breathing. The old man who had invited Weiss to take part ran from his place in the firing squad, stuck his rifle into the *milicien*'s ear and shot. Bits of skull spattered the ground, and the body went still.

Early that evening, Weiss walked alone through Alboussière. He suddenly came upon the condemned man's corpse, twisted and blood-drenched on an old wagon of hay. His shoes had been stolen. The execution, thought Weiss, had been a 'bungled and repugnant affair'. He hoped never to see another.

Weiss did not come across Captain Binoche until the next morning, when the officer asked the eight Americans to teach his men to use the new weapons dropped by US Navy and Army Air Forces planes. Binoche took the Americans and ten French trainees to an abandoned farm outside the village for a short course on bazookas, heavy machine guns and other specimens of the growing *maquis* armoury. The first weapon was the bazooka, a shoulder-mounted tube that fired three-and a half-pound rockets to a distance of about 300 feet. Weiss recalled, 'Scruby described it as a simple if inefficient anti-tank weapon, bordering on the useless.'

Private Settimo Gualandi lifted the bazooka onto his shoulder to demonstrate the correct way to hold it. Corporal Reigle loaded a rocket into the back. Gualandi fired at the target, an empty farm-house sixty feet away. The French students were astounded to see the projectile miss the house, soar over its roof and explode a few seconds later in a meadow. The commotion brought out a frantic shepherd, who shouted at the GIs not to murder his flock. Chagrined, the American experts gave a French peasant fighter a chance at the weapon. His first shot went straight into the house and blew up inside, as it was designed to do.

It fell to Private Weiss to demonstrate the Browning M2 .50 calibre heavy machine gun. Like Gualandi, he missed his target. When a young *résistant* took three turns, he hit the house every time. Weiss, who 'had been outdone by a wily Frenchman', was no longer sure who was teaching and who learning. The two sides laughed about the role reversal, and Weiss reflected that the *maquisards* probably 'knew more about fighting than we did'.

In his room at the Hôtel Serre, M. Haas the banker recorded steady Allied gains on his wall map. The Germans officially surrendered Marseilles and Toulon to the Free French on 28 August. Once engineers had repaired the two harbours, supplies would flow to the Seventh Army in the south and help it connect to General Eisenhower's armies in the north. Weiss watched M. Haas's strings stretch to take in more and more Allied territory. On 31 August, when Valence finally fell to the Americans and Free French, M. Haas adjusted the map. Weiss did not know that Ferdinand Lévy, the intelligence officer to whom he had given a pack of Camels for saving him, had lost his own life liberating the town.

In between missions for the Resistance that included guarding the ground for Allied airdrops, Weiss gathered his nerve to invite the hotel's 'theatrical' redheaded girl for an afternoon stroll. Walking into the countryside, they struggled to communicate in broken French and English. Giving up on conversation, they fell onto the grass. Weiss remembered, 'She dug her heels into the ground for leverage and pressed hard against me, whispering, "*Prenez-moi, cheri, prenez-moi.*"' The French girl waited for the eighteen-year-old American to take the initiative, but Weiss lost courage. As they were about to quit in frustration, Royal Air Force planes streaked overhead and strafed German positions in the Rhône Valley. The interruption gave them the excuse to return to the hotel, where they went to their separate rooms.

The American GIs, the *résistants* and the Parisian refugees shared convivial dinners under the Serres' impeccable supervision at the hotel. Weiss enjoyed evenings with Binoche and his deputy, Lieutenant Paul Goichot, who chided him about his American naïveté. The two French officers felt the teenager had much to learn about wine, women and war. One evening, Binoche, in a playful mood, asked Weiss if he liked to shoot rabbits. Weiss, whose Brooklyn boyhood had afforded no such opportunity, said he didn't know. Binoche invited him 'rabbit hunting' the next morning, and Weiss was too timid to refuse. He went to bed wondering why Binoche had not asked one of the country-bred Americans like Scruby or Garland.

In the morning, Weiss turned up outside the village ready for rabbits. Two things surprised him. Binoche was not among the group of about twenty hunters, and the weapons were 9-millimetre Sten submachine guns and Lee Enfield rifles. Weiss asked, 'Why do we need all this heavy artillery for hunting rabbits?'

Ferdinand Mathey, the gendarme major who had commanded the firing squad in Alboussière, laughed. 'Rabbits? *Cher* Stéphane, the only rabbits we are hunting today are Germans.'

Weiss already had doubts about Mathey, and the policeman's joke at his expense did nothing to remove them. Mathey's handling of the *milicien*'s execution had left a bad taste, and a day hunting Germans with him was something Weiss would rather have avoided. Mathey, fitted out in his gendarme tunic with kepi and cavalry boots, announced that their objective was a farm in the valley below. Informants had told him German troops were hiding there. Without explanation, Mathey and the other *résistants* began the operation by firing their weapons into the air as if in celebration. 'What a fuck-up,' thought Weiss. Any Germans in the farmhouse would be alerted. If this was how Mathey fought a guerrilla war, Weiss did not like it. While the men marched down the hillside in a column behind Mathey, Weiss imagined the forewarned Germans preparing their defences. Silently, Weiss conceived his sharpest criticism of Mathey's strategy, 'It smacks of a Simmons-planned operation.'

They reached the valley floor after an hour of hard hiking. About thirty yards from the house, with no trees or other protection ahead of them, they stopped in full view of the occupants. 'The farm was well built for defense,' Weiss observed, 'and I anticipated a helluva fight. Every window, every door, of which there were many, could be a gunport for the enemy.' Mathey did not position anyone behind the house to prevent a German escape, and Weiss regretted the lack of hand grenades to force the Germans away from the windows. On Mathey's orders, the *résistants* dashed forward. Two or three men covered one group, then rushed ahead to stop and cover the next. The first wave ran to the front door and kicked it open, firing as a few *résistants* propelled their way into the house. The first room was empty, but voices called from the back. Three unarmed Frenchmen with hands high stepped hesitantly forward. Although Weiss thought the three were probably collaborators, he gave the one nearest him a cigarette. The suspect Frenchmen said the Germans had fled a few minutes earlier. Weiss, angry that Mathey had given them warning, was not surprised.

In a car they requisitioned from a local inhabitant, Mathey, Weiss and a driver scoured the countryside in search of the Germans. Local farmers said the Germans had gone east, towards the River Rhône. They followed that route for hours over rough roads without food or drink. The day was ending when they saw the lights of Soyons, one of the villages Weiss and his squad had passed through after their escape from Gaston Reynaud's farm. Mathey told Weiss to stay with the car and pump air into its tyres, while he and the driver walked into Soyons. Weiss worked the hand pump, until a blast suddenly hurtled him into the car's fender. Hearing the screams of women and men, Weiss ran about sixty yards towards 'a terrible, eerie scene in the fading light of day'.

A huge tree, its roots ripped from the soil, lay on its side blocking the road. Around it lay corpses, blood and debris. Dazed men and women came out of their houses to help the injured. An old woman in a black peasant smock implored Weiss to come into her blast-damaged cottage. Inside, a young man who may have been her son was kneeling on the dirt floor. By dim candlelight, Weiss saw the boy's ripped clothing and blood gushing from a wound in his thigh. Her son needed a doctor, morphine and bandages. There was nothing Weiss could do. Helpless, he went outside.

Ferdinand Mathey staggered towards him, his shoulder bleeding badly. The gendarme major told him that he had been helping a group of French *résistants* and their German prisoners to move a tree that the Germans had placed across the road to cover their retreat, when a booby trap exploded. The bomb had killed at least twenty-five people, French and German. Many more were wounded. Coming out of shock, Mathey asked where the driver was. Weiss answered, 'I thought he was with you.' They realized the man was dead.

Weiss took the wheel of the car to drive Mathey, the young man with the thigh wound from the cottage and several other victims to a makeshift infirmary. It was the first of many trips ferrying the wounded between the blast site and the clinic. As he drove one badly injured German prisoner, the two enemies struggled to communicate. They arrived at the clinic and waited in the car for a doctor. 'We looked at each other,' Weiss wrote, 'sitting in the cramped seats of the little car, both shocked at our misfortune.' The German produced snapshots of his wife and child. This was Weiss's first intimation of humanity in a German uniform. He longed to reciprocate, but he had left his family photographs at Gaston Reynaud's farm. The German went into the clinic without realizing that the American who helped to save his life was Jewish.

TWENTY-ONE

After all, what kind of Army would we have if every man
did what he pleased – if soldiers were permitted to throw
their clothing in a heap, to spit on the floor, to burn the
lights at all hours, or to sleep until noon?

Psychology for the Fighting Man, p. 346

AT THE END OF HIS DAY RABBIT HUNTING and ambulance driving in
Soyons, Steve Weiss returned exhausted to Alboussière. The seven
other GIs had moved out of the Hôtel Serre, and he found them in a
chalet that Captain Binoche had borrowed for their use. All of his
comrades, except Bob Reigle, were sleeping. Weiss told Reigle about
the bungled raid on the farmhouse and the booby-trapped tree. Reigle
had news for Weiss. An American paratroop officer from the Office of
Strategic Services (OSS) had come to Alboussière to invite the squad to
join the OSS. One of the clandestine service's Operational Group (OG)
sections needed men to replace its wounded. Weiss said he preferred to
remain with the Resistance. Reigle argued that, as Americans, they
belonged with the OSS. When the rest of the squad woke up, they took
a vote. The tally was seven for the OSS and one for the Resistance. The
one was Weiss, who thought his friends were making a mistake. 'We
were with the French,' Weiss said later, 'but we were going to be with
the Americans. Otherwise, there was no reason.' To Weiss, returning
to US command, when he was already fighting Germans alongside the
French, did not justify leaving the only officer he had ever trusted.

The men packed their gear. In front of the Hôtel Serre, the Serre
family, M. Haas and his sisters, the maids Élise and Simone, the

redhead with whom Weiss had almost had an affair and the hotel's chef bid the Americans farewell. When Captain Binoche thanked them for their contribution to French liberation, Weiss said goodbye as if leaving a father.

Weiss thought their driver, a pilot in the Free French Air Force, drove 'as if he were maneuvering a P-40 fighter plane at breakneck speed over narrow, winding roads. I doubted if we would reach our destination alive'. The car braked at a bend to avoid running into three *maquisards* at a roadblock. One of the *résistants*, seeing the Americans, asked, 'Anyone from Brooklyn?' When Weiss spoke up, the Frenchman called to someone in the bushes. 'On cue,' Weiss wrote, 'stepping onto the road as if she were a headliner on the Orpheum Theatre Circuit, an attractive woman in her early thirties approached the car and greeted us in an educated Brooklyn accent.' The GIs got out of the car to talk to her. Offering her a cigarette, Weiss asked, 'What on earth are you doing here?' A tear tumbled from her eye, and she hugged each GI in turn.

The woman told her story. She was in France at the beginning of the Nazi occupation, when Americans were neutral and the Germans left them alone. She became an enemy alien after the United States entered the war in December 1941. In September 1942, the Germans responded to the internment of German citizens in the United States by sending Americans between the ages of sixteen and sixty-five to camps. Rather than be confined with the other American women at Vittel, she went into hiding. With the help of French friends, she moved around the country. It had been two hard years, but speaking to someone from Brooklyn was almost as good as being home. She and Weiss reminisced about the old neighbourhood and 'dem bums', the Dodgers. Weiss gave her two packs of Camels, and they left her with the *maquis*.

Their next stop was nearly thirty miles from Alboussière, a safe house that Company B, 2671st Special Reconnaissance Battalion, had established on a farm outside the village of Devesset. Code named Operational Group (OG) Louise, the battalion had established its headquarters in a farmhouse on high ground with a clear field of fire.

The commanders, Lieutenants Roy Rickerson and William H. McKenzie III, welcomed the eight recruits into their large living room. Weiss thought Rickerson 'was framed like a middle weight, and pound for pound every bit as tough'. One team member, Sergeant Adrian Biledeau, lay on a sofa with his leg in a cast, having broken his thigh and ankle parachuting into France with the rest of the OG on 18 July. Louise was one of six OGs in the Ardèche, with each OG divided into two sections. The standard OG contingent deployed a captain in command of three lieutenants and thirty NCOs. With attrition, unit size shrank until it recruited downed American aircrews or stragglers like the eight GIs from Charlie Company. Most of Rickerson's section came from French-speaking corners of the United States, like Louisiana, Maine and upstate New York near the Canadian border. Speaking French with North American accents, most of the team had an easy time communicating with both *résistants* and civilians. Their names were as French as any in the region: Pelletier, Boucher, Gallant, Biledeau, Gagnon, Collette, Laureta, Dozois and Fontenot. Even Rickerson, despite his English name, came from Bossier City, Louisiana.

The atmosphere at the OSS headquarters was collegial, almost like a fraternity house. Without realizing it, Steve Weiss had indirectly achieved his goal of transferring to Psychological Warfare. Psychological Warfare, as the overseas branch of the Office of War Information (OWI) where Weiss had worked in New York, had begun its existence as part of the same organization as the OSS. Called the Office for the Coordinator of Information, the agency performed both public and secret information functions at the beginning of the war. It was only in 1942 that President Roosevelt split the organization into the OWI and OSS, with the Coordinator, General William 'Wild Bill' Donovan, taking command of the OSS. One of the OSS's missions in Europe was the same as Psychological Warfare's: to inspire people under German occupation to fight for the Allies. Its additional tasks were to harass German forces, cut German communications and provide weapons and logistical support to the Resistance. Weiss had thus been recruited to a former part of the unit he had initially applied for, but all he wanted was to return to Binoche and the Resistance.

Lieutenants Rickerson and McKenzie had an impeccable record of achievement since parachuting into France six weeks earlier. After liaising with the local Resistance and taking Sergeant Biledeau to a hospital to set his fractured leg, Rickerson and McKenzie established their operating base. Five days later, they went into action blowing up two bridges. French engineers with Rickerson cut the cable at one end of a suspension bridge fifty miles north of Avignon at Viviers before destroying its foundations with eight 20-pound charges on the bridge's suspension cables. The technique knocked out the bridge so that it fell intact to block the river, forcing a barge laden with petrol for German forces to turn back. McKenzie meanwhile demolished a railway bridge near Viviers. Six days later, on 29 July, OG Louise launched an assault that was nothing less than astounding for a small group of a dozen Americans with fewer than a hundred *maquis* allies. They attacked a German garrison of 10,000 men northwest of Lyons in the town of Vallon, destroying a fuel depot, heavy artillery and most of the Germans' vehicles. They also left about two hundred German troops dead. Then, using airdropped 37-millimetre anti-tank guns, they attacked a German column as it retreated north.

On 25 August, the battalion suffered a setback when a failed ambush of German troops forced the *maquis* to withdraw and the Americans to fight their way to safety. Rickerson suffered 'superficial if bloody wounds' that he did not mention to the Charlie Company recruits. At Chomerac on 31 August, Lieutenant Rickerson and two Free French officers convinced the German commander that an Allied army surrounded his forces. Three thousand eight hundred Germans surrendered to the tiny band.

Weiss had become part of one of the most successful guerrilla operations of the war in Europe, and the more he learned about Rickerson, whom the men called 'Rick', the more he admired him. The lieutenant's professionalism persuaded Weiss that joining the American unit was right after all. He thought that 'unlike Simmons, Rick's feats of arms proved him to be an officer worthy of command. I needed that.' Rickerson assigned Weiss to guard the radio operator, Sergeant Frank Laureta of Denver, Colorado, while he made his transmissions to Algiers. German radio detection vans operated throughout the area. If one tuned into Laureta's frequency and Germans broke into the house, Weiss would be Laureta's last line of defence.

Rickerson outlined the unit's next mission: to attack the German 11th Panzer Division, one of the Wehrmacht's toughest in France, near Lyons. France's third most populous city had been liberated on 2 September, but the German Nineteenth Army was using routes around it on their retreat to Germany. The 11th Panzers were the Nineteenth's rear guard. Rickerson estimated the 11th's strength at fifty Panther heavy tanks, a dozen Mark IV medium tanks, four mechanized infantry battalions and an armoured artillery regiment.

Weiss was astonished that Rickerson would send a dozen OSS paratroopers, eight Charlie Company riflemen and about a hundred French part-time guerrillas against a German armoured division. 'It can't be done. We'll be wiped out,' he muttered. Rickerson, who either ignored or didn't hear the teenage private, discussed with McKenzie the weapons and equipment the operation required. They gave a shopping list to radio operator Frank Laureta, who went upstairs with Weiss to transmit to OSS Algiers. Laureta pulled his communications equipment out of a cubbyhole in the attic, fixed an antenna to the roof, wired it to his radio set, put on the headphones and encoded the message. Weiss asked him if he believed the army would actually deliver the men and equipment Rickerson was asking for.

'Yes, why not?'

Weiss told him the 36th Infantry Division's supply sergeants were reluctant to hand out so much as 'a chalky D-ration chocolate bar'. Laureta advised the young soldier to wait and see.

Three nights later, on schedule, a black B-24 Liberator bomber flew through the dark sky over a drop zone guarded by Rickerson's team, the eight Charlie Company troops and some *maquisards* with horses, carts and trucks. Dozens of crates and a few men fell to earth. A few parachutes failed to open, smashing cargo onto the ground. The team took the new men and supplies for the Lyons operation back to the safe house. They ate dinner, during which Weiss appreciated the friendliness between officers and men, the banter and the professionalism. It was at least as good as it had been with Captain Binoche, perhaps better owing to the easy access to supplies. 'This is the kind of war I want to fight,' he thought, 'with guys you can rely on.'

In the Ardèche with OG Louise, Steve Weiss was constantly on the move. He went with the team to cut telephone and telegraph lines, and he accompanied Lieutenant Rickerson on a mission to destroy the last bridge over the Rhône. As radio operator Frank Laureta's guard, he kept an eye out for German radio detectors. One van approached the house, its antenna scanning the airwaves from the road. Laureta was not transmitting at the time, and the van drove on. The Germans were withdrawing from the Ardèche, and Rickerson prepared his unit to move north to face the 11th Panzer Division near Lyons.

Months of tension followed by a lull affected Weiss's health. His stomach ached, and he lost his normally voracious appetite. His malady, with symptoms of influenza and amoebic dysentery, was debilitating. Dr John Hamblet, OG Louise's medical officer, prescribed pills that failed to effect a cure and certified the patient unfit for the scheduled attack on the 11th Panzers. When Sergeant Scruby and the six other Charlie Company infantrymen left with Lieutenant McKenzie and his OSS group for Lyons, Weiss feared that none of them would come back alive.

TWENTY-TWO

Fatigue can quickly reduce a fighting spirit.

Psychology for the Fighting Man, p. 293

THE LAST GERMAN UNITS WITHDREW from the area around Devesset. Also gone from the region by September 1944 were Lieutenant William H. McKenzie's OSS team and the seven Charlie Company riflemen, who were pursuing the German 11th Panzer Division near Lyons. With no word from McKenzie for two days, Lieutenant Roy Rickerson closed down the safe house, returned the keys to its French owners and packed his unit's equipment onto trucks and jeeps. An ailing Steve Weiss sat at Rickerson's side as the lieutenant drove the lead car through the mountains northeast to Lyons. Rickerson stopped on the way to see an old friend, Lieutenant Paul Boudreau, recuperating in the village of Annonay. Boudreau, commander of Operation Betsy, had taken a .50 calibre round from an American fighter plane. Doctors who removed the bullet from his thigh feared that a postoperative infection would force them to amputate his leg. Penicillin was in short supply in the Ardèche, but Allied ships were delivering medical supplies daily to Marseilles. Rickerson made sure that, with the roads recently secured, his friend was taken there.

Rickerson's convoy pushed on to Lyons, on whose periphery the 36th Division had fought when the Free French Army liberated the city on 2 September. Operational Group Louise settled into the Grand Nouvel Hôtel, where several other OSS OGs were residing. At last, Rickerson learned what happened to Lieutenant McKenzie. When his OSS and Charlie Company troops reached Lyons, the 11th Panzers had already retreated. The valorous but suicidal battle that Weiss had dreaded did not take place. His friends from Charlie Company had fought in Lyons, beside the *maquis*, against *Milice* snipers on the rooftops. They rejoined the 36th Division in time to take part in the siege of Bourg-en-Bresse. So far, no orders had come for Weiss.

Dr John Hamblet asked Weiss to sit with a wounded pilot in their hotel. The airman's hands were charred with burns from German anti-aircraft fire that sent his flaming B-24 Liberator bomber crashing into a French forest. The pilot was crippled with pain that medication did little to alleviate. Weiss stayed in the room for four hours at a time, but the pilot rarely spoke. When he did, he said that he could not remember whether he had given the order for his seven crewmen to bail out. Uncertainty and guilt intensified his depression. The fact that B-24 crews called their aircraft 'flying coffins', because they had only one exit door and often caught fire when hit, did not lessen his sense of culpability. Weiss locked the window to keep him from jumping.

To Weiss's delight, Captain François Binoche arrived in Lyons and invited him to dinner with his Ardèche *maquisards*. They ate as lavish a dinner as wartime scarcity allowed in a simple restaurant. Rhône wines enhanced the jubilant mood. Amid the heady conversation, Weiss learned that some of his Resistance comrades belonged to the Communist Party. In Alboussière, he had not given any thought to their politics. Now, their sympathies made him suspicious. He queried Binoche, who answered, 'Of course, there are Communists among us. Why shouldn't there be?' Binoche thought it natural that French fighters, both conservatives and Communists, should band together against the occupier. Weiss advised Binoche, as he had been taught in America, not to trust Communists. Binoche waved aside his concerns: 'I didn't give a damn about a man's political persuasion during the struggle, as long as he was willing to fight. I don't give a damn now.' Binoche left Lyons soon afterwards to command a unit of the French 5th Armoured Division that was fighting its way towards Germany. His *maquis* comrades who were not regular army lingered in Lyons.

Social life in Lyons abounded in the weeks following its liberation, as Allied soldiers and *résistants* discovered more reasons and more ways to enjoy themselves. Weiss attended parties given by the American, British and French military. The Jedburgs, small British-American-French special forces teams, hosted a jamboree in a local hostelry. Weiss was touched that they had set a place at the banquet table for one of their fallen. Towards the end of the evening, a sexily clad young woman caught Weiss's eye and he spontaneously kissed her on the lips. The other soldiers laughed when he realized 'she' was a man in drag.

It did not take the teenage GI long to redeem his heterosexuality at a house of ill-repute commandeered for the week by his Ardèche *maquis* friends. While the Frenchmen lounged in the main room among half-dressed courtesans, Weiss paired off with one of the women. A dozen years older and more experienced than Weiss, she provided his most pleasurable night of the war. However, when he encountered her in a Lyons street the next day, he was so embarrassed to be seen in her company that he turned down her invitation to take a friendly promenade. Afterwards, he felt ashamed.

His few days in Lyons ended when Rickerson's OG, along with the other OSS OGs, rebased to Grenoble. The Alpine capital of the Isère department had resumed a kind of normality since his last visit on 23 August, when he and Jim Dickson went AWOL to revel in the city's liberation. The OSS requisitioned a girls' school as a barracks in which each soldier had his own room. Young French women worked as waitresses, while the heavy work fell to German prisoners of war. In Grenoble, the OSS liaised with the Resistance units who would assist it in the battles to come. Weiss looked forward to taking part in the OSS campaign in the Vosges Mountains, the great natural barrier between the lower Alps and the Alsace plain. However, he was not certain of his status. Was he a special forces soldier or a rifleman in the 36th Infantry Division?

Officially, Weiss was missing in action. On 25 September 1944, the War Department sent a Western Union telegram to William Weiss at 275 Ocean Avenue, Brooklyn, New York. The message from the Army

Adjutant General, Major General James Alexander Ulio, was identical
to seven others sent to the families of the rest of the Charlie Company
riflemen who had vanished from the ranks a month earlier:

> The Secretary of War desires me to express his deep regret that your
> son Private Stephen J. Weiss has been reported missing in action
> since twenty-fifth August in France. If further details or further
> information are received you will be promptly notified.

The telegram did not say that Steve had been killed, but similar notices
to other families had been followed by announcements that sons,
brothers or fathers were dead. William Weiss regretted that he had
allowed his son to talk him into signing his enlistment papers. He
went to his room, where he sat alone in silence every Armistice Day,
and wrote a letter to the War Department.

Major General Ulio, a sixty-two-year-old career officer who had
become Adjutant General in 1942, sent William Weiss a follow-up
letter the next day. 'I know that added distress is caused by the failure
to receive more information or details,' Ulio wrote, as he had written
to thousands of other fathers. 'Therefore I wish to assure you that at
any time additional information is received it will be transmitted to
you without delay, and, if in the meantime no additional information
is received, I will then communicate with you at the expiration of
three months.' He added,

> Experience has shown that many persons reported missing in action
> are subsequently reported as prisoners of war, but as this information
> is furnished by countries with which we are at war, the War
> Department is helpless to expedite such reports. However, in order
> to relieve financial worry, Congress has enacted legislation which
> continues in force the pay, allowances and allotments to dependents
> of personnel being carried in a missing status.

William Weiss pressed the War Department for more information
about his son, adamantly refusing to believe the boy was dead. The
Pentagon did not know Steve Weiss was alive and on active service

with the OSS. Too many American soldiers had gone missing in Europe for the military to know what had happened to them all, and some did not want to be found.

On 27 September, the day after General Ulio wrote to his father, Private Weiss accompanied an American paratrooper, Abe Rockman, to services for Yom Kippur, the Day of Atonement. The venue was a Grenoble synagogue that had miraculously been untouched during the German occupation. (Grenoble had been in the Vichy zone under direct French control until November 1942, when Axis troops occupied the Vichy area in response to the Allied invasion of French North Africa. The Germans took most of the region, but they allocated the areas near the Italian border, including Grenoble, to Italy. Many French Jews fled to Grenoble, where Italian officers refused to turn Jews over to the Germans. When Italy capitulated to the Allies in September 1943, Wehrmacht and SS troops moved in and transported many of Grenoble's Jews to the death camps in Poland.) The congregation included the remnant of the Jewish community who had managed to evade the German extermination programme. At the service, the French Jews welcomed the two Americans in Yiddish and French. Weiss recalled, 'One ageing Jew placed his head on my chest and cried with relief and sadness. Suddenly, I was gloating, my eyes full of tears. The Nazis had tried methodically to destroy a race and here was living proof of their failure.' When prayers concluded, Weiss and Rockman stopped to speak to two young Jewish women with scarves wrapped around their hairless heads. They were afraid to ask whether the women had been shaved by Germans or by vengeful Frenchmen who believed they had been lovers of German soldiers. The Americans felt the women had been unjustly treated either way.

The US Army magazine, *Yank*, took notice of Lieutenant Rickerson's Operational Group in late September. A photographer captured images of the special forces soldiers, including Steve Weiss, while they were waiting in Grenoble for their next assignment. One photograph was of Weiss singing alongside his OSS comrades in a Grenoble church. Someone sent the magazine to Weiss's family in Brooklyn, which assured them that their son was alive.

Weiss, determined to play a meaningful part in the war, applied to remain with Rickerson and the OSS as they moved north and east in the wake of the retreating German army. He met Major Alfred T. Cox, a Reserve Officers' Training Corps-trained officer from Pennsylvania's Lehigh University and OSS commander in southern France. Rickerson had already told Cox he wanted to keep Weiss. Weiss volunteered to parachute with the OSS behind enemy lines, despite having had no paratroop training. Cox admired the youngster's spirit and officially requested the Seventh Army to reassign Weiss to the OSS. The reply came back from a Seventh Army staff officer: no. The 36th Division needed experienced infantrymen, especially a first scout like Weiss, and it wanted him back in the line immediately. 'It never dawned on me,' Weiss reflected later, 'to have said to Major Cox in Grenoble, "No, Major, I'm not going back. You might as well call the MPs."' Something in the teenager prevented him from challenging authority, just as he had never contradicted his father. It did not occur to him that he could question those above him. He had served under two brilliant and considerate officers, Binoche and Rickerson. Now, despite his dread of placing himself again under Captain Simmons's command, he did not doubt his duty to obey.

However much Weiss objected to leaving the special forces, the Seventh Army staff officers were correct that the infantry needed riflemen. From the time Weiss and the seven others were separated from the 36th Division near Valence on 25 August, the Division had fought almost every day without rest. With the 3rd and 45th Infantry Divisions, it engaged the German Nineteenth Army for a week at Montélimar. The Germans nonetheless escaped, and the three divisions pursued it eastwards.

The Germans retreated as quickly as their transport and the road system allowed. The Americans followed, unable to prevent the Germans from launching counter-offensives where the terrain favoured them. Ascending the heights of the Vosges Mountains, the German defenders gained the advantages they enjoyed in Italy: rugged summits from which to fire on the pursuing forces, good cover and weather that often neutralized the Americans' air superiority.

Long-time veterans of the 36th Division with memories of the hated Italian theatre found it hard to endure again.

The US Army was losing more men in northeast France than it could replace. The official US Army casualty figures for the European Theater of Operations in 1944 were 47,423 in July, 59,196 in August and 30,937 in September. More than 70 per cent of the casualties came from the infantry. Weiss blamed General George C. Marshall, the Army Chief of Staff, who 'froze the Army at 7.7 million men, and allocated 3.2 million of the "best and brightest" to the Air Force. By reducing the Army from two hundred divisions to eighty, he placed the responsibility of success on the 750,000 frontline soldiers worldwide, and I was one of them, as part of a chain gang.' Without rear echelon units being rotated into combat, giving the regular infantry divisions time off, the bulk of the fighting fell to fewer than 10 per cent of the men. Respite would come only with death, injury, capture or desertion.

Senior officers were aware of the system's shortcomings, both on the GIs and the Allied campaign. The commander of the 80th Infantry Division, Major General Horace Logan McBride, discussed the dearth of troops in late 1944 with the Assistant Chief of Staff for G-1 (Personnel), Colonel Joseph James O'Hare, of the Twelfth Army Group. Between the West Pointers from the class of 1916, O'Hare was 'Red' and McBride was 'Mac'. Mac wrote:

> To me the personnel system of the Army during the war has functioned abominably. It has been the greatest single obstacle in the training and fighting of a combat division.
>
> Until the replacements are considered a class of supply, just like ammunition, gasoline or rations, and a reserve built up in the units prior to entry into combat, the problem will never be satisfactorily solved. The first day of combat brings its casualties and replacements for these casualties, under the present system, do not become available to the unit until 3 or 4 days later. Consequently, the unit's effective strength decreases during the first, second and third day to a point where the fighting strength of the rifle units approaches zero. Furthermore, in order to keep these units going it is necessary to

feed replacements in during actual combat with a resultant injustice to the individual concerned and a failure to raise the combat efficiency of the unit corresponding to the number of replacements absorbed. We have had occasions where squad and platoon leaders received replacements after dark and had to move forward in the attack before daylight, not even getting a chance to see their men to be able to recognize them.

McBride's letter underscored an aspect of the replacement strategy that militated against Weiss's transfer to the OSS: 'The return to the Division of previous members of the Division is of vital importance,' General O'Hare replied to Mac a few days later. Conceding that troop resupply remained inefficient, Red cautioned,

However, we now find ourselves totally out of infantry rifle replacements because of the War Department's inability to ship the numbers that are necessary and were requisitioned. For example, 25,000 infantrymen were requisitioned for November, but at the present date only 13,000 have arrived, and the remaining 12,000 of the November requisition will arrive some time in December. Further, the requisition of this category for December was for 67,000, but the War Department has stated that it will be able to furnish only 30,750, so you can see that when the supply is so small and the demand is as great as it is, we are forced to have necessary control measures.

While the Army had sound reasons for returning Steve Weiss to the infantry, he sensed it was treating him 'just like ammunition, gasoline or rations' to be fed into the frontline. The OSS needed the skills of a now-experienced Resistance and special forces operative just as much as Charlie Company required a first scout, but bureaucratic inflexibility gave precedence to the demands of a soldier's original unit. When Weiss was ordered back to the 36th, Lieutenant Rickerson and his men said they were sorry to lose him. On 3 October, he turned 19 and soon left Grenoble doubting he would live to see 20.

* * *

An OSS sergeant drove him from Grenoble to Lyons, the best place to catch a ride on a supply truck heading east. The non-com suggested Weiss take a short rest in Lyons before returning to the front. Friends of his, he said, could offer him a room for a few days. 'I was slow to answer,' Weiss wrote, 'but in the end I reluctantly agreed.'

The sergeant's friends were a married couple in their early thirties named Ronnie and Olga Dahan. They lived in a two-bedroom apartment with their nine-year-old son, Gerri, who was away at a school in the countryside. After introductions and a few drinks, the Dahans lent Weiss the boy's room. As Weiss came to know the couple, they confided details of their life. They had fled their home in Paris when the Germans occupied the city on 14 June 1940. Olga was British and faced internment as an enemy alien with the other British women at Frontstalag 194 in the Vosges resort of Vittel. Ronnie had an even more pressing reason for flight: he was Jewish. After France and Germany signed the Armistice of 22 June 1940 dividing France into occupied and unoccupied zones, the Vichy government of Marshal Philippe Pétain assumed control of Lyons. Jews felt marginally safer under Vichy rule than in the German-occupied north. On 11 November 1942, in response to the Allied invasion of French North Africa, Germany occupied Lyons along with most of the other areas under Vichy jurisdiction. Mussolini's Italy was allowed to seize a small part along its border with France. When the Nazis arrived in Lyons, the Dahans had no escape route. Ronnie Dahan paid the Spanish consul a vast sum to declare his apartment a neutral Spanish residence that could not be violated. (The American Embassy in Paris in 1940 had issued similar documents to American citizens in France to prevent the Germans from requisitioning their properties. The Germans for the most part honoured them until Hitler declared war on the United States in December 1941.)

Lyons fell under the terror of Gestapo chief Klaus Barbie. A zealous SS functionary since 1935, Barbie detained Jews, Roma, Communists, homosexuals, Freemasons and suspected *résistants*. His ferocity, which included torturing to death the Resistance leader Jean Moulin in 1943, made life for Jews hiding in Lyons more precarious than in almost any other part of France. Barbie, who did much of the torturing himself, boasted in a letter to his superiors of rounding up forty-one children from a Jewish care home and sending them to their deaths. Despite the Spanish consular certificate on the Dahans' door, the Germans raided the flat one day only hours after Ronnie had gone out. A suspicious Gestapo official took an interest in their son, Gerri. Setting the boy on his lap, he casually asked when he had last seen his father. Gerri replied, 'About a week ago.'

Ronnie Dahan spent some nights at home during the German occupation, but he disappeared early each morning. While Steve Weiss was his guest, he took him to his place of refuge. It was a short walk from his and Olga's flat through streets 'crowded with push carts, itinerant peddlers, and shabbily dressed apartment dwellers'. Before they arrived, Ronnie asked Weiss not to reveal to Olga anything he saw. Weiss wondered why, especially since the Germans had left. Dahan explained that his safe house belonged to a young woman named Laure. 'You can't hide in a sewer twenty-four hours a day,' Ronnie told him. 'If the dogs don't find you, the rats will. See what I mean? What's required is a safe house, unknown to your family, an ordinary place that you can enter and leave without raising a neighbor's suspicions. Laure offered that chance to me.' Laure was Ronnie's mistress. 'She was slender, dark-haired, and of medium height with angular Mediterranean features,' Weiss remembered. It was a short visit, during which Ronnie gave her some money. Seeing how close the two were, Weiss refrained from moralizing. 'Whatever their level of intimacy,' he wrote, 'stranger things had happened during the Occupation than one woman hiding another woman's husband.'

After Klaus Barbie left Lyons with the rest of the German forces, the city was the scene of savage battles between the *Milice* and the *maquis* that the French regular army was barely able to control. When fighting ended, Jews and other targets of Nazi persecution came out of hiding. The city was in no state – bridges destroyed, industries bombed, buildings demolished and food scarce – to offer the whole population the sustenance it needed. Lyons that October was as cold as winter, and most houses lacked coal for heating.

Ronnie and Olga introduced Weiss to a woman traumatized by having witnessed the Gestapo beat her father to death in a public street. She was in her thirties, and the murder had happened a few months earlier. Ronnie asked Steve to appear at her hospital bed, an American soldier in uniform, to assure her that the liberation was real and the Germans would not return. Her own family, the Dahans and a few other friends gathered around her and introduced Private Stephen J. Weiss of the United States Army. She and her children, they said, were safe at last. Her husband sat beside her. Weiss wrote, 'She looked straight through me without a flicker of recognition, nor did she understand what her friends were saying.' When Ronnie told Steve later that her husband had found another woman, Weiss reflected, 'I felt aggrieved and out of my depth.'

Weiss stayed with Ronnie and Olga for nine days, during which he recovered from his dysentery, flu and nervous disorder. He now had to return to duty. The Dahans were disappointed and made him promise to return at the end of the war. With the Germans withdrawing from France at speed, they believed their reunion was not far off. Steve had grown close to Ronnie, a fellow secular Jew and wise older brother figure, and to Olga, one of the few civilians he met whose first language was English. They made him feel part of their family. Reflecting years later on his time in France, Weiss said, 'The relationship I did make, which was for life, was with the family in Lyons.'

Nineteen-year-old Steve Weiss left Lyons alone, hitching rides with any Allied driver who would give him a lift while incessant rain drenched him and his duffel bag. A morbid fear of serving again under Captain Simmons and reliving the inhuman life of a combat infantryman overwhelmed him. He went anyway.

TWENTY-THREE

The Army is organized throughout for one single purpose
– fighting.

Psychology for the Fighting Man, p. 325

BY THE END OF SEPTEMBER 1944, the US military in the European
Theater of Operations found itself waging war on an unexpected
front. While its divisions battled the Wehrmacht in eastern France,
American service personnel, in league with French criminals, were
plundering Allied supplies. This too was a shooting war, in which
Americans fought one another. Victory over the Nazis depended on
defeating the criminals. Soldiers at the front could not fight without
weapons, ammunition, rations, petrol, boots and blankets. Some
couldn't survive without cigarettes. A front-page story in the
Washington Post reported, 'This was demonstrated most forcibly last
September when Patton's tanks reached the Siegfried Line and ran dry,
while "Army trucks were backed up the whole length of the Champs
Elysees with GIs selling gas by the canful and cigarettes by the
carton."' An army study of the problem admitted,

> The organization of the Military Railway Service in Northern
> France did not provide for adequate protection of freight in transit.
> In Southern France, Military Police units were assigned to the
> Military Railway Service for this purpose. Almost from the
> beginning of operations on the Continent, the problem of protecting
> supplies in transit was of major magnitude, particularly in Northern
> France during the first five months of operation.

Allied use of the railways expanded as troops pushed back the German lines. By 15 August, one functioning line carried supplies from the port of Cherbourg to Le Mans. By 1 September, Allied rail services reached Paris and its network of lines to most of the country. From July's daily total of only 1,520 tons of freight, shipments increased to 11,834 tons a day by September. All that bounty in war-starved France, unguarded by Military Police, tempted black market merchants who had flourished under the German occupation. Allied deserters, as well as serving officers and men, cooperated with the criminal underworld to drain the lifeblood of the frontline soldier. Many of the thieves were former infantrymen, as the army weekly magazine, *Yank*, noted,

> They went AWOL from their units, which were mostly moving on beyond Paris, and stayed behind where the market and the money were. They moved into the upper brackets and became racketeers. Some of these men had minor criminal records in civilian life. When the opportunity for profitable crime came into their Army life they seized it. The biggest profits were in gasoline and trucking rather than rations, so most GI gangsters switched to these rackets.

Yank added that some combat soldiers were 'temporarily AWOL from the front, who came back to Paris looking for a brief fling at the bright lights, liquor and women, and found things so pleasant they forgot about going back to their units'. In late September 1944, the US Army Provost Marshal's office arrested twenty-seven American deserters working on the black market in Paris. One of them, who had been a truck driver, had 51,000 French Francs (about $1,000) from illegal sales of petrol.

Lacking enough Military Policemen to prevent large-scale pilfering, the army withdrew troops from combat to protect trains, convoys and supply dumps. Soldiers rode in goods vans, patrolled railway yards and stood guard at depots. For any combat soldier, guard duty in Paris was a welcome respite from battle. In late September, as the menace grew, the army looked for guards among the troops who had just won the forty-day battle for Brest.

Soon after the Americans conquered the port, which fighting and German demolition had rendered unusable to Allied shipping, nineteen-year-old Private First Class Harold G. Barkley of Quincy, Illinois, rejoined the 2nd Battalion, 38th Infantry Regiment. Having suffered a severe shoulder wound from a phosphorus-tipped bullet fired by a tank's machine gun in Normandy, he had been evacuated to a hospital in England. Speaking to other 2nd Infantry Division soldiers at their bivouac near Brest at Saint-Divy, he learned that most of the men in his squad were dead. The survivors were preparing for transfer east to confront the German border fortifications known as the Siegfried Line. One lucky battalion, though, would go to Paris as train guards. A lottery among VIII Corps regiments awarded the assignment to the 38th Infantry. Commanders of its three battalions drew straws to determine which would go to Paris and which to the German frontier. The winner was Lieutenant Colonel Jack K. Norris, commander of the 2nd Battalion.

On 26 September, while trucks carried most of the division towards Germany, the 2nd Battalion travelled to Paris. Among them were Private Barkley and Corporal Alfred T. Whitehead. 'My thoughts went back to Timmiehaw in Normandy,' Whitehead wrote. 'He said I'd make it to Paris, and now I was on my way.' Barkley and Whitehead made no mention of each other in their war recollections, despite the fact they were in the same battalion. Both remembered Paris duty as their best in France. They reached the darkened city at about midnight on 1 October. Barkley and the rest of Company G settled into the Hôtel Nouveau in the eastern suburb of Vincennes. Whitehead, whose Headquarters Company was billeted near the Eiffel Tower at 1 avenue Charles Floquet, went straight to a bar. He wrote,

> The people there were all friendly and gave me all I wanted to drink, and wouldn't let me pay for a thing, but I watched them all closely, not trusting any of them – I remembered the two GIs with their heads cut off. I walked back to our vehicles where I spent the night under a truck.

While guard duty was safer than combat, it was nonetheless an important job. Whitehead, Barkley and their comrades resented the black marketeers, who deprived frontline infantrymen like themselves of necessities for survival. Neither questioned their orders for dealing with looters: shoot to kill. Barkley's son Cleve, based on his father's reminiscences, wrote, 'Thugs and AWOL soldiers working as black marketeers were relieving some supply trains of as much as 95% of their cargoes before they reached the supply dumps at the front.' Whitehead was disgusted that 'French renegades were looting supply cars of all descriptions, along with the aid of numerous American GIs who gave a black name to the whole business, while causing shortages of food and fuel on the front lines.' The Battalion history recorded, 'They knew what it was to go without cigarettes, and a clean change of clothes; now while engaged in guard duty, they did their utmost to prevent wastage or theft of these sorely needed supplies.'

Both Whitehead and Barkley rode in open trucks on trains that moved slowly to frontline supply depots. Trains made frequent stops, when their armed guards jumped off and patrolled both sides of the tracks to deter thieves. A journey could take a few days, and the men slept in shifts. Whitehead wrote that an officer in the uniform of a full colonel ordered the diversion of several carriages from a station near the Belgian border. Whitehead's platoon sergeant refused. 'Hell,' the 'colonel' said, 'I outrank you, sergeant, and I am going to switch these cars off.' Whitehead claimed that, as the 'colonel' attempted to detach the rolling stock, the sergeant shot him dead.

The Battalion's unpublished history noted that Headquarters Company 'daily staged an informal guard mount under the famed Eiffel Tower. The guard detail, very "spoony" looking in their white gloves, newly painted helmets, and polished boots, was always a source of interest to the French people who crowded around to watch each day's ceremony.'

Whitehead got drunk on his time off as often as he had in Texas and Wisconsin. He also frequented Paris's many whorehouses. Barkley rarely drank and avoided the brothels of Pigalle, the risqué quarter that the GIs called Pig Alley. Yet it was Barkley, an otherwise conscientious soldier, who robbed a train. His escapades with the black market began innocently, while he was guarding a depot in Paris. A Frenchman asked him if he had anything to sell, and Barkley pulled from his pocket a tin of polish for waterproofing boots. Neither spoke the other's language. Barkley made a gesture as if he were spreading the unguent on bread and said, 'Mmm.' This seemed to satisfy the Frenchman, who paid Barkley a hundred francs. Another man offered him a bottle of cognac in exchange for a five-gallon jerrican of petrol. The can Barkley gave him held more water than petrol, but the Frenchman's bottle turned out to contain more water than cognac.

One night, Barkley and two other soldiers crept into the railway yard. They searched out a goods van filled with looted fur pelts left behind by the Germans. Barkley convinced himself that, belonging to no one, the pelts would not be missed. The three GIs grabbed bundles of fur and fled. Barkley delivered his to two young women, Paulette and Elaine, he had befriended a few weeks before. They kissed him again and again in thanks. This was the extent of his black market career, for which other train guards might have shot him dead.

Al Whitehead rotated between protecting supply stores and guarding trains. On one train that stopped somewhere outside Paris, he noticed two black GIs approaching. One of them stopped and said, 'Hey, look, they got a guard on this train.' That was enough for Whitehead to level his Thompson sub-machine gun at them and say, 'Yes, and all I want you to do is lay your hands on this train. That's all I want you to do. By God, I'm just itching to fill you full of lead.'

Paris was becoming lawless, as goods stolen from the army flooded the city's black market. Joyriders used contraband petrol to prowl the capital in cars that they had not been allowed to drive under the Germans. American cigarettes were so abundant that they were selling for $1.60 a pack, about a third less than the usually cheap French cigarettes. On 13 October, two American deserters, Privates Morris Fredericks and Turner Harris, robbed a café in Montmartre and made off with $42,000 in jewellery, bonds and cash from the owner and his customers. The two soldiers, one white and one black, had been living for the previous two months in a hotel on sales of stolen army petrol. Three other deserters were apprehended in another Paris hotel with 11,000 packs of cigarettes. Deserters fought gun battles in the streets with MPs and Parisian gendarmes.

The 2nd Battalion's efforts were, Wade Werner reported from Paris in the *Washington Post*, 'cutting thefts down to manageable proportions'. He explained, 'It has been found that men who themselves suffered shortages at the front as the result of pilfering now are the best watchdogs for the supply trains.' Commanders praised the men for 'a job superbly done in efficiently organizing and accomplishing the duties of guarding the thousands of tons of supplies'. By early November, the Paris idyll was drawing to a close. The men mustered in a Paris auditorium to receive new orders. A colonel took the stage and declared, 'Half of you sitting here today will probably not make it back. We're going to crack the Siegfried Line!' The men were stunned. Harold Barkley whispered to a friend, 'I wonder which half he was talking about.'

Al Whitehead sent a telegram to his wife, Selma, in Wisconsin. It amused him that the cable's arrival would make her fear for a moment that he had been killed in action. He imagined her relief, when she read, 'You are more than ever in my thoughts at this time. All my love, Al.' He had photographs taken at a photographer's studio to send to her. As he left the studio, he noticed a crowd in which two Frenchmen were about to shave the heads of young women for having slept with Germans. 'It made me mad anyway,' he wrote, 'and in a flash I waded in and pistol whipped the two Frenchmen, ran them both off, and left the crowd standing there with mouths agape.'

On 10 November, Whitehead's battalion boarded a train at the Gare de Montparnasse. The next morning at eleven o'clock, as the train moved slowly east, 2nd Division artillery unleashed all its guns on the German lines. Along with mortar and small arms fire, the volley commemorated the Armistice of 1918. This time, there would be no Armistice. The Allies demanded Germany's unconditional surrender. Whitehead, Barkley and the rest of the men heading towards the Siegfried Line sensed they would fight until the war or their own lives came to an end.

TWENTY-FOUR

Most serious of all the causes for an epidemic of
dissension is the bad leader.

Psychology for the Fighting Man, pp. 326–7

THE MEN OF THE US 36TH INFANTRY DIVISION had fought a hard,
relentless war in the six weeks since their retreat from Valence and the
disappearance of Steve Weiss's squad. Their next engagement began a
day after Valence and lasted a terrifying week. The struggle for what
became known as the Montélimar Battle Square ended without a
victor, as the battered German Nineteenth Army escaped the Seventh
Army's trap on 30 August. Then, owing to a shortage of artillery
shells, the 36th failed to stop the Germans on Route Seven. Pursuing
the enemy at midnight on the 30th, General Dahlquist hoped to
engage the Germans before they regrouped. The next day, the 36th
Division reversed its setback of 24 August by liberating Valence. On
2 September, the Free French Army captured Lyons with vital assistance from the 36th. France's third largest city, which was 260 miles
north of the August invasion beaches, had fallen to the Allies two
months ahead of Operation Dragoon's original schedule. Troop
morale soared.

Despite formidable Wehrmacht resistance, the Texas Division
initially advanced on foot at the astounding rate of ten miles a day.
On 7 September, the 36th crossed the River Loue and trudged
through mud and forest to the River Doubs. Engineers reconstructed
a steel bridge that the Germans had blown, allowing men and tanks
to cross to the eastern bank and continue their pursuit of the enemy.

On 9 September, the heaviest autumn rains in years burst over France. Two days later, north of the Burgundian market town of Autun, Allied forces from the Riviera linked up with the troops who had landed at Normandy. Operation Dragoon had achieved its primary objective, joining its forces to Eisenhower's.

The momentum that had propelled the Seventh Army from the Mediterranean to Lorraine was drowning in the early autumn storms. The Americans suffered shortages of men and supplies. Operation Dragoon's three advancing American divisions – the 3rd, 36th and 45th – lost 5,200 men in September. Only 1,800 replaced them, a shortfall of 3,400 soldiers. The 36th alone suffered another 1,045 casualties at the beginning of October, reducing its strength from 14,306 to around 10,000. Once again, the army was unable to replace most of them. The survivors, deprived of sleep and under constant threat of death, exhibited signs of severe strain. New men coming into the line at this time were usually killed within five days, and they too had to be replaced. The 36th's daily advance of ten miles in the first half of September slowed to a few yards in the second half and came to a standstill by the beginning of October.

'October was upon us,' wrote CBS correspondent Eric Sevareid, 'the October of eastern France, which is filled with dull cloud masses, the smell of manure in the villages, and the freezing rain which never ceases, so that one exists in a perpetual twilight and moves in a sodden morass of wet clothing and yellow clay.' With the change in weather, Sevareid detected a change in the war:

> The parade and pantry were finished; for the first time the enemy had beaten us to the high ground with time enough to organize a stand. His supplies were rushed to him in a hurry from their near-by stores within the Reich, while ours moved painfully through the mountains from the southern ports hundreds of miles away, the frozen drivers falling asleep at their wheels, frequently to die ignominiously in the mud of the ditches. Tempers grew short, there were long silences in any conversation, the honeymoon with the French civilians ceased by mutual withdrawal, and our men, who had known so much more war than most of those who invaded

from England, remembered the Italian winter and began to long again for home.

Morale collapsed among both replacements and veterans, as units fought below strength owing to delays in dispatching replacements to the front. Until then, the 36th led the army's infantry divisions in the number of decorations it received: 266 to its officers and 963 to the enlisted men. Major General John E. Dahlquist, the 36th Division's commander, observed in September 1944 that his troops were losing both efficiency and aggressiveness. He also detected a steep decline in morale, which he measured in a manner familiar to military commanders throughout history: the percentage of men who avoided battle. Some soldiers were deliberately wounding themselves, and many did their best to contract trench foot and other illnesses. Some troops held back when ordered forward. Dahlquist wrote of 'desertions among the line infantry companies in combat (50–60 per division) and the ever-present straggler phenomenon'. Courts martial convicted 1,963 soldiers in the European Theater of Operations of outright desertion and another 494 for 'misbehavior before the enemy' (which often included desertion in battle). Most received sentences of about twenty years at hard labour, and all but one of 139 death sentences for desertion were commuted. Special and Summary Courts Martial convicted more than 60,000 troops of AWOL, and a further 5,834 cases of AWOL were serious enough to be tried by the more formal General Courts Martial that handed out sentences averaging fifteen years at hard labour. Dahlquist attributed some of the desertions to the heavy loss of officers and non-coms and their replacement by those lacking both field experience and acquaintance with the men they commanded. Desertion was an indication of poor leadership. Earlier in the war, Major General J. A. Ulio, the army's Advocate General, had written, 'All officers, particularly those of company grade, and all non-commissioned officers, must understand that absenteeism is a serious reflection on leadership. They must develop that spirit of comradeship and responsibility among the men which is the best deterrent to absenteeism.'

There was an added consideration, of which Dahlquist was aware: men who had survived the previous winter in Italy's Apennines 'had little stomach for another winter's operations in French mountains'. Even soldiers who had not fought in Italy felt they had endured enough by late 1944. An army investigation noted, 'The troops who had been fighting continuously all the way across France developed the feeling that they had done their part and should be afforded some relief.' The Seventh Army's other two divisions, the 3rd and the 45th, had the same problems that the 36th did with officer casualties, morale loss and desertions. The 3rd Division commander, Major General John E. 'Iron Mike' O'Daniel, complained that his troops had lost the fighting spirit they brought with them to the beaches in August. One regiment of the 45th Infantry Division suffered forty-five troops coming off the line with 'combat fatigue' in one week. Matters were exacerbated by the rain and mud, which caused skin infections and trench foot in conditions that did not allow soldiers to wash. Trapped in foxholes under enemy fire, the troops fought knee-deep in their own excrement. Furthermore, chronic shortages of ammunition, due to the long supply route from Marseilles to the Alps, meant that when the Americans caught up with the Germans, they were not always able to attack. The GIs called the failure to support them with sufficient ammunition a typical SNAFU, 'Situation Normal, All Fucked Up'.

The commander of Weiss's 143rd Regiment, Colonel Paul D. Adams, reported to General Dahlquist that his men were experiencing physical and mental breakdowns that had dramatically increased desertions, self-inflicted wounds and combat exhaustion. Officers feared the remaining troops would not stand up to German counter-attacks. General Dahlquist saw that the men of the 36th Division, even when they were willing to fight, were too exhausted to do it properly. The official army history recorded, 'Colonel Paul D. Adams, commanding the 143rd Infantry of the 36th Division, reported [to Dahlquist] an almost alarming physical and mental lethargy among the troops of his regiment, and General Dahlquist, the division commander, had to tell [VI Corps commander] General [Lucian] Truscott that the 36th had little punch left.' Adams's 143rd Regiment was, in Dahlquist's view, his best. If its men were suffering, morale was probably lower in the 141st and 142nd. Most of the riflemen in all three regiments had been given no respite from combat since they hit the beach near Saint-Raphaël two months earlier on 15 August.

Colonel Adams told Dahlquist the men needed time off: 'You give them three days and they'll be back in shape without any trouble. Just leave them alone, let them eat and sleep for the first day, make them clean up the second day, and do whatever they want the rest of the time, and they'll be ready to go.' The 36th had no choice but to raise the men's spirits. Otherwise, unnecessary deaths and desertions would doom the assault on the High Vosges.

Enlisted men were not the only victims of battle fatigue. When the Germans attacked Colonel Adams's 1st Battalion forward of Remiremont in early October, he and the battalion commander, Lieutenant Colonel David M. Frazior, led a reserve company into the battle to repel them. After reinforcing the line, Adams and Frazior drove back to base in an open jeep. Frazior fell asleep in mid-conversation, and Adams pretended not to notice. He regarded Frazior as 'one of the finest men and one of the best battalion commanders anybody could ever have'. In the morning, Frazior announced, 'It's time for me to quit, because I'm in no shape to command this battalion.' Adams advised him to get more sleep, but Frazior was adamant that his exhaustion rendered him incapable of battlefield command. Adams knew that Frazior did not lack courage. In Italy, he lost part of his hand fighting the Germans. Recuperating in a hospital in North Africa, he deserted to rejoin the battalion in time to lead it in the invasion of France. Frazior's determination and integrity were never in doubt. Adams relieved him of command, but kept him in the regiment as his executive officer.

Sensitive to the depth of his officers' and men's fatigue, Adams lodged a request with General Dahlquist to establish rest camps. Dahlquist approved, and the 36th's first centre for rest and recreation opened in early October ten miles west of Remiremont in the resort of Plombières-les-Bains. The 36th established a second rest camp at Bains-les-Bains a month later. In both, the soldiers were given drugs to let them sleep for at least a day, issued clean uniforms, allowed to shower and given hot food. After three days, which included enter-tainment and access to physicians and chaplains, the troops returned to duty. While this had a positive effect on the men who made it to the rest centres, there were not enough reserves to spare a majority of them from the frontline.

The 36th Division grew desperate for ammunition, petrol, rations, blankets, winter clothing and, most of all, men. It nonetheless assisted the French in liberating Dijon and reached the River Moselle on 21 September. Its weary men did not go much further. Their next mission, in the words of Seventh Army's G-2, intelligence section, was to 'clear approaches to passes of the VOSGES in zone, to seize terrain from which to launch an offensive designed to carry the Seventh Army through the VOSGES defenses to STRASBOURG and over the RHINE'. German units fortified the Vosges' natural obstacles with bunkers, landmines, machine gun emplacements and artillery to bleed the Americans for every yard they took.

While much of the Seventh Army's VI Corps dug into the foothills, the Germans were reorganizing their units on the heights and absorbing troop reinforcements from home. American supply lines stretched more than four hundred miles from the Mediterranean, but the Germans had edged closer to their supply bases in Alsace and Germany itself. For the first time, the Germans expended more artillery shells than the Americans. Autumn showers grounded Allied air support, increasing the defenders' advantage in the mountains. If the American system was breaking down, so were the men. Division historian Colonel Vincent M. Lockhart put it succinctly: 'Almost every adverse factor of combat faced the 36th Division in late September and October 1944.' Correspondence among senior officers increasingly referred to shortages of troops, ammunition, rations and winter clothing. The commanders observed it, but the men lived it. As more and more were killed, captured and wounded, and as others ran away, the need for manpower was greater than ever.

That need, for Charlie Company of First Battalion, 143rd Regiment, included Private Stephen J. Weiss. Weiss, taking one ride after another towards the 36th Division, passed much of the war-wrecked equipment that both the Allied and German armies had abandoned. Riding beside drivers of jeeps and trucks, he observed thousands of rear echelon troops who had never come near a battle.

Every French town seemed to be filled with 'pencil pushers' entertaining French women in cafés. Many of these 'civilians in uniform,' as Weiss called them, were supplying their girlfriends with food and cigarettes intended for frontline troops. Tales of GIs working with the black market to steal and sell American petrol and other supplies, mainly from the port at Marseilles, bothered him. So did his conviction that the rear echelon boys were not pulling their weight. Although there were more than three million American troops in Europe, no more than 325,000 were in combat at the same time. The infantry, barely 14 per cent of the total American military presence in Europe, suffered 70 per cent of the casualties. Weiss's sense of injustice, compounded by his misgivings about Captain Simmons, gnawed at him all the way to the front.

Weiss reported to the headquarters of VI Army Group, the main component of General Alexander Patch's Seventh Army, in Vittel. The brass had commandeered the 1920s Hôtel de l'Ermitage, one of the Alpine spa's most luxurious establishments. Weiss met a fellow ex-trainee from Fort Blanding named Santorini in the hotel's elegant art deco lobby. Santorini, who was working in counter-intelligence, mentioned that his colonel needed a photolithographer. Weiss, with his year's experience in photolithography for the Office of War Information in New York, was an ideal candidate. The colonel interviewed Weiss and requested authorization from the 36th Division for his transfer to counter-intelligence. Not many troops were trained in photolithography, encouraging Weiss to believe he would avoid returning to Captain Simmons after all. The next morning, however, division turned the colonel down.

'Rebuffed and angry, I packed my meagre belongings, thanked the colonel and Santorini for their efforts on my behalf and left in search of the 36th,' Weiss wrote. Division headquarters was fifty miles east of Vittel in the town of Remiremont, about a day's drive on France's narrow and crowded rural highways. Weiss walked to the road and put out his thumb.

The 36th Division had captured Remiremont on 23 September. On 24 September, it moved its Command Post forward to Éloyes and on 1 October to an old house in the town of Docelles beside a bombed-out bridge over the River Moselle. In Docelles, their advance stalled. The division's Command Post was stuck in Docelles for twenty-one days, its longest time in a single location since the August invasion. 'The 36th was back to the old Italian situation of mud, mountains and mules,' one officer wrote, 'but we had very few mules.' The next main objective, Bruyères, was only seven and a half miles away. However, against entrenched German positions, high mountains, dense forests, rain and mud, it might have been a hundred.

On 8 October, a new replacement joined the ranks of Weiss's Company C, 1st Battalion, 143rd Regiment, at Docelles. He was Private First Class Frank Turek, a good-looking, 22-year old Polish-American draftee from Hartford, Connecticut. His arrival, however, did little to fill the void left by the many men who had disappeared from the ranks. Four days later, Columbus Day, Thursday, 12 October, Steve Weiss walked into 36th Division headquarters. The 143rd Regiment's executive officer, Lieutenant Colonel David Frazior, recalled his relief on learning that Weiss, following the other seven men from the missing squad, had returned: 'I remember it distinctly, because we were so glad to get them back!' Unfortunately for Weiss, Frazior was not at divisional headquarters to express his relief. Instead, a 'bored headquarters clerk' ignored him for a few minutes before asking what he wanted. Weiss gave his name and unit. Looking at his file, the clerk told him his family had been informed he was missing in action. Weiss thought of his mother, father and sister in Brooklyn. 'I was sure they were overwhelmed with anxiety,' he wrote. The clerk showed no interest in Weiss's problems and failed to offer him coffee from a pot brewing nearby. An officer came in and asked Weiss if he would consider working in his headquarters office. He would, but their superiors quickly rejected the request. That afternoon, Weiss took a lift four miles forward of Docelles to Charlie Company's Command Post in a forest halfway to Bruyères.

Captain Simmons had yet to return from the aid station, where he had gone for treatment of a sniper's bullet in his neck. Commanding Company C in his absence was the executive officer, Lieutenant Russell Darkes. Darkes, a twenty-four-year-old Officer Candidate

School (OCS) graduate from Mount Zion, Pennsylvania, did not acknowledge Private Weiss's return. While not expecting a warm homecoming, Weiss resented being treated 'just like ammunition, petrol or rations'. It bothered him that no officers shook his hand, despite needing him so much that they rejected his transfer to the OSS and several other units. No soldier, according to a survey of GI opinion called 'What the Soldier Thinks', welcomed such impersonal treatment. 'Men resent being treated as "manpower" in the abstract,' the report on troops who fought between December 1942 and September 1945 stated. 'They want to retain their essential dignity as human beings.' One soldier wrote on his survey form, 'Treat them as men not dogs.'

Officially, army policy was for officers to put their men first. 'The good leader had faith in human nature,' Colonel L. Holmes Ginn, Jr, of the Army Medical Section, wrote in his report on combat exhaustion. 'He knew his men, he was their friend, he insisted they be treated as human beings, he looked after their wants, and he was firm but just in his dealings with them.'

While Weiss stood in a cavernous farmhouse Command Post that had no furniture or other sign of human habitation, only one person spoke to him. It was his old platoon sergeant, a tall and amiable Texan named Lawrence Kuhn. Kuhn smiled and said, 'Reigle told me you were alive.'

Weiss, grateful for the only greeting on offer, asked Kuhn about his squad leader, Sergeant Harry Shanklin. Kuhn hesitated, then said, 'Shanklin's dead.' A German patrol had killed him in a firefight near the River Moselle a few weeks before. Weiss felt sick, remembering Shanklin's friendly grin and 'boyish good looks'. Twenty-two-year-old Shanklin had led him from the beach at Saint-Raphaël all the way to Valence, sustaining the squad's morale and protecting them from unnecessary danger. 'When Harry Shanklin was killed,' Weiss said, 'I was devastated.' A few hours later, as the sun was setting, Weiss moved up to a woodland clearing where the men of Charlie Company were coming off the line for the night.

The first friends he saw were Bob Reigle and Settimo Gualandi, who had been with him in the Resistance and the OSS. Reigle and

Gualandi, now a sergeant, were happy to see him. The three GIs rested on the soft earth, and Weiss asked about Sergeant William Scruby. Reigle had bad news. Scruby, whose ingenuity had saved them from death or capture in the irrigation canal near Valence, was gone. A mortar shell blew his leg off two weeks before, and he was unlikely to survive. Sheldon Wohlwerth had taken German machine gun rounds in his chest, and he too had been evacuated with little hope of making it. Weiss noticed that the other three guys from their Resistance service, Fawcett, Garland and Caesar, were also absent. Of the eight, only Reigle, Gualandi and now Weiss himself were in the line. The other men in their old squad were replacements. This was bad enough, but Weiss was assigned to another squad where he knew no one.

'I was just 19,' Weiss recalled. 'When I got back, half of the others were dead. I felt so alienated, so non-existent.' Every man there had troubles, and Weiss's were no worse than anyone else's. However, returning from the land of the living, he detected changes in the others that they did not see in themselves. The men around him, especially Reigle and Gualandi, were not as he remembered. Combat exhaustion was etched into each face as sharp as a bullet hole.

Weiss recognized an ex-trainee from Fort Blanding, thirty-year-old Private Clarence Weidaw, quietly eating his rations. Weiss walked over and said, 'Weidaw, it's me, Steve.' Weidaw went on eating. 'Weidaw's gone mute on us,' another soldier said. 'The Krauts had him trapped in a hayloft. He wouldn't surrender, so after they pulverized the hayloft and set it alight, Weidaw jumped and escaped under a hail of fire.' Since then, the private had not said a word.

'Why did you come back?' Weiss's friends asked. Reigle said he should have stayed away. All that he and Gualandi had known since their return were 'S-mines, booby-traps, mortars, machine guns and heavy-duty artillery', but not sleep or a few hours out of danger. 'Why did you come back?' Weiss wasn't sure. He said maybe it was because he was loyal. 'Loyal,' his comrades laughed. 'Are you kidding? You'll be dead in a month.' As if confirming their prediction, a German reconnaissance plane soared overhead and, undoubtedly, reported their position to its artillery batteries. This was war, the real war, the infantry war, and Weiss was back in it.

Weiss's first night on the line turned freezing, unbearable for soldiers in summer uniforms. Lieutenant John D. Porter, a platoon commander in the Vosges, wrote, 'Poor supply of a critical Class II item, winter clothing, was responsible for much of the trench-foot and respiratory diseases.' Some of the men sought warmth in a farm-house. Weiss joined them inside. Suddenly, German artillery peppered the ground around the house. Outside, men asleep in tents, 'vulnerable and unprotected, were pulverized … Screams and shouts mingled with the whine and crump of shells.' Weiss and the others ran out of the house to assist the wounded, but the shelling cut them off from one another. Weiss took shelter in a covered pen, where two goats trembled in fear. More shells shattered the pen's door and roof. Weiss wrote that, when the barrage stopped,

> I ran into the woods. Thirty men had been killed and wounded, their thin canvas tents had been torn to shreds. Tent poles were splintered; blood-stained blankets and combat packs were strewn all over the tangled earth … More medics and stretcher bearers arrived from Docelles by ambulance to care for the wounded and to collect the dead.

'No foxholes had been dug,' Weiss observed, one of many signs that the men were too exhausted to take the basic precautions they had taken earlier in the war.

The next day, the squad waited in a barn to collect bullets and grenades, knowing that fresh supplies meant more combat. With so many dead and so few to replace them, platoon Sergeant Kuhn asked Weiss to take over as squad leader with the rank of staff sergeant. He refused. 'I didn't want the responsibility for eleven other guys,' he said. Instead, he settled for assistant squad leader as a buck sergeant. A lieutenant he had never met came out of a bunker a night later to issue orders. Weiss was to lead the eleven men of his new squad through a dense mass of trees into no man's land. Weiss's first scout was trembling, and the second scout stared towards an infinite horizon. The men were not in any shape to face the enemy, but they marched behind Weiss through the moonless night forward of the American lines. Waist-high bushes wet with autumn rain drenched the troops' summer uniforms. None of the landmarks that the lieutenant had described was there. In the dense woods, the men sensed Germans behind every rock, a booby trap in every tree and a landmine under every step. When the second scout starting quivering, Weiss assured him he would be fine. He felt that the GI was reacting like 'a sane young man to insane circumstances'.

The squad came back without finding any Germans. The lieutenant upbraided Weiss for failing to achieve the objective. 'Easy for him to complain,' Weiss wrote, 'from his large protected dugout wrapped around him like a full length fur coat.'

Weiss overheard a Southern soldier in a foxhole nearby. 'You never see any Jews up on the front,' he drawled. 'They're always behind the lines working as doctors or dentists.' It was bad enough returning to the infantry and fighting in freezing mountains, but he resented this reminder that the Nazis were not the only racists in the war. For the first time, 'The thought of clearing out entered my mind.'

This was Day One of the offensive to capture Bruyères. To reinforce the village's natural protections, which included the Vologne River to the south and tank-resistant marshlands on two sides, German engineers had felled and booby-trapped large pine trees to block the roads. Interlocking machine gun positions surrounded the village, and strongpoints in sturdy stone houses guarded the passes. One American platoon commander wrote, 'The discovery of a machine gun battalion in the defense of Bruyères alerted US Intelligence that the Kraut intended to make a permanent stand in this sector. Machine gun battalions were never used unless the enemy was attempting to hold the position permanently.'

At 0800 hours that morning of 15 October, elements of the 36th Division moved through the Forêt-de-Faite to take the first objective, called Hill A. The Germans responded with small arms and automatic weapons fire, but the T-Patchers pushed about four hundred yards forward to another hill overlooking the village.

Renewed mortar and artillery fire stalled the American advance at the summit.

The squad dug in for protection against the night's German artillery and mortars. Between impacts, they discussed their reasons for staying in the army. An older veteran told Weiss he would have left the outfit but for one reason: 'Blackmail.' Weiss did not understand. 'Married with a kid,' he said. A German shell exploded near their foxhole. 'I'd leave in a flash, but for the wife and kid.' Another artillery round rattled the earth, and the soldier raised his voice: 'No government allotment check means no support for the wife and no milk for the baby.' A new replacement, aged 38 and with a wife and baby back in Brooklyn, sought counsel from Weiss the veteran. 'What can I do to stay alive?' he asked. Suddenly, the teenaged soldier was playing 'old man' to someone twice his age. He had no answer, but he tried: 'Watch me, and do as I do. Don't be too cautious, and don't be too aggressive. Choose somewhere in between.' It was pure Hollywood, and Weiss felt like a fraud. Nothing guaranteed survival.

When the sun rose on 16 October, the Japanese-American or 'Nisei' 442nd Regimental Combat Team, recently incorporated into the 36th following its unparalleled achievements on the Italian front, advanced through German roadblocks towards Hill B. American engineering units tried to clear the roads of the fallen trees and ordnance that the Nisei regiment had penetrated, until the Germans fired and drove them back. All morning, the Germans deployed fresh artillery shells from their home bases to devastate the Americans between Laval and Bruyères. More GIs were dying, and there were no troops to replace most of them.

At 0730 hours that morning, German artillery pounded the American positions to an intensity that no human psyche was constituted to withstand. Private Stephen James Weiss of Company C, First Battalion, 143rd Regimental Combat Team, 36th US Infantry Division, shook with each tremor of the earth. His foxhole was no protection from the assault of steel and fire. Men around him were dying. It was more than he could take. He went over the hill.

BOOK III
MILITARY JUSTICE

TWENTY-FIVE

'Giving up' is nature's way of protecting the organism
against too much pain.

Psychology for the Fighting Man, p. 347

STEVE WEISS WANDERED DEEP INTO THE FOREST, each step taking
him further from the artillery that rocked the ground behind him. He
stumbled onto a footpath, unconsciously following its course through
a thick pine labyrinth. A light rain soaked his shoulders and spread
down his body. Shivering with cold and dragging his rifle, Weiss
walked for two and a half hours. The trail took him to a clearing near
a small village. French 2nd Armoured Division tank crews, mostly
Arabs and Berbers from North Africa, were roasting fresh lamb over
a log fire. They offered Weiss a share of their food, but what he wanted
was a place to sleep. They showed him a barn just beyond their circled
tanks. At the top of a ladder, he carved a bunk in the hay and lay
down beside his rifle. Coma-like unconsciousness overcame him. It
was just before noon on 16 October.

A day or two later, Weiss woke up. When he went outside to
relieve himself, his Arab hosts gave him something to eat. In a brief
conversation, Weiss and the tankers discovered they had all fought in
Italy and were first-timers in France. Weiss returned to the loft and
fell immediately to sleep.

At the 36th Division headquarters in Docelles on 19 October 1944, a
General Court Martial convened to consider the case against
Lieutenant Albert C. Homcy for violating Article of War 75,

'Misbehavior before the enemy'. His alleged offence was refusing to obey an order to lead unqualified service troops, all of them cooks, bakers and orderlies, against German tanks the previous August. Homcy's counsel, Major Benjamin F. Wilson, Jr, raised a peremptory challenge to one member of the court panel. As a result, the president of the court, Lieutenant Colonel David P. Faulkner, withdrew. Another member, Major Harry B. Kelton, replaced him. Lieutenant Homcy, who had been cited in Italy for 'exceptionally meritorious conduct … under almost constant enemy artillery and mortar fire', could not easily be charged with cowardice. Yet he had disobeyed an order. Homcy testified that he could not, in accord with his duties as an officer, lead untrained men to certain death. His admission that he had disobeyed a direct order from a superior officer left the court little option but to convict him, because the officers on the panel would not rule on the legality or wisdom of orders. The court sentenced him to dishonourable discharge, forfeiture of pay and fifty years at hard labour. Five members of the court submitted a clemency petition that recommended suspending his sentence and allowing him to return to duty. The 36th Division Judge Advocate, however, rejected clemency and confirmed sentence.

The court, as subsequent disclosures at the appellate level made clear, had been under undue influence from the 36th Division's commander, General Dahlquist. Lieutenant Colonel David Faulkner had been the main conduit of Dahlquist's pressure, which explained why defence counsel Wilson had asked for him to be removed from the panel. The other officers, as they would later testify, knew of Dahlquist's insistence on convictions 'for the good of the service'. Court member Captain Lowell E. Sitton admitted that he felt 'intimidated' and 'vividly' recalled 'that severe pressures were applied to court martial boards in his [Dahlquist's] division at or about the time of [Homcy's] trial to make findings of guilty "for the good of the service" without regard to the rights of the individual or the merits of the particular case in question'. The president of the court, Major Kelton, and other officers on the panel remembered being subjected to the same influence. Court member Captain Eldon R. McRobert said Dahlquist came to him personally:

He said that we were not doing our job, as we were being too lenient to the soldiers being tried, that we should find more of them guilty and if they were found guilty then we should assess a stronger sentence than we had been doing. He also gave us a very strong reprimand that we had not been doing our job and made a statement to the effect that if it were not so much trouble he would make this a matter of record and report it on our military records.

McRobert further recalled a meeting between the court martial board and Dahlquist during Homcy's trial:

After the Court-Martial Board left General Dahlquist's headquarters, after he had given the verbal reprimand, we had discussed among all members present and I am sure that I remember without exception that each of us felt that our private rights had been invaded and that General Dahlquist had no authority to do what he had done.

Another panel member, Captain Isidore Charkatz, stated that Dahlquist intervened directly in other cases, including that of a soldier found 'not guilty of a crime by reason of insanity'. Dahlquist called Charkatz a few days after the verdict and 'gave me a strong verbal reprimand ... I was asked to take a letter to each member of the Board to be read and signed and then returned to the General.'

Former Lieutenant, now Private, Homcy was sent to the Disciplinary Training Barracks in Green Haven, New York, to begin fifty years at hard labour.

On 22 October, Weiss woke up again in the barn. Coming outside, he spoke to the North African tank crews and discovered his slumber had lasted six days. He thanked his hosts and retraced his steps through the forest. A few hours later, he snapped to attention in front of Captain Allan Simmons at Charlie Company's new forward Command Post. Simmons was calm, more disappointed than vengeful. 'You could have told me,' he said, in an unprecedented expression of sympathy. 'Don't you remember that, when we first met in Italy, I offered to be your priest, rabbi, friend and confidant, that you could come to me with your troubles?' Weiss did not recall Simmons speaking to him at all when he joined the 36th Division the previous June in Italy. Unable to speak, he wanted to say, 'You never gave a damn. Aloof as always! You played it safe and never led from the front. Where the hell were you, when the fighting started, when the rest of us got knocked about? How come our casualty rate is consistently over one hundred per cent a month and you, your second in command, Lieutenant Russell Darkes, and the company first sergeant are still around?'

Simmons had, however, been wounded by shrapnel during the River Rapido crossing in Italy. When Simmons was taken to an aid station, his executive officer, Lieutenant Russell Darkes, crossed the river under fire. In an unpublished memoir, Darkes wrote that he and other Company C survivors 'ended up in a shell hole on the German side of the River and were absolutely pinned down ... We finally made our way across the foot bridge in spite of the precarious condition, to the American side of the River. Upon our return, we discovered that the Battalion Commander and several of his staff members were either killed or wounded during the night.' The army awarded then twenty-four-year-old Darkes the Silver Star for his actions that day. Weiss was unaware of the risks his company officers had taken, because he had not seen them leading from the front since he joined the division.

Weiss kept silent, which may have spared him a court martial for desertion or going Absent Without Leave. Simmons did not press charges. All Weiss had to do was return to his squad. Weiss, though, did not move. He felt incapable of going back into the line. Would the captain let him unload rations and equipment for a few days, at least until he was fit to fight without endangering anyone else? He knew that other company commanders had assigned traumatized soldiers to non-combat duty to give them time to readjust. For officers, reassignment appeared to be automatic. When Lieutenant Colonel David Frazior was too exhausted to lead the 1st Battalion, Colonel Adams had simply made him his executive officer. Simmons declined Weiss's request with one word, 'Dismissed.'

* * *

Captain Simmons's handling of Steve Weiss was a distinct contrast to the way another officer, Lieutenant Audie Murphy of the 3rd Division, treated a distressed man in his unit. Murphy, who had landed in the south of France at the same time as the 36th Division and had fought his way north across the same country, had been promoted from staff sergeant to lieutenant because he was an excellent soldier. When ordered to push through German lines and hold a position for another unit to cross through, he ordered his men to move out. One of the men, however, was sitting under a tree crying and shaking. Murphy gently shook him by the shoulder. This exchange followed:

'I can't take it any more, lieutenant.'
  'What's come over you?'
  'I don't know. I got the shakes.'
  'You can't make it.'
  'If I could, I would. I'm not fooling.'
  'Stick around the C.P. The krauts may hit this spot.'
  'Yessir. I'm ashamed, but I can't help it.'
  'Have you got something on your mind?'
  'Nosir. I just started shaking.'
  'Can you sleep?'
  'I haven't slept in a week.'
  'You better report to the medics.'
  His head goes back to his knees, and the sobbing starts again.
  'What's wrong with that joe? Battle-happy?' asks Candler.
  'Looks like he's taken all he can.
  'I know how he feels. Many's the time I've just wanted to sit down and cry about the whole damned mess.'

Weiss had taken all he could, but no one sent him to a medic. Instead, Captain Simmons returned him to the line in the hillside forests beyond the village of Bruyères. Since his departure, the 36th Division had captured Bruyères in a costly five-day battle that ended on 20 October. The final phase of the conquest was house-to-house fighting on 18 and 19 October. 'No quarter was given and none was asked,' wrote one platoon commander. 'The Germans fought desperately and would not even permit aid men to care for or evacuate the wounded.' The American forces in that struggle were Weiss's 1st Battalion of the 143rd Regiment and the Japanese-American 442nd. So many of the Japanese-Americans had been killed and wounded that their rifle companies were down to about thirty soldiers each.

Shortly after his return to duty, Weiss climbed into a trench with two other sergeants. A frontline stalemate was settling in. Ordinary soldiers on both sides seemed to avoid pointless battles and artillery exchanges. The unspoken understanding collapsed that evening, when a newly minted second lieutenant came up to the line. The twenty-year-old junior officer, with puppy-like curiosity, patrolled the squad's positions and inspected the men's equipment. The veterans, knowing his actions were unnecessary, observed him cynically and prayed the enemy would ignore his frenetic activity. As the lieutenant was leaving, he tripped on a flare that shot into the sky and showered light on both sides of the line. The Germans, who must have taken the illumination for the prelude to an attack, unleashed their artillery on the American foxholes. Weiss and the other men crouched deeper into the earth, wishing the inexperienced officer dead. When it was over, Captain Simmons sent the lieutenant to another outfit – sparing either the lives of the men in Charlie Company or the lieutenant's own.

Everyone was jumpy during the lull in the Allied offensive. Dug in along the frontline near the hamlet of Brechifosse the next night, Weiss heard a noise that he mistook for a German patrol and grabbed one of the many grenades he had stacked in his foxhole. He pulled the pin and was about to hurl the grenade, when his foxhole buddy told him the only sound was the wind. No Germans were coming their way. Weiss tried to force the pin back in. His hands shook and sweat seeped from his forehead, the seconds passing. If the grenade exploded, he and the other soldier would be killed. If he threw it, the Germans would unleash another cascade of artillery. Controlling his panic, he disarmed the grenade. Weiss was now certain that he had become a danger not only to himself but to the other men.

When morning broke cold and wet, the company's first sergeant relayed a message to Weiss from Captain Simmons. As punishment for his six days' absence, Weiss was ordered to dig a latrine in rocky, nearly frozen ground. No one was permitted to help him, and he had only a small retrenching tool to scrape a hole to the regulation six feet long by a foot deep. This was army 'chickenshit' at its worst, especially with Weiss in constant danger and reaching his psychological limit. As he bent his back to the task, the rain soaked his flimsy uniform and his squad gathered around in sympathy. One of them implored, 'Don't let him do this to you.' Only years later would Weiss admit, 'I never confronted Simmons or disobeyed his order to dig, because I was too young, naïve and intimidated by rank.'

On the night of 26 October, Private First Class Frank Turek's squad leader ordered him to find a Company B patrol in the woods. Turek, who had not been on patrol before, was terrified. His nerves were so jittery that he fired two rounds into a dead German. He found Company B, but he got lost on the way back to his foxhole. 'I was jumpy,' he remembered, 'and I just couldn't stand looking at the trees fearing that there was a Jerry behind them and every move out there in front affected me.' Turek met Steve Weiss on the line. Weiss remembered the new replacement's anxiety. 'I also remember how clean his uniform was,' he said. 'It was pristine.' Having arrived only two weeks earlier, Turek was new to combat. The Polish-American youngster told Weiss, 'No way am I staying here.' Weiss noticed his anxiety, as much the consequence of pre-war trauma as of fear of battle.

On completing high school, he had gone to work at the Royal Typewriter Company factory in Hartford. A severe case of miliaria, popularly known as prickly heat, forced him to quit after three months. The rash covered his upper body, which was as embarrassing as it was painful. He said later, 'I felt that I was being strangled, so I decided to visit my physician and he said that I give the job up [sic], give my nerves a rest.' Turek, who was unemployed and lived at home with his mother and father, became fretful when gangrene infected his father's leg. On 24 March 1943, about the time the leg was amputated, the army drafted him. During basic training, Turek's miliaria rash returned. Medical officers attributed the outbreak, resembling shingles, to nervousness. One army physician prescribed medication, but it had no effect. Another diagnosed his condition as psychosomatic.

The night of 27 October was terrifying for Turek, who was on guard duty in a forward foxhole. The sound of every falling leaf made him jump with fright. Needing sleep, he asked other troops nearby to take the watch for him. It was not clear to him in the darkness which side was sending artillery shells overhead. When his foxhole buddy explained that the Germans were shelling 200 yards away, Turek panicked, beat his head with his fists and collapsed in terror.

Other soldiers in the outfit were also at the edge of endurance that night. Clarence Weidaw, the soldier who had not spoken a word since the Germans nearly shot and burned him in a hayloft, and Jim Dickson, who had gone AWOL with Weiss in August during Grenoble's liberation, had had enough. Weiss himself was dangerously overstressed, as his near-fatal episode with the hand grenade proved. Few of Charlie Company's riflemen on the frontlines had faith in Captain Simmons, and they complained that he led from the rear. 'You could never find Simmons,' Weiss said, 'even behind the lines.' Weiss, Weidaw and Dickson confided their fears to one another, and they reached a unanimous decision. At four o'clock in the morning on 28 October, six days after Weiss had returned to duty, the three GIs climbed out of their hillside foxholes and left the line.

Private First Class Frank C. Turek deserted early the same morning, although Weiss was not aware of it. Another deserting soldier from Charlie Company encountered Turek in the woods, and together they hitched a ride in a military vehicle whose driver must have known they were running away. He dropped them in a small town. They did not know its name, but it was the only hiding place they could find.

The 36th Division, as a War Department survey discovered, had the highest rate of desertions in the European Theater of Operations (ETO). 'The longer the 36th stayed in the line,' the Observers Board stated, 'the greater the incidence of disciplinary problems and psychosis cases, as reflected in the number of court-martials, stragglers, and hospital admissions for exhaustion.' Sixty-three infantrymen from the

36th Division were convicted of violating Article of War 75, 'Misbehavior before the enemy', which usually meant desertion under fire. Even without the deserters who were never apprehended, this was more than in any other division in the ETO.

On 28 October, at least five men from Charlie Company – Weiss, Weidaw, Dickson, Turek and another soldier whose name does not appear in the records – were no longer on the line. One regimental platoon commander, Lieutenant Robert D. Porter, described the battle they missed that morning: 'The enemy fired as rapidly as his guns would permit. Men were blown to bits but others took their places. American dead and wounded lay where they had fallen over enemy trenches they were assaulting, inside enemy dug outs, on top of enemy already dead or dying.' The task of the soldiers who fought was not made easier by the absence of their comrades who had run away.

While their company was engaged in fierce combat, Weiss, Weidaw and Dickson were heading south away from the Vosges. Truck drivers gave them lifts along roads jammed with military supply convoys and the wreckage of earlier fighting. Reactions to the rogue GIs varied. Soldiers who had been at the front, including the truckers who delivered ammunition to the firing line, were invariably helpful. 'Overseas most combat soldiers are sympathetic towards other fellows who go AWOL,' one survey of frontline infantry soldiers noted. However, rear echelon troops, who had yet to hear or see combat, were wary. 'Most mess sergeants,' Weiss wrote, 'rejected our plea for food and gave us scraps that even a dog would reject.'

By this time, the US Army Provost Marshal estimated that thousands of deserters were on the run in France. It would have been impossible for so many to remain at large without other soldiers keeping their secret and French civilians giving them shelter. Some deserters hid with French women, while others found a home among black market criminals. Weiss, Dickson and Weidaw, however, had no plan beyond a vague hope that the Military Police would not catch them. If they had been more meticulous, they would have chosen a better hiding place than the US Army's airfield near Lyons.

The three deserters slept in a hangar, coming out occasionally to watch C-47 cargo planes deliver supplies and troops. The troops were replacements for the dead and injured, but also for those, like Weiss and his companions, who had run away. P-47 Thunderbolts flew out on daylight missions over the German lines northeast of Lyons, and not all of the 'Jugs' returned. The three infantrymen wasted time at the base, where sooner or later someone would arrest them. It did not take Weiss long to conclude, 'Our venture was doomed from the start.' They were young, unsure of themselves and frightened. They had not discussed their future, Weiss thought, 'because we had none'. Their four options, as to most other deserters in eastern France, were to hike across the border into Switzerland, where the authorities interned downed airmen from both Axis and Allied armies in tolerable detention camps and regarded those who came on foot without weapons as refugees; make their way across France to Spain; live with sympathetic French families under false identities; or go to Paris and join the black market. They did not consider any of these. Instead, they went into Lyons.

Weiss was riding a bus in the city centre, when he noticed his former host Ronnie Dahan standing at the back. Dahan ignored him. It must have been obvious from Weiss's unkempt appearance that he had deserted. Dahan exited without shaking Weiss's extended hand. Weiss realized that Dahan, who had endured the worst of the German occupation, could not afford difficulties with the United States Army. The Dahans would not be able to hide Weiss, and he had no other friends in Lyons.

Back at the airfield later that afternoon, the three GIs pondered their predicament. They were not hard-core deserters, like those pilfering Allied supplies in the criminal underworld. If they remained at the base, arrest was certain. Dickson and Weidaw decided to report to a medical station and request treatment for nervous exhaustion. Physicians in the European Theater of Operations treated 102,989 'neuropsychiatric casualties,' and the two soldiers felt they qualified for medical attention. Weiss did not like the idea, saying the doctors would probably call the Military Police to arrest them. Dickson and Weidaw wanted to try it anyway. What else could they do? Weiss bid them goodbye with foreboding. Two days after leaving the line with his friends, Weiss was on his own. He wrote, 'I was overcome with loneliness.'

The army was swifter to notice his disappearance from the line near Bruyères than it had been at Valence in August, and the War Department dispatched a second telegram to William Weiss. It announced that his son was again missing in action. 'My mother and father were very depressed, very wiped out,' Steve Weiss recalled. Somehow, the first time he disappeared they retained hope he would emerge alive. The second telegram, though, had a shattering effect on the household. 'It was like a morgue,' Weiss said. The Weisses received family and friends at home, as if for a funeral. In France, Steve was unaware of the misery the desertion was causing his family.

Weiss hitchhiked back towards the 36th Division and Captain Simmons. Near the Lower Vosges town of Vesoul, he spent a night in a barn. When he woke up, his desperation was complete. He could not go any further. If the army had spread the burden of combat more fairly by rotating troops, he thought he could fight again. Troops in the rear had never faced battle, and most men at the front had never had a rest. It seemed unjust. He wrote later, 'Fair play was all I demanded, that each man do his duty and take a turn at the front.' That was not going to happen. 'If one day, you're the guy pulling more than the other guys, the next day someone takes your place,' he said. 'Not in the army.' Weiss saw only an army that had abandoned him to a commander with no regard for his life or well-being, an army that had refused to allow him to continue fighting with the OSS, an army that denied him every alternative assignment he had been offered and an army that had no more consideration for the ordinary dogface combat soldier than it did for equipment to be replaced when it ceased to function. This army was stronger than he was, and its chain of command retained a hold on his sense of duty. He did not question its legitimacy, even when he believed it unfair. 'I was so depressed I didn't give a shit,' he explained later. 'If you want to shoot me, shoot me.'

On Monday morning, 30 October, two American deserters surrendered to Military Police in the town of Vesoul. The first was Private First Class Frank Turek, who was soon turned over to MPs from the

36th Division. They drove him to their new headquarters at Bruyères, where First Lieutenant Herman L. Tepp of the Military Police 'ordered him to return to his company and sent him by vehicle to his company kitchen train'. Turek was back in service. The second was temporary Sergeant Weiss, who left the barn at about ten o'clock that morning and surrendered to an American Military Police patrol.

Captain Richard J. Thomson, Jr, of the 67th Military Police Company, whom Weiss remembered as 'a captain who never heard a shot fired in anger', placed him under arrest. Thomson, after throwing Weiss into a stockade dug into the wet earth, made a written report: 'The soldier was dressed in uniform at the time of surrender. Soldier made the following voluntary statement: Soldier admitted being A.W.O.L. from his unit since 27 October 1944.' The MPs gave the prisoner a cup of coffee and a cigarette. If they shot him then and there, Weiss thought, 'It would be a relief, not a tragedy.'

TWENTY-SIX

There are strains which no man, however tough-minded,
can endure.

Psychology for the Fighting Man, p. 353

ON 2 NOVEMBER, STEVE WEISS reported to the division psychiatrist,
Major Walter L. Ford, in one of a group of hospital tents where medical staff treated the physically and mentally wounded. The Judge
Advocate General's office relied on Ford to determine whether accused
soldiers were psychologically fit to stand trial or should be discharged
from the army under Section VIII of Army Regulation 615-360 for
'inaptness or undesirable habits or traits of character'. (The traits
included insanity and homosexuality.)

When Weiss arrived at the hospital tent to see Ford, physicians and
nurses were treating hundreds of wounded Japanese-Americans from
the 442nd Nisei Regiment. There was neither silence nor a private
place to conduct the interview, because the Nisei had suffered more
than eight hundred killed and wounded in the previous week. Forty-
eight hours earlier, the regiment had rescued a trapped section of the
141st Regiment that the press had dubbed the 'lost battalion'. The
section, smaller than a battalion with only 211 men, had advanced so
far beyond American lines that it was cut off. For a week, German
forces on all sides besieged the men. Dug into slit trenches in a thick
forest above Biffontaine, they ran out of food, water and ammunition. The division dropped supplies by air, most of which fell into
German hands. For a week, the Nisei advanced up steep 'Banzai Hill'
through mud, forest and thick brush against superior German forces

to win the day. However, they lost more than 800 men killed and wounded. (The 442nd did not achieve sufficient strength to return to combat until March 1945 in Italy. It was probably the only American combat regiment in Europe that did not record a single desertion.) The survivors of the rescue party lay all around Weiss, while Major Ford quizzed him about his state of mind.

Weiss responded desultorily to the physician's questions, more aware of the suffering Japanese-Americans around him than of the psychiatrist. Ford questioned Weiss for a half hour, but he did not ask him about his reasons for deserting, his lack of trust in his commanding officer or his belief that the military machine treated ordinary soldiers unfairly. Ford declared that Weiss, despite having 'psychoneurosis, anxiety, mild', was competent to face a court martial.

While Weiss discussed his sanity with the division psychiatrist, Private First Class Frank Turek left the line again. 'On 2 November,' Military Police Lieutenant Herman Tepp wrote, 'Turek reported to me at S-1 [Personnel] Section, 143rd Infantry in the vicinity of Decimont, France, and he stated that he refused to go to his company. I again ordered him to his company and he stated that he refused to go.' The army had no alternative but to prosecute him.

Like Weiss, Turek had to meet Major Ford for psychological assessment. After a similar half-hour discussion, Ford reported that the twenty-two-year-old Polish-American private 'was suffering from psychoneurosis, mixed, chronic, mild and that this is a long standing emotional disorder which makes it difficult for the soldier to adjust during periods of stress'. Although Ford concluded that Turek's mental health was more damaged than Weiss's, the authorities deemed he should stand trial for desertion. The maximum penalty for his offence was death.

Turek's court martial convened in Bruyères on 6 November 1944, three days after his psychiatric appraisal. An old, unheated chapel, part of the complex where General Dahlquist had established divisional headquarters on 31 October, served as the courtroom. The town bore the scars of the three-week battle that the Americans had won at high cost, and there was no mood of forgiveness for those who had shirked their duty. The specification was clear: 'In that Private First Class Frank J. Turek, Company C, 143rd Infantry, at or near Brechitosse [sic], France, on or about 28 October 1944, ran away from his company, which was then engaged with the enemy.'

The prosecution made a peremptory challenge to remove Captain Eldon R. McRobert from the panel, and the defence challenged Captain Lowell E. Sitton. Both officers were excused. That left ten officers on the court martial panel, who effectively served as judge and jury. Major Benjamin F. Wilson, Jr, and an assistant, Captain Robert W. Plunkett, defended Turek. The Trial Judge Advocate or prosecutor was Captain John Stafford, assisted by Captain Jess W. Jones. The prosecution established that the 143rd Regiment was 'tactically before the enemy' near Brechifosse on 28 October, the morning that Turek deserted. It called only one witness, Lieutenant Raymond E. Bernberg, who confirmed that Turek's regiment was facing the enemy that day. The defence did not contest his testimony. Captain Stafford declared, 'The United States rests.'

Major Wilson introduced Major Ford's psychiatric report as Defence Exhibit A and called Private First Class Turek to testify under oath. Turek admitted leaving his company on 28 October. Wilson asked him about his first patrol. The court reporter, Corporal Maxwell Resnick, recorded Turek's reply with numerous spelling and punctuation errors:

Well Sir, we were just going into combat, the first time for any of us. We arrived at the front to relieve this outfit about noon of that day I don't recall the time. During the daytime it was alright. About dusk my squad leader came and said that I and other men go out and contact B Company on patrol. On the way over to B Company about five hundred yards away from our position I saw a man laying on the side of the road and I was in the rear with two fellows in front of me. I nudged one of the fellows and said, 'Do you see that fellow' and he said 'Yes' and he said he was a 'Jerry'. I took the safety off my rifle and pumped a couple of shells into it and I went to the front of the men and we moved on ... I was jumpy and I just couldn't stand looking at the trees fearing that there was a jerry behind them and every move out there in front affected me.

Defence counsel Wilson asked him about the effect that shell fire had on him, and Turek replied that the night after his first patrol 'every leaf I heard falling on the ground had me jumping'. On guard duty in a foxhole, he went to find someone to relieve him so he could sleep. His testimony continued:

> It was so dark that if anyone took my place, I don't believe that he would be able to find his own hole and come back. I fell into a couple of foxholes and got out, but I couldn't see anything, do nothing. I went back to the hole and heard these shells coming over. I thought they were our own shells. I asked my buddy who was doing the shelling and he said, 'Those are the Jerries.' And he said he thought it was two hundred yards in front of us, and I did not know what to do. I started beating my head and felt like a caged animal and since then I was on edge all the time.

The Trial Judge Advocate's cross-examination rehearsed the same events, and Turek had little to add. Turek's replies to Captain Stafford's final questions, however, determined the outcome of the trial.

> Stafford. Would you go back and fight if you had the opportunity?
> Turek. I don't know that is hard to say.
> Stafford. Would you or would you not go back and fight if given the opportunity?
> Turek. No, Sir.

Major Wilson's own final questions in response allowed Turek to tell the court about his childhood traumas, the amputation of his father's leg, his loss of a job due to psychosomatic skin rashes and problems at home that continued to worry him. An officer on the court martial panel asked him whether he deserted alone, and Turek answered that another soldier had gone with him. The court retired to consider its verdict. It found Turek guilty. After a second deliberation, it sentenced him to 'be dishonorably discharged the service, to forfeit all pay and allowances due or to become due, and to be confined at hard labor at such place as the reviewing authority may direct for twenty-five (25) years'. At three o'clock in the afternoon, the court martial was completed.

The next morning, 7 November 1944, at 9.30, in the same chapel in Bruyères where Frank Turek had been convicted, another General Court Martial convened to try Private First Class Stephen J. Weiss. The presiding officer, Major James T. Clarke of the 155th Field Artillery Battalion, sat in the sanctuary at a long table with fourteen other officers, seven on either side. Many of them had judged Private First Class Turek the day before. The senior officer on the court martial panel was Lieutenant Colonel David P. Faulkner of 36th Division headquarters staff. In common with other courts martial at the time, the court judging Private Weiss included no enlisted men. Only one member of the court, Second Lieutenant Bertram M. Lebeis, was a qualified lawyer. Most of the officers, from Lieutenant Colonel Faulkner down to Second Lieutenant William Steger, were not combat veterans. Behind the panel loomed a cross from which defendant Steve Weiss thought the crucified Christ was judging the judges.

The defence counsel was Major Benjamin F. Wilson, Jr, who had defended Turek and, a few weeks before that, Lieutenant Albert C. Homcy, on the same charges of 'misbehavior before the enemy'. Although Weiss would later complain that Wilson was not a lawyer, the major had more legal experience than most other officers on courts martial. As the Washington Appeals Court Judge George E. MacKinnon later noted, 'Major Wilson had very considerable training in and experience with the law. He had completed two years of law school prior to entering the service, completed a service course in Military Justice, and continued his study of military justice at the Artillery School, the Advance Infantry Course, and at the Inspector General's School.' Wilson's court martial experience included more than three hundred cases in which he had served as a member of the court, a Trial Judge Advocate (prosecutor) or defence counsel. Judge MacKinnon observed that Wilson was 'much better qualified to defend an accused in a court martial proceeding than many fully licensed lawyers'. However, Wilson's heavy caseload deprived him of time to speak with his clients and to prepare a thorough defence.

Wilson was not the only officer present who had taken part in Lieutenant Homcy's court martial. Major Harry B. Kelton, Captain Lowell E. Sitton, Captain Isidore Charkatz and First Lieutenant Charles Hickox had all served on the panel that, under pressure from General Dahlquist, found Lieutenant Homcy guilty on 19 October. Another judge on the Weiss panel, Lieutenant Raymond E. Bernberg, had originally been named as a witness for the prosecution against Weiss. His sworn statement that Weiss had been before the enemy when he deserted formed part of the prosecution's case. Normal procedure should have allowed him to recuse himself or the defence to challenge him for cause, but he remained a judge. The prosecutor or Trial Judge Advocate was the same as in the Homcy and Turek cases, Captain John M. Stafford. In the nearly three weeks since Homcy's trial, General Dahlquist had not withdrawn his demand that officers produce guilty verdicts and harsh sentences 'for the good of the service'.

The defence and prosecution tables were in the nave, between the congregants' pews and the chancel rail. The Trial Judge Advocate, Captain Stafford, and his assistant prosecutor, Captain Jess W. Jones, faced the court from one side of the aisle. On the other were defending counsel Wilson and his assistant, Captain Robert W. Plunkett, as well as Weiss himself. Looking up at the court, the altar and the cross, nineteen-year-old Weiss felt insignificant before the full weight of the judiciary, the military and the Almighty. The ritual commenced with the swearing in of the court. The court reporter, Corporal Russell C. Trunkfield, recorded the trial in a shorthand notebook.

Trunkfield's official transcript noted that neither the prosecution nor the defence, when asked, raised a challenge to remove any member of the court. It was not clear why Major Wilson, who had challenged Lieutenant Colonel Faulkner in the Homcy trial, did not challenge him in Weiss's case. Faulkner, whom Wilson knew to be the conduit of Dahlquist's insistence on more convictions and harsher sentences, remained on the panel judging Weiss. The record stated, 'The members of the court and the personnel of the prosecution were sworn.' The trial transcript continued:

The accused was then arraigned upon the following charges and specifications:

Charge: Violation of the 75th Article of War.

Specification 1: In that, Private Stephen J. Weiss, Company C, 143rd Infantry, being present with his company while it was engaged with the enemy, did, in the vicinity of Laval, France, on or about 16 October 1944, shamefully abandon the said company and seek safety in the rear.

Specification 2: In that, Private Stephen J. Weiss, Company C, 143rd Infantry, being present with his company while it was engaged with the enemy, did, in the vicinity of Brechitosse [sic], France, on or about 28 October 1944, shamefully abandon the said company and seek safety in the rear.

The penalty for violating Article 75, 'Misbehavior before the enemy', was 'death or such other punishment as a court-martial may direct'.

Weiss, through Major Wilson, lodged his plea to the charge and both specifications, 'Not guilty.' The facts were not in dispute. Weiss had already admitted deserting. Before anyone advised him of his right to remain silent, he had confessed his desertion to the Military Police, division officers, his defence counsel and the division psychiatrist, Major Walter L. Ford. Weiss's admission weakened his case, leaving the prosecution nothing to prove. While preparing for trial, Major Wilson did not ask what lay behind Weiss's desertion. Nor did he probe his client about his state of mind. Neither Major Wilson nor psychiatrist Ford asked him why he was afraid to return to the line but not to die by firing squad.

The Trial Judge Advocate, Captain Stafford, 'made no opening statement to the court' and called the prosecution's first witness, Major Robert L. O'Brien, to the witness stand. O'Brien, the 143rd Regiment's adjutant, testified as an expert. Assistant Trial Judge Advocate Captain Jess W. Jones conducted the direct examination.

O'Brien told the court that he spent part of each day in the field with the regiment and confirmed that it had been engaged with the enemy on 16 and 28 October, the days that Weiss left the line. Major Wilson, in cross-examination, asked O'Brien how he knew that Company C of the 143rd Regiment had been 'before the enemy' on the relevant dates. O'Brien replied, 'Because, in addition to being Adjutant of the Regiment I am Historian of the Regiment and spend four hours in the evening with officers of the Regiment getting the records in shape. I know they were [before the enemy].' Having established the unchallenged fact that Weiss's company had been 'before the enemy' on 16 and 28 October, O'Brien was excused. The prosecution did not produce any eyewitnesses to Weiss's desertion. It did not have to, because of Weiss's pre-trial statements. The Trial Judge Advocate had no further witnesses.

Captain Stafford introduced Government Exhibits One and Two, copies of two extracts 'of the morning report of Company C, 143rd Infantry dated 3 November 1944'. These extracts stated Charlie Company's dispositions on the dates in question. The prosecution rested.

The defence requested a recess to give time for one of its witnesses to reach Bruyères, and the court adjourned until one o'clock.

When the trial resumed after lunch, the defence called its first witness. Private Stephen J. Weiss stood, and Major Wilson addressed the court, 'The accused had his rights explained to him in connection with making a statement – sworn or unsworn – or remaining silent and desires to take the stand and make a sworn statement.' Weiss swore to tell the truth and took his place beside the altar. He stated his name, rank, company and regiment to the prosecutor, who asked, 'Are you the accused in this case?'

Major Wilson proceeded for the defence. 'Weiss,' he asked, 'how old are you?'

'Nineteen, sir.'

Wilson's direct examination elicited from the defendant that he had completed high school at the age of sixteen, taken college courses in psychology, pathology and chemistry at night and worked for the Office of War Information before he enlisted in the army. In a rapid exchange of questions and answers, Weiss provided a précis of his military career: training for seventeen weeks at Fort Blanding; rifle instruction at Fort Meade; waiting at Replacement Depots in Oran, Algeria, and Caserta, Italy; joining the 36th Division north of Civitavecchia on 12 June 1944; and serving as a first scout in Company C, 143rd Regiment, 36th Infantry Division, from that time until late August 1944 on the outskirts of Valence. As 36th Division officers, the trial judges did not require additional background on the campaigns that Weiss had fought in Italy and France. Major Wilson asked, 'Have you ever shot at a German?'

'Yes, sir.'

Wilson asked Weiss to tell the court about the Valence battle and 'the circumstances under which this separation occurred'. Weiss's account was the briefest of summaries, a few hundred words to relate a tale that a veteran could spend hours telling his grandchildren. Weiss's testimony was preserved, with the court reporter's misspellings, in the official transcript:

> It was night and we ran into enemy opposition. I was first scout and we were proceeding on a mission to destroy a machine gune [sic] next [sic] which was parallel to the road. On either side of the road it was open terrain. The Germans shot at us. They fired two shots and I fired one back at them. They threw two grenades at me and I got down into a ditch on the side of the road. The company commander had instructed us that my squad was to flank this position and wipe it out. The tank destroyers couldn't come up; they couldn't see the target. We went out and started to flank the gun when the tank destroyers moved up and opened fire on us. We decided to go back to our outfit and started out but we were unable as we ran into German machine guns. We came to an irrigation ditch and stayed there until next morning.

Weiss continued telling in headline form what he had done with the Resistance and the OSS, neglecting to mention that he had attacked a farmhouse where German soldiers had been hiding and chased the Germans across country to Soyons. Nor did he include in his testimony his missions to guard OSS parachute drops of men and equipment. Major Wilson asked how long he had served 'with this Recon outfit'.

'I stayed with the outfit from approximately September 2nd to October 9th.'

The questions and answers established that Sergeant Scruby and the other men of his squad left the OSS at Lyons, which court reporter Corporal Trunkfield, consistently spelled 'Leone'. Weiss explained that he did not return to the 36th Division when the rest of the squad did, because he was sick. When he recovered, he hitchhiked to Charlie Company's Command Post in the Vosges.

Major Wilson asked, 'Did you report to your company commander after this?'

'Yes, sir.'

'Who is your company commander?'

'Captain Simmons.'

'Did he ask where you had been?'

'Yes, sir.'

'Was he satisfied with your story?'

'Yes, sir.'

'Do you know whether or not Captain Simmons received any communication from this Paratrooper Recon outfit as to your activities when you were with them?'

'He received a citation for our fighting.'

'What date did you return to your Company – Company C?'

'October 10th.'

Major Wilson did not ask about Major Cox's official request for Weiss's transfer to the OSS and Weiss's offer to parachute with the OSS into enemy territory. This would have indicated to the court that Weiss was not a coward seeking to avoid the war, but a soldier who had found his métier with the special forces rather than under a company commander he distrusted. Weiss had not had time to explain his case to his counsel before the trial. He was also, as he said later, too depressed to make his condition clear to the court.

'Weiss,' Wilson asked his client, 'what caused you to leave your company on or about 16 October 1944?'

'I came back to the company and I was pretty nervous on account of the Valence deal. I nearly got killed there. I also found out that a lot of my buddies who I palled around with had been killed or wounded. I didn't think the war was natural for America and was pretty shaken up. The fellows had been killed or wounded.'

Wilson's next line of questioning established that Weiss went to a village on 16 October and returned after 'eight days', although he had in fact returned six days later. It further demonstrated that Weiss returned of his own will. When Wilson asked for the date he returned to the company, Weiss's response was confused: 'I believe that was on the 25th of October, or the 28th of October.'

'Was your company at the time you returned engaged with the enemy?'

'Yes, sir.'

'What caused you to leave again?'

'It was artillery, sir. The shells coming in. I seemed to go all to pieces and broke down. I felt tired and worn out.'

Rather than pursue this line of inquiry, which might have revealed a psychological state that pointed towards treatment rather than punishment, Major Wilson posed no further questions.

The Assistant Trial Judge Advocate, Captain Jess W. Jones, conducted the cross-examination. 'Weiss,' he began, 'where did you say you were located when you were with the Maquis?'

'Right across the Rhone River from Valence.' The question was irrelevant, because Weiss's service with the *maquis* was not disputed and was not an offence. In the next exchange, Weiss admitted leaving the line on 16 October.

'Why did you leave the line on the 16th?' Captain Jones asked.

'Because I broke down inside; the artillery shells were coming in and I shook all over and just went to pieces.'

'Now, did you leave the organization again on the 28th of October 1944?'

'Yes, sir.'

'Were you tactically before the enemy on the 28th?'

'Yes, sir.'

'Why did you leave then?'

'Intensified artillery barrage. I went to pieces again.'

'Do you know what the 75th Article of War is?'

'Yes, sir.'

'On the 16th of October 1944 did you understand what that was?'

'Yes, sir.'

'Tell the court just how you left on the 16th of October? When did you leave? At what time of day?'

'It was early in the morning, about seven-thirty.'

'How did you leave without anyone detecting you?'

'I don't know if anyone detected me or not.'

'Did you walk away?'

'I got up and ran down the hill.'

'Was there shelling at the time?'

'Yes, sir.'

The next questions concerned Weiss's two-and-a-half-hour flight through the woods, which ended with his arrival near a village. There was no reference to the French North African armoured crew who gave him shelter.

'When you left this first time did you know you were leaving your organization?' Jones asked.

'Do you mean did I realize it?'

'Yes.'

'Yes, I realized it.'

'Did you definitely make up your mind? Had you been thinking about it the night before?'

'No, sir.'

'When did you make up your mind to leave your organization?'

'When the artillery fell, sir.'

'When you got away from the artillery fire – say down to the foot of the hill – what did you think about down there?'

'I could hear it and was shaking.'

'On the next day, did you feel it was your duty to return to your company?'

'I was still nervous, sir.'

'Were you trembling the next day?'

'Yes, sir.'

'Did you feel a duty to return to your company?'

'I felt a duty, sir.'

'Did you make an attempt to go back the next day?'

'I thought it over, sir.'

'What conclusion did you come to?'

'I wasn't fit; I would be a detriment to my unit.'

'When you finally did decide to go back to your organization what made you pick that particular day to go back?'

'My mind was clearer and I realized in the full sense of the word that I had a duty to fulfill to my organization.'

'And what did you do then?'

'I returned to my unit, sir.'

Weiss, in response to more prosecution questions, said that he was bivouacked with the company in a 'little town' on 24 October and went into the line on 25 October. The Germans were firing rifles and machine guns, he recalled, but no heavy artillery. The Assistant Trial Judge Advocate asked when he left the company again, and Weiss answered it had been 28 October at about four in the morning. 'What made you leave at that time?' Captain Jones asked.

'The artillery barrage, sir.'

'How did you get away? Did anybody see you when you left?'

'I imagine the soldiers saw me.'

'What did you do when you left?'

'I walked down the road for a while. I got a "hitch" on a truck and went through a few villages I can't remember by name. I stayed in a barn and cried.'

'What were you crying about?'

'I was all shaken up inside.'

'How long were you gone?'

'Two days, sir.'

'Until the 30th?'

'Yes, sir.'

'What happened then?'

'I turned myself in to the MPs.'

'Where?'

'At Vesoul.'

Captain Jones asked why Weiss went to Vesoul, to which he responded, 'It was just as good a place as any. It was a town and I wanted to get away from the artillery.'

'I ask you on both of these times when this artillery barrage started coming in, did you really try to stay there?'

'Yes, sir.'

'What went through your mind at that time?'

'My mind was cloudy. I couldn't think straight.'

Captain Jones's cross-examination ended without his having asked Weiss if anyone else had deserted with him. The names of the two deserters with whom he left the line on 28 October, Privates Clarence Weidaw and James (Jim) Dickson, were not entered into the court record. Nor was there mention of the desertion of Frank Turek and another soldier from the same Company C that morning, although Turek had been in the defendant's chair only twenty-four hours earlier. These were significant lapses. If at least five men from one company were so disgruntled that they left the line simultaneously, it would not have reflected well on their commander or, possibly, on the army itself. No one asked whether Weiss had faith in Captain Simmons. No one asked if he would have stayed in the war under another commander, as he had requested to do with French Captain Binoche and OSS officers Lieutenant Rickerson and Major Cox. While the prosecution would have weakened its case by drawing the court's attention to other desertions and general dissatisfaction with the company commander, the defence was remiss to leave these facts out of the trial record. Weiss had deserted with two other soldiers. Where were they? Why were they not on trial? If others were being treated for medical conditions, why wasn't Weiss?

The court intervened to ask three questions, none of which was relevant to the case. 'When you were cut off from your company close to Valence, what did the tank destroyer open up on you with?'

'Three inch guns, sir.'

'How close were they?'

'Some hundred yards.'

'During the period you were with the Maquis did you undertake any sort of demolition? Did you engage in any fighting against the Germans during that time?'

'No, sir.'

Weiss's confusion at this point appeared overwhelming. His time with the Resistance was not germane to the case against him. His trial was for deserting on 16 and 28 October near Bruyères, not for having been cut off from his company at Valence in August. Moreover, his answers were neither accurate nor to his benefit. He had attempted to engage the Germans at a farmhouse with Major Mathey's *maquis* group, and he had also assisted Captain Binoche in demolishing a bridge over the River Rhône.

Major Wilson, undoubtedly noticing the discrepancy, refreshed Weiss's memory. 'When you were with the Maquis did you undertake any sort of demolition?'

Weiss answered, 'Yes, sir.'

'What did you do?'

'We blew up one bridge that would hinder the "Jerries" from coming through.'

Defence counsel had clarified part of the record, but its relevance to the charge and specifications was nil. Major Wilson was done, and the Assistant Trial Judge Advocate, Captain Jones, undertook a short re-cross-examination about Valence, where Weiss's squad was cut off from the rest of the company. 'When you were first fired on by this tank destroyer outfit was that the first time that you ever noticed being afraid very much?'

'Yes, sir.'

'Was that before you got with the Maquis or after?'

'Before, sir.'

'You say you went out with the Maquis and blew up a bridge?'

'Yes, sir.'

'Were you afraid at that time?'

'The nearest Germans were four miles away and they were just an occupying force.'

Captain Jones had no further questions, and the court began its re-examination of the witness.

'When you were with the Paratroopers near the Swiss border did you hear any artillery over there?'

'No, sir.'

'You fought with the Paratroopers over there?'

'One engagement.'

'What was the nature of the fight?'

'There was no fight; we expected a fight. We went up to the Italian-Swiss border and went up into the mountains and we expected to be subjected to "Jerry" fire but there were no "Jerries" and we got out safely.'

The trial record continued, 'There being no further questions by the prosecution, the defense, or the court, the witness was excused and resumed his seat next to his counsel.'

The defence called its next witness, Sergeant Settimo Gualandi. Gualandi swore to tell the truth, and the defence counsel asked how long he had known Weiss. 'Since March, sir,' he replied, which meant they had met while training at Fort Blanding in Florida. Major Wilson's questions allowed Gualandi to tell the court that he and Weiss had hit the beaches of southern France together, served in the same squad and were separated from their company at Valence. 'From the time you landed in France up to Valence did Weiss show any indication of being afraid?' Wilson asked.

'No, sir. Not at all.'

'Was your squad ever sent out on patrol?'

'Yes, sir.'

'Was Weiss along with you?'

'Yes, sir.'

'In the vicinity of Valence were you and Weiss together on a mission to destroy a machine gun next [sic]?'

'Yes, sir.'

'Will you tell the court what happened when you were sent out on that mission?'

'We were pinned down and our squad was sent back just a little way in order to go around and flank it out. Weiss was first scout. We were following him and he was pocketed right under the machine gun nest and the tanks came creeping up the road and opened fire; we were right near them. They were on our right and we couldn't get back.'

'Was there any of our own fire in the vicinity?'

'It was all German at that time when we were on the right flank.'

'Then what happened?'

'We couldn't get back because of the machine gun shooting so we pulled back – I would say 100 yards – and we stayed in a ditch over night. The next morning our company had already pulled out and we didn't know where they were so we went into an open field to a house and set up our own security there. Some French policemen came around on a bicycle and seen us and left right away. Pretty soon they came back – two men and a civilian came back with police uniforms. They took us out, four at a time. We went through Valence and across the Rhone River.'

'How many American soldiers were in the group that was cut off?'

'Eight of us.'

'Do you recall some of the names of the others?'

'Sergeant Scruby. He got wounded. There was Segle [sic].'

The exchange that followed elicited from Gualandi a summary of the squad's service with the Resistance and the OSS. Major Wilson then asked whether Gualandi had gone on missions with the paratroopers. 'We just went right along with them wherever they went,' Gualandi answered. 'We didn't have a special mission.'

'How did you get back to your outfit from the Paratroopers?'

'We stayed there about two days and decided we had better get back. Major Cox wrote a letter for us explaining to the commanding officer of the 143rd that we had been fighting with the Maquis and joined the Paratroopers and were under military control and on duty all the time. He wrote the letter to the general and we hitch-hiked back.'

'When you got back what happened?'

'We turned into the company commander.'

With that conclusion to the defence's questions, the Assistant Trial Judge Advocate began his cross-examination. 'Sergeant,' he said, 'did the accused return to the company with you?'

'No, sir. He left us. He got sick when we came up to Leone [sic]. He stayed back with the Paratroopers.'

'Now,' the prosecutor asked, 'were you in his squad on or about 16 October 1944?'

'After he came back he got into a different squad.'

'Were you ever around or near him when a fight was going on?'

'He joined up when we had been pulled back for a rest. Then we went up to the line again and he was with us.'

'Did he appear, at the time you saw him, to be very nervous?'

'No, sir. He seemed all right to me.'

'Did you ever see Weiss at any time in which it appeared that his nerves were out of control?'

'No, sir.'

The prosecutor asked whether Sergeant Gualandi recalled Weiss rejoining the company for the second time on 28 October and returning to the line. He did remember.

'When you got up there did you receive an artillery barrage?'

'We moved into the 142nd position and there was a barrage.'

'Was there a barrage the first morning? A "Jerry" barrage?'

'I can't recall, sir. I couldn't swear to it.'

'Can you recall whether there was a "Jerry" barrage around four o'clock in the morning?'

'I can't recall, sir.'

'You say you were with the accused on the 28th?'

'Yes, sir.'

'Did he appear extraordinarily nervous to you in any way?'

'No, sir. He appeared all right.'

The court reporter noted, 'There being no further questions by the prosecution, the defense, or the court, the witness was excused and withdrew.'

As Gualandi left the stand, Weiss sensed that his friend's testimony buttressed the prosecution's case more than his own. Gualandi's assertion that Weiss was not nervous in combat undermined the contention that incoming artillery had caused his panic. 'While listening to Gualandi,' Weiss wrote, 'I realize that all the men on the Detail are commissioned officers, from lieutenant to colonel; there is not an enlisted man among them.' If there had been frontline enlisted men on the court, he felt, they would have understood his state of mind. Rear echelon officers lacked the experience on which to judge the fear and discontent that could drive a combat infantry enlisted man to desert.

Major Wilson introduced Defense Exhibit A, the findings of Division Psychiatrist Major Walter L. Ford. Dated 2 November 1944, the day Ford interviewed Weiss for 'pending charges', the 'Psychiatric Report in Disciplinary Cases' comprised two pages. On page one, Major Ford wrote in a barely legible hand,

> This soldier was assigned to the Div. in June 1944. He three 3 weeks of combat above Rome and made the invasion of S. France. His unit was surrounded near Valence & he was listed as MIA for 43 days. During this time he was fighting with the Maquis and a Spec. Serv. Recon. unit from which he received a citation. He tells that he has gradually become more tense & 'nervous.' He has battle dreams & difficulty in sleeping. He noticed a warped fear of riding in cars and an intolerance to noise. He left his unit on 27 Oct. as he felt he could not tolerate combat any longer.

The form on which Major Ford wrote his analysis required him to complete the sentence, 'In my opinion he is suffering from: (Medical Diagnosis with brief explanation of this condition in lay terminology) ...' Ford wrote, 'Psychoneurosis, anxiety, mild. This is an emotional condition which makes it difficult for this soldier to control his behavior in combat.'

Under 'Recommendation', he answered, 'Recommend that the above condition be considered as extenuation to be evaluated in connection with other evidence.' The second page of the report was a standard set of questions for use by the court. Most concerned Weiss's ability to understand the court proceedings, to which Ford answered, 'Yes.' On questions of criminal responsibility, Ford answered five questions about the accused's state of mind:

1. Was he at the time of the alleged offense suffering from a defect of reason resulting from disorder of the mind? *No.*
2. Did such defect of reason prevent him from knowing the nature and quality of the act which he was doing? *No.*
3. Did such defect of reason prevent him from knowing the consequences of such an act? *No.*
4. Or, if he did know, was his mental state such that he was unable to refrain from such act? *No.*

Regarding behaviour, the report asked, 'Was the accused suffering at the time of the offense from any emotional or physical disorder which might have affected his behavior?' Ford's answer was, 'Yes.'

With its submission of Ford's report, the defence rested.

The prosecution recalled Private Weiss. Assistant counsel Captain Jones asked, 'Weiss, are you prepared to go back and fight?'

'In another capacity, sir.'

'Are you willing to go back to Company C, 143rd Infantry, and fight?'

'I don't feel fit, sir.'

'Have you made up your mind that you are not going back, Weiss?'

'I have not made up my mind, sir. I feel I'm losing my mind.'

'Have you ever tried exercising your mind, Private Weiss? You have made up your mind, however, that you would fight in another capacity?'

'Off the line, sir.'

'Will you or will you not go back and fight?'

'I don't understand the question, sir.'

'I think you understand my question, Weiss. Will you go back into your line company and fight?'

'I don't think I can, sir.'

The prosecution and defence made closing arguments to the court, which the court reporter did not record in the trial transcript. The fifteen officers of the court martial retired to reach a verdict.

Weiss, seated beside Major Wilson, awaited judgment. The court returned a short time later, indicating there had not been much discussion. Major Clarke, the President of the Court, asked Weiss to stand. The trial transcript recorded:

> Upon secret written ballot, two-thirds of the members present at the time the vote was taken concurring in each finding of guilty, the court finds the accused:
> Of Specification 1: Guilty
> Of Specification 2: Guilty
> Of the Charge: Guilty.

Two-thirds of the court meant that five of the fifteen officers had decided Weiss was not guilty. In a civilian trial, he would have gone free. Military courts convened under their own rules, codified in the 1920 *Court Martial Manual* as revised in 1943. On a majority vote, Weiss was guilty of violating Article of War 75 and faced the death penalty. Having delivered its verdict, the court was informed that Private Weiss had no previous convictions for any offence, civilian or military. It was also told that Weiss's basic pay was $60 a month, less $22 a month to dependants and $6.40 a month for government insurance. When asked whether the information was correct, Weiss answered, 'All but my pay, sir. I receive $70 per month with combat pay.'

The court retired again to deliberate sentence. Weiss waited without showing emotion. By secret, written ballot, the fifteen officers considered the choices available to them under the law: to send Weiss to prison or to order him 'shot to death by musketry'. The court marched back to the long table a few minutes later, a duration that made clear there had been no debate. Sitting beside the fourteen other officers with the altar behind them, Lieutenant Colonel Faulkner asked Weiss to stand. The chapel was by now as cold as the snow-bound town outside. 'Private Stephen J. Weiss, Army serial number 128033,' Faulkner pronounced, 'you are to be dishonorably discharged from the service, to forfeit all pay and allowances due or to become due, and to be confined at hard labor, at such place as the reviewing authority may direct, for the term of your natural life.'

Three-fourths of the court, the record showed, concurred in the sentence. That would have been eleven of the fifteen officers. 'The court then, at 1430 o'clock, P.M., 7 November 1944, proceeded to other business.'

The trial that decided the fate of nineteen-year-old Private Stephen J. Weiss had taken five hours, including at least one hour for lunch, to condemn him to prison for the rest of his life.

'They didn't kill me physically,' Weiss wrote, 'but at nineteen, my life over, I was nothing more than a living dead man. If they killed me on the spot, it would have been all right, because I didn't give a damn.'

The fifteen officers in the court martial of Stephen J. Weiss were not the only Americans to cast votes that Tuesday. In the United States, the electorate went to the polls to choose between Franklin Delano Roosevelt and Thomas E. Dewey for president and commander-in-chief. By the time Roosevelt learned the public had given him overwhelming support to serve an unprecedented fourth term, Steve Weiss was stomping the ground to prevent his feet from freezing. Around him in his cell were convicted murderers, rapists, thieves and other deserters. This was where he began nearly a year before, when deserters in a stockade on the Anzio beachhead warned him that he would end up like them. He did not believe it then, and he could barely believe it now.

TWENTY-SEVEN

The guard house may not be any help at all – sometimes
it even makes things worse.

Psychology for the Fighting Man, p. 355

PRIVATE STEVE WEISS LEFT THE BRUYÈRES stockade at the end of
November 1944, shackled with other convicts and shipped west on a
succession of cargo and passenger trains. Several days of changing
trains brought the prisoners to the Gare de l'Est in Paris. A Military
Policeman met Weiss at the station, and Weiss got into his jeep. When
the MP did not bother to put him in handcuffs, Weiss asked why. The
answer was obvious, 'You've got some place to go?'

There was only one place, the Loire Disciplinary Training Center
(DTC), more than a hundred miles away near Le Mans. The MP
drove in an uncovered jeep through the darkness of post-liberation
Paris, whose landmarks Weiss was too numb to savour. They exited
the city by a western gate and, just past Versailles, turned off
National Route 10 for a late-night breakfast. The policeman and his
charge ate without speaking, amid cigarette smoke and kitchen
fumes, at an army canteen for military truck drivers. When they
finished, the MP did not linger. Icy winds battered their faces as they
sped through a bleak landscape scarred by the titanic struggle of a
few months earlier. Pastures and meadows made no impression on
Weiss, whose court martial sentence of hard labour for the rest of his
'natural life' had deprived him of all feeling. For the nineteen-year-
old, 'life' was an unimaginably long time. The jeep passed the town
of Le Mans, which General Patton's Third Army had liberated on 8

August, and crossed the River Sarthe to continue west past more frozen meadows. Leaving the road, the MP manoeuvred along two-wheel tracks to an unmarked square of land where another MP was waiting.

The driver asked for receipt of delivery, as if Weiss had been a consignment of boots. The jeep rumbled away, leaving the teenage convict alone with the prison guard. Looking at the barren terrain, Weiss wondered where the DTC was. The guard told him it did not exist yet. Weiss and the other inmates were going to build it.

The stockade had been farmland until 17 October 1944, when the 2913th Guardhouse Overhead Detachment of MPs arrived from Britain to transform it into a penitentiary. German prisoners of war laid the rudiments of a prison that awaited 4,500 US Army convicts. By the time of Weiss's arrival, the only structures were three single-storey brick hovels that had been farm buildings. One served as a clinic. The other two were the mess hall and the camp office. The prisoners had to construct everything else, from the cages they would be kept in to the watchtowers from which they would be shot if they attempted to escape. Weiss was assigned to a pup tent with another inmate for the rest of the night. In the morning, black truck drivers from racially segregated Services of Supply units delivered wood, barbed wire, nails and other materials for the prisoners to construct their new home. Work details broke the frozen ground with picks to make punishment pits and to plant fence posts along the base perimeter. The men worked quickly and for long hours. When they were not working, they lined up outdoors for meals from the camp kitchen and shared a communal latrine. Short of blankets, they slept in their clothes.

The inmates' uniforms were neither warm nor waterproof. Incessant rain soaked their jackets, trousers and combat boots. They batted their bodies with cold hands to keep from freezing. Those who contracted pneumonia were taken to military hospitals off base and returned to work as soon as they recovered. The camp canteen had little hot food, and prisoners survived mostly on cold rations. 'However, to be fair,' Weiss wrote, 'we didn't get enough food on the front either.'

Weiss observed the camp's staff of Military Police, most of whom had been civilian police officers before the war. His opinion of them was not high. The staff sergeant in charge of the guard detail carried a tent pole that he used to beat prisoners who annoyed him. He had been a policeman in New York, but the city was no bond between him and Weiss. Behind his back, Weiss called him 'Bow Legs'. His nickname for one huge MP, who had been a beat cop in Chicago, was 'Big Al'. The commanding officer, Lieutenant Colonel Henry L. Peck, had been a building contractor in the United States. Weiss recalled, 'Sometimes I'd see him walking to his office, a dour, inaccessible, crisp looking officer, and wondered how he reconciled his position as a prison administrator, trapped in a backwater, riding herd on a bunch of misfits, when fighting colonels were leading men at the sharp end.' Having been at the 'sharp end' and, in his own mind, failed, Weiss knew that it held fewer dangers for a colonel than a dogface infantryman. It troubled him that, at the Disciplinary Training Center, there was neither training nor rehabilitation. The men were 'simply warehoused'.

Disciplinary Training Centers were intended as a progressive alternative to the army's 'Disciplinary Barracks', where only the worst offenders were caged. The new name pointed towards a reformed philosophy of punishment, whose guiding idea was that convicts remained soldiers capable of being retrained for service. The 'Prisoner's Handbook' for another DTC stated that the purpose of confinement was 'honorably restoring to the army those of you who can demonstrate by your attitude, conduct, aptness, and bearing that you are worthy of such action'. The practice at most DTCs never matched the theory. At the Lichfield DTC in Staffordshire, England, guards were so brutal to prisoners, especially convicted deserters, that they were court martialled. As Weiss discovered, the Loire DTC had no programme to rehabilitate any prisoner or 'honorably' to restore him to service. It did have a rigorous regime of hard labour, gratuitous cruelty, petty privations and insufficient, inedible food.

Guidelines set by the Theater Provost Marshal, Major General Milton A. Reckord, stipulated that 'prisoners should be treated neither with such laxity that confinement might appear an attractive alternative to duty, nor with a severity that would create undue resistance to any possibility of rehabilitation.' His directives required that prisoners housed in buildings sleep on 'wooden pallets or wooden bunks, without mattresses or springs; while those housed in shelter tents [like Weiss] may be provided bed sack with a minimum amount of straw'. Regarding diet, General Reckord's instructions stated, 'Meat will not be provided solely for the comfort of the prisoner except under most unusual circumstances.' He added, 'Light shall not be made available for the comfort of the prisoner. It may, however, be used to facilitate work and instruction.'

By the second week of December, the outlines of the camp were becoming visible: cages, each as large as a football field, in which the prisoners pitched their two-man tents; underground solitary confinement holes sealed with iron bars; barbed wire surrounding the camp and dividing it into sections; and watchtowers from which MPs with .30-calibre machine guns were prepared to shoot anyone who stepped outside the wire. The Provost Marshal's Office reported that the men soon constructed the basic compound, comprising 'a large area surrounded by a double apron fence, 14 feet high. Eleven cages kept the prisoners segregated according to the crime which they had committed.' Weiss was confined with the other deserters, all of them serving from twenty years to life. This was nothing like his father's war.

TWENTY-EIGHT

Anger shared, controlled and directed to the single
purpose of destroying the enemy, is a powerful force for
survival and for victory.

Psychology for the Fighting Man, p. 325

CORPORAL ALFRED T. WHITEHEAD had much to be grateful for
when Thanksgiving came to the Schnee Eifel region on 23 November
1944. Since the return of his 2nd Battalion from Paris ten days before,
the frontline along the Belgian-German border had been static. The
38th Regiment had dug deep trenches and fashioned log cabins from
the ubiquitous pines. It had also constructed a small church that
would not have been out of place on the frontier in Davy Crockett's
time. Cooks delivered hot food much of the time, and some of the
better hunters supplemented their diet with venison. Charles B.
MacDonald, an infantry captain and later the leading historian of the
Siegfried Line campaign, wrote, 'It was also true that the Germans on
the other side of the line were for the most part content to emulate the
Americans in keeping the sector relatively quiescent.' For the infantry,
despite making regular patrols and braving mortar and artillery
rounds, the battlefield did not get much better.

To celebrate Thanksgiving, Headquarters Company rotated to a
rest area near the Belgian town of Saint Vith. As they pulled out of
the line, Whitehead perched on the tailgate of one of the trucks beside
another soldier. After about ten miles, the men saw an ambulance
burning beside the road. It must have been hit by German artillery.
Before they could react, the Germans shelled them. 'A roaring

explosion rocked the truck,' Whitehead wrote, 'and metal fragments flew up only inches from my head, going right through the hand of the non-com sitting next to me.' The truck raced for safety to a bend in the road, where the driver fell dead. Whitehead and another soldier jumped off and ran through a snowbound field. The other soldier said he had been hit, and blood gushed from his foot. Medics picked him up, and the troops resumed their journey.

Their billet was an old farmhouse with a front porch that reminded Whitehead of 'those back home in Tennessee'. The camp provided rare luxuries like hot showers, clean uniforms and USO shows. Thanksgiving turkey was served with all the trimmings, but the road-side shelling had rattled Whitehead so much that he could not enjoy it. As he had done in childhood to escape his stepfather, he sauntered into the woods alone in search of game. There was nothing worth shooting until sunset, when a large 'jack rabbit' bounded into his line of sight. He shot it, but, without an appetite, gave it to a Belgian farmer.

Back on the line a week later, Whitehead alternated between patrols and standing watch. For the first time, he heard the famous voice from Radio Berlin of an American woman who called herself 'Midge at the Mike'. The GIs called her 'Axis Sally', but her real name was Mildred Elizabeth Gillars. She had quit her job teaching English in Berlin in 1935 to broadcast for the Nazis. From December 1941, when the United States entered the war, her target audience was the US military. 'I'm afraid you're yearning plenty for someone else,' her sultry voice cooed to homesick GIs. 'But I just wonder if she isn't running around with the 4-Fs way back home.' Her appeals for troops to surrender and enjoy 'eggs and bacon frying' failed to impress Whitehead. 'That kind of propaganda bullshit didn't move us in the slightest,' he wrote.

On 11 December, the 106th Infantry Division relieved the 2nd along the thinly defended frontlines. The 2nd moved west by motor convoy through Saint Vith to Camp d'Elsenborn, just behind the Elsenborn Ridge, in Belgium. This was the assembly point for a proposed attack on the highway between Krinkelt in Belgium and Dreiborn in Luxembourg. The objective was control of the

Schwammenaeul Dam on the River Roer, where the Germans stood ready to flood American forces moving towards the Rhine. On 13 December, the 2nd Division left Elsenborn for a Belgian village called Rocherath. From there, the 9th Infantry Regiment attempted to breach the German lines. The 38th stayed just behind, waiting to pour through any opening the 9th made, but German resistance at a fortified customs house near the Wahlerscheid road junction stopped the offensive dead.

An indecisive battle continued until 15 December. That afternoon, cooks brought hot food up to the line where the 38th Regiment waited to follow the 9th into battle. 'To the veterans, it was like the Kiss of Death,' wrote Cleve Barkley, based on his father's reminiscences. 'Although delighted to wolf down hot chow, they knew that this gesture meant only one thing: They'd be going into action – soon!'

Early on the morning of 16 December, the 2nd Battalion of the 9th Regiment penetrated the German lines to capture prisoners and pillboxes, followed by the 3rd Battalion of the 9th Regiment. Whitehead's 2nd Battalion of the 38th Infantry Regiment came forward: 'When we reached our attack point, we no longer had the protection of the dense forest. Here the enemy had cleared a large killing zone to the front of their forts, filling it with massive, formidable objects, wire and mines.' The 2nd Battalion led the 9th Regiment into the fray. Captain Charles B. MacDonald wrote,

By midnight the 2nd Battalion [38th Infantry Regiment] held a substantial bridgehead within the Wahlerscheid strongpoint and another battalion was filing silently through the gap. One battalion swung northwest, the other northeast. From one position to another, the men moved swiftly, blowing the doors of pillboxes with beehive charges, killing or capturing the occupants, prodding sleepy Germans from foxholes, and capturing seventy-seven at one blow at the customshouse.

Whitehead claimed no small part of the credit for victory. He allegedly destroyed 'sixteen enemy emplacements, including several pillboxes with a flamethrower', achievements other veterans of the battle doubted. Whitehead also wrote that his platoon leader submitted his name for a Silver Star. The 2nd Battalion pushed another 1,500 yards through the Monschau Forest, where German artillery and machine gunners opened up on them. By 17 December, the offensive had gone as far as it could.

Nature that day took Germany's side. Fog and sleet made life miserable for the GIs and grounded Allied planes. While Whitehead was digging a slit trench, a mail orderly ran up to him. 'You are surrounded,' he recalled the young man saying. 'The Germans have broken through, taken the water dump, the mail dump and all the Christmas presents are gone!' Whitehead answered, 'You're crazy as hell.' The 9th and 38th Regiments were deep inside German territory. Neither they nor their commanders knew that Field Marshal Gerd von Runstedt had launched the mass counter-offensive that the newspapers would call 'the Battle of the Bulge'. When Whitehead realized the mail orderly was not lying, he thought that 'we'd all but won the war, when this staggering bit of bad news hit us'. The 38th Regiment's advance was about to reverse itself.

The 38th hastily pulled back from Wahlerscheid's crossroads to the Elsenborn Ridge. The Germans appeared to be on the way to achieving their objective of driving a wedge between the Allied armies and seizing the Belgian port of Antwerp, which had opened to Allied ships only on 26 November. By evening, the 2nd Battalion had fought a rearguard action to make its way to Rocherath. 'Not knowing the larger strategy of the situation,' Whitehead wrote, 'we were all bitching, and I was wondering out loud why-in-the-hell those people in the rear couldn't hold what we'd already taken.' Frontline troops would pay the price for the failure of command and intelligence to notice the buildup. For the next three days, the 2nd Division and the other forces arrayed along the German frontier waged a struggle for survival. The inexperienced 99th Division was nearly destroyed. Positions changed hands many times, orders were lost and men died when their own side mistakenly fired on them.

'No pity was given by us or the enemy,' Whitehead wrote. 'Our wounded and dying who fell in to the roads, or those fighting in foxholes, were run over and ground to pieces by the German tanks.' Whitehead joined a dawn patrol on 19 December. Entering a house, he saw an SS officer coming at him with a bayonet. Knocked down by the officer's rifle butt, Whitehead said he moved quickly enough to stab the German with a trench knife. The struggle went on, until Whitehead shot him with his .45. The encounter was remarkably similar to one he described on Hill 192 in Normandy. 'During these three days there had been no time to rest, except for short 10–20 minute periods could any of us close our eyes,' he remembered. 'Many a time I'd reach down and grab some snow and rub it in my face to keep awake, while saying to myself, "I'm okay, I'm okay."'

Although Whitehead's account of his bravery from 16 to 19 December seemed unbelievable, some soldiers achieved at least one of the many feats he claimed for himself: calling in artillery on his own position to eliminate Germans who had overrun it; disabling Panther tanks with bazookas and shooting the crews as they climbed out; and hiding in a house with Germans inside and sneaking out wearing a German coat. All of these things happened, but it is unlikely the same man was responsible for them all. Nothing in his service record confirms these tales of derring do, but there is no doubt Whitehead was entitled to a share in the 2nd Battalion's Distinguished Unit Citation for 'outstanding courage, skill, and fearless initiative demonstrated by all personnel'.

Three days of fighting, house-to-house and hand-to-hand, in the twin towns of Krinkelt and Rocherath ended with the 38th's withdrawal under fire. By 20 December, most of the 2nd Division had withdrawn about three miles to the heights at Elsenborn, 'a long natural ridge and a far tighter and more defensible position than the scattered roads and villages of the border'. From there, US forces could shell the Germans below. Whitehead recalled that officers never used the word 'withdrawal', preferring 'move to different positions'.

At least 1,030 2nd Division troops received treatment for wounds in the first three days. Hundreds of others were dead, had deserted or were taken prisoner. Al Whitehead was alive, free of injury and had not run away. Nor was he in a German prison camp, like Sergeant Frank 'Hardtack' Kviatek, who had trained him at Camp McCoy, Wisconsin.

By Christmas, the German offensive was concentrating further south against the US 101st Airborne and other units in Bastogne. Around Elsenborn, 38th Regiment troops dug slit trenches most of Christmas Day and celebrated with cold K-rations. A few days later, overseeing a burial detail of Germans, Whitehead betrayed callousness that was unusual even in a man who had been long in battle: 'I put my pick through their heads, pried them up, and dragged them over to the edge of a pit that had been dug, then shoved them in. The other men in the detail, new replacements, didn't like the way I was doing the job, and stared at me in disbelief.'

The right side of his abdomen had been hurting for several days, and he requested painkillers from the dispensary. The doctor, whom he had known at Camp McCoy, examined him and said, 'My God, Whitehead, this war's over for you.' Whitehead was incredulous. The doctor explained, 'You've got to have an operation for appendicitis. You'll have to go back to England, and then it will probably be back to the States for you.'

Alfred Whitehead of 4th Platoon, Company D, 63rd Infantry Training Battalion, Camp Wolters, Texas. Whitehead is in the third row, seventh from left, and his friend 'Timmiehaw', who was killed by a 'bouncing Betsy' mine, is second from left in the same row.

(*Above*) A US MP with two Italian black marketeers caught selling American cigarettes in Naples, November 1944. (*Right*) American deserters like Whitehead were not the only black-market dealers. Here, a British sailor does business in London's Cutler Street, which came to be known as 'Loot Alley'.

(*Opposite*) According to Whitehead's autobiography, *Diary of a Soldier*, this is Omaha Beach, D-Day, 6 June 1944. Whitehead identifies himself as the third soldier from right, at the front of the landing craft.

In April 1944, Whitehead heard an address given by General George S. Patton – 'Old Blood and Guts' (which for some US soldiers meant 'Our blood, his guts'). Patton was in favour of shooting deserters and slapped a shell-shocked soldier in Sicily.

General Bernard Law Montgomery, under whom John Bain fought as part of the British 8th Army, differed in style from Patton, if less so in content: 'There will be no more belly-aching and no more retreats.'

John Bain at fourteen, the age at which he boxed in the finals of the Schoolboy Championships of Great Britain.

John Bain, of the Argyll and Sutherland Highlanders, in 1940, before his transfer to the Gordon Highlanders, the regiment from which he deserted.

Although Bain did not serve time there, the Military Detention Barracks at Aldershot was the archetypal British military prison. Its nickname, 'the Glasshouse', which derived from its roof, came to stand for any military prison.

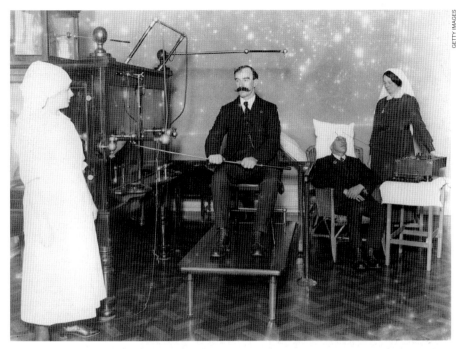

Experimental medical equipment being used to treat British First World War soldiers suffering from shell shock. *Fortune* magazine reported that 'twenty-five years after the end of the last war, nearly half of the 67,000 beds in Veterans Administration hospitals [in the United States] are still occupied by the neuropsychiatric casualties of World War I.' (*Below*) By the Second World War, at least some commanders favoured providing psychiatric care in forward aid stations, which is where this US soldier, here being administered a sedative, was sent.

The artillery barrage at
El Alamein inspired John
Bain's poem 'Baptism of
Fire' (published under
his adopted name of
Vernon Scannell): 'And,
with the flashes, swollen
thunder roars / as, from
behind, the barrage of big
guns / begins to batter
credence with its din
/ and, overhead, death
whinnies for its feed …'.
Scannell was fortunate
(or claimed to be), and
was able to tell his son in
a poem that 'my spirit,
underneath, / Survived
it all intact'. He died in
2007, aged eighty-five.

TWENTY-NINE

Such a sufferer from war shock is not a weakling, he is
not a coward. He is a battle casualty.

Psychology for the Fighting Man, p. 353

ONE EVENING IN LATE DECEMBER, an infantry captain came to the
Loire Disciplinary Training Center near Le Mans. The prisoners lined
up outdoors at his makeshift desk to hear the captain's proposal.
A veteran recovering from battlefield wounds, the captain invited
volunteers for the frontlines. The German counter-offensive that
began in the Ardennes Forest on 16 December was taking thousands
of Allied lives, and the army needed men to replace them. It would
grant freedom to any inmate who returned to fight. When the war
ended, records would be wiped clean and discharges would be honourable. A few convicts signed up, demonstrating bravery that Weiss
admired.

When Weiss faced the captain, he volunteered for any duty, including mine disposal, apart from the infantry. His mental condition,
which had received no medical attention, made infantry combat
unimaginable. The captain said it was the infantry or nothing. Weiss
later wrote, 'I turned him down cold.'

Before sunrise every morning, the camp bugler blew reveille. Men
who slept in their uniforms for warmth needed no time to dress. They
queued to brush their teeth and headed to the mess hall to wait for
powdered eggs or porridge. Someone yelled at Weiss one dark morning on the way to breakfast, 'Get the lead out.' He responded, 'Blow
it out your ass.' It was a mistake. An MP pushed his face into the

mess hall's brick wall. After an hour frozen to the spot, Weiss heard the staff sergeant behind him shouting, 'So, this is the son of a bitch who won't follow orders?' Before Weiss could answer, a fist slammed into the side of his face and cracked his skull into the brickwork. 'My eyes stung, blood rushed down my cheek and dripped on the ground,' Weiss wrote. 'Bow Legs' dragged him to the administration office, kicking him all the way.

An officer ordered Weiss to explain himself. Bleeding and humiliated, he said that he had thought the person telling him to 'get the lead out' in the dark was a fellow prisoner. Otherwise, he would have kept his mouth shut. 'Bow Legs' challenged Weiss to put on the gloves. Before Weiss could answer, the officer ordered him to shut up and get out. That would have been the end of it, but the staff sergeant selected Weiss for further torment. He took particular satisfaction in catching Weiss visiting another prisoner's cage and beating the hell out of him with his tent pole. Weiss was as bitter as he was powerless.

Two prisoners from the 82nd Airborne Division could not take the Loire DTC any longer and cut through the wire one night. At morning roll call, no one answered to their names. Guards were irate, prisoners elated. 'I was not only pleased with their accomplishment,' Weiss wrote, 'but delighted they had lulled the staff into thinking that as prisoner athletic instructors, a soft billet, they would stay behind the wire.' The convicts bet cigarettes on whether the two paratroopers would be captured.

Four days later, Staff Sergeant 'Bow Legs' dragged the two escapees through the wire into camp. The other prisoners watched disconsolately as he kicked the paratroopers and beat them with his tent pole. 'Bow Legs' shoved them underground into a punishment hole, where they languished for a week on bread and water. When the week was up, the army transferred them to federal prison in the United States. Official policy stated that 'those having no salvage value were sent to the U.S.'.

The directive on 'Treatment of U.S. Soldiers in Confinement' from the Theater Provost Marshal, Major General Milton A. Reckord, stated, 'Cruelty or unusual punishments will not be tolerated.' That did not prevent brutality from characterizing the camp regime, whether by design or due to lack of supervision of the more sadistic guards. One afternoon when there was no rain, the guards took the men on a march outside the base perimeter. One prisoner strayed to the left, and a guard shouted, 'Hey, you, get back in the line.' When the man slipped to the side of the column again, the same MP aimed his .45-calibre revolver and fired. The man fell. Grabbing his bleeding leg, he cried out in agony. Some of the prisoners went to his aid, while the others stared in disbelief. Another guard called for the medics, who came about an hour later in an ambulance to take him to a hospital. The other prisoners concealed their outrage at the guard, who was not punished.

Steve Weiss met two other deserters from the 36th Division, Jim Dickson and Frank Turek. The last time Weiss saw Dickson, in Lyons, he was on his way with Clarence Weidaw to a medical station to seek treatment for psychoneurosis. The doctors accepted that Weidaw, who had gone silent after having nearly been burned alive by Germans, needed treatment. They returned Dickson to the division, whose court martial board convicted him of 'misbehavior before the enemy' and sentenced him to twenty-five years' hard labour. 'I remember running into Dickson at the DTC,' Weiss said, 'but we never had much in common. He was not trustworthy.' The two soldiers, who had deserted together on 28 October, avoided each other after their initial meeting at the DTC.

Frank Turek, who had deserted from the 36th on the same day as Weiss, had not been with Charlie Company long enough for them to have become friends. 'We talked a bit,' Weiss said. 'We did not know each other. What I remember about him, and that behavior I admired, was that he was able to directly assess, for whatever it was worth, that being up on the front was too dangerous [for him] to exist. I couldn't do that. I wavered.'

Once construction of the camp was complete, time passed slowly. There were no books to read, little work to do, no sports programme and no rehabilitation or counselling. Hard labour became anything but hard. 'It was calisthenics, marching, a lot of hanging around,' Weiss said. 'I was leading a bunch of fellows, maybe an hour or two a day, in calisthenics.' Some of the inmates, black and white, formed a choir to entertain the other prisoners. Their repertoire consisted of what Weiss called 'the typical songs that white and black would know'. One of the most popular was 'Swing Low, Sweet Chariot'. Black-white cooperation in the choir did not imply that relations between the races were relaxed. A Texan Weiss had known in the 36th Division resented sharing quarters with black prisoners. 'He was a tough hombre, tall, slender, a Gary Cooper type,' Weiss said. The Texan attacked one black prisoner, who fought back with all he had. The other inmates urged them on, and the guards ignored the fracas. 'It was a good slugfest,' Weiss said. 'I'd call it a draw.'

A majority of the inmates at the Loire DTC were black enlisted men, most of whom had been convicted for 'non-military crimes' like murder, rape, larceny, armed robbery, petty theft and other violations of civilian criminal law. Army records showed that black soldiers received harsher penalties than whites convicted of the same crimes, and they were more likely to be put to death. There were two methods for administering the death penalty in the army: shooting and hanging. 'Hanging is considered more ignominious than shooting,' an army circular of 8 July 1943 noted, 'and is the usual method, for example, in the case of a person sentenced to death for spying, for murder in connection with mutiny or for a violation of Article of War 92 [rape]. Shooting is the usual method of a person sentenced to death for a purely military offense, as sleeping on post.'

When courts martial condemned soldiers to death, someone had to execute the sentence. All American troops in the European Theater of Operations were trained to fire rifles, qualifying them for firing squads. Few if any had the skills of a hangman. With more men sentenced to hang than to be shot, a hangman had to be found.

The army's initial proposal was to hire a local executioner, but a French liaison officer at US Army G-1 (Personnel) Headquarters 'expressed doubt that a French national could be found as a hangman because hanging is not a method of execution in France'. Unwilling to employ the guillotine, the army searched for an American hangman.

On 16 September 1944, Lieutenant General John C. H. Lee, commander of the Services of Supply in Europe, appealed to all base section commanders for a hangman. His 'OUTGOING CLASSIFIED MESSAGE' stated:

> Classified confidential survey requested to be made of your Command to determine whether any EM [enlisted man] is a qualified hangman. If qualified EM is located, determine whether he will volunteer for such duty. Report name, rank, ASN [Army Serial Number], and organization of all volunteers by TWX [Teletype Writer Exchange] giving qualifications.

Corporal Eric Klick of the 4237th Quartermaster Sterilization Company volunteered, but he had merely witnessed rather than taken part in a few executions in the United States. Two other potential executioners stepped forward, Private Second Class John C. Woods of the 5th Engineer Special Brigade and Private First Class Thomas Robinson of the 554th Quartermaster's Depot. Lieutenant Colonel Allen C. Spencer of the Adjutant General's office wrote to General Lee that Woods's experience had been limited to his 'having been assistant hangman twice in the state of Texas and twice in the state of Oklahoma'. A simple check of Woods's claims would have shown that the electric chair had replaced the noose in both states: Oklahoma in 1911, when Woods was seven; and Texas in 1923, when he was twenty. Private First Class Robinson of New York City had been a baker. Nonetheless, the army appointed Woods its official hangman and Robinson his assistant.

While the generals wanted enlisted men to conduct the hangings, just as only enlisted men served on firing squads, the executioner needed a higher rank than buck private. This was quickly rectified, as Major General Milton A. Reckord, Theater Provost Marshal, wrote on 28 September: 'G-1 has promised to provide the grade recommended by me for the hangman in order to compensate him in a small measure for the work he is to perform. I am recommending the hangman be made a Master Sergeant and the assistant hangman a T/3 [Technician Third Grade].'

At a stroke, Buck Private Woods was promoted to Master Sergeant Woods, leapfrogging Private First Class (contradictory records refer to him as both PFC and Corporal) Robinson to outrank him by two grades.

In October, Woods and Robinson began a pilgrimage through France in an army truck lugging their portable scaffold on a trailer. Army policy directed that hangings for rape take place in the communities where the offence was committed. The victims and their families were invited to witness American military justice, proof that the the United States Army condemned mistreatment of the local population. When hanging in the community proved impracticable, executions took place in DTCs.

Woods and Robinson's peregrinations took them in mid-December to the Loire Disciplinary Training Center, where Steve Weiss was detailed to help erect the gallows for the hanging of two men. One had been convicted of murder, the other of raping a Frenchwoman. Both were black. The War Department's 'Procedure for Military Executions' of 12 June 1944 laid down guidelines for every aspect of putting soldiers to death by hanging, as well as 'by musketry'. Weiss, who had long conversations with hangman Woods, saw the forty-one-year-old sergeant as a 'small framed Texan from San Antonio, the bottom of his overseas cap resting at eye level, wearing a .45 automatic on each hip'. Not only did Woods sport the two .45s in matching holsters like a cowboy, he regaled Weiss with tales of hangings he had done. One of his claims was to have hanged more than three hundred men in fourteen years. This was an unlikely statistic for a man who had become a military executioner only two months before and whose prior record had included self-claimed assistance at only four hangings. When Weiss and the other inmates completed the scaffold at the top of a rise beside the camp, Woods made a show of testing the drop, the trap door and the rest of the equipment. To Woods's eye, everything was in working order.

What the army manual called 'the ceremony' began when a detail of MPs unlocked the condemned man's cage and put him in handcuffs. The other Death Row inmates erupted in fury, screaming and banging tin cups against their cages. The rest of the prisoners stood at attention beside their pup tents. The MPs led the condemned man through the camp and out the gate to the gallows. Weiss, who was standing nearby, watched the black soldier mount the steps. The commanding officer, the chaplain and the medical officer, as prescribed in the manual, were waiting for him at the top. With them was Sergeant Woods. The commanding officer read out the sentence and, as the manual required, asked, 'Do you have any statement to make before the order directing your execution is carried out?' The convict had nothing to say.

Sergeant Woods stepped forward holding out a hood that, according to the regulations, was 'of black sateen material, split at the open end so that it will come well down on the prisoner's chest and back. A draw string will be attached to secure the hood snugly around the neck.' Weiss wrote, 'Woods placed a black hood over the man's head, tied a rope around his neck and sprang the trap door.' The convict disappeared, the regulations stipulating that 'the lower portion of the scaffold will be covered to conceal the body of the prisoner from the spectators after the trap is sprung'. The medical officer, who was required to certify death, pulled aside the green canvas cloth. Weiss saw that the condemned man was still breathing. The doctor pressed a stethoscope to the writhing chest and shook his head. Weiss realized the man's neck had not broken, leaving him to writhe at the end of the rope unseen by everyone except Weiss and the medical officer. Fifteen minutes later, the body went still. The doctor listened again. The man had at last strangled to death.

The regulations stipulated a different procedure. 'Every precaution will be taken to prevent the protracted suffering of the prisoner,' Adjutant General A. E. O'Leary had instructed in an order of 8 July 1943. The 27 September 1944 directive from the Judge Advocate updated the order: 'In the event the construction proves to be defective, the rope breaks or the execution is not successful, the procedure will be repeated until the prescribed punishment has been administered.' No precaution had been taken to prevent 'protracted suffering', and the doctor did not suggest cutting the man down to be hanged again.

As with the French firing squad that shot the *milicien* in Alboussière, the hanging had been botched. Both experiences left Weiss sick. A few days later, he was ordered to assist at the hanging of the second black convict. Woods was no more efficient than he had been at the previous execution, and the second man also strangled slowly to death. Weiss gave Woods the benefit of the doubt, writing, 'Whether it was Woods' failure to kill quickly or whether the fault lies in hanging as a method, that allowed the condemned to linger inhumanely, may never be known.'

From D-Day in Normandy to the autumn of 1945, the Judge Advocate General's official history noted, seventy soldiers '– all enlisted men – had been executed in the European Theater of Operations'. Of this number, fifteen were white, and fifty-five, nearly 80 per cent, were black.

The bodies of the executed prisoners were sent to a First World War cemetery near Fère-en-Tardenois, where they were interred in unmarked graves. Their families were not informed how they died or where they were buried, another violation of procedure. Some families received a second telegram, following the announcement of death, saying the soldier had died of 'willful misconduct'. The War Department officially instructed, 'If the next of kin or other relatives of the deceased desire the body, the officer designated to execute the sentence will, if practicable, permit its delivery to them for burial.' In practice, this almost never happened. Weiss, already convinced that the army was unjust to the living, observed that it was unfair to the dead as well.

Journalists were not permitted to cover executions. Instructions from Brigadier General Ralph B. Lovett, Adjutant General for the European Theater of Operations, on 14 December 1944 to 'All Officers Exercising General Court-Martial Jurisdiction' were clear: 'Appropriate information will be made available to the press after an execution has been carried out ... Under no circumstances will any such release include the name of the soldier or identify the organization of which he was a member.' Reporting details of the execution of 'our boys' might have harmed morale on the home front.

* * *

Steve Weiss spent the winter of 1944–5 doing calisthenics and mulling over his crime. Despite his mental dislocation, the camp psychiatrist did not interview him. The Loire DTC offered the teenage soldier no psychological care, no rehabilitation and no training. Weiss had every reason to believe that he would spend the rest of his life there, because the army had not informed him that two days after his trial the 36th Division's judge advocates had reviewed his sentence. 'The sentence is approved,' Major Harry B. Kelton, the Adjutant General in General Dahlquist's headquarters, wrote on 9 November, 'but the period of confinement is reduced to twenty (20) years.'

After the court martial, the War Department sent a telegram to William Weiss to inform him his son was alive. 'When the telegram came that I was back on duty, there was a big celebration,' Steve Weiss remembered. 'All the family, the extended family, got together at the apartment and celebrated.' He was alive, no longer missing in action, no longer presumed dead. He was, however, a deserter. 'It didn't seem to be an issue,' Weiss recalled. The family's response to his desertion might have been shame, 'if I had a different kind of father'. Far from rejecting his son, the First World War veteran wrote to the War Department demanding a fair hearing for him:

I am writing to you in reference to my son, Pvt. Stephen J. Weiss, #12228033 … It will interest you to know what has been done to a boy who enlisted in the Army at the age of 18, who gave his blood to the Red Cross at various times, who saved every penny to buy bonds, who could not wait for his graduation from high school to sign up with the army.

After five months' training, he was sent overseas, arrived in Africa, fought at Anzio beachhead. We received two telegrams from the War Dept. that he was missing in action. He was attached to the Seventh Army, 143rd Infantry, and fought his way into the southern part of France.

While he was lost from his outfit, he attached himself with a paratroop outfit. In Yank magazine of November 12, 1944, the story will tell what 13 guerrillas did as he was one of a band of irregulars, soldiers who were lost from their outfit. They blew up bridges, hampered the German transportation. For days they were living in a hay loft; they finally attached themselves to the French Underground, with the Marquies [sic] of France, who looked after them. One day they came with French Police uniforms and dressed in them and were taken in back of the lines. If they were caught they would have been shot as spies. My boy reported to his outfit, sick, starved and in a state of psychoneurosis. The medics laughed at him.

They gave him a General Court Martial because he was away from his outfit and accused him of leaving his outfit in the line of duty under fire with the enemy; his sentence was handed out, life in prison. The reviewing authority reduced the period of confinement to 20 years and suspended the execution of dishonorable discharge until the soldier's release from confinement, forfeiture of all pay and allowances. He has been confined since Nov. 7, 1944. My desire is that you please take action in this matter as my wife is very sick and my father who is an old man, won't live much longer if this condition keeps on. If ever a boy of 18 was given a raw deal, my boy received same. He has had frozen feet and a skin infection; every letter we receive from him tells of what he is going through. This is the thanks he received for giving his all for his country. Please investigate this; all that I ask is that my boy be restored to duty and given a square deal. I am a Purple Heart man, having fought in the last war.

The Adjutant General, Norman B. Nusbaum, wrote to the Commanding General asking that 'this office be furnished information upon which to base a reply, together with a copy of the Staff Judge Advocate's Review, if available'. Although Weiss's father had not kept him out of the army in 1943, he was doing all he could to free him from prison in 1945. In his view, the army was treating the common soldier no better in this war than it had when it tried to deny his 77th New York Division the honours of victory in 1919. In the meantime, the military authorities were slowly addressing the case of Private Stephen J. Weiss.

Treating combat exhaustion through courts martial was proving to be a failure. Among the consequences for the armed forces was the steady loss of good soldiers to prisons, when psychiatrists might have rendered them fit for further service. Its effect on the men themselves was incalculable. Because the war had damaged their mental health as surely as bullets had their bodies, they needed treatment rather than punishment. Among the senior officers who began to understand this problem was Major General John E. Dahlquist, Weiss's former commander. Although he had demanded in 1944 that division courts martial bring in more guilty verdicts and harsher sentences for desertion, he had changed his mind by February 1945. At the time, his division was suffering more desertions than any other. On 27 February, he wrote to Lieutenant General Ben Lear, the Deputy Theater Commander:

> The problem of war weary men in the Infantry of the old divisions which fought in Italy is one of the most serious we have ... Medically, these men are alright [sic]; that is, the doctor is not able to find anything wrong with them. They do not qualify as exhaustion cases, therefore they cannot be reclassified for other duty under present regulations. Yet, these men should be removed from the Infantry because they have lost their 'zip' and tend to weaken the fighting spirit of the new men.
>
> ... For the past month, we have been gradually ridding our ranks of the bad exhaustion (psychoneurotic) cases and the war weary where possible. This must be handled very quietly however, for if any intimation that we were doing such a thing got noised around, our aid stations would be flooded with infantrymentrying [sic] to get reclassified.

Combat infantry commanders, like Dahlquist, were daily confronted with the reality that some men could not help breaking down. Rear echelon officers, however, were not ready to recognize the problem. Major General E. S. Hughes, on reading a copy of Dahlquist's letter, wrote to General Lear, 'I do not agree with General Dahlquist that men who have lost their zip should be removed from the Infantry. I think General Dahlquist over-stresses both physical and mental fatigue.'

Parts of the army apparatus were changing. The Army Medical Corps sent psychologists to Detention Training Centers in the spring of 1945 to discover from inmates themselves what made them desert. One visiting psychologist at the Loire DTC asked to examine Steve Weiss. Weiss recalled, 'I reported to a medium sized, dark-haired, scholarly man wearing glasses, in a small office in one of the camp's administrative buildings.'

The army psychologist asked him, 'How do you feel?'

'I don't know,' Weiss answered. 'I don't feel anything.'

This initiated a conversation in which, for the first time since he joined the army, Weiss discussed what he had done, what had been done to him and his impressions of both. The full story that he had kept inside, even at his court martial, came rushing out: his alienation from Captain Simmons, his experiences in combat, his service with the Resistance and the OSS, his sense of abandonment when he returned to the 36th Division, the deaths of his friends, his fears and his breakdown under artillery barrages. The psychologist was more sympathetic than Weiss had expected from someone who was also an officer. The psychologist put the young soldier's confusion into context, explaining that Weiss had turned his anger at Captain Simmons against himself. What Weiss ought to have done to preserve his sanity, he said, was to confront Simmons rather than run away. He said, 'Enduring prolonged combat left you with very little choice, hang tough another day or withdraw. You chose the latter, because it was no longer possible to tolerate that amount of anxiety.' For the first time since Weiss enlisted, someone understood him.

The psychologist said that Weiss's desertion did not mean he was a failure. 'Rather,' he explained, 'it seems that you simply tried to reduce the threat of being overwhelmed emotionally without having accumulated the required coping tools.' The vocabulary of psychological analysis was new to Weiss. The psychologist let Weiss absorb his words before concluding, 'Someone has made a horrible mistake.'

'What's that, sir?'

'You don't belong here. You belong in a hospital.'

At this time, officers at Disciplinary Training Centers reported that half the men convicted of desertion and absence without leave were suffering from 'combat fatigue'. At the Loire DTC, 90 per cent of the convicted deserters were, like Weiss, from infantry rifle companies. The psychologist who examined Weiss recommended that the charges against him be dropped and the young soldier returned to duty.

Weeks passed during which Weiss heard nothing. He endured the prison routine, slowly losing hope that he would ever leave. In April, President Roosevelt died. In May, the Red Army conquered Berlin, Hitler committed suicide and Germany surrendered. Some American troops in Europe were being prepared for service in the Pacific, where the war against Japan still raged. History was passing Weiss by. One day in June, a colonel from the Judge Advocate General's office arrived at the Loire DTC to interview Weiss. Having studied the psychologist's report, the colonel had to determine whether the young soldier merited a second chance. On him alone depended Weiss's future: another twenty years in prison or a return to the United States Army. Weiss waited in front of the colonel's desk, watching him study the case file. The colonel asked, 'Will you fight in the Pacific?'

Weiss stood at attention and answered, 'Yes, sir.'

It was the right answer. Weiss had not changed his mind about returning to the infantry. General Eisenhower had given an order, which every infantryman knew, that no soldier who had fought in two theaters of operations would be sent to a third. Weiss had fought in the Mediterranean Theater of Operations in Italy and southern France and in the European Theater of Operations in eastern France. He could not be forced to fight in the Pacific Theater. The colonel, who was apparently unaware of Eisenhower's directive, approved Weiss's release from prison and restoration to the service. Weiss was free, but he was not going to the Pacific. He was on his way to Paris. The last laugh was his.

THIRTY

For love there is no substitute. For the pangs of separation
there is no perfect cure, except winning the war and
getting home to the loved ones again.

Psychology for the Fighting Man, p. 342

AL WHITEHEAD WAS ANYTHING but a cooperative patient at the First
Hospital of the Seine Base Section in Paris. When a nurse attempted
to relieve him of his weapons soon after his arrival in early January,
he clung to his .45 calibre pistol and kept it under his pillow. He ate
little, months of short rations in the field having reduced his appetite.
Unable to sleep, even with tranquillizers, he paid someone in the
hospital to bring him 'calvadose [sic], cognac, or anything else he
could get his hands on'. A bottle of calvados arrived. Whitehead took
it to the kitchen, mixed it with a can of grapefruit juice and drank it
all. As he recalled later, he slept for three days.

When he woke, an American nurse informed him that, following
his recovery from appendicitis, he was shipping out. 'That was the
best news I'd heard since my arrival, so I didn't ask where – I assumed
it would be back to my division, since the pain in my side had
subsided.' The 2nd Division at this time, 11 January 1945, was still
holding the Elsenborn Ridge in Belgium. The army dispatched
Whitehead to the 94th Reinforcement Battalion, a replacement depot
in Fontainebleau south of Paris.

Whitehead arrived at the depot at 10 o'clock on the morning of 12
January, and he did his best from that moment not to fit in. He
resented being a replacement, waiting to be sent to a new outfit. The

2nd Division, he wrote, was where he belonged. However, he recognized he was suffering from 'combat fatigue and would have been a detriment to myself and others'. When a sergeant upbraided him for filling his cigarette lighter with petrol, as he had done at the front, he threatened to kill him. Most of the officers and non-coms at the depot, like the majority of replacement enlisted men there, had not seen action. Whitehead had been in combat continuously from D-Day through to 30 December 1944, and he had earned the Silver Star, two Bronze Stars, Combat Infantry Badge and Distinguished Unit Citation. As far as he was concerned, he did not have to take shit from anyone. And he didn't. When a young lieutenant issued him a bolt-action, First World War vintage rifle for guard duty, he told him to take the 'peashooter' and 'shove it up his ass'. Unable or unwilling to accept he was no longer on the frontlines, he demanded a Thompson sub-machine gun and a trench knife.

Steve Weiss resented being forced to return to Charlie Company, but Al Whitehead was enraged that the army was not sending him back to his old outfit. By January 1945, with a desperate need to replace men lost during the Germans' Ardennes offensive, the policy had changed. The army sent veterans who had recovered from wounds or illness wherever they were needed, not necessarily back to their old divisions. After six days at the depot, Whitehead was fed up and requested a three-day pass. The first sergeant, company commander and chaplain in turn told him to wait, and he cursed them all. As he stormed out the front gate, a sentry called out, 'Halt or I'll shoot.' Whitehead shouted back, 'Go to hell.'

When Whitehead marched out of the depot, he could have done what many soldiers in the rear had done before him: desert *to* the front. Steve Weiss's battalion commander, Lieutenant Colonel David M. Frazior, had done just that in 1943, when he left a military hospital in North Africa to rejoin his men for the invasion of Italy. At about the same time, three nineteen-year-old privates left their unit in Algeria to fight in Tunisia. After hitching rides to reach the front 800 miles to the east, they were confronted by Major John T. Corley of the 1st Infantry Division. Corley did not condone their offence, but he put them into battle. 'You certainly went AWOL in the right direction,' he said. (Corley was promoted to lieutenant colonel and given command of the 3rd Battalion of the 26th Infantry Regiment, indicating that his superiors at least tacitly accepted his decision to put the AWOLs into combat.)

A month before Whitehead walked off the base, an American Red Cross volunteer, Virginia von Lampe of Yonkers, New York, deserted her post in Paris. Although under military discipline, Miss von Lampe headed east in search of the 'Battered Bastards of Besieged Bastogne', as newspapers had dubbed the 101st Airborne Division. Surrounded by Germany's 47th Panzer Corps while the Battle of the Bulge raged, the men were running out of ammunition and food. Their acting commander, General Anthony McAuliffe, had just made history by rejecting the Germans' surrender demand with one word, 'Nuts!' A week before General Patton's Third Army broke through as promised to relieve Bastogne, Ginny von Lampe made it into the maelstrom. She explained to a bemused major inside the city, 'I've got some donuts for the fellows, Sir.' He held her as a spy, until she proved her nationality by naming the winner of the 1943 World Series – no great difficulty for a New Yorker – as the Brooklyn Dodgers.

Whitehead, walking through Fontainebleau to an American Service Club, had not considered deserting *to* the action. The 2nd Infantry Division, still fighting the Battle of the Bulge that January, was in such desperate need of veteran fighters that it would in all likelihood have taken him back. Instead, Whitehead went looking for a drink. MPs at the American Service Club refused him admittance, because he had no pass. As he left in search of a bed in a brothel, he thought, 'Well, it's death either way you look at it. If I go back up front with that damned peashooter I'll be killed, and if I go AWOL I'll be shot. I might just as well go to Paris and live it up.' That is exactly what he did.

In Paris the next day, 19 January, he checked into the hotel at 1 avenue Charles Floquet, where he had lodged while on train guard duty. The hotel proprietress hesitated to give him a room, until he assured her he had a thirty-day furlough and was not a deserter. His room had 'creaky furniture and faded wallpaper', and the bathroom was down the hall. He drank wine and cognac until he passed out.

Like many soldiers at the end of a long period of tension, he slept for several days. Sleep, though, did not mean peace. Recurrent nightmares of being under artillery barrages made him break into cold sweats. In the dreams, his younger brother, Uel, appeared helpless on the battlefield. After several days of bad dreams and intermittent sleep, he went out to eat.

He ordered soup and bread in a small café. The waitress, who had a pronounced limp, took pity on him and added some fried eggs and potatoes to his plate. He got into a game of craps with a Frenchman, winning several hundred dollars. (Whitehead, in the telling, never lost at gambling.) As he was leaving, two MPs came in. They asked him his division, and he said the 2nd. This was no longer true. Since leaving the hospital, he had been attached to the 94th Reinforcement Battalion at Fontainebleau. When the MPs demanded his pass, he proffered the .45 he had refused to surrender to the nurse. According to Whitehead, the MPs wanted no trouble with him and left.

The waitress gave him the key to her furnished room in a cheap hotel nearby and told him to wait for her there. She returned from work at about midnight. A romance and business partnership, similar to many others between American deserters and their French girl-friends in Paris, began that night. 'So we took up a life together,' Whitehead wrote, 'this little French girl with a limp and myself.' Her name was Lea, 'a pretty girl with dark hair, blue eyes, and a beautiful smile that played hide-and-go-seek with the dimples in her cheek.' She taught him rudimentary French, introduced him to museums and took him to movies and plays. It was the farm boy's first experience of a cultural life he had not known in Tennessee. When he wore old clothes that Lea gave him, no one took him for a soldier. 'By that time,' he wrote, 'I decided I was a civilian.'

In the café where Lea worked, he met other deserters. They, however, were German. One was an officer, 'a blond-haired, blue-eyed man of about thirty-five, with a combat hardened personality like my own'. The officer had served in Paris during the occupation, but he did not retreat with his division. Paris, five months after its liberation, was home to deserters from most of the armies in Europe. Living in an underground network of black market conmen, pimps, thieves and gangsters, ex-soldiers of a dozen nationalities evaded American Military Police and French gendarmes whose job was to hunt them down.

The presence of so many armed men outside military control wreaked havoc in post-liberation Paris. A US Army legal study noted, 'Of course, no black market could have grown in any liberated country without cooperation of American military personnel. Cupidity is not an exclusive characteristic of foreigners.' French civil courts were more lenient towards black market thieves than were American courts martial. The French Director of Military Justice denounced his country's military tribunals for 'unjustified leniency'. The problem for the US military was not punishment so much as finding the deserters who supplied American equipment to the black market.

Late one night, MPs raided the hotel where Al Whitehead was living with Lea. As they knocked on the door, Whitehead crawled out of the window clasping his .45 and waited on the ledge until they left. It was time to move. The couple rented an apartment the next morning. The modest flat, at the River Seine end of the tree-shaded avenue de la Motte Picquet, was less likely to be searched than a hotel. In the new place, he and Lea confided their life stories to each other. Her father had been a village policeman, who sent her to a convent to separate her from a young man she loved. She hated her father and had bitter memories of convent life. At the first opportunity, she fled to Paris. When the Wehrmacht occupied Paris, she became the mistress of a German officer. Whitehead admitted he had a wife in Wisconsin. Because he could not write to her without risking capture, Lea sent a letter in French to Whitehead's mother. Whitehead hoped his mother would tell Selma he was alive. Al and Lea survived on her earnings as a waitress, but it was not enough.

Another deserter advised Al he could make money with an American black market gang based in a hotel near the Arc de Triomphe. Al went to the shabby lodging off the avenue Foch to find them. A uniformed American soldier sat in the lobby, as if keeping watch. Whitehead was too cautious to speak to him, but he returned to the hotel the next morning. The same GI was there. Again,

Whitehead left without saying anything. When he paid a third visit, he said to the soldier, who was reading a newspaper, 'I guess you're going to tell me this is your day off.'

'Hell, no. I'm AWOL,' the soldier said. 'What are you going to do about it?'

'I'm going to join you.'

Whitehead met the gang's leader, a sergeant and 'ex-paratrooper; a short, stocky soldier with blond, curly hair'. The seven-man gang included veterans of the 82nd Airborne, 2nd Armored, and the 1st, 3rd and 8th Infantry Divisions. The sergeant, suspicious that Whitehead might be a police informer, put him to the test: he could join their gang if he stole an army six-by-six truck. Within minutes, Whitehead spotted an American supply truck stopped in traffic and climbed in. He pressed his .45 against the head of the driver, a black enlisted man, and said, 'Get out and run down to that red neon sign, and keep going and don't look back, or I'll shoot you right between your eyes.'

Whitehead passed, taking his place in one of many gangs of ex-soldiers terrorizing Paris. His group planned robberies in the sergeant's hotel room as if preparing military operations. Among the tools of their trade were French and US Army uniforms, a vast array of stolen weapons, forged passes and hijacked vehicles. Whitehead wrote that 'we stole more trucks, sold whatever they carried, and used the trucks to rob warehouses of the goods in them.' For the next few months, the gang used combat tactics to rob military warehouses. Like a night patrol, they stealthily crept behind guards and knocked them out cold before seizing the loot. Their activities spread to Belgium, where they stole civilian cars to sell in France.

Gangland operations gave Whitehead a bigger thrill than battle. One night, he and his accomplices spotted a blue Buick in front of a military headquarters. Its two stars made it clear the owner was an American general. The gang jumped into the car and forced the driver out. As they drove off, MPs fired at the Buick. Whitehead and the others shot back, but apparently no one on either side was killed. The car had so many bullet holes, though, that the thieves abandoned it. On other occasions, they disguised themselves as Military Policemen. Real MPs saluted them in the streets, and they had fun checking the passes of off-duty GIs. When they robbed cafés, they made their geta-way in jeeps with the gendarmes giving futile chase on bicycles.

The paratroop sergeant's gang was one of many rampaging through Paris in the months after the city's liberation. Like other deserter mobs in Paris, they were 'armed to the teeth with .45s, rifles and Thompson sub-machine guns'. Whitehead himself always carried his Colt .45 automatic plus three smaller .25 calibre pistols that he hid in his pock-ets and boots. The Paris press compared life in the city to Prohibition-era Chicago, and it put the violence down to the same cause: American gangsters. The army's Criminal Investigation Branch had to deal with a crime wave for which it was unprepared, as it noted:

> In the eleven month period from June 1944 (the month of the invasion) through April 1945, for example, C.I. agents handled a total of 7,912 cases, of which 3,098, or nearly 40 percent, involved misappropriation of U.S. supplies. Greater yet was the proportion of crimes of violence (rape, murder, manslaughter, assault) which supplied 44 percent of the C.I. work, leaving the remaining 12 {sic} percent for such crimes as robbery, burglary, housebreaking, riot and mutiny.

Time magazine reported, 'Informal G.I. markets have sprung up around the Arc de Triomphe, in the Place Pigalle, under the Eiffel Tower, in bistros, restaurants, around jeeps pausing in traffic jams.' Prices for goods the GIs provided were exorbitant. The Criminal Investigation Branch reported that a fifty-carton box of cigarettes went for $1,000 and twenty pounds of coffee for $200. The sellers were both deserters and serving soldiers, and the goods were invari-ably contraband. Betraying considerable pride in his audacity as a gangster, Whitehead wrote, 'We robbed every café in Paris, in all sectors except our own, while the gendarmes went crazy.' The gang showed up at cafés and ordered cases of cognac and champagne. After the owners loaded the boxes onto their jeeps, the men turned their weapons on them. They stole money from patrons and customers alike. Whitehead recalled raiding cafés regularly for three months without interference from the police. The gang robbed private houses, whose bedsheets and radios were 'easy to fence'.

Profits from stolen petrol, cigarettes, cognac, champagne, cars and weapons were making the gang's members rich men. Within six months, Whitehead reckoned his share at $100,000. This was probably an exaggeration. The Theater Provost Marshal's 'History: Criminal Investigation Branch' estimated that 'profits realized through illicit traffic in essential US Army goods had reached nearly $200,000'. That was the achievement of months of stealing by more than 150 officers and men of the 716th Railway Battalion until their apprehension at the end of November 1944. Whitehead could not send the money home, because the army had declared a 'Prohibition Against Circulating Importing or Exporting United States and British Currencies' on 23 September 1944. Whitehead hid his money under the bed at his and Lea's apartment, until he invested in a café and small hotel. He put both in Lea's name and let her manage them.

Al Whitehead prospered amid the highlife of underworld Paris, occasionally straying to brothels and often getting drunk. He ran into one soldier on leave from his old 2nd Division and escorted him to an establishment where he covered the prostitutes' fees for them both. The soldier, who seemed more envious than disturbed by Whitehead's clandestine life, said he was returning to the 2nd somewhere near the German-Czechoslovakian border. Whitehead wished he could go back as well, but the soldier warned he would be shot like Private Eddie Slovik had been the previous January. 'Well, buddy,' Al said, 'what difference does it make whether the Germans kill me, or our own army shoots me – I'm still one dead son of a bitch.' Nonetheless, he stayed in Paris.

The city that spring lost its allure for Whitehead. His gangland activities were dying down, and he had little to do. On 7 May, the radio announced the Allied victory in Europe. He recalled the announcer saying, '*Le guerre ce fini! Le guerre ce fini!*' Despite his seven months in Paris, Whitehead's French was rough at best. (The announcer may have said, '*La guerre, c'est fini!*') He went outside to take photographs of Allied flags flying in the streets that he included in his self-printed diary, and he went back to the apartment alone to brood. 'That day and night everyone in Paris and the rest of Europe was celebrating, but I just stayed in my apartment thinking about it all.' He wandered aimlessly through Paris, occasionally finishing along the banks of the Seine. At the end of June, he told Lea he wanted to go home. The only way to do that was give to himself up to the United States Army.

The easiest course for Whitehead to follow was to walk into any Military Police post. Instead, he said that he took a train to Czechoslovakia to find the 2nd Division. In Whitehead's absence, the division had fought its way into Germany and captured Leipzig. On 1 May, it moved into Czechoslovakia. Whitehead stated that he surrendered in Czechoslovakia, but the division had left for an encampment outside Rheims on 18 June. An army telegram of 13 December 1945 recorded Whitehead's 'apprehension in Rheims, France, on or about 1 July 1945'. On 12 and 13 July, most of the Second to None Division, including Whitehead's Headquarters Company, sailed from Le Havre to New York.

Whitehead nonetheless wrote that he reached the 2nd Division in Czechoslovakia and reported to a first sergeant, who ordered him to his former platoon. After a few days in the company stockade, he was transferred to the division's authority. Because Whitehead's last posting was with the 94th Reinforcement Battalion at Fontainebleau, it ordered him transferred there. With fifteen other handcuffed prisoners, charged with rape or murder as well as desertion, he rode in a truck to another stockade about six hours away.

Whitehead slept on the floor of a cell with fifty other inmates on the second floor of an old prison building. In the morning, guards moved him to a ground floor cell on his own. He wrote that he was 'restless' and angry at being shipped from one place to another. He decided to escape, chipping at the mortar between the bricks to dig his way out. He had not made much progress by six o'clock that evening, when he was led outside and put into a jeep that took him to Fontainebleau. There, the 9th Reinforcement Battalion locked him in a cell with three other prisoners.

'During his confinement at this depot,' the 'Informal Routing Slip' noted, 'Cpl. Whitehead gave no difficulty, performed his work satisfactorily and, in view of the fact that he was not apprehended, but gave himself up, there apparently was no reason to think he might escape.' While persuading guards that he was resigned to his fate, Whitehead was filled with resentment. The sentry assigned to watch him was Private First Class Robert C. Shumate, whom Whitehead referred to in his diary as 'a corporal'. A corporal himself, Whitehead may not have wanted to admit taking orders from a private. In the morning, Shumate ordered Whitehead and two other prisoners to clean a large house on the base. Whitehead hated Private Shumate. 'He had us emptying ash trays and waste baskets, all the while saying, "None of you guys are going to escape from me. I'm not going to be pulling your time." I thought, "You stupid jerk, in just about five minutes I'm going to show you just how stupid you really are."'

Whitehead saw himself as a battle veteran, 'a professional soldier', and looked down on Private Shumate as 'a punk recruit'. When Shumate ordered him to tidy an office in the house, he found blank passes on the desk and secreted them in his clothing. The passes would allow him to roam freely in Paris without trouble from MPs. The work completed, Shumate marched the three inmates to the mess hall for lunch. Whitehead sat outside, saying he was too sick to eat. Shumate threatened to shoot him if he tried to escape, and Whitehead answered, 'Why, I like it here ...' Shumate led the other two prisoners inside. The stockade report stated that Shumate in fact put Whitehead to work in the mess hall, while the other two prisoners were assigned to duty in the kitchen. 'Due to the relative location of the kitchen and Mess Hall in the M.P. billets,' the stockade report noted, 'it is impossible for one man to keep both rooms under observation at the same time.' At about 1.30 in the afternoon, Whitehead was either sitting outside, as he wrote, or working in the mess hall, according to the official report. The differing accounts agreed on one thing: a minute later, he escaped. According to the report, 'He did escape at approximately 1330 hours.' He did not go far, as he recalled: 'I rolled over behind the rock fence I was sitting on, and raking out a depression in the leaves, I camouflaged myself with them completely.'

Whitehead had some unexpected good fortune, as the report on his escape noted: 'On 23 July 1945, at about 1330 hours, four (4) members of the MP detachment were not present for duty for the following reasons: One man was called for by personnel for rectification of his records. One man was having a profile made, and two men were on pass.' Whitehead, without realizing it, could not have timed his flight better.

'A search for the escaped prisoner was begun immediately,' wrote First Lieutenant John F. Connolly of the 9th Reinforcement Depot's Provost Marshal's Office. 'The town was checked and also the railroad station. A vehicle covered route N 7 to Paris and returned by route N 5. No trace of the prisoner was found.'

Lying camouflaged in the leaves, while guards searched for him, he lay as still as a sniper the rest of the day. When bells tolled midnight, he crawled out of his lair. He removed his prison fatigues, under which he was wearing a full dress uniform. The camp offered no obvious route of exit, because high walls enclosed it on all sides. However, one wall surrounded a house that opened onto the road outside the camp. He climbed the wall and broke into the house. It was too dark inside for him to find the back door to the street, so he forced open a window and jumped out.

MPs and gendarmes patrolled the roads. Whenever a jeep approached, Whitehead leapt into a doorway. He found a hiding place near the railway station and waited until morning. At about seven o'clock, a passenger train readied to depart. Whitehead jumped on, although he had no idea where it was going. As he sat down, he asked a conductor the train's destination. The man answered, 'Paris.' That was good enough.

THIRTY-ONE

Each man, no matter how strong mentally and physically, has his limits beyond which the strongest will cannot drive him.

Psychology for the Fighting Man, pp. 320–1

ON 25 APRIL 1945, Soviet and American forces linked at the River Elbe. With Germany occupied, Adolf Hitler dead and the Third Reich vanquished, the Wehrmacht high command surrendered unconditionally in a schoolhouse at Rheims at 2.41 on the morning of 7 May. Hostilities officially ended the next night, when mass celebrations erupted throughout Great Britain. The *Daily Express* front page declared, 'Songs and Dancing All Night', while the *Daily Mail* trumpeted, 'All quiet till 9 p.m. – then London crowds went mad in the West end.' When Winston Churchill appeared outside the Ministry of Health in Whitehall, revellers sang, 'For He's a Jolly Good Fellow'.

John Bain did not sing along. The twenty-three-year-old veteran, having served king and country for nearly five years, was recuperating from the wounds that he had suffered in both legs near Caen in Normandy. His bitterness over time lost outweighed his relief that the European war had ended. While many aspiring writers in uniform expected the war to inform their poetry, novels and plays, Bain regretted the utter waste of his youth. Moreover, his two-and-a-half-year suspended sentence for deserting at Wadi Akarit in North Africa hung over him. If he committed another offence, no matter how minor, a court martial would add it to any prison term it imposed.

During his convalescence at the Winwick Hospital in Cheshire, he had twice gone Absent Without Leave. His first AWOL occurred when, wearing hospital blues and hobbling on crutches, he lingered in Manchester beyond the limit of his one-day pass. The delay resulted from a serendipitous encounter with a young Scottish woman in the Auxiliary Territorial Service, Maxie McCullough. 'All the other girls, they've all done it,' she told him. 'Lots of times, most of them. I'm the only one. I'm the only virgin. I hate it.' As desperate to dispose of her virginity as Bain was to assist, Maxie tried to sneak the drunk, crippled soldier through her barracks' perimeter fence. MPs caught him and sent him back to Winwick. The second AWOL was by design, when he kept an assignation with Maxie at a Manchester YMCA. The couple's quest for a private place to make love, in those days when hotels required proof of matrimony, ended with Bain's arrest again by MPs. Winwick's hospital commandant called him a 'Bolshie' and locked him for several days in one of the former mental asylum's padded cells.

Luckily for him, he was not prosecuted for going AWOL. The hospital commandant, tired of dealing with him, transferred Bain to the Cameron Highland Regiment's 'penitential stone barracks' at Hamilton in Scotland. Its convalescent depot, 'more military in character than medical', required him to wear military uniform and perform both physical training and sentry duty. His legs were healing, and he could walk without aid. However, immobility in his left ankle postponed his return to active service.

When VE-Day arrived, all he had to do was remain in the barracks until his discharge erased his suspended sentence. He chose not to wait, convinced that 'if I stayed in the army any longer I would be finished, I would become a brown automaton, a thing without imagination, intelligence, ambition'. Slinging a haversack with his few possessions over his shoulder, he deserted again.

'I really loathed the army,' he explained years later in a radio interview. 'I wasn't cut out for that sort of life. And I just up and left, because I couldn't hang around. It meant waiting something like six months to a year, waiting for my de-mob number to come up. And I thought, well, I joined up for the duration, so I'm off.' A truck driver gave him a lift to London's northern outskirts at Cricklewood. John Bain, no longer the dazed warrior who had 'floated' away from Wadi Akarit in 1943, knew what he was doing. He wrote, barely concealing his glee, 'I was on the run.'

With at least twenty thousand troops 'on the trot', Britain's major cities teemed with more deserters than during the war itself. Many had escaped their units at home, while others returned from hiding in France, Italy, Belgium, Holland and Germany. Most were British, but among them were Americans, Canadians and other Allied troops. The British government's decision to prolong wartime rationing and national identity cards well into the peace left men without documents ineligible for legal employment, food, petrol and clothing. Inevitably, they lived outside the law and turned to professional criminals for forged papers. Capture meant years in the 'glasshouse', military prison, for them and potential fines or up to six months' imprisonment for anyone who aided them. Among the many deserter 'accomplices' were Mr and Mrs W. Mackie of rural Devonshire, who received fines of $80 (around £20) each for harbouring two American soldiers in a stable near their cottage. The County Magistrates' Court imposed a $40 (£10) fine and two years' probation on the Mackies' nineteen-year-old daughter, Dorothy, who had a child by one of the Americans. The seventy-year-old father of a British deserter was placed on probation in 1945 for having hidden his son at home since the Dunkirk evacuation of June 1940.

Bain's eighteen-year-old sister, Sylvia, had moved to London from the family's house in Aylesbury. He went to her flat in Shepherd's Bush, where she was living with her boyfriend and another young couple. Her young man was a painter named Cliff Holden, whom she had met at the house of another painter, Lucian Freud. The couple were Peter Ball, a nineteen-year-old English lad with a thick beard, and a pretty French girl named Yvonne, who had escaped from occupied France to work in London as an artist's model. Sylvia introduced her brother to them as 'Vernon', the name by which he was known before he enlisted. It was a benediction of his return to civilian life.

Vernon ate macaroni cheese in the kitchen with Sylvia, Cliff, Peter and Yvonne. When Vernon and his sister were on their own, he confided to her that he had deserted. His immediate need was for civilian clothes and a place to sleep. Sylvia offered both, but he worried that her boyfriend might object to harbouring a deserter. 'Oh, Cliff won't mind,' she said. 'He's on the run himself. So is Peter.'

Bain was propelled into a vast network of anarchists, conscientious objectors and deserters. Underground London in the summer of 1945 included Bakunin-reading anarchists like Cliff, as well as criminal deserters living off stolen military supplies and robbery. Cliff burned Bain's Gordon Highlander uniform in the kitchen fireplace and lent Bain a dark blue shirt, 'a useful colour since it would not show the dirt'. Peter gave him a pair of sandals that would be good until autumn. He used Sylvia's clothing coupons and a little money he had to buy thick corduroy trousers. 'And so began the first summer of my desertion, a time of excitement, anxiety and tentative growth,' he wrote. He frequented the pubs of Notting Hill, Soho and Fitzrovia, most of them hangouts for other deserters and literary bohemians like Dylan Thomas. His reading, abandoned when he entered the ranks, resumed. It was as catholic and undirected as before: Rilke, Kafka, Baudelaire, Yeats and Auden.

Cliff got him a job at an unlicensed factory in a shed off the Euston Road, where they both worked for cash making dolls' heads for a former merchant marine named Pat. With his earnings, Bain rented a small flat in Chalk Farm. The companies that Pat supplied suddenly stopped paying him, leaving him unable to meet his wage bill. To compensate, he gave Cliff and Vernon 200 dolls' heads each. Without a job, Vernon could no longer afford his rent and, in his slang for running off without paying, 'did a bunk'. Pat invited him to lodge at his family's house in exchange for chores that included looking after his two small children.

His London life became aimless, public houses providing him with companionship of sorts. A man in a Charlotte Street pub helped him to find work as an electrician at the Coliseum Theatre. This required checking the bulbs in lanterns for the chorus to carry onstage and shining a spotlight on the lead performer during a crucial scene. One night, Bain's failure to remove a crimson filter from the beam gave the star 'a distinctly diabolical appearance'. No more adept with electricity than he had been with the safety of his Bren gun in Normandy, he fumbled with the light until it toppled over. Rather than wait to be fired, he slipped away.

It was not long before he moved in with a girl named Jackie in Covent Garden's Monmouth Street. She suggested his dolls' heads could earn him a little money, if she sewed bodies and dresses onto them. Bain the deserter could not approach reputable toyshops, so they sold a few dolls in a pub. Their takings paid for drinks, but not much else. Another money-making scheme that Cliff introduced him to was selling Indian perfume in a street market, again raising enough for beer rather than rent. One evening in a pub with Jackie, he had a better idea. He would take up boxing again, as a professional.

An ad in the *Boxing News* asked good amateurs who wanted to turn pro to contact a trainer named Willie Dalkin. Bain went to Bill Klein's Gymnasium in Fitzroy Square in search of Dalkin, who arranged a test bout for the eleven-stone six-pound (160 pound) middleweight. Bain turned up at Klein's basement gym the next day, with trunks, shoes and a mouth-guard he bought with borrowed money, to face a tough Irishman. Although out of shape from drinking and smoking, he deployed a strong left jab and a right-cross that nearly sent his opponent to the mat. Dalkin took him on.

Bain cut down his alcohol consumption and trained hard, sparring regularly at Klein's gym. 'Very good fighters trained there,' he recalled, 'but not the top rank. I sparred with Freddie Mills a couple of times, a painful experience.' (Mills became world light-heavyweight champion in 1948.) Bain fought his first professional match at Ipswich, a six-rounder against a more seasoned boxer from Romford. The bout began badly for Bain, who was knocked down in the first round. In the second and third, however, he took control. He won by a knockout in the fourth. The Boxing Control Board certified John Bain's professional status with a ten-shilling licence. Dalkin arranged two more six-round bouts that he won, admittedly 'against pretty poor opposition', and began grooming him for eight-rounders against better fighters.

One night in Charlotte Street's Fitzroy Tavern, Bain confessed to someone he had just met, 'probably boastfully', that he was on the run. His drinking companion warned him that London was a dangerous place for deserters. The police were on the lookout for them. He had just seen a whole café full of men in Soho dragged into the police's Black Maria.

About half of Britain's 20,000 deserters lived in London. Another 20,000 men conscripted to work in the coal mines had also deserted, a crime then equal to desertion from the army. One Labour Member of Parliament, Captain John Baird, appealed to the government to grant an amnesty to deserters. 'These young men had been failures in the war,' *The Times* summarized his Commons speech on 29 November 1945, 'but he was convinced that many of them would "make a better job if it" in peace-time.' His was a lone voice.

Police and some newspapers blamed deserters for what the *Daily Telegraph* called 'one of the greatest outbreaks of gangsterism since the end of the 1914–1918 war'. London's Commissioner of Metropolitan Police reported an increase of 34 per cent in indictable crimes over 1938, the last year before the war. Deserters were responsible for 9 per cent of crimes solved, a significantly high proportion for 20,000 men in a population of forty-seven million. A prominent criminal from Seven Dials near Covent Garden, Billy Hill, recalled that there was never a shortage of deserters for armed robberies. The violent crimes of a minority of deserters, rather than the post-war army's need for soldiers, forced the police to take action.

Police in late 1945 and early 1946 blocked off sections of London to trap deserters by picking up men with suspect documents. On 14 December 1945, more than two thousand London policemen, supported by British, American and Canadian MPs, launched 'Operation Dragnet'. While they cordoned off four square miles of London to check identity cards, burglars broke into a shop and 'hauled away a safe containing $800'. Of the 15,161 men dragged in for questioning, only four turned out to be deserters: an American officer and three enlisted men. London's *Evening Star* newspaper condemned police for using 'Gestapo' tactics.

* * *

If Bain had been in the West End during Operation Dragnet or in the Soho café during the police raid, it would have meant a second court martial and two terms in military prison. The man in the pub who had witnessed the Soho raid suggested Bain leave London. He was studying medicine in Leeds, which, he said, had fewer deserters and fewer police dragnets. Its cost of living was lower, and it offered an unexpectedly rich cultural life – theatre, opera, a good university and public lectures. Thinking it over later, Bain decided to move. It meant giving up professional boxing and his girlfriend. Jackie cried when he told her, but she refused to go with him.

Knowing that British Army desertion files listed a Gordon Highlander private named John Bain, he changed his name to Vernon Scannell. His memoirs provided no reason for the choice of Scannell. His son, John Scannell, explained over beer in one of his father's regular Fitzrovia pubs, 'He told me the name Scannell was pinched from a passport in a brothel just around the corner from here.' Vernon Scannell liked his new name, not least because it severed another tie to his father.

Leeds to most Londoners was nothing more than a bleak outpost of the industrial north, uninviting and uninteresting. 'At first,' Scannell wrote, 'I hated it.' The squalor of its Victorian slums shocked him, and the local accent 'seemed harshly alien, not hostile perhaps, but excluding'. The medical student he had met in London let him sleep on his floor, but he soon moved to 'a tiny attic room that leaked rain' in the Chapeltown district. The Chapeltown building turned out to house the North Leeds Communist Party, making it less than ideal for avoiding police scrutiny. In the freezing winter of early 1946, Scannell pictured Leeds as a battle zone with smog 'blinding the city in clouds of yellowish grey like poison gas', northeast winds 'waiting to bayonet you at street corners' and 'pavements booby-trapped with ice'.

Leeds, though, came to appeal to him more than London. He wrote that 'in a sense I was born there, or should I say I was re-born there ...' His rebirth was as a poet. 'I started to write poems on my own,' he recalled, 'and singularly bad they were too, though I did not at the time realize how awful. Life was charged with wonder and danger and promise.' He turned twenty-four on 23 January, unemployed, in hiding and without legal identity.

Kenneth Severs, a Ph.D. candidate at Leeds University and editor of the *Northern Review*, met Scannell in a pub. Through Severs, Scannell obtained an introduction to the university's celebrated Professor of English, Bonamy Dobrée. Dobrée took a liking to the twenty-four-year-old aspiring poet and arranged for him to sit in on university courses, including a tutorial with the literary critic George Wilson Knight. Dobrée and Knight gave his reading more direction: 'For the first time I read Faulkner, Dostoevsky, Forster. I discovered Hopkins and was slap-happy with syllables for weeks afterwards ...' While pursuing in earnest the education his enlistment had interrupted, he wrote poems, many about Leeds, and sent them to literary journals. He garnered the rejections that were every young poet's rite of passage, until the left-wing *Tribune* magazine published one. John Middleton Murry's *Adelphi* and the *Chicago Poetry Journal* followed suit, printing two each. Scannell wrote, 'I was delighted to believe, quite mistakenly, that this was the beginning of a successful literary career.'

Meanwhile, at Westminster, pressure to solve the 'deserter problem' grew. Labour Member of Parliament Woodrow Wyatt planned to table a question in the House of Commons in November 1946: 'To ask the Minister without Portfolio whether he will consider making arrangements to offer some inducement to persuade deserters who have been at large for more than nine months to return to their units.' When party whips prevailed upon him to withdraw a question that would highlight governmental failure to deal with the issue, Wyatt wrote to Prime Minister Clement Attlee: 'The position seems to be that some twenty thousand deserters are loose in the country without Identity Cards, Ration Books, etc., and are therefore virtually outlaws ... It is obviously a situation which no society can tolerate indefinitely.'

The Minister of Defence, Albert Alexander, told Parliament on 22 January 1947 that deserters who surrendered before 31 March would have 'any mitigating circumstances taken into account when their cases are determined'. This fell short of an amnesty, and the War Office was forced to disclose that only 1,158 men out of 20,000 had turned themselves in during the 'leniency period'.

Artists Herbert Read and Augustus John, with writer Osbert Sitwell and others, formed the Deserters Amnesty Campaign. In a letter to *The Times*, they reminded readers of 'the almost total failure of the "surrender scheme" announced by the Minister of Defence last January'. They appealed for an amnesty: 'We are convinced that the only real solution to the deserter problem, from both the practical and the human points of view, is the granting of a general amnesty to these men – before they drift into becoming full-time criminals ...' At this time, the prime minister's office noted that, far from deserters turning themselves in, more than seven hundred men a month were adding to their numbers with fresh desertions.

Vernon Scannell's loose arrangement with Leeds University entitled him to membership of the Student Union, where he took advantage of its sports facilities to train and join the boxing team. He became Northern Universities Champion in three weight divisions: welter, middle and cruiser. His status as a professional remained secret, lest he be disqualified from amateur competition.

Although boxing and literature studies took up much of his time, he had little money and led a lonely existence in his attic room. His ever-present fear of capture, 'an overshadowing presence that darkened my consciousness', revealed itself in his poem 'On the Run':

> If sleep should come, the stairs might thunder,
> The door burst open, boots lam bone
> And split the skin, manacles' anger
> Bite wrists and scratch the brain:
> It might be fact or dream exploding.
> Either way, it could happen.

One Sunday afternoon, while Scannell read *Crime and Punishment* in his attic, it did happen: 'There was a sudden banging of heavy feet on the stairs and the next moment my door burst open and two men in plain clothes charged into the room, grabbed me and pulled me to my feet.' One of the policemen said, 'We know all about you.' Bain spent the next 'five miserable days' in a 'cell with lavatorial tiled walls and a wooden bunk and three grimy-looking blankets'. Military guards took him by train to Aberdeen, where he was put back into uniform in a cell with two other deserters.

The junior officer assigned to defend him at the court martial told him his only option was to plead guilty. Bain wrote to Bonamy Dobrée and George Wilson Knight in Leeds. Both teachers sent books and offered to testify in his defence.

When Bain appeared before a court of three officers, his counsel entered a guilty plea and asked the court to take into consideration his client's combat record in North Africa and Normandy. The court permitted the defendant to speak, and Bain explained that he had found his nearly five years in the army 'both in and out of action, totally destructive of the human qualities I most valued, the qualities of imagination, sensitivity and intelligence'. He had no choice, he said, but to escape.

The President of the Court, reading in his notes that the defendant hoped to become a writer, asked him what he wrote. 'Poetry,' answered the defendant. He later recounted the court's reaction: 'And they looked at each other with a wild surmise and said, "Well, send him to a psychiatrist. He's clearly mad."' The psychiatrist's report led to his transfer to Northfield Military Hospital, a mental asylum, near Birmingham. The confinement would lead to the poem 'Casualty – Mental Ward', which included,

> Something has gone wrong inside my head.
> The sappers have left mines and wires behind,
> I hold long conversations with the dead.

He remained there for many weeks, during which he twice saw a young captain serving as the unit's psychiatrist. At their second session, the psychiatrist told him, 'If you are ill – and I don't think you are – then this is the last place to get well.' He referred Bain to a Medical Board, which would probably release him. The captain advised him to 'keep your nose clean in the meantime'. He did as he was told and waited. 'After a short spell,' he wrote, 'I was discharged, quite honourably, suffering from "an anxiety neurosis".'

His freedom, so long sought, was tinged with guilt. He wrote,

> The shades of all those men who had done nothing worse than I and were now serving long prison sentences rose to accuse me. But they were not my only accusers. I had survived a war in which many men, some of them my friends, and all with as much to live for as I, had been killed; they lay in the sands of Libya or in the orchards and meadows of Normandy and, however clean they kept their noses, no Board would give them their discharge. They, too, accused, and they accuse me still.

A former army colleague told him about the captain they had seen desert from the Mareth Line in 1943. During an artillery barrage, John Bain as company runner had 'looked to see how he [the captain] was getting on, and he wasn't there. He deserted. He'd gone back. He ran away in the middle of an attack. I never knew what happened to him.' Now, he learned that the captain had been promoted to major and was still serving. If he had any qualms about the inequities of military justice that sent privates to the Mustafa Barracks and awarded promotions to officers, they vanished.

THIRTY-TWO

They may not realize it, but often the truth is they have
become homesick. They are longing for those upon whose
presence and affection they have long depended. They
want their wives or mothers.

Psychology for the Fighting Man, p. 334

WHEN ALFRED WHITEHEAD'S TRAIN ARRIVED from Fontainebleau
at the Gare de Lyon on 24 July 1945, he took the Metro, which he
called the 'underground streetcar,' to his apartment in the avenue de
la Motte Picquet. In a full dress uniform and with stolen passes from
the prison office, he had little to fear from Military Police in post-
war Paris. He did not know, however, what to expect from Lea.
When she opened the door, they stared at each other in silence.
Something had changed in the month since he left. It took him a
moment to realize what it was. Another American soldier had moved
in.

She whispered to him to wait in the bathroom, while she told her
new lover to leave because her husband was coming home. Whitehead
considered killing them both. His mind, as already evidenced by his
contradictory decisions to surrender and escape, was confused.
Jealousy demanded revenge, but murder would send him back to the
stockade and probably the gallows. He waited in the bathroom.
When the other GI left, Lea gave Al a glass of wine. He had nothing
to say to her. 'I hadn't been faithful to my wife,' he thought, 'so I had
no room to talk. But I never did forgive her.' After downing more
wine, he fell asleep in her bed.

The summer of 1945 saw Paris gradually returning to normal. Although the black market provided some illegal bounty to the city's residents, regular supplies of basics were reaching the city from the country and harbours. Bands of deserters were still on the run, but the army had more men available to hunt them down. Whitehead, although he carried concealed weapons, avoided his old gang. He drank more, gambled and sought the company of other women. His dissolute life made him consider, as other deserters had, joining the French Foreign Legion. The Legion asked no questions and, at the end of five years' service, allowed its veterans to resume life with a new identity. 'But,' he wrote, 'I had grown to hate war and was tired of killing.'

On 12 December 1945, a freezing day in Paris, Whitehead was drunk again. He missed Selma, pitied himself and wanted to go home. Walking back to the apartment, he made a decision. He changed out of his civilian clothes, put on his US Army dress uniform and wrote a farewell letter to Lea. Outdoors, he attracted a policeman's attention by shooting out streetlights with two ivory-handled .25 automatics. The gendarme approached with weapon drawn and ordered the American to raise his hands. 'I never put my hands up for the goddamned German Army,' Whitehead claimed to have shouted, 'and I sure as hell am not going to put them up for a two-bit French cop.' The policeman attempted to disarm him, but Whitehead claimed he turned over only one pistol. They could negotiate for the other at the station.

The gendarme took him to the police post at 69 rue de Fondary in the Fifteenth Arrondissement. American MPs arrived soon afterwards. Whitehead's account of his arrest differed significantly from that of the MPs who took custody of him. He contended that he had asked the French police to call for the MPs, who came and offered to release him. The MPs' report stated clearly that the French police apprehended him and called the American authorities on their own initiative. Whitehead contended that he gave a third .25-calibre pistol to the MPs as a souvenir. While driving in the jeep with them to their headquarters, he said he produced two more pistols from his boots.

He wrote, 'I can still see their shocked faces.' Nothing in their report mentioned the additional weapons. Whitehead went further, claiming he produced yet one more .25 automatic for the 'desk sergeant' when he arrived. By Whitehead's count, he had given over six automatic pistols to French and American police. The official police report said he had only one pistol with three bullets.

Whitehead said he told the gendarmes his name was Joe Givodan, but identified himself immediately to the MPs as Corporal Whitehead. Corporal Richard S. Capone, Company C, 787th MP Service Battalion, provided another version:

> I questioned the soldier and he said his name was George and handed me a pass (class 'B') which read George Wasko. The French police turned over to me a 25 Cal. Pistol, Werk Erfurt, Serial No. 2993 and a clip with 3 rounds of ammunition.
>
> I frisked the soldier and found dog tags bearing the name of Alfred T. Whitehead and also a set of Officers dog tags bearing the name of Nixon. I asked him how long he was AWOL and he continued to lie and to say that Whitehead was his buddy. When I asked the soldier his serial number he seemed at a loss of an explanation.
>
> We proceeded to the Booking Station at No. 8 Rue Scribe and found the man to be Alfred T. Whitehead. I turned the soldier over to the Duty Officer Lt. Ball. Then I returned to Patrol Duty.

This account contained nothing of the bravado with which Whitehead characterized his behaviour, producing pistols like a magician and bravely rejecting MPs' offers of release. 'They were still telling me to go back to my outfit,' he wrote, 'and I was still drunk and telling them I had overstayed my leave.' The MPs, on the contrary, appeared from the record to have behaved professionally. They locked him up at eleven o'clock that night. In the morning, the Judge Advocate General's Office preferred charges against Whitehead for violation of Article of War 61 in having been Absent Without Leave for 304 days. If the war in Europe had not ended in May, the charge would have been desertion with the possibility of a death sentence.

First Lieutenant Julius Hochstein of the Judge Advocate's Office assigned First Lieutenant Eugene T. Owen to investigate the charges on 17 December. Two days later, Owen submitted his report:

> Witnesses requested by him [Whitehead], and other witnesses whose expected testimony was not fully and satisfactorily indicated in statements attached to the charges … were thereafter, if reasonably available, examined by me in his presence. He was allowed to examine and cross-examine witnesses as he wished, with my assistance, and make such statements and arguments as he wished in his own behalf, after due warning as to his rights and privileges.

Asked on a form whether he had any 'reasonable ground for belief that the accused is, or was at the time of any offense charged, mentally defective, deranged or abnormal,' Lieutenant Owen answered, 'None.' In the statement, 'In my opinion he _____ be eliminated from the service,' Owen wrote, 'should.' He completed the sentence 'I recommend _____' with 'A General Court Martial.' On 22 December, Lieutenant Hochstein referred the charges for trial.

Whitehead made no mention of Lieutenant Owen or the fact that Owen allowed him to call witnesses in his defence. Instead, he complained of mistreatment by officers he said had placed him in solitary confinement for fourteen days on bread and water because he would not answer their questions. While awaiting trial and looking out of his cell window, Whitehead wrote, he saw Lea walking towards the prison, threw her a note warning her not to visit him and saw MPs bring her inside. When he pretended for her safety not to know her, he claimed she left in tears.

Whitehead wrote that he spent Christmas alone in a punishment hole that was only four feet by six feet, because he refused to answer an officer's questions. He did not state what the officer wanted to know. At the end of fourteen days, the officer threatened him with a third week in the hole if he didn't tell him everything, whatever that may have been. Rather than return to solitary, Whitehead wrote, 'I was hustled into a courtroom like a bum instead of a soldier: no bath, unshaven, and without being given a comb for my hair.' He remembered the court martial taking place in late December, but court records indicated it began on the morning of 2 January 1946.

As in the court martial of Steve Weiss, no enlisted men sat on the court martial panel. The senior officer among the six judges was Major George F. Shaw of the Signal Corps. For reasons not specified in the court martial transcript, the Trial Judge Advocate, his assistant and the defence counsel were excused. A second Assistant Judge Advocate, Lieutenant Sheridan H. Horwitz, and assistant defence counsel, Lieutenant Harry Cohen, argued the case. Lieutenant Horwitz introduced two exhibits for the prosecution, the Morning Reports of 19 January and 23 July 1945. The first listed Corporal Whitehead as AWOL and the second as having 'escaped confinement.' He asked whether defence counsel agreed to the stipulation that 'the accused, Corporal Alfred T. Whitehead, returned to military control of the United States on 12 December 1945.' The defence agreed, and the prosecution rested.

The defence case made no opening remarks to the court. Lieutenant Cohen said, 'The accused having been advised of his rights in this case elects to make an unsworn statement.' Captain David L. Sprechman, as the court's 'Law Member' who had had legal training, delineated Whitehead's three options: a sworn statement, which allowed cross-examination by the prosecution and the court; an unsworn statement, which excluded cross-examination but carried little weight with the court; and remaining silent, for which 'no one in this court can comment on your failure to take the stand and your failure to take the stand will not be considered as an admission of guilt'. Sprechman asked the accused whether he understood the choices. Whitehead answered, 'I think so, sir.'

Whitehead stuck by his decision to make an unsworn statement. He took the stand without taking the oath, and only Lieutenant Cohen questioned him. His short testimony covered little more than a page of the court martial transcript. Cohen asked his name, military organization, whether he was the accused in the case and his date and place of birth.

Cohen continued, 'What happened when you were four years old?'

'My father got killed, sir.'

'And what did you do?'

'I went to work on a farm.'

'How much schooling have you had, Whitehead?'

'Not any.'

'Where did you work?'

'On a farm for Walter K. Parnell.'

The next questions established he had not been prosecuted for any criminal offence as a civilian and had been in the army for three years.

'Have you had any combat, Whitehead?'

'Seven months.'

'How many campaigns have you been in?'

'I been in, sir? Normandy to Germany, sir, about four or five.'

'Were you wounded?'

'Well, yes, sir, I was.'

'How many times?'

'Twice.'

'And what did you do when you were wounded?'

'I kept on fighting. I knew I'd get it if I stayed there.'

'Have you ever been court martialed before, Whitehead?'

'No.'

'Is there anything else you would like to tell the court about yourself?'

'No, sir, I do not.'

The court excused the witness, and Lieutenant Cohen declared, 'The defense rests.'

The court reporter did not record the defence's closing argument, and the Assistant Trial Judge Advocate did not make one. The court retired briefly. When it returned, Whitehead stood to attention. On the charge and both specifications, the verdict was 'Guilty.' The court deliberated a moment before pronouncing sentence. The maximum penalty for violation of Article of War 61 was life at hard labour. The court was lenient, declaring that Whitehead 'be dishonorably discharged the service, to forfeit all pay and allowances due or to become due, and to be confined at hard labor at such place as the reviewing authority may direct for five years'.

Whitehead wrote that the court did not afford him the opportunity to explain his exhaustion and his desire to return to the 2nd Division rather than to a new division as an unknown replacement. The court record, however, made it clear that he could have said anything he wanted. Moreover, he was fortunate the prosecution did not ask him how he survived in Paris during his two periods of desertion. His criminal activities, as recounted in his memoir, would have earned him the death penalty. At 10.25 that morning, the court 'proceeded to other matters'.

EPILOGUE

These are real battle casualties, just as much as if they had lost a leg.

Psychology for the Fighting Man, pp. 352

AFTER HIS PARIS COURT MARTIAL, Whitehead served time in the Delta Disciplinary Training Barracks in the south of France and in federal penitentiaries at Fort Hancock, New Jersey, and at Fort Jay and Green Haven, New York. When the army remitted half of his five-year sentence, he walked out of Green Haven with $25 and a brown tweed suit on 17 May 1948. His wife, Selma, was waiting for him. His parole terms could not have been more irksome: to work as a farm labourer for the stepfather he had joined the army to escape in 1942. Two years later, he used the skills he had mastered cutting GIs' hair during the war to become a barber. Al's Barber Shop opened sometime in the early 1950s in the Gilsville Family Center on Sam Davis Road in Smyrna, Tennessee. He and Selma moved into a small house on Maple Street and raised three children.

Whitehead felt aggrieved about his dishonourable discharge, which he thought was unfair to a soldier who had fought and been decorated. He believed that, by proving he had been wounded, he could convince the authorities his desertion had its origin in his medical condition. In March 1949, Dr R. C. Kash of Lebanon, Tennessee, examined him and wrote,

I find a one-inch scar over a depression from which bone appears missing at the right front-parietal region of the skull. Also there are some scars on the dorsum of the right hand at the articulation of the metacarpal and first phalanx of the right index finger, said to have been received in a bayonet engagement.

These scars are neither old nor recent. I think it is reasonable to believe that they are of approximately four or five years' duration.

In response to Whitehead's appeal that year to the Pentagon's Clemency and Review Board, the Board reviewed his file. In his favour, it noted, 'Applicant had an otherwise good record. He landed in France on D-Day and fought in France, Belgium and Germany.' On the other hand, the Board's report commented, 'He claims to have been twice wounded but to have kept on fighting ... There is nothing of a medical or psychiatric nature in the file to excuse his conduct.' The fact that he was carrying a false identity card and a concealed weapon when French police apprehended him in December 1945 also counted against him. The Board recommended that 'the case *be not* reviewed by the Army Board on Correction of Military Records for the reason that there is no record of error or injustice in the case'.

Eighteen years later, a lawyer with offices in the same shopping centre as Al's Barber Shop, C. Alex Meacham, took up Whitehead's case. Meacham, following President Jimmy Carter's January 1977 amnesty for Vietnam War draft evaders, wrote to the White House on 14 March 1977:

I am writing on behalf of a very good friend of mine, Mr. Alfred T. Whitehead, a copy of whose Enlisted Record and Report of Separation-Dishonorable Discharge is enclosed herewith.

Mr. Whitehead was in combat in World War II from December 1943, until December 1944. During this time he was wounded twice, and after the second wound his army records and medical records were lost or misplaced. Through an unfortunate misunderstanding, this led to his being counted as AWOL and he was Court-martialed and given time in Military Confinement. At that time, he also received a Dishonorable Discharge from the army.

... He has never been able either to get copies of his records or the case re-opened. He feels strongly that he was wrongfully Court-martialed and sentenced when his true records were not available to the court ...

... I am requesting that due consideration be given to clearing Mr. Whitehead's record.

Meacham's letter was disingenuous at best, although certainly based on information Whitehead had supplied. Whitehead apparently neglected to tell Meacham that he simply ran away from the Replacement Depot at Fontainebleau. Rather than return to the 2nd Infantry Division on the frontlines, he went to Paris. He did not seem to mention to his lawyer, as he wrote in his privately printed memoir of 1989, that he stole Allied supplies, shot at Military Policemen and escaped from a stockade. If he had, Meacham could not have written that Whitehead's seven months' absence from military duty was the result of 'an unfortunate misunderstanding'. However, the Army Board for Correction of Military Records upgraded Whitehead's discharge from 'dishonorable' to 'general' on 27 October 1978. Whitehead's son, Alexander T. Whitehead II, wrote, 'The day it arrived in the mail was only the second time in my life I ever saw my father, while sober, cry. The other was at the funeral of his mother.' Although a 'general' discharge ranked below 'honorable', it was probably more than Whitehead, if he had told the full story of his desertion, was entitled to. The Board did not reverse the guilty verdict.

His former comrades in the Indianhead Division did not forget him or his desertion. He attempted to take part in one of their annual reunions in Columbus, Georgia, in 1970. Division veteran Jesse Brode later wrote that Whitehead 'was told to leave as he was not a member and could not become a member'.

In the spring of 1986, forty years after his court martial, Al Whitehead flew alone to Paris. 'Everything was different,' he wrote. 'Where the old hotels once stood, there were apartment houses. I was drinking and felt like I'd walked twenty miles trying to find a hotel like the ones I knew.' The hotels Whitehead remembered were more like rooming houses, where people lived and ate year round. Most had long since disappeared. Whitehead had also changed. Aged 64, he was not the bold young soldier discovering the city of light. His hair and thick moustache had turned white. Paris's black markets and American MP patrols had long since disappeared, and the modern city so disoriented Whitehead that he returned to the airport and slept on a bench in the terminal.

When he woke up in Charles de Gaulle Airport, he went back to Paris in search of familiar haunts. He changed dollars into francs, no longer enjoying the black market rate, and wandered from one street to another. As the sun was setting, a taxi took him to the Seventh Arrondissement café where he met Lea in 1945. He wrote, 'I walked inside and stood there for a moment, the memories rushing back to those days long ago.' He got drunk again and asked the woman behind the bar whether she knew of a room where he could sleep. She walked him outside, where a young, dark-haired man was waiting. The three of them went to a squalid room on the top floor of an old building. Whitehead, convinced his companions were a prostitute and her pimp, said he wanted a bed but not the girl. He offered money to the man, who threw it in his face. Whitehead the old soldier, black marketeer and ex-convict felt his wartime anger rising. 'That's when I got tough with them,' he wrote. 'He backed off and we went downstairs with them in front.'

In a nearby alley, two juvenile delinquents spotted him. He was an obvious target, drunk and, in his own words, 'a harmless old Joe with my white moustache and several days snow white beard on my face'. The thieves would not have expected a sixty-four-year-old American tourist to resist, but Whitehead squared off with his back against the wall to avoid an attack from behind. In his imperfect French, he shouted that he had 'kicked the shit out of bastards like them in the war, and by God I could do it again!'

When the first youth threw a punch, Whitehead seized his arm, threw him over 'commando style' and broke his arm. The second youngster pushed him into the wall. Whitehead grabbed the boy's face and rammed his knee into his groin. He reached for a pocket-knife he usually carried, and the youngsters ran away. Whitehead hid under a van for ten minutes until he was certain they would not be back with reinforcements. He took a taxi to the airport and flew home. It was his last trip to Paris.

Whitehead returned to West Yarmouth on Cape Cod, Massachusetts, where he had moved Al's Barber Shop from Tennessee a few years earlier. One of his customers, Thomas Lindsay, remembered meeting him in 1991. 'I listened to his stories while in the chair,' Lindsay wrote, 'and bought a copy of his book which he had stacked by the door.' The memoir did not conceal his desertion, his black market career and his prison record from the customers in his shop.

Whitehead died on 26 January 1996 in Cape Cod, five days before his seventy-fourth birthday. His family buried him at Coon Prairie Cemetery in Westby, Wisconsin, not far from the family farm where as a young recruit he had courted Selma Sherpe. It was the only place, during his stays with Selma and her family, he had ever known happiness. His son recalled, 'For years Dad just went through the motions of being alive. He never laughed, rarely smiled and was always distant in mood.' The son's regret for his father was that he 'died a long time ago in the fields and hedgerows of France'.

In February 1953, shortly after he was returned to office as prime minister, Winston Churchill declared a general amnesty for wartime deserters as part of the celebrations for the coronation of Her Majesty Queen Elizabeth II. Deserters hiding in Britain were free to take up legal occupations, and those overseas could at last return home. The post-war 'manhunt' that had preoccupied the civil and military police for more than seven years was over.

The amnesty came too late to affect Vernon Scannell, who had been discharged as medically unfit and had returned to Leeds. After nine months of study there, he moved to London and then to various small towns in England. His colourful post-war career took him from boxing with a travelling fair to teaching at minor public schools. At one prep school, Hazelwood in Limpsfield, Surrey, his students included a future editor of *The Times*, Simon Jenkins. Jenkins recalled his teacher with affection, writing that he imparted two important messages: 'One was the supremacy of boxing and the other of poetry.' None of his students knew that he had been a professional boxer or a published poet. Jenkins added, 'All he communicated was a vague and distant preoccupation, as of a man with much to hide and only a little to give, even if that little was infinitely precious. He was out of John Le Carré.'

Vernon Scannell married Josephine Higson in 1954 and had six children. After one of their infant sons died, the marriage gradually fell apart. His novels, poems, reviews and poetry readings produced barely enough money to provide for his large family. His son John remembered him as a man who enjoyed drinking to excess and having punch-ups well into his sixties. His desertion from Wadi Akarit, while known to his wife and children, was something he did not publicize in either his poems or early volumes of memoirs. Then, in 1987, he wrote the full story in *Argument of Kings*. As part of the publicity for the book, BBC Radio's prestigious *Desert Island Discs* invited him to discuss his work and choose the eight pieces of music he would take to his imaginary isle.

Scannell's voice in the BBC recording sounded deep and distinctly highbrow, more Oxford don than working-class kid from Buckinghamshire who had spent more time in the ring than the classroom. The vocabulary was redolent of easy familiarity with the classics of prose and poetry. The combination of boxing and poetry was, he admitted, 'a bit of an odd mixture or so people think. There were other boxer poets. John Keats, although he wasn't a boxer, was a considerable fighting lad. Certainly Byron was. He had a bare-fist champion in his entourage and used to spar with him ... T. S. Elliot took it up. And Bernard Shaw.'

Michael Parkinson, one of the BBC's most astute interviewers, asked him about his desertion. Scannell described the scene at Wadi Akarit the morning the Seaforth Highlanders went through the Gordons' lines to attack the Roumana Ridge. 'They were easy targets for the German machine gun fire,' he said.

They took the positions, and we moved up. It was by this time light. The sun was up. There were corpses lying all over the place, our own people who earlier had just been going past us and exchanging insults. To my unbelieving horror, I had not seen this before, my own people, my own friends went around looting the corpses, taking watches and wallets and that sort of thing. Off their own people ... Suddenly, I was sick of the whole thing and just turned around and walked away. And nobody stopped me.

After their eight musical selections, guests on *Desert Island Discs* were asked which books, apart from Shakespeare and the Bible, they would like on their island. Scannell chose a five-volume edition of English poetry and the collected poems of W. H. Auden. The final item permitted on the island was a luxury. For Scannell, there could have been nothing else: 'A mass of A-4 writing paper and something to write with.'

Discussing his Wadi Akarit desertion for the first time in public affected him more than he had expected. His son John, with whom he was staying in London, remembered that day:

I was meant to meet him here [in the pub] afterwards, and he didn't show up. He disappeared for the entire afternoon. My father never dramatized anything. He was absolutely honest. It [discussing his desertion] seemed to trigger off exactly the same event. He walked from the studio, and simply turned up about three hours later at his publisher's, Jeremy Robson's, place: 'I don't know how I got here.'

The ex-deserter received official vindication as he grew older. The Royal Society of Literature elected him a Fellow in 1960, and he won the Heinemann Award for Literature a year later. The Queen granted him a civil list pension in 1981 for services to literature, and the Imperial War Museum sponsored a ceremony for the launch of *Argument of Kings*. His was never an easy life. He moved frequently and battled the British Inland Revenue over unpaid taxes on income from readings of his poems. He spent a few months in Brixton Prison for drunk driving, a severe sentence that was especially harsh because the magistrate did not like him stating his profession was poet.

Vernon Scannell, who had run three times from the armed forces and wrote often of the military's dehumanizing impact, never let go of his war years. He relived them in his poems and became a champion of other Second World War poets, who were in his view as good as those who emerged from the First. The finest of them, he wrote in *Not without Glory: Poets of the Second World War*, was Keith Douglas. Douglas was the young officer who had deserted *to* the front at El Alamein and died in Normandy at about the time Bain was wounded.

In Scannell's own poetry, as well as in his memoirs, his favourite motif was violence, sometimes in the boxing ring, often in war and, most of all, in the battles of the human heart. It was no coincidence that one of the finest collections of his poetry was titled, 'Of Love and War'.

On 11 May 1970, he wrote from his cottage in Dorset to his friend James Gibson about a new poem, 'Walking Wounded'. The image of soldiers, whose injuries did not require stretchers, making their way through the North African desert had haunted him for years. He told Gibson that 'it was so damned hard to write':

> I think I had to wait so long to write the poem because the merely descriptive poem does not greatly interest me: I had to see what allegorical or symbolic meaning the image possessed. And slowly I came to see that the Walking Wounded represented the common human condition: the dramatically heroic role is for the few. Most of us have to take the smaller wounds of living and we have to return again and again to the battlefield, and perhaps in the long run this is the more important, even the more heroic role.

The poem conjured an image of bandaged soldiers that John Singer Sargent had captured in his First World War masterpiece, *Gassed*:

> And then they came, the walking wounded
> Straggling the road like convicts loosely chained,
> Dragging at ankles exhaustion and despair.
> Their heads were weighed down by last night's lead,
> And eyes still drank the dark ...

... And when heroic corpses
Turn slowly in their decorated sleep
And every ambulance has disappeared
The walking wounded still trudge down that lane,
And when recalled they must bear arms again.

Vernon Scannell, born John Vernon Bain, died on 17 November 2007 at the age of eighty-five. Just before his death, he posted an entry on a Gordon Highlander war veteran website: 'Would like to know what happened to Gordon Rennie and William "Bill" Grey.' The site did not post a response.

Steve Weiss was living in California in 1991 when former Lieutenant Russell Darkes finished writing his unpublished manuscript, 'Twenty-five Years in the Military'. The memoir, which circulated among veterans of the 36th Division, mentioned an incident that occurred in Italy a few months before Weiss joined the division near Rome. The commander of Company C at that time, Captain Horton, called his officers together to discuss a planned assault up Mount Sammucro. Company C, like most other American rifle companies in the Second World War, had six officers, of whom one was a captain and five were lieutenants. One of the five lieutenants, named Greenly, had recently been killed. Darkes wrote,

Captain Horton immediately called all platoon leaders to assemble at the very crest of the mountain to issue his attack order before darkness approached. It was to be a night attack. Suddenly, there was a sharp crack with a light 'thud'. After several seconds trying to determine what happened, Lt. Simmons from Belfast, Maine, and I, Lt. Russell Darkes, noticed that Captain Horton and the other two lieutenants were lying very still and bleeding profusely from their heads. All three of them were killed instantly by one lone bullet fired by a German sniper from the 'A' Company area.

Command of the company fell to Lieutenant Allan Simmons, who was promoted to captain. The other survivor of that freak rifle round, Lieutenant Darkes, became company executive officer.

Reading about this event for the first time, Weiss was shocked. It made him consider that there was a reason for Captain Simmons's caution and distance. To witness three of his comrades felled by a single bullet must have had a traumatic impact. Weiss, by 1991 a practising psychologist, had studied trauma and the way it could drive a man into himself. It had happened to his father during the First World War, and it seemed to have affected Simmons in the Second. Steve Weiss, who felt he had an excuse for deserting, suddenly thought that Simmons had an excuse for not taking risks, not getting close to the men and not providing moral support. By 1991, however, this lesson had no use.

Weiss made many post-war trips to France, where he found people who had helped him during his time with the Resistance and the OSS. He renewed his friendship with Free French commander François Binoche and the couple who had given him a room in Lyons, Ronnie and Olga Dahan. In the spring of 2011, he returned to Bruyères, where the 36th Division had sentenced him to hard labour for the rest of his 'natural life'. To anyone who did not know his story, he might have been any other American octogenarian on vacation. But Americans of his generation in French villages were rarely tourists. Men old enough to have fought in the mountains and villages of the now-prosperous French countryside were searching for the youth and laughter they left there.

Weiss is a thin, elegant man, who carries himself with dignity. His demeanour makes him seem like a retired officer, back upright and eyes that look straight at everyone he speaks to. We were in Bruyères to find the courtroom where the army had tried him for 'misbehavior before the enemy'. Despite his eighty-six years, he needed no more help to march through Bruyères than when he was nineteen.

Steve Weiss let me explore the town, which had once been the frontline between the Wehrmacht and the United States Army, with him. A few hours earlier, he had been to the military cemetery at Epinal to see the grave of his friend, Sergeant Harry Shanklin. It was the only time he cried, he told me, during his entire trip. Shanklin was twenty-two when he died near the River Moselle. It bothered Weiss that Shanklin did not live to have a wife, children, a career or a chance to reflect on what happened during the war. The thought weighed on Weiss, who saved his own life by doing something he could not help – running away.

By the time of our promenade in Bruyères that balmy April afternoon, Weiss was in a better mood. We knocked on the doors of old people who were children in 1944 to ask if they knew where the 36th Division headquarters had been. No one was sure. One prim, white-haired matron in a cotton dress wondered why we wanted to know. When we told her that Steve had been a GI in the 36th Infantry Division, she threw out her arms. She was 14 when they liberated the town from the Boche, she said, too young to kiss a GI. Now, she kissed Steve on both cheeks. Then she sobbed.

A little later, I suggested to him that his desertion might have saved him from an early death or a serious wound. But there were wounds. He said, 'Look what I had to do to get right again. I spent years on the psychiatrist's couch. I became a psychologist because of it, in terms of the war. I had to put the whole thing back together again.'

Weiss remembered a compound that included a headquarters building, a stockade and a chapel, where his trial took place. In 1944, winter snow veiled the town. The spring of 2011 was clear, almost hot. Townspeople directed us to several building complexes, where they thought the 36th might have made its headquarters. One was a large Catholic school attached to a stone chapel. Another was the local hospital, whose chapel was just outside the main building. Weiss stared at them in turn, walked around them and concluded his normally letter-perfect memory just was not up to it. It did not matter. He had fought in Italy and France, won medals, deserted and been convicted somewhere in this Vosges village. He had served time in the Loire Disciplinary Training Center and in the confines of his memory, where the trial was re-enacted for years. Finding the former court-room was, anyway, something I had asked him to do. I thought it might bring out elements of his story that were not in the official transcript. If the room where the court martial took place on 7 November 1944 was a key, we didn't find it.

ACKNOWLEDGEMENTS

MY LAST BOOK, *Americans in Paris: Life and Death under Nazi Occupation*, dealt with expatriates who stayed in wartime Europe when wisdom seemed to dictate departure. While I was writing their story, a young woman who was then living with one of my sons asked about people who fled. Did I know whether many American and British soldiers had deserted during the Second World War? I didn't, and I soon discovered that not many other people did either. Much had been written about military deserters during the First World War, creating a body of literature that contributed to the campaign for their posthumous exoneration. My research into the subject of American, British and Commonwealth Second World War deserters turned up surprisingly few books that mentioned them. William Bradford Huie's 1954 *The Execution of Private Slovik* was almost the only lengthy discussion of the subject, although it focused on the one man who was executed rather than the 150,000 or so who survived.

Desertion by the men of the 'greatest generation' remained for the most part taboo. Their stories lay in archives, police files, psychiatric reports and court martial records. To uncover so much material and to explore an under-exposed subject required considerable help, and the assistance afforded me in various and disparate quarters deserves more gratitude than I am able to express here.

I hereby thank Charlotte Goldsmith for asking the question about deserters that initiated this exploration. I must also thank my friends Goldie Hawn and Kurt Russell, who over wine on a restaurant terrace in Dubrovnik cut short my indecision over the book's title by asking why I did not call it simply *Deserter*. While I was writing this book, a son, Lucien Christian Charles, was born to me and his mother, Anne Laure Sol, in Paris. His birth provided added inspiration as I struggled to make sense of everything I learned while researching. My work meant neglecting him at a time I shouldn't have, and I ask his forgiveness. My older children, stepchildren and grandchildren tolerated absences and moodiness, tolerance for which I owe them apologies as much as thanks.

I worked on the book for the most part in the United States, France and Britain, where a legion of friends, collaborators and colleagues provided support of all kinds. In the United States, I particularly want to thank Dr Tim Nenninger and Richard Boylan of the National Archives and Records Administration in College Park, Maryland; Mary B. Chapman, Jeffrey Todd, Lisa Thomas and Joanne P. Eldridge of the Clerk of Court's Office, United States Army Legal Services Agency, Arlington, Virginia; Elizabeth L. Garver, French Collections Research Associate at the Harry Ransom Center, University of Texas at Austin; Austin researcher Wendy Hagenmeier; Paul B. Barton, Director of Library and Archives, George C. Marshall Foundation; Colonel Lance A. Betros and Major Dwight Mears of the Department of History, US Military Academy, West Point, New York; also at West Point, Dr Rajaa Chouairi; Cleve Barkley and the Friends of the Second Infantry Division; and the staffs of the US Army Military History Institute, Carlisle Barracks, Pennsylvania, and the National Personnel Records Center. I could not have completed the book as it is without the valuable contributions of Abigail Napp, Cora Currier, Christopher and Jennifer Isham, Mary Alice Burke, Jim Gudmens, Tony Zuvich, Jeff and Anne Price, Dr Conrad C. Crane, Dr Richard W. Stewart, Dr David W. Hogan, Don Prell, Joe Dillard and John Bailey.

In Britain, I must thank, first of all, Steve Weiss. In addition, I am grateful to John Scannell and his sister Jane Scannell for their time and support in helping me to understand their father, Vernon Scannell. Scannell's friend, Paul Trewhela, provided me with valuable material and the introduction to the Scannell family. I must thank my fellow writers Brian Moynahan, Colin Smith, Artemis Cooper and Max Hastings for advice and background material on the war. Professor Hugh Cecil of Leeds University and Cathy Pugh of the Second World War Experience Centre gave me valuable recorded interviews with British soldiers who recalled the deserters with whom they served during the war. I must also thank Anya Hart Dyke and Andrew Parsons; Verity Andrews and Nancy Fulford of the University of Reading Special Collections Service; and the staffs of the London Library, the National Archives at Kew, the British Library, the Liddell Hart Centre for Military Archives at King's College London, and the Imperial War Museum.

In France, where I wrote most of the book, my thanks must go to Lauren Goldenberg, Amy Sweeney, Charles Trueheart of the American Library in Paris, Alexandra Schwartz, Rose Foran, Alice Kaplan, Selwa Bourji, Stéphane Meulleau, Hildi Santo Tomas, Gil Donaldson, Sylvia Whitman and Jemma Birrell of Shakespeare and Company Bookshop and the staffs of the Archives Nationales de France, the Bibliothèque Nationale de France and the Musée des Collections Historiques de la Préfecture de Police de Paris. Acknowledgement must be made and praise given to the men and women who own and work at some of my favourite cafés in southern France: Café de l'Hôtel de Ville in Forcalquier, Les Terraces in Bonnieux, Café de France in Lacoste, Chez Claudette in Saint-Romain and the Café du Cours in Reillanne – ideal locales for writing, editing and daydreaming over coffee and tobacco.

I should also like to thank those who kindly offered me refuges from the distractions of urban life: the trustees and staff of the Lacoste campus of the Savannah College of Art and Design, who generously appointed me writer-in-residence during the hot summer of 2010; the music conductor Oliver Gilmour, for lending me his luxurious house in Dubrovnik; Roby and Kathy Burke, whose villa in Haute Provence could not have been bettered for tranquillity and beauty in which to work; Taki and Alexandra Theorodarcopulos in Gstaad; Simon and Ellie Gaul for a room in their spectacular spread beside Grimaud; and Emma Soames for the loan of her country house in southern France as the ideal setting in which to complete the work. My thanks also to Daniel and Véronique Adel for helping me find a house to rent not far from theirs in the Luberon.

Much gratitude must go to my editors, Ann Godoff at Penguin Press in New York and Martin Redfern at Harper Press in London.

Their guiding hands (and spirits) are evident on every page. If any names are left out of this list, it is not intentional.

NOTES

Introduction

p. x 'a twenty-five year old American' William Bradford Huie, 'Are
Americans Afraid to Fight?' *Liberty*, June 1948, p. 80.

p. xv 'It is always an enriching' Charles B. MacDonald, *The Siegfried Line
Campaign*, US Army in World War II, European Theater of Operations,
Center of Military History, US Army, Washington, DC, 1993 (originally
published, 1963), p. xi.

p. xv 'The mystery to me' Ernie Pyle, *Brave Men*, New York: Henry Holt,
1944, p. 164.

p. xvi 'American Army deserters' Dana Adams Schmidt, 'Deserters, Gangs
Run Paris Racket', *New York Times*, 23 January 1945, p. 5.

p. xvi 'The French police fear' Dana Adams Schmidt, 'Americans Leave
Dislike in France,' *New York Times*, 12 November 1945, p. 5.

p. xvii 'American men have no' Committee of the National Research
Council with the Collaboration of Science Service as a Contribution to
the War Effort, *Psychology for the Fighting Man, Prepared for the
Fighting Man Himself*, Washington, DC: The Infantry Journal (and
Penguin Books), 1943, p. 13.

p. xviii 'What war can ever' John Keegan, *The Battle for History* (Toronto:
Random House, 1995), p. 9.

BOOK I: BOYS TO SOLDIERS

ONE

p. 4 'The East Side' 'Storm of Protest May Save Parade', *New York Times*,
6 April 1919, pp. 1 and 4.

p. 4 'as Commander in Chief' 'Appeal to Wilson for Parade of the 77th,'
New York Times, 6 April 1919, p. 1.

p. 5 'The 77th fought' 'History of the 77th', *New York Times Magazine*, 4
May 1919, p. 80.

p. 5 'the foreign-born, and especially the Jews' Richard Slotkin, *Lost Battalions: The Great War and the Crisis of American Nationality*, New York: Henry Holt, 2005, p. 76.

p. 6 'There are citizens' President Woodrow Wilson, 'State of the Union', 7 December 1915. Full text at http://teachingamericanhistory.org/library/index.asp?document=1328. Also quoted in Gary Mead, *The Doughboys: America and the First World War*, New York: Overlook Press, 2002, p. 365.

p. 6 'Every building had' '2,000,000 Out to See Veterans Pass By', *New York Times*, 7 May 1919, p. 1.

p. 6 Of the deserters Robert Fantina, *Desertion and the American Soldier, 1776–2006*, New York: Algora Publishing, 2006, p.112. See also 'Punishing the Army Deserter', *New York Times*, 16 June 1918, p. 7.

p. 7 Britain shot 304 soldiers Cathryn Corns and John Hughes-Wilson, *Blindfold and Alone: British Military Executions in the Great War*, London: Cassell, 2001, pp. 484–503.

p. 7 'The time has come' 'A Million Cheer 77th in Final Hike of War Up 5th Av.', *New York Times*, 7 May 1919, pp. 1 and 5.

p. 7 'The neighborhood was' Steve Weiss, email to the author, 17 April 2010.

p. 8 'I didn't know' Steve Weiss, Interview with the author, London, 7 October 2009.

p. 9 'Seems like yesterday' Stephen J. Weiss, 'War Dance (1943–1946)', unpublished manuscript, second draft, London, 2009, pp. 24–5. Weiss has written two drafts of his memoir, which are hereafter referred to as WD/First Draft and WD/Second Draft.

TWO

p. 10 The nineteen-year-old volunteer's Vernon Scannell, notes for his author's biography for his novel *The Big Time*, Scannell papers, University of Reading Archives, Special Collections Service.

p. 10 'that dark and grey' Vernon Scannell, *Argument of Kings*, London: Robson Books, 1987, p. 112. [Hereafter, Scannell, *Kings*.]

p. 10 'I was supposed' Vernon Scannell, Interview, Imperial War Museum, London, 21 October 1987, Tape No. 10009 (Four reels, 120 minutes), transcribed by the author. [Hereafter, Scannell, IWM Interview.]

p. 10 'If you did revert' *Ibid*.

p. 11 'singularly ignorant of' *Ibid*.

p. 11 'Are you over 18' Vernon Scannell, *Drums of Morning: Growing Up in the Thirties*, London: Robson Books, 1992, p. 200. [Hereafter, Scannell, *Drums*.]

Notes

p. 11 'The recruiting officer' *Ibid.*

p. 11 'The Army was' *Ibid.*

p. 12 'disliked the army' Vernon Scannell, *The Tiger and the Rose: An Autobiography*, London: Hamish Hamilton, 1971, p. 3. [Hereafter, Scannell, *Tiger*.]

p. 12 'early days in' Scannell, *Kings*, p. 17.

p. 12 'By nature I was' Vernon Scannell, 'Coming to Life in Leeds', *The Listener*, 22 August 1963, galley proof in Vernon Scannell Collection, Box 4, Vernon Works: The Walking Wounded, A, T and TCCMSS Letters Recip, Miscellaneous, Folder: Scannell Letters [Corris, Eric C], Harry Ransom Center, University of Texas.

p. 12 'not so much' Vernon Scannell, *A Proper Gentleman*, London: Robson Books, 1977, p. 103. [Hereafter, *Gentleman*.]

p. 12 'working class but' Scannell, *Kings*, p. 77.

p. 12 "Vernon? What's that?" Vernon Scannell, Interview with Michael Parkinson, *Desert Island Discs*, BBC Radio, 29 November 1987. [Hereafter, Parkinson interview.]

p. 12 'A lot of the chaps' Scannell, IWM Interview.

pp. 12–13 'My comrades were' Scannell, 'Coming to Life in Leeds'.

p. 13 'I became ashamed' Scannell, *Tiger*.

p. 14 'They had no respect' Scannell, IWM Interview.

p. 14 'It was defeat' Alan Moorehead, *The African Trilogy: The North African Campaign, 1940–43*, London: Cassell, 1998 (originally published by Hamish Hamilton, 1944), p. 381.

p. 15 'a full scale retreat' *Ibid.*, pp 385–6.

p. 15 Worst of all Artemis Cooper, *Cairo in the War, 1939–1945*, London: Penguin, 1998, p. 189.

p. 15 'Every vehicle was' S. F. Crozier, *The History of the Corps of Royal Military Police*, Aldershot: Gale and Polden, 1951, p. 74.

p. 16 'that His Majesty's' General C. J. E. Auchinleck to the Under-Secretary of State, the War Office, 7 April 1942, British National Archives, CAB 66/25/32.

p. 16 During the First World War Sir Percy James Grigg, Memorandum by the Secretary of State for War, 14 June 1942, British National Archives, CAB 66/25/32.

p. 16 'With the increase' Crozier, *The History of the Corps of Royal Military Police*, p. 177.

p. 17 'a shilling a day' Wilf Swales (968), Interview with the Second World War Experience Centre, Leeds, England, recorded on 21 June 2001.

p. 17 Two leaders in Donald Thomas, *An Underworld at War: Spivs, Deserters, Racketeers and Civilians in the Second World War*, London: John Murray, 2003, pp. 187–8.

p. 17 'The number of' Crozier, *The History of the Corps of Royal Military Police*, p. 178.

p. 17 This deserter band Thomas, *An Underworld at War*, p. 186.

p. 17 'My military advisers' Sir Percy James Grigg, Secretary of State for War, Memorandum to the War Cabinet, 'Death Penalty for Offences Committed on Active Service', 14 June 1942, British National Archives, CAB 66/25/32.

p. 18 'If legislation is' Ben Shephard, *A War of Nerves*, London: Jonathan Cape, 2000, p. 239.

p. 19 'softness in education' Letter from General Archibald Percival Wavell, former Commander-in-Chief Middle East, to Chief of the Imperial General Staff General Alan Brooke, 31 May 1942. Brooke wrote to Wavell on 5 July 1942, 'I agree with you that we are not anything like as tough as we were in the last war. There has been far too much luxury, safety first, red triangle, etc., in this country.' Quoted in David French, *Raising Churchill's Army: The British Army and the War against Germany, 1939–1945*, Oxford and New York: Oxford University Press, 2000, pp. 1 and 242.

p. 19 The first units French, *Raising Churchill's Army*, p. 140.

p. 19 'a fairly constant' Edgar Jones and Simon Wesseley, '"Forward Psychiatry" in the Military: Its Origins and Effectiveness,' *Journal of Traumatic Stress*, Vol. 16, August 2003, p. 413 (complete article, pp. 411–19).

p. 19 'Recent desertions show' Auchinleck to War Office, 19 July 1942, British National Archives, WO 32/15773. See also David French, 'Discipline and the Death Penalty in the British Army in the War against Germany During the Second World War', *Journal of Contemporary History*, Vol. 33, No. 4, October 1998, pp. 531–45.

p. 20 'The place we see' Vernon Scannell, *Soldiering On: Poems of Military Life*, London: Robson Books, 1989, p. 29. [Hereafter, *Soldiering On*.]

p. 20 'I do remember' Scannell, IWM Interview.

p. 21 Some of the more Cooper, *Cairo in the War, 1939–1945*, p. 214.

p. 21 'who for their own' Douglas H. Tobler, *Intelligence in the Desert: The Recollections and Reminiscences of a Brigade Intelligence Officer*, self-published, Gold Bridge, BC, 1978, p. 45. See also French, *Raising Churchill's Army*, p. 139.

p. 21 'The 51st Highland' J. B. Salmond, *The History of the 51st Highland Division, 1939–1945*, Edinburgh: William Blackwood and Sons, 1953, p. 29.

p. 22 'An Arab was' Scannell, IWM interview.

THREE

p. 23 **'If Steve Weiss'** Alfred T. Whitehead, with contributing material by Selma B. Whitehead, *Diary of a Soldier*, printed privately by Alfred T. Whitehead and Selma B. Whitehead, 1989, p. 3. [Hereafter cited as Whitehead Diary.] My copy is signed, apparently by the author, 'My Old Barber, Al, 6/17/91.'

p. 23 **Whitehead asked her** The CCC was phased out late in 1942, as young men were needed for the armed forces. At its height, the CCC employed more than 300,000 volunteers. Among CCC enrollees were the actors Robert Mitchum, Walter Matthau and Raymond Burr, as well as the boxer Archie Moore, baseball player Stan Musial and Admiral Hyman Rickover. See 'Conservation: Poor Young Men', *Time*, 6 February 1939, http://www.time.com/time/magazine/article/0,9171,771421,00.html.

p. 24 **His Social Security** *Social Security Death Index, Master File*, Provo, UT: Social Security Administration, No. 410-28-8395, Tennessee, Issue date: before 1951.

p. 24 **And the US Census** US Bureau of the Census, *Fifteenth Census of the United States, 1930*, District Eleven, Putnam, Tennessee, Roll 2269, p. 8B, Enumeration District 13. NARA, T626, Roll 2,667. The Census does not list any female member of the household old enough to have been Alfred's mother, but it gives the names and ages of seven girls (four older than Alfred, three younger) between the ages of 5 months and 19 years.

p. 24 **'They had me working'** Whitehead Diary, p. 2.

p. 25 **'She followed me'** *Ibid.*, p. 3.

p. 25 **'After his platoon'** York, Alvin C., Citation, Medal of Honor recipients, World War I, US Army Center of Military History, Washington, DC, June 8, 2009. http://www.history.army.mil/html/moh/worldwari.html.

p. 26 **'At night'** Whitehead Diary, p. 12.

p. 26 **Training lasted seventeen** John Ellis, *The Sharp End: The Fighting Man in World War II*, London: Aurum Press, 1990, p. 13. Ellis wrote that, towards the end of the war, 'some American infantrymen arriving in north-west Europe had received only six weeks training'.

p. 28 **'I had numerous'** Whitehead Diary, p. 19.

FOUR

p. 29 **'the Scottish soldier'** Patrick Delaforce, *Monty's Highlanders: 51st Highland Division at War, 1939–1945*, Brighton: Tom Donovan, 1991, p. 4.

p. 30 'I watched my Jocks' *Ibid.*, p. 43.

p. 30 'the biggest artillery' John Bierman and Colin Smith, *Alamein: War without Hate*, London: Penguin, 2003, p. 276.

p. 30 'And, with the flashes' Vernon Scannell, 'Baptism of Fire', Alan Benson Collection of Vernon Scannell, 1948–2007 (2008-10-07P), Box 4, Folder 4.1 Scannell – Correspondence, 2001, January–May.

p. 30 'One of the most memorable' Vernon Scannell, IWM Interview.

p. 31 'And the worst' Scannell, *Soldiering On*, p. 41.

p. 31 'When you're in action' Vernon Scannell, IWM Interview.

p. 31 'I enlisted in' Keith Douglas, *Alamein to Zem Zem*, London: Faber & Faber, 2008 (originally published Editions Poetry, 1946), p. 1.

p. 31 'I like you, sir' *Ibid.*, p. 15.

p. 33 The 8th Army lost Bierman and Smith, *Alamein: War without Hate*, p. 334.

p. 33 'After Alamein they' Scannell, IWM interview.

p. 33 'And at the gap' Scannell, *Soldiering On*, p. 42.

p. 34 'by common consent' Moorehead, *The African Trilogy*, p. 381.

p. 34 After the conquest *Ibid.*, pp. 75–6.

p. 35 'Then leave the dead' Keith Douglas, *Complete Poems*, Oxford: Oxford University Press, 1978, p. 100.

p. 35 'The ancient law' Moorehead, *The African Trilogy*, p. 262.

p. 36 'a cushy pen pushing' Scannell, *Tiger*, p. 94.

p. 37 'We were going' Scannell, IWM Interview.

p. 37 'I have seen strong' Ellis, *The Sharp End*, p. 69.

p. 38 'After the sun' Scannell, *Kings*, p. 13.

p. 38 'John felt immense' *Ibid.*, p. 20.

p. 38 'They [the Seaforths]' Parkinson interview.

p. 38 'Once daylight came' B. S. Barnes, *Operation Scipio: The 8th Army at the Battle of Wadi Akarit, 6th April 1943, Tunisia*, New York: Sentinel Press, 2007, p. 233. (This well-researched volume contains the written and oral testimony of many participants in the battle.)

p. 39 'We then could' *Ibid.*, p. 206.

p. 39 'an almost trance-like' Scannell, *Kings*, p. 21.

p. 39 'We had on this day' Barnes, *Operation Scipio*, p. 242.

p. 39 The Seaforths had lost Major G. L. W. Andrews, I/C, 5th Battalion, 5th Seaforth Highlanders, testimony at http://51hd.co.uk/accounts/andrews_wadi-akarit.

p. 40 'Then he saw' Scannell, *Kings*, p. 23.

p. 40 'My own friends' Parkinson interview.

p. 40 'He sees the shape' Vernon Scannell, *Of Love and War: New and Selected Poems*, London: Robson Books, 2002, p. 40.

FIVE

p. 41 'We learned there' Whitehead Diary, p. 22.

p. 41 'Both as individuals' *Ibid.*, p. 23.

p. 43 On 3 October Second Battalion Staff, 'The Second Battalion, 38th Infantry, in World War II', 1945 (edited with permission of Lieutenant Colonel Jack K. Norris by Cleve C. Barkley, 1985), p. 4.

SIX

p. 44 'Their talk always' Allan Campbell McLean, *The Glasshouse*, London: Calder and Boyars, 1969, p. 7.

p. 45 'From now on' Scannell, *Kings*, p. 50.

pp. 45–7 'a mixture of snarl and smile … sleep' Scannell, *Kings*, pp. 52–8.

p. 47 'Are you going back' Parkinson interview.

p. 48 'All he cared' Scannell, *Kings*, p. 25.

p. 48 Along the route Scannell, *Kings*, p. 70.

p. 49 'as a kind of amulet' Scannell, *Drums*, p. 4.

p. 49 James Bain had John Scannell, Interview with the author, London, 15 February 2011.

p. 49 The couple had Parkinson interview.

p. 49 'one of his little jokes' Scannell, *Drums*, p. 7.

p. 50 'I do not recall' *Ibid.*, p. 9.

p. 50 'What I felt' *Ibid.*, p. 12.

p. 50 For reasons left Parkinson interview.

p. 51 'I also remember' Vernon Scannell, IWM Interview.

p. 51 'tragic and mythopoeic' Scannell, *Drums*, p. 71.

p. 52 'the boxing Bain brothers' *Ibid.*, p. 132.

p. 52 'He enlisted among' Vernon Scannell, 'The Unknown War Poet', Alan Benson Collection of Vernon Scannell, 1948–2007, 2008-10-07P, Box 4, Folder 5.1, Scannell Correspodence – 2007, January–March, Harry Ransom Center, University of Texas.

p. 53 'Our interview with' *Drums*, p. 188.

p. 53 '… He could conceal' Vernon Scannell, *Of Love and War*, p. 50.

SEVEN

p. 54 'support and defend' Steve Weiss, Interview with the author, London, 28 June 2010.

p. 54 'Today, twenty-five years' 'The Psychiatric Toll of Warfare' *Fortune*, December 1943, p. 141.

p. 55 'Although seemingly glamorous' WD/Second Draft, p. 27.

p. 55 'map reading, aerial' *Ibid.*

p. 55 'gave a false impression' *Ibid.*, p. 29.

p. 55 rigid enforcement of petty rules 'Chickenshit. This graphic description, used both as noun and adjective, signifies what is mean, petty and annoying, especially as applied to regulations. Thus, when an infantryman in a rest area finds himself restricted because his dogtags are not worn around his neck, or his shoes are unshined, or he has been detected in the act of robbing the village bank, he complains that there is too damned much chickenshit around.' Joseph W. Bishop, Jr, 'U.S. Army Speech in the European Theater', *American Speech*, Vol. 21, No. 4, December 1946, p. 248. (Full article pp. 241–52.)

p. 55 an army that had expanded Maurice Matloff, *Strategic Planning for Coalition Warfare, 1943–1944*, Washington, DC: Center of Military History, US Army, 1990, p. 388.

p. 56 'Weiss experienced no' Steve Weiss, Interview with the author, London, 7 October 2009.

p. 56 'stomp his ass' WD/Second Draft, p. 28.

p. 56 'If you don't change' *Ibid.*

p. 56 *Time* magazine reported 'Medicine: In Uniform and Their Right Minds', *Time*, 1 June 1942.

p. 56 'the cold hard facts' Edward A. Strecker, *Their Mothers' Sons: The Psychiatrist Examines an American Problem*, Philadelphia and New York: J. B. Lippincott, 1946, p. 6. Dr Strecker added, 'In the vast majority of case histories, a "mom" is at fault.' American mothers, he believed, spoiled their sons. Alongside 'momism', he blamed 'progressive education' for turning out young men incapable of adapting to the military. No politicians saw votes in condemning American motherhood, and his remained a minority view.

p. 56 The army Adjutant General Major General J. A. Ulio, Adjutant General, US Army, to Commanding Generals, Army Ground Forces, Army Air Services, Services of Supply, commanders of all ports of embarkation *et al.*, 3 February 1943, NARA RG492, Box 2029 (NND 903654), Records of Mediterranean Theater of Operations, US Army, Records of the Special Staff, JAG Headquarters Records, Decimal Correspondence 250.401 to 251.

p. 56 Secretary of War Letter from Secretary of War Henry L. Stimson to Director of the Bureau of the Budget Harold D. Smith, 22 October 1943, and Text of Executive Order 9367, 9 November 1943, Deserter File, George C. Marshall Foundation, 1600 VMI Parade, Lexington, VA.

p. 57 'in May, 1942' Letter from Brigadier General M. G. White to General George C. Marshall, Chief of Staff, 9 November 1942, Deserter File, George C. Marshall Foundation, 1600 VMI Parade, Lexington, VA.

p. 57 'nearly as many' Elliot D. Cooke, *All But Thee and Me: Psychiatry at the Foxhole Level*, Washington, DC: Infantry Journal Press, 1946, p. 8.

p. 57 'A hundred or more' *Ibid.*, p. 16.

p. 58 'ungainly, artistic and bright' Steve Weiss, Interview with the author, Paris, 17 July 2010.

p. 59 'When, in 1943' Cooke, *All But Thee and Me*, p. 71.

p. 59 'Commanding Generals, Army' War Department, The Adjutant General's Office, Washington, 'Subject: Absence Without Leave and Desertion', 3 February 1943, pp. 1 and 2, NARA, RG 498, Box 306, General Correspondence, 250–250.1.

p. 60 'As long as it takes' Cooke, *All But Thee and Me*, p. 93.

p. 61 'Yes, sir, I was' *Ibid.*, pp. 149–50.

p. 62 'If a soldier' *Ibid.*, pp. 153–4.

p. 62 'Within a few weeks' Reynolds Packard, *Rome Was My Beat*, Secaucus, NJ: Lyle Stuart, 1975, p. 110. Packard wrote that US military censors would not permit him and other correspondents to file reports on the black market or deserters.

p. 63 'Complaints are coming' Norman Lewis, *Naples '44*, London: Eland Books, 1983 (originally published London: William Collins, 1978), pp. 32–3.

p. 63 'One soon finds' *Ibid.*, p. 120.

p. 64 'Unlike the field marshal' WD/Second Draft, pp. 36–7.

p. 64 German artillery dug Charles M. Wiltse, *The Medical Department: Medical Service in the Mediterranean and Minor Theaters*, Washington, DC: Office of the Chief of Military History, Department of the Army, 1965, p. 227.

p. 65 The division suffered John Huston made a documentary film in 1945, *The Battle of San Pietro*, for the War Department. Its realism and the shocking effects of the fighting on the men of the 36th Division led the army to withhold the film from distribution.

p. 65 The two-day 'battle of guts' Wiltse, *The Medical Department*, p. 244.

p. 65 'My fine division' Fred L. Walker, *From Texas to Rome*, Dallas, TX: Taylor Publishing, 1969, p. 311. See also Bruce Brager, *The Texas 36th Division: A History*, Austin, TX: Eakin Press, 2002, pp. 158–77, and Eric Morris, *Circles of Hell: The War in Italy 1943–1945*, London: Hutchinson, 1993, pp. 251–2.

p. 65 'The 36th had' Raleigh Trevelyan, *Rome '44: The Battle for the Eternal City*, New York: Viking Press, 1982, p. 310.

p. 66 'flat and barren' Mark Clark, *Calculated Risk: The War Memoirs of a Great American General*, London: Harrap, 1951, p. 7.

p. 66 'Under armed military' WD/Second Draft, p. 6.

p. 67 'I turned a corner' Trevelyan, *Rome '44*, p. 239.

p. 67 'Fuck it,' the GI Packard, *Rome Was My Beat*, p. 133.

p. 68 Weiss was unaware Albert J. Glass *et al.*, eds., *Overseas Theaters: Neuropsychiatry in World War II*, Vol. II, Medical Department, U.S. Army in World War II: Clinical Studies, Washington, DC: Government Printing Office, 1973, pp. 997–8.

p. 68 'It is my opinion' Raymond Sobel, 'Anxiety-Depressive Reactions After Prolonged Combat Experience – the "Old Sergeant Syndrome"', Frederick R. Hanson, ed., *Combat Psychiatry*, Special Supplement, *The Bulletin of the U.S. Army Medical Department*, Vol. 9, November 1949, p. 141. See also, 'The Psychiatric Toll of Warfare', *Fortune*, December 1943, pp. 141–3, 268–70 and 27–83. *Fortune* wrote, 'We know for example that about one third of all casualties now being returned to the U.S. from overseas are neuropsychiatric ... around 10,000 men a month are being discharged from the Army for psychiatric reasons' (p. 143).

p. 68 'I thought Hal' WD/Second Draft, p. 7.

p. 69 A study of 'Who's Afraid?', *Time*, 22 November 1943. John Dollard of the Yale Institute of Human Relations conducted the survey.

p. 69 'In past wars' General George C. Marshall, 'Biennial Report of the Chief of Staff of the US Army, July 1, 1943, to June 30, 1945, to the Secretary of War', *Yank* magazine, 19 October 1945, p. 7.

EIGHT

p. 71 'a drench of pure horror' Scannell, *Kings*, p. 58.

p. 71 'The NCO advancing' *Ibid.*, p. 60.

p. 72 'the bitter, clenched' *Ibid.*, pp. 64–5.

p. 73 'Three years penal' *Ibid.*, p. 66.

p. 75 'All day long' Ray Rigby, *The Hill*, London: W. H. Allen, 1965, p. 8. (Sidney Lumet directed the film version of the story in 1965 with Sean Connery.)

p. 75 A staff sergeant *Ibid.*, p. 211.

p. 76 'Each time he' Joseph Heller, *Catch-22*, London: Jonathan Cape, 1962, p. 130.

p. 76 Bain wanted to Scannell, *Kings*, p. 72.

p. 76 Every night in *Ibid.*, pp. 74–6.

p. 78 'When I lie' Algernon Methuen, *Anthology of Modern Verse*, London: Methuen, 1921, p. 62.

p. 79 'embarrassed, even a' Scannell, *Kings*, p. 81.

p. 79 'I'd use one' *Ibid.*, p. 83.

p. 80 'All right, he thought' *Ibid.*, p. 87.

p. 80 'You'll be confined' Vernon Scannell, 'Mourning the Dead', *Epithets of War*, London: Eyre and Spottiswoode, 1969, p. 27.

p. 81 'It was outrageous' Scannell, *Kings*, p. 92.

p. 81 'Where do you come' *Ibid.*, pp. 98–9.

p. 83 'But I'll get' Vernon Scannell, 'Compulsory Mourning', *Epithets of War*, p. 31.

p. 83 'I'd have promised' Michael Parkinson interview.

p. 84 'satisfied with the living' Hansard Debates, 10 October 1944, vol. CDIII, cc 1589-90W, http://hansard.millbanksystems.com/written_answers/1944/oct/10/mustapha-detention-barracks-alexandria.

NINE

p. 86 From Northern Ireland Second Battalion Staff, 'The Second Battalion, 38th Infantry, in World War II', p. 4.

p. 86 'As rough as' Whitehead Diary, p. 45.

p. 86 'I never knew' *Ibid.*, p. 44.

p. 87 'wound up joining' *Ibid.*, p. 46.

p. 87 The 116th Regimental Captain James R. Darden, 'Operations of the 1st Division in the Landing and Establishment of the Beachhead on Omaha Beach, 6–10 June 1944', Staff Department, Advanced Infantry Officers Course, The Infantry School, Fort Benning, GA, 1949–50, p. 8.

p. 87 The Big Red One Antony Beevor, *D-Day: The Battle for Normandy*, London: Penguin, 2009, p. 7.

p. 87 'a raincoat, gas' 'They were issued three K type and three D type rations. Riflemen were issued 96 rounds each and BAR teams 900 rounds; 60 mm crews 20 rounds of mortar ammunition. Every man carried five grenades and in addition each rifleman carried four smoke grenades. Every man wore special assault jackets with large pockets and built-in packs in the back.' Darden, Staff Department, Advanced Infantry Officers Course, p. 13.

p. 87 'We were instructed' Whitehead Diary, p. 48.

p. 88 'Bodies and pieces' Whitehead Diary, p. 50.

p. 89 'Big naval barrage' Whitehead Diary, p. 53.

p. 89 'The following afternoon' Edward O. Ethell and Paul Caldwell, *The Thirty-Eighth United States Infantry*, Pilzen: Planografia, Novy Vsetisk and Grafika, June 1945, p. 8.

p. 90 'I was waiting' Whitehead Diary, p. 56.

p. 90 Four of 2nd Division's Edwin P. Hoyt, *The GI's War: American Soldiers in Europe During World War II*, New York: Da Capo Press, 1991, p. 407.

p. 91 'Only a limited' Second Battalion Staff, 'The Second Battalion, 38th Infantry, in World War II', p. 5.

p. 91 'They doggedly defended' Whitehead Diary, p. 57.

p. 91 **The contest for Trévières** Second Battalion Staff, 'The Second Battalion, 38th Infantry, in World War II', p. 10.

p. 91 **'Then,' Whitehead wrote** Whitehead Diary, pp. 59–60.

TEN

p. 92 **'The machinery had'** Scannell, *Tiger*, p. 92.

p. 93 **At 0800 the next** Scannell, *Kings*, p. 144. In an account of this event he wrote in 1997, Scannell recalled that Captain Forbes came below (rather than call the men on deck). See Vernon Scannell, 'Why I Hate the Celebration of D-Day ... and What it Was Like to Be There', *New Reporter*, May 1997, p. 8. See also Wilfrid Miles, *The Life of a Regiment*, Vol. V: *The Gordon Highlanders, 1919–1945*, Aberdeen: The University Press, 1961, p. 25.

p. 93 **'the world's pet uncle'** Vernon Scannell, 'Robbie,' *Of Love and War*, p. 42.

p. 93 **'Jesus Christ, no'** Scannell, *Kings*, p. 119.

p. 93 **In March, the Highland** Salmond, *The History of the 51st Highland Division, 1939–1945*, p. 137.

p. 94 **The Highland Division conducted** Delaforce, *Monty's Highlanders*, p. 123.

p. 94 **'there were thousands'** David Reynolds, *Rich Relations: The American Occupation of Britain, 1942–1945*, London: HarperCollins, 1995, p. 353.

p. 94 **'The war was'** Frankie Fraser, interview in *Bad Boys of the Blitz*, documentary film first broadcast on British Channel 5, Tuesday, 3 May 2005 at 8 p.m. See also http://menmedia.co.uk/manchestereveningnews/tv_and_showbiz/s/156716_must_see_tv_bad_boys_of_the_blitz. According to Fraser, he killed two people in a raid on Wandsworth Prison in 1943 to free another deserter. http://www.madfrankiefraser.co.uk/frankiefraser.htm?story/book1.htm~mainFrame

p. 95 **In April 1944** 'GIs Major Crime in London is AWOL', *New York Times*, 20 April 1944, p. 6.

p. 95 **'The Provost Marshal's'** 'Army & Navy – Malefactors Abroad', *Time*, 1 May 1944.

p. 95 **'They also trapped'** 'London AWOL Roundup Traps a One-Star General', *Chicago Daily Tribune*, 18 May 1944, p. 6.

p. 95 **Five nights later** Thomas, *An Underworld at War*, pp. 215–16.

p. 95 **'An awful lot'** Timothy Sharland (4266), Interview, Second World War Experience Centre, Leeds.

p. 96 **'For crying out'** Scannell, *Kings*, p. 126.

p. 96 **On the perimeter** Patrick Delaforce, *Monty's Highlanders*, p. 124.

p. 97 'The men we get' Major General Harold Freeman-Attwood to General Headquarters, 3rd Army, 30 May 1943, British National Archives, WO 231/10 (War Office, Directorate of Military Training), 'Lessons Learned from Operations in Tunisia', 1943 May–July.

p. 97 'The resistance to' Reynolds, *Rich Relations*, p. 356.

p. 97 That meant not sending Delaforce, *Monty's Highlanders*, p. 123.

p. 97 'We can do very' David French, '"Tommy is No Soldier": The Morale of the Second British Army in Normandy, June–August 1944', in Brian Holden Reid, ed., *Military Power: Land Warfare in Theory and Practice*, London: Frank Cass, 1997, p. 162.

p. 97 'But the truth' Vernon Scannell, 'Why I hate the celebration of D-Day', p. 8.

p. 97 'We have got' David French, *Raising Churchill's Army*, p. 245. See also French, '"Tommy is No Soldier"', in *Military Power*, Reid, ed., p. 162, for a psychiatric survey of 600 British troops between October 1943 and April 1944.

p. 98 Believing the war French, *Raising Churchill's Army*, p. 244.

p. 98 When the flotilla passed Miles, *The Life of a Regiment*, Vol. V, p. 252.

p. 98 'the LCI circled' Scannell, 'Why I hate the celebration of D-Day', p. 8.

p. 99 'What I with' Vernon Scannell, 'War Wounds', original transcript, Alan Benson Collection of Vernon Scannell, 1948–2007, 2008-10-07P, Box 4, Folder 5.1, Scannell – Correspondence – 2007, January–March, Harry Ransom Center, University of Texas.

p. 99 The LCI had trouble Scannell, 'Why I hate the celebration of D-Day', p. 9.

p. 99 'There was only' Miles, *The Life of a Regiment*, Vol. V, p. 253.

p. 100 'We seized the' Scannell, 'Mercenaries', *Epithets of War*, p. 32.

p. 100 During the night Salmond, *The History of the 51st Highland Division, 1939–1945*, p. 145.

p. 100 'He had managed' Scannell, *Tiger*, p. 96.

p. 100 'It seemed impossible' Scannell, 'Robbie,' *Of Love and War*, pp. 42–3.

p. 101 Their first week Delaforce, *Monty's Highlanders*, p. 128.

p. 101 At first, the wounds French, '"Tommy is no soldier"', in *Military Power*, Reid, ed., p. 163.

p. 101 The percentage of Beevor, *D-Day: The Battle for Normandy*, p. 111.

ELEVEN

p. 102 'Maybe the war' WD/Second Draft, p. 7.

p. 102 Troops in Italy The phrase was first coined by a disgruntled British soldier, who wrote a letter to British Member of Parliament Nancy Astor complaining of official neglect of soldiers in Italy and signed it, 'D-Day Dodger'. When Lady Astor innocently repeated the term, she received widespread condemnation. There had been four D-Day amphibious landings in Sicily and Italy before Normandy. British 8th Army squaddies composed 'The Ballad of the D-Day Dodgers' to the music of 'Lily Marlene'. One verse went:

> *We're the D-Day Dodgers out in Italy,*
> *Always on the vino, always on the spree.*
> *Eighth Army scroungers and their tanks*
> *We live in Rome – among the Yanks.*
> *We are the D-Day Dodgers, over here in Italy.*

p. 103 A sergeant about The 36th Division was composed of three regiments (the 141st, the 142nd and 143rd) of about five thousand men. Each regiment was divided into three battalions.

p. 103 'locked within himself' WD/Second Draft, p. 9.

p. 104 'The two of us' *Ibid.*, p. 9.

p. 104 a blatant violation Article Two of the Convention Relative to the Treatment of Prisoners of War, Geneva, 27 July 1929, states: 'Prisoners of war are in the power of the hostile Government, but not of the individuals or formation which captured them. They shall at all times be humanely treated and protected, particularly against acts of violence, from insults and from public curiosity. Measures of reprisal against them are forbidden.'

p. 105 'We never found' WD/Second Draft, p. 10.

p. 105 'I discover that' *Ibid.*, p. 11.

p. 105 Weiss did not Military psychiatrists reported that it was common for soldiers under stress to call out for their mothers, wives or girlfriends. *Psychology for the Fighting Man*, the book printed in England for Allied soldiers who would land in France, explained, 'They may not realize it, but often the truth is they have become homesick. They are longing for those upon whose presence and affection they have long depended. They want their wives or mothers.' *Psychology for the Fighting Man, Prepared for the Fighting Man Himself*, op. cit., p. 334.

p. 106 'most divisions took' WD/Second Draft, p. 12.

p. 107 'The stench of' *Ibid.*, p. 13.

p. 107 'I was nothing' *Ibid.*

p. 108 'Lying in a fold' *Ibid.*, p. 14.

p. 108 'Of all the lousy' *Ibid.*, p. 15.

p. 109 'All advanced' Alan Moorehead, *Eclipse*, New York: Harper & Row, 1968, p. 18 (originally published London: Hamish Hamilton, 1945). The British soldier Alex Bowlby, who fought throughout the Italian campaign, had the same impression: 'The view from the mountain was – mountains. There seemed no end to them.' Alex Bowlby, *The Recollections of Rifleman Bowlby*, London: Cassell, 1999 (reprinted 2002) (originally published London: Leo Cooper, 1969).

p. 109 **'If they keep'** WD/Second Draft, p. 15.

p. 109 **'He was in every'** Steve Weiss, Interview with the author, Paris, 17 July 2010.

p. 109 **The Italian campaign** Russell J. Darkes, 'Twenty-five Years in the Military', typescript, Lebanon, PA 17042: A. Archery & Printing Place, 1991, p. 33. (As Lieutenant Darkes, he was executive officer of Company C, Weiss's unit. His typescript is lodged at the Russell Darkes Collection, AFC/2001/001/48329, Veterans History Project, American Folklife Center, Library of Congress, Washington, DC.

p. 110 **'so despised by'** Lewis, *Naples '44*, p. 119. K-rations were 'Field Rations, Type K', issued to US troops from 1942 to carry in the battlefield. Lightweight if not nutritious, they were packages of dried goods for breakfast, lunch and dinner that included small cans of meat, crackers and cigarettes. These were distinguished from the slightly more substantial 'C-rations', combat rations. When the army was able to set up kitchens close to the front, which was rare in Italy, the men had hot food.

TWELVE

p. 112 **'The smell of war'** Scannell, *Kings*, pp. 149–50.

p. 112 **After their landing** Salmond, *The History of the 51st Highland Division, 1939–1945*, p. 141.

p. 113 **A green flare shot up** Scannell, *Kings*, pp. 153–4.

p. 113 **In the middle** Scannell, *Tiger*, p. 97.

p. 114 **Captain Urquhart commandeered** Delaforce, *Monty's Highlanders*, p. 129.

p. 114 **'B and C Companies'** Miles, *The Life of a Regiment*, Vol. V, p. 256.

p. 114 **By the time** Delaforce, *Monty's Highlanders*, p. 129.

p. 114 **They also took prisoners** J. B. Salmond, *The History of the 51st Highland Division, 1939–1945*, p. 143; Delaforce, *Monty's Highlanders*, p. 129; and Wilfrid Miles, *The Life of a Regiment*, Vol. V p. 256.

p. 114 **The company bagpiper** Scannell, *Kings*, p. 156.

p. 115 **'I told you'** *Ibid.*, p. 136.

p. 116 **'They would live'** Norman Craig, *The Broken Plume: A Platoon Commander's Story, 1940–1945*, London: Imperial War Museum, 1982, p. 146.

p. 116 **'a great dark cave'** Scannell, *Kings*, p. 158.

p. 117 **'The lucky bastards'** *Ibid.*, p. 160.

p. 117 **'They were confident'** Miles, *The Life of a Regiment*, Vol. V, p. 257.

p. 117 'The fact must' Salmond, *The History of the 51st Highland Division, 1939–1945*, pp. 144–5.

p. 117 'during the whole' Russell and Burrows quoted in: Delaforce, *Monty's Highlanders*, p. 143.

p. 118 'People get lost' Lieutenant Hugh Temple Bone, Imperial War Museum, Catalogue number: Documents 1464, Second World War, private papers. Quoted in French, *Raising Churchill's Army*, p. 139.

p. 118 'The fury of' Scannell, *Kings*, p. 165.

p. 119 At first light *Ibid.*, pp. 170–1.

THIRTEEN

p. 121 They had pitched Steve Weiss, Interview with the author, London, 28 June 2010.

p. 122 Combat troops turned WD/Second Draft, p. 22.

p. 122 'Dear God' Bowlby, *The Recollections of Rifleman Bowlby*, p. 118.

p. 122 'Whoever dreamed this' Norman Lewis, *op. cit.*, p. 101.

p. 123 'freedom of speech' President Roosevelt enumerated the Four Freedoms in a speech to Congress on 6 January 1941, before American entry into the war. They subsequently became the war goals. See the *Congressional Record*, 1941, Vol. LXXXV, Part 1, 1941.

p. 123 'The sheer irony' Vincent Sheean, *This House against This House*, New York: Random House, 1945, p. 297.

p. 123 'His face was' Steve Weiss, email to author, 29 July 2011.

p. 123 The new divisional Jeffrey J. Clarke and Robert Ross Smith, *Riviera to the Rhine, United States Army in World War II: The European Theater of Operations*, Washington, DC: Center of Military History, US Army, 1993, p. 38.

p. 124 'Desertions became wholesale' Packard, *Rome Was My Beat*, p. 110. Packard wrote that censors blocked his stories on the black market and deserters.

p. 124 'twenty-five mile hikes' WD/Second Draft, p. 40.

p. 125 The 36th Division Jacques Robichon, *The Second D-Day*, London: Arthur Barker, 1969 (originally published in French as *Le Débarquement de Provence: 15 Août 1944*), p. 191.

p. 125 A Royal Navy crew WD/Second Draft, p. 39.

p. 125 'I immediately sensed' *Ibid.*, p. 40.

p. 126 'One soldier came' Ernie Pyle, 'The Death of Captain Waskow', Scripps Howard News Service, 10 January 1944. Reynolds Packard wrote that Pyle told him in Italy that he managed to persuade Scripps Howard to publish the piece, which unusually for him was about an officer rather than an enlisted man, by emphasizing that the GIs shook the dead man's hand. Packard quoted Pyle on the GIs, 'They are really dull. Sometimes they are tough and mean. But my editors won't let me write about anybody except these goddamn GIs. I'm tired of being called the letter writer for the doughfoot.' Packard, *Rome Was My Beat*, p. 113.

FOURTEEN

p. 127 **Near the Forêt de Cerisy** S/Sgt Charles R. Robb, Jr (Army Serial Number 37529161) of Company F, 9th Regiment, wrote on the Yahoogroup 'Friends of US 2nd Division' site (Message 8401), 'Now I have to give him (Whitehead) credit for the story of the two American soldiers that lost their heads, over two girls. Well, true or untrue, this same story was passed along to us and we again were warned not to fraternize with the French, especially the women.'

p. 127 **'One was a group of strange'** Whitehead Diary, p. 62.

p. 128 **'Snipers were seldom'** Cleve C. Barkley, *In Death's Dark Shadow: A Soldier's Story*, published by the author, 2006, p. 124.

p. 128 **'I sat right down'** Whitehead Diary, p. 65.

p. 128 **'This was hedgerow'** *Ibid.*, p. 66.

p. 129 **'The hedgerows themselves'** Walter M. Robertson, *Combat History of the Second Infantry Division in World War II*, Baton Rouge, LA: Army and Navy Publishing Company, 1946, p. 29.

p. 129 **Whitehead's 2nd squad** email from Cleve C. Barkley to the author, 9 April 2012.

p. 129 **'I'd get an enemy'** Whitehead Diary, p. 70.

p. 130 **Despite Whitehead's impression** Edward W. Wood and Raleigh Ashbrook, *D + 1 to D + 105: The Story of the 2nd Infantry Division*, Czechoslovakia: G-3 Section, 2nd Division Headquarters, 1945, p. 11.

p. 130 **Whitehead wrote of** Whitehead Diary, p. 71.

p. 130 **'started serenading the'** *Ibid.*, p. 72.

p. 130 **'a showy mathematical'** Paul Fussell, *Doing Battle: The Making of a Skeptic*, Boston: Little, Brown, 1996, p. 134.

p. 130 **'A second division'** Whitehead Diary, p. 73.

pp. 130–1 **'The "Rhino" was'** The General Board, United States Forces, European Theater, 'Armored Special Equipment', Center of Military History, Department of the Army, Washington, DC, 1945, File R475/4, Study No. 52, p. 14.

p. 131 **'He was dead'** Whitehead Diary, p. 75.

p. 131 **The next day** Second Battalion Staff, 'The Second Battalion, 38th Infantry, in World War II', p. 18.

p. 132 **'I don't believe'** Whitehead Diary, pp. 77–8.

p. 132 **The mine that** The toll of the 2nd Division troops killed during the war in Robertson's *Combat History of the Second Infantry Division in World War II*, pp. 38–9, lists Schwerdfeger, Sanchez and Turner as having died in combat on the same day. But the date given is 26 July 1944, not 11 July, the date of the assault of Hill 192. General Robertson wrote that, on 'that bloody day of July 26', the 38th Regiment advanced on Saint-Jean-des-Baisants. It is not clear why Whitehead confused the dates of the Hill 192 and Saint-Jean-des-Baisants battles.

p. 133 **The 38th Infantry** Barkley, *In Death's Dark Shadow*, p. 144.

p. 133 **One of the eighty-three** Second Battalion Staff, 'The Second Battalion, 38th Infantry, in World War II', p. 22.

p. 133 **His service record** 'Personnel Records Section', in File, Whitehead, Alfred T., CM ETO 309739, Office of the Clerk of the Court, U.S Army Judiciary, 901 North Stuart Street, Suite 1200, Arlington, VA 22203-1837. (Whitehead's Court Martial File CM ETO 309379 hereafter referred to as Whitehead Court Martial File. Most pages in the file are unnumbered.)

p. 133 **Many 2nd Division** Whitehead Court Martial File.

p. 133 **'I went a little'** Whitehead Diary, p. 82.

FIFTEEN

p. 134 **At almost the** Eric Sevareid, *Not So Wild a Dream*, New York: Alfred A. Knopf, 1946, p. 436. CBS News reporter Sevareid landed in the south of France just after the first wave of troops and sent the first reports to the United States via Rome.

p. 134 **A fabulous armada** Clarke and Smith, *Riviera to the Rhine, United States Army in World War II*, p. 92.

p. 134 **'experienced the magnitude'** WD/Second Draft, p. 42.

p. 135 **Weiss and the other** Winston S. Churchill, *The Second World War*, Vol. VI: *Triumph and Tragedy*, Boston: Houghton Mifflin, 1953, p. 94.

p. 135 **'a ringside seat'** Clarke and Smith, *Riviera to the Rhine, United States Army in World War II*, p. 22.

p. 136 **Dawn broke dry** *Ibid.*, p. 108.

p. 136 **'absolutely petrified'** Robichon, *The Second D-Day*, p. 190.

p. 136 **For this feat** Clarke and Smith, *Riviera to the Rhine, United States Army in World War II*, p. 111. Murphy won, among other honours, the Medal of Honor, Distinguished Service Cross, Silver Star with First Oak Leaf Cluster, Legion of Merit, Bronze Star Medal with 'V' Device and First Oak Leaf Cluster, Purple Heart with Second Oak Leaf, European-African-Middle Eastern Campaign Medal with One Silver Star, Four Bronze Service Stars (for nine campaigns) and one Bronze Arrowhead (for the assault landings at Sicily and southern France). After the war, he became an actor in Hollywood and was killed in an aeroplane crash in 1971.

p. 137 **'Here we saw'** Winston Churchill, *Triumph and Tragedy*, p. 95.

p. 137 **The 141st Regiment** Steven J. Zaloga, *Operation Dragoon: France's Other D-Day*, Oxford: Osprey Publishing, 2009, p. 47. Zaloga added, 'Each of these [strongpoints] was in turn made up of two or three resistance nests (*Widerstandsnester*), which were clusters of bunkers usually a platoon in strength with more machine guns, mortars, and light guns than a normal infantry formation.'

p. 137 **'prove myself a man'** Jacques Robichon, *The Second D-Day*, p. 190.

p. 137 **'webbing and leather'** WD/Second Draft, p. 43.

p. 138 **'The 143rd Infantry'** Clarke and Smith, *Riviera to the Rhine, United States Army in World War II*, p. 115.

p. 138 **They soon eliminated** *Ibid.*, p. 121. See also John A. Hyman, 'From the Riviera to the Rhine', *T-Patch* (36th Division newspaper), First Anniversary Supplement, 1945, republished at texasmilitaryforcesmuseum.org/36division/archives/frame/hymans1.html. The 142nd Regiment was unable to land at Camel Red below Saint-Raphaël, owing to the strength of German underwater defences. They ended up on Green Beach.

p. 138 **In Saint-Raphaël** WD/Second Draft, p. 45.

p. 138 **Ten hours after** J. Zaloga, *Operation Dragoon*, p. 50.

p. 139 **'an example of'** Samuel Eliot Morison, *The Invasion of France and Germany*, Boston: Little Brown, 1957, p. 91.

p. 139 **'I was hugged'** Steve Weiss, 'Infantry Combat: A GI in France, 1944', in Paul Addison and Angus Calder, eds., *Time to Kill: The Soldier's Experience of War in the West, 1939–1945*, London: Pimlico, 1997, p. 332.

p. 140 **'For the first'** Eric Sevareid, *Not So Wild a Dream*, p. 440.

p. 140 **On 17 August** Weiss, 'Infantry Combat: A GI in France, 1944', in Addison and Calder, *Time to Kill*, p. 332. Operation Dragoon, according to the American version, took its name from the mispronunciation of the town of Draguignan, an early objective of the invasion. Winston Churchill insisted he changed the name from Operation Anvil to Dragoon, because the Americans had dragooned him into it.

p. 140 **'more like a Broadway'** WD/Second Draft, p. 46.

p. 140 **The mayor invited** 'GI Stories of the Ground, Air and Service Forces in the European Theater of Operations', Orientation Branch, Information and Education Division, Headquarters, Theater Service Forces, European Theater (TSFET), 1945, republished at www.lonesentry.com/gi_stories_booklets/36thinfantry/index.html.

p. 140 **Called** *maquisards* **and** Clarke and Smith, *Riviera to the Rhine, United States Army in World War II*, p. 42.

p. 140 **'Many of them'** 'OSS Aid to the French Resistance in World War II: Operational Group Command, Office of Strategic Services: Company B – 267 1st Special Reconnaissance Battalion', Archives Nationales de France, Paris, File 72 AJ/84/I/Pièce 5, p. 9.

p. 141 **'[Jim] Dickson and'** WD/Second Draft, p. 47.

p. 142 **'Hordes of men'** *Ibid.*, p. 48.

SIXTEEN

p. 144 **This was a serious** Article of War 86 stated: 'Misbehavior of Sentinel. Any sentinel who is found drunk or sleeping upon his post, or who leaves it before he is regularly relieved, shall, if the offense be committed in time of war, suffer death or such other punishment as a court-martial may direct; and if the offense be committed in time of peace, he shall suffer any punishment, except death, that a court-martial may direct.' Typical sentence for sleeping on post was five years at hard labor. See Memorandum from Headquarters, Western Base Section, SOS ETOUSA, 'Subject: Discipline', 26 February 1944, NARA, RG498, Box 362, Classified General Correspondence, 1945, 230.5-250.

p. 144 **Whitehead's squad leader** Whitehead Diary, p. 86.

p. 145 **'We sometimes accidentally'** *Ibid.*, p. 97.

p. 145 **'The last objective'** Robertson, *Combat History of the Second Infantry Division in World War II*, p. 48.

p. 145 **'bomb damage had'** Whitehead Diary, p. 100.

p. 146 **'the French people'** *Ibid.*, p. 101.

p. 146 **'The tactic was'** Wood and Ashbrook, *op. cit.* D + 1 to D + 105.

p. 146 **'Afterward, I was'** Whitehead Diary, p. 107.

p. 147 **Brest, where** Robertson, *Combat History of the Second Infantry Division in World War II*, p. 51.

BOOK II: SOLDIERS TO DESERTERS

SEVENTEEN

p. 151 **about twelve hours** Clarke and Smith, *Riviera to the Rhine, United States Army in World War II*, p. 155.

p. 151 **The 143rd had** Lockhart, *T-Patch to Victory: The 36th Infantry Division from the Landing in Southern France to the End of World War II*, Texas: Staked Plains Press, 1981, p. 24.

p. 152 'the 36th Division' Hyman, 'From the Riviera to the Rhine', p. 5.

p. 152 'Sure, but let's' WD/Second Draft, p. 49.

p. 152 Two young Frenchwomen *Ibid.*, p. 50.

p. 152 He had a more Louis-Frédéric Ducros, *Montagnes Ardéchoises dans la guerre*, Vol. III: *Combats pour la libération: du 6 juin 1944 au 7 septembre 1944*, Valence, 1981, p. 351.

p. 153 A Charlie Company WD/Second Draft, p. 51.

p. 153 They went to *Ibid.* Article of War 107 states, 'Soldier to make good time lost. Every soldier who in an existing or subsequent enlistment deserts the service of the United States or without proper authority absents himself from his organization, station, or duty for more than one day … shall be liable to serve, after his return to a full-duty status, for such period as shall, with the time he may have served prior to such desertion, unauthorized absence, confinement, or inability to perform duty, amount to the full term of that part of his enlistment period which he is required to serve with his organization before being furloughed to the Army reserve.' See *Revision of the Articles of War, 1912–1920* (two vols.), Hearing of the Subcommittee of the Committee on Military Affairs. US Senate, 66th Congress, 1st session on S.64. A bill to establish military justice, 1919. House Report 940, 66th Congress, Second session, Hearing of the Special Subcommittee of the Committee on Military Affairs. House of Representatives, 66th Congress, Second session, 1920, The Articles of War, Approved June 4, 1920, pp. 27–8.

Article 107 was less severe than Articles 58 and 75. Article 75 stated, 'Misbehavior before the enemy. Any officer or soldier who, before the enemy, misbehaves himself, runs away, or shamefully abandons or delivers up or by any misconduct, disobedience, or neglect endangers the safety of any fort, post, camp, guard, or other command which it is his duty to defend, or speaks words inducing others to do the like, or casts away his arms or ammunition, or quits his post or colors to plunder or pillage, or by any means whatsoever occasions false alarms in camp, garrison, or quarters, shall suffer death or such other punishment as a court-martial may direct.'

p. 153 Weiss and the others WD/Second Draft, p. 51.

p. 154 '[General] Dahlquist dispatched' Clarke and Smith, *Riviera to the Rhine, United States Army in World War II*, p. 156.

p. 154 A Free French intelligence Arthur Layton Funk, *Hidden Ally: The French Resistance, Special Operations, and the Landings in Southern France, 1944*, New York and London: Greenwood Press, 1992, p. 167.

p. 155 Dahlquist's order to *Ibid.*, p. 168.

p. 155 Just before dark Weiss, 'Infantry Combat: A GI in France, 1944', in Addison and Calder, *Time to Kill*, p. 334.

p. 155 Weiss found a spot *Ibid.*

p. 156 'Lying there, I waited' Weiss, *Ibid.* In WD/Second Draft, p. 58, Weiss wrote, 'I rise and run ten yards before hitting the ground. As I do, a potato masher, a German hand grenade, explodes next to my waist, sending pods of earth and bits of metal skyward. Gulping air, I get up again, rush another ten yards, and slam into the ground. Wham! The second potato masher explodes by my right hip, tossing dirt and metal everywhere; I repeat the maneuver for the third time; the grenade explodes almost on top of me. My unknown and dedicated assailant tosses one more, but by now I'm out of range and close enough to leap into the ditch beside the road. Some squad members and Simmons have already taken cover.'

p. 156 'As the C.O.' WD/First Draft, p. 64.

p. 156 Considering what to do *Ibid.*

p. 157 'Within seconds, men *Ibid.*

p. 157 'We stopped and waited' Lockhart, *op. cit.*, p. 76.

EIGHTEEN

p. 158 The aborted battle Lockhart, *op. cit.*, p. 74.

p. 159 'Morning came, clear' Weiss, 'Infantry Combat: A GI in France, 1944', in Addison and Calder, Time to Kill, p. 335.

p. 159 'We were angry' Weiss, 'Infantry Combat: A GI in France, 1944', in Addison and Calder, *Time to Kill*, p. 335.

p. 159 In Valence, the population Lockhart, *op. cit.*, pp. 78–9.

p. 160 Back in the irrigation canal Weiss, 'Infantry Combat: A GI in France, 1944', in Addison and Calder, *Time to Kill*, p. 67.

p. 160 Weiss gained respect Steve Weiss, Interview with the author, Paris, 17 July 2010.

p. 161 'There's something else' WD/Second Draft, p. 58.

p. 161 Gaston Reynaud greeted Lockhart, *op. cit.*, p. 79. Ducros, *Montagnes Ardéchoises dans la guerre*, p. 385.

p. 161 'The hayloft, partially' WD/Second Draft, p. 59.

p. 161 In Valence, Louis Steve Weiss, email to the author, 3 August 2010.

p. 162 Lévy belonged to Ducros, *Montagnes Ardéchoises dans la guerre*, p. 385.

p. 162 'Automobile tires grate' Steve Weiss, email to the author, 3 August 2010.

NINETEEN

p. 164 'Passing slowly through' Steve Weiss, 'Infantry Combat: A GI in France, 1944', in Addison and Calder, *Time to Kill*, p. 336.

p. 164 **Only a few hours** Ducros, *Montagnes Ardéchoises dans la guerre*, p. 348.

p. 165 **The four Americans** *Ibid.*, p. 385.

p. 165 **Sergeant Scruby and** WD/Second Draft, p. 63.

p. 166 **Another black Citroën** *Ibid.*

p. 166 **One of the boatmen** Ducros, *Montagnes Ardéchoises dans la guerre*, p. 385.

p. 166 **'twisted and broken'** WD/Second Draft, p. 63.

p. 166 **That morning at** Ducros, *Montagnes Ardéchoises dans la guerre*, p. 386. See also Lockhart, *op. cit.*, p. 81.

p. 168 **'Standing next to'** WD/First Draft, p. 76.

TWENTY

p. 169 **The guests at** WD/First Draft, pp. 76–7.

p. 170 **An impeccably dressed** WD/Second Draft, p. 66.

p. 170 **Homcy was a career** United States Court of Appeals, District of Columbia Circuit, Albert C. Homcy versus Stanley R. Resor, Secretary of the Army, 455 F.2d 1345, opinion by Circuit Judge George MacKinnon. http://cases.justia.com/us-court-of-appeals/F2/455/1345/168414/. See also File, Homcy, Albert C., CM271489, Office of the Clerk of the Court, US Army Judiciary, 901 North Stuart Street, Suite 1200, Arlington, VA, 22203-1837.

p. 170 **'I didn't think'** Court Martial Transcript, p. 25. File, Homcy, Albert C., CM271489, Office of the Clerk of the Court, US Army Judiciary, 901 North Stuart Street, Suite 1200, Arlington, VA, 22203-1837.

p. 171 **'I really admired'** Steve Weiss, Interview with the author, Paris, 17 July 2010.

p. 172 **'The explosion shattered'** WD/Second Draft, p. 67.

p. 172 **Steve Weiss embraced** Steve Weiss, Interview with the author, Paris, 17 July 2010.

p. 173 **'A mob?'** Eric Sevareid, *Not So Wild a Dream*, pp. 454–5.

p. 173 **'Of medium height'** Stephen J. Weiss, WD/First Draft, p. 78.

p. 174 **'I rationalized that'** *Ibid.*, p. 79.

p. 174 **'Stocky, with square'** *Ibid.*, Also WD/Second Draft, p. 69.

p. 175 **'Scruby described it'** WD/Second Draft, p. 70.

p. 176 **Weiss did not know** Ducros, *Montagnes Ardéchoises dans la guerre*, p. 351. Lévy died fighting in the Valensolles quarter of the town hours before it fell.

p. 176 **'She dug her'** WD/First Draft, p. 81.

p. 176 **The American GIs** Weiss, 'Infantry Combat: A GI in France', in Addison and Calder, *Time to Kill*, p. 339.

p. 177 **Ferdinand Mathey** WD/Second Draft, p. 72.

p. 177 **Mathey, outfitted in** *Ibid.*

p. 177 **'The farm was'** WD/First Draft, p. 72.

p. 178 **'a terrible, eerie'** Weiss, 'Infantry Combat: A GI in France', in Addison and Calder, *Time to Kill*, p. 340.

p. 179 **'We looked at'** *Ibid.*

TWENTY-ONE

p. 180 **'We were with'** Steve Weiss, Interview with the author, Paris, 17 July 2010.

p. 181 **'as if he were'** Weiss, 'Infantry Combat: A GI in France', in Addison and Calder, *Time to Kill*, p. 340.

p. 182 **'was framed like'** WD/First Draft, p. 87.

p. 182 **One team member** John Whiteclay Chambers, *OSS Training in the National Parks and Service Abroad in World War II*, Washington, DC; US National Park Service, 2008, p. 546. See also 'OSS Aid to the French Resistance in World War II, Operational Group Command, Office of Strategic Services: Company B – 2671st Special Reconnaissance Battalion', Grenoble, France, 20 September 1944, Archives Nationales de France, Paris, 72 AJ/841/I/Pièce 5.

p. 182 **The atmosphere at** NARA, File H, 350.05.1 (ETO-131), Study No. 131, prepared by Major Ray K. Craft, Chief, Psychological Warfare Section, 1945.

p. 183 **Lieutenants Rickerson and McKenzie** Funk, *Hidden Ally*, p. 220.

p. 183 **'superficial if bloody'** Chambers, *OSS Training in the National Parks and Service Abroad in World War II*, p. 342.

p. 183 **At Chomerac on 31** 'OSS Aid to the French Resistance in World War II, Operational Group Command, Office of Strategic Services: Company B – 2671st Special Reconnaissance Battalion', Archives Nationales de France, Paris, 72 AJ/83/II/Pièce 1. The OSS's report noted that the Operational Groups with 4,000 *résistants* 'held off the full strength of 22,000 Germans, including elements of SS infantry and armoured divisions, airborne glider troops and mountain infantry, all diverted from the front in Normandy or from defensive positions in the south'.

p. 183 **'unlike Simmons, Rick's'** WD/Second Draft, p. 76.

TWENTY-TWO

p. 186 **Rickerson's convoy pushed** Funk, *Hidden Ally*, p. 252.

p. 187 **To Weiss's delight** WD/Second Draft, pp. 81–2.

p. 187 Binoche left Lyons Douglas Johnson, 'Obituary: General François Binoche', *The Independent*, 27 May 1977.

p. 188 It did not take WD/Second Draft, p. 82.

p. 189 'I know that added' Steve Weiss's personal papers, London. (Copy provided to the author on 4 August 2010.)

p. 190 The US Army magazine Steve Weiss, email to the author, 14 November 2010.

p. 191 'It never dawned' WD/Second Draft, p. 100.

p. 192 The official US The General Board, United States Forces, European Theater, 'Reinforcement System and Reinforcement Procedures in the European Theater of Operations', Center of Military History, Department of the Army, Washington, DC, File: 200.3/2, Study No. 5, 1945, p. 20.

p. 192 'froze the Army' WD/Second Draft, p. 85. Weiss's figures are accurate, as confirmed by General George C. Marshall in 'Biennial Report of the Chief of Staff of the United States Army, July 1, 1943, to June 30, 1945, to the Secretary of War', reprinted in *Yank* magazine, US Army, Washington, DC, 19 October 1945, p. 7. US Army Chief of Staff Marshall wrote that available American manpower 'physically fit for war service lay between 15 and 16 million'. Of that total, some were needed for naval and merchant marine service, as well as in the production of armaments to supply the American forces and the other allies. Army ground forces numbered 3,186,00 in all theatres (Pacific, European and Mediterranean). American peak mobilization for all services and ancillary military support was, according to Marshall, fourteen million. This compared to the Soviet contribution of twenty-two million, the British Empire's twelve million and China's six million. The Germans mobilized seventeen million.

p. 192 'To me the personnel' The General Board, European Theater, 'Combat Exhaustion', US Army, Office of the Chief Clerk, Military History, General References Branch, File: R704/11, Study No. 91, 1945, pp. 127–8.

p. 193 'However, we now find' *Ibid.*, p. 129.

p. 194 'I was slow' WD/Second Draft, p. 85.

p. 196 'She looked straight' *Ibid.*, p. 87.

p. 196 'The relationship I did' Steve Weiss, Interview with the author, Paris, 17 July 2010.

TWENTY-THREE

p. 197 'This was demonstrated' 'High Officer Reveals: 12,000 Yanks AWOL in Europe, Half of Them in Black Market', *Washington Post*, 26 January 1945, p. 1.

p. 197 'The organization of' Colonel L. A. Ayres and Lieutenant Colonel P. R. David, 'Military Rail Service', The General Board, United States Forces, European Theater of Operations, Center of Military History, Department of the Army, Washington, DC, File R321/7, Study No. 123, p. 7.

p. 198 Allied use of *Ibid.*, p. 12.

p. 198 'They went AWOL' Allan B. Ecker, 'GI Racketeers in the Paris Black Market', *Yank* magazine, 4 May 1945, p. 2.

p. 198 'temporarily AWOL from' *Ibid.*

p. 198 'In late September' '27 Paris GIs Held in Paris Black Marketing', Associated Press, *Washington Post*, 22 September 1944, p. 2.

p. 199 Soon after the Americans Barkley, *In Death's Dark Shadow*, p. 216.

p. 199 'My thoughts went' Whitehead Diary, p. 128.

p. 199 Barkley and the rest Second Battalion Staff, 'The Second Battalion, 38th Infantry, in World War II', p. 41. Although Harold Barkley remembered staying at the hotel near the Eiffel Tower, the battalion history stated that Company G's billet was the Hôtel 'Nouvelle' [probably Nouveau], 20 rue de Paris, in the suburb of Vincennes. Whitehead and the rest of Headquarters Company stayed at 1 avenue Charles Floquet.

p. 199 'The people there' Whitehead Diary, p.130.

p. 200 'Thugs and AWOL' Barkley, *In Death's Dark Shadow*, p. 216.

p. 200 'French renegades were' Whitehead Diary, p. 129.

p. 200 'They knew what' Second Battalion Staff, The Second Battalion, 38th Infantry, in World War II', p. 41.

p. 200 Whitehead wrote that Whitehead Diary, p. 132.

p. 200 'daily staged an' Second Battalion Staff, 'The Second Battalion, 38th Infantry, in World War II', pp. 41–2.

p. 200 Yet it was Barkley Barkley, *In Death's Dark Shadow*, pp. 229–30.

p. 201 Al Whitehead rotated Whitehead Diary, p. 134.

p. 201 Joyriders used contraband Robert Sage, "Paris Protests Waste of Gas by Joy Riders', *Chicago Daily Tribune*, 26 October 1944, p. 5.

p. 201 On 13 October 'Black Market Deals of U.S. Soldiers Told', Associated Press, *Chicago Daily Tribune*, 26 December 1944, p. 3. See also, 'MP Killed in Fight as Black Market Gang is Broken Up', Associated Press, *Washington Post*, 8 January 1945, p. 1.

p. 202 'cutting thefts down' Wade Werner, 'MPs in France Check U.S. Supply Thefts', *Washington Post*, 20 December 1944, p. 2. Werner filed his article on 4 December, but it was delayed – presumably to clear military censorship.

p. 202 'a job superbly done' Ethell and Caldwell, *The Thirty-Eighth United States Infantry*, pp. 18-19.

p. 202 Al Whitehead sent Whitehead Diary, p. 135.

TWENTY-FOUR

p. 203 **The men of** Clarke and Smith, *Riviera to the Rhine, United States Army in World War II*, p. 89.

p. 203 **Despite formidable Wehrmacht** *Ibid.*, p. 196.

p. 204 **Operation Dragoon's three** *Ibid.*, p. 210.

p. 204 **The 36th alone** Clarke and Smith, *Riviera to the Rhine, United States Army in World War II*, p. 283; Summary of Activities: North African Theater of Operations, US Army, 1 October 1944, Vol. VIII, Copy No. 31, Analysis and Control Section Office C/s NATOUSA, NARA RG 498, UD 1018, Box 1.

p. 204 **'October was upon us'** Eric Sevareid, *Not So Wild a Dream*, pp. 472–3.

p. 205 **Until then, the 36th** Summary of Activities: North African Theater of Operations, US Army, 1 October 1944, Vol. VIII, Copy No. 31, Analysis and Control Section Office C/s NATOUSA, NARA RG 498, UD 1018, Box 1.

p. 205 **'desertions among the line'** Clarke and Smith, *Riviera to the Rhine, United States Army in World War II*, p. 291.

p. 205 **Courts martial convicted** The General Board, European Theater, 'Military Justice Administration in the Theater of Operations,' US Army, Office of the Chief Clerk, Military History, General References Branch, File: R250/1, Study No. 83, 20 November 1945, pp. 3–4 and 4.

p. 205 **Most received sentences** *Ibid.*, p. 69.

p. 205 **'All officers, particularly'** Major General J. A. Ulio, Adjutant General, US Army, to Commanding Generals, Army Ground Forces, Army Air Services, Services of Supply, commanders of all ports of embarkation *et al.*, 3 February 1943, NARA RG492, Box 2029 (NND 903654), Records of Mediterranean Theater of Operations, US Army, Records of the Special Staff, JAG Headquarters Records, Decimal Correspondence 250.401 to 251.

pp. 205–6 **'had little stomach'** *Ibid.*

p. 206 **'The troops who'** The General Board, European Theater, 'Combat Exhaustion', US Army, Office of the Chief Clerk, Military History, General References Branch, File: R704/11, Study No. 91, 1945, p. 7. On p. 2 of the same report, the authors wrote, 'There was a total of 102,989 neuropsychiatric casualties in the European Theater of Operations and a vast majority of these were combat exhaustion cases. The majority of these casualties occurred in combat divisions ... The condition occurred among all types of individuals and was encountered in two widely separated periods of combat.'

p. 206 **'Colonel Paul D. Adams'** *Ibid.*, p. 291.

p. 207 **'You give them'** Clarke and Smith, *Riviera to the Rhine, United States Army in World War II*, p. 292.

p. 207 **'one of the finest men'** Lockhart, *op. cit.*, p. 115.

p. 207 **Sensitive to the depth** *Ibid.*, p. 118.

p. 207 **The 36th established** The General Board, United States Forces, European Theater, 'Report on the Army Chaplain in the European Theater', Center of Military History, Department of the Army, Washington, DC, File: 322.01/4, Study No. 68, 1945, p. 88.

p. 208 **The 36th Division** Major Irvin F. Carpenter, 'The Operations of the 3rd Infantry Division, VI Corps (Seventh United States Army), in the Crossing of the Meurthe River and the Breakout from the Vosges Mountains, 20–27 November 1944 (Rhineland Campaign),' Staff Department, The Infantry School, Fort Benning, GA, 1949–50, pp. 5–6. Major Carpenter included a military description of the Vosges: 'The VOSGES MOUNTAINS begin in the forested hills around KAISERSLAUTERN and extend generally southward, dividing the plains of ALSACE and LORRAINE with SAVERNE GAP, being that point, which divides the mountains into the LOWER AND HIGHER VOSGES. South of SAVERNE, the HIGHER VOSGES rise steeply to heights of over 4,000 feet and continue southward to the 4,600 foot heights overlooking BELFORT GAP. From a military viewpoint, the LOWER VOSGES present a greater problem or obstacle than do their counterpart. To the North, the mountains have very steep western approaches and are densely forested, whereas, to the South, the western approaches rise more gradually and are less densely forested except for a sharp decline to the East onto the plains of ALSACE. There are four major passes through this mountain range. In order from North to South, they are as follows: SAVERNE GAP, which provides entrance to STRASBOURG; SAALES PASS, which provides entrance to SELESTAT and STRASBOURG; SCHLUCHT PASS, which provides entrance to COLMAR; and, BELFORT GAP, which provides entrance to MULHOUSE. These mountains, in their entirety, presented quite a formidable barrier to any proposed breakthrough and favored the enemy along the entire front.'

p. 208 **'clear approaches to'** G-2 History, Seventh Army Operations in Europe, Seventh United States Army, quoted in Carpenter, 'The Operations of the 3rd Infantry Division', p. 4.

p. 208 **While much of** Lieutenant John D. Porter, 'The Operations of the 442nd Regimental Combat Team in the Vosges Mountains, 29 September–20 November 1944, Rhineland Campaign (Personal Experience of a Platoon Leader),' The Infantry School, General Section, Military History Committee, Fort Benning, GA, Advanced Officers Course, 1946–7, p. 7.

p. 208 **'Almost every adverse'** Lockhart, *op. cit.*, p. 131.

p. 209 **Although there were** Samuel A. Stouffer *et al.*, *Studies in Social Psychology in World War II: The American Soldier*, Vol. II: *Combat and Its Aftermath*, Princeton: Princeton University Press, 1949, pp. 61–2. Stouffer wrote that it was 'always surprising to the uninitiated how small a part of a modern army ever comes into contact with the enemy'.

p. 209 **The infantry, barely** Gerald Linderman, *The World Within War: America's Combat Experience in World War II*, New York: Free Press, 1997, p. 1.

p. 210 **'The 36th was'** Lockhart, *op. cit.*, p. 131.

p. 210 **On 8 October** Testimony of Private First Class Frank C. Turek, in Turek, Frank J., CM297854, Court Martial File, Office of the Clerk of the Court, US Army Judiciary, 901 North Stuart Street, Suite 1200, Arlington, VA, 22203-1837.

p. 210 **'I remember it'** General David Frazior to Colonel Vincent M. Lockhart, quoted in letter from Lockhart to Steve Weiss, 20 April 1991, Steve Weiss, personal papers. Lockhart added in his letter to Weiss, 'Too bad that stupid bastard who was your company commander didn't see it that way.'

p. 210 **'I was sure'** WD/Second Draft, p. 89.

p. 211 **No soldier, according** Information and Education Division, US Army Service Forces, 'What the Soldier Thinks: A Digest of War Department Studies on the Attitude of American Troops, December 1942–September 1945', Washington, DC: Government Printing Office, 1945, p. 2.

p. 211 **'The good leader'** The General Board, European Theater, 'Combat Exhaustion', US Army, Office of the Chief Clerk, Military History, General References Branch, File: R704/11, Study No. 91, 1945, p. 7.

p. 211 **'When Harry Shanklin'** Steve Weiss, Interview with the author, Vosges, France, 30 April 2011.

p. 212 **'I was just 19'** Steve Weiss, interview with the author, London, 7 October 2009.

p. 213 **'Poor supply of'** Lieutenant John D. Porter, 'The Operations of the 442nd Regimental Combat Team in the Vosges Mountains, 29 September–20 November 1944, Rhineland Campaign (Personal Experience of a Platoon Leader)', The Infantry School, General Section, Military History Committee, Fort Benning, GA, Advanced Officers Course, 1946–7, p. 25.

p. 213 **'vulnerable and unprotected'** WD/Second Draft, p. 91.

p. 213 **'I ran into'** WD/Second Draft, p. 92.

p. 213 **'I didn't want'** Steve Weiss, interview with the author, London, April 2009.

p. 214 **'The discovery of'** Lieutenant John D. Porter, 'The Operations of the 442nd Regimental Combat Team in the Vosges Mountains,

29 September–20 November 1944, Rhineland Campaign (Personal Experience of a Platoon Leader)', The Infantry School, General Section, Military History Committee, Fort Benning, GA, Advanced Officers Course, 1946–7, p. 23.

p. 215 **The squad dug** WD/Second Draft, p. 95.

p. 215 **At 0730 hours that morning** 'Original Record of Trial of Weiss, Stephen J., 12228033, Private, Company C, 143rd Infantry, APO 36, US Army, 7 November 1944', official transcript, p. 12. Office of the Clerk of the Court, US Army Judiciary, 901 North Stuart Street, Suite 1200, Arlington, VA, 22203-1837. (Hereafter referred to as 'Weiss Court Martial Transcript File'.)

TWENTY-FIVE

p. 220 **'that severe pressures'** United States Court of Appeals, District of Columbia Circuit, Albert C. Homcy versus Stanley R. Resor, Secretary of the Army, 455 F.2d 1345, opinion by Circuit Judge George MacKinnon. http://cases.justia.com/us-court-of-appeals/F2/455/1345/168414/.

p. 221 **'He said that'** *Ibid.*

p. 221 **'After the Court-Martial'** *Ibid.*

p. 221 **Former Lieutenant, now** Letter from Colonel Schultz, Headquarters, Eastern Branch, US Disciplinary Barracks, Green Haven, New York, 7 January 1946, Weiss Court Martial Transcript File, p. 25. File, Homcy, Albert C., CM271489, p. 194, Office of the Clerk of the Court, US Army Judiciary, 901 North Stuart Street, Suite 1200, Arlington, VA, 22203-1837, p. 194. Homcy served until 7 January 1946, the day on which he was both released from prison with a dishonourable discharge and re-enlisted in the US Army as a private. He received an honourable discharge from his 1946 enlistment on 24 August 24 1946. See Albert C. Homcy versus United States, 536 F.2d 360 (Fed. Cir. 1976).

p. 222 **'ended up in'** Darkes, 'Twenty-five Years in the Military', p. 23.

p. 223 **'I can't take it'** Audie Murphy, *To Hell and Back*, New York: Picador, 2002 (originally published New York: Henry Holt, 1949), p. 236.

p. 223 **'No quarter was'** Lieutenant John D. Porter, 'The Operations of the 442nd Regimental Combat Team in the Vosges Mountains, 29 September–20 November 1944, Rhineland Campaign (Personal Experience of a Platoon Leader)', The Infantry School, General Section, Military History Committee, Fort Benning, GA, Advanced Officers Course, 1946–7, p. 11.

p. 224 **The American forces** Clarke and Smith, *Riviera to the Rhine, United States Army in World War II*, p. 344.

p. 224 A frontline stalemate First Lieutenant John D. Porter, 'The Operations of the 442nd Regimental Combat Team in the Vosges Mountains, 29 September–20 November 1944 (Rhineland Campaign) (Personal Experience of a Platoon Leader)', The Infantry School, General Section, Military History Committee, Fort Benning, GA, 1947, pp. 6 and 12.

p. 225 'I never confronted' WD/Second Draft, p. 100.

p. 225 'I was jumpy' Testimony of Private First Class Frank C. Turek, in Turek, Frank J., CM297854, Court Martial File, Office of the Clerk of the Court, US Army Judiciary, 901 North Stuart Street, Suite 1200, Arlington, VA, 22203-1837.

p. 225 'I also remember' Steve Weiss, Interview with the author, the Vosges, 30 April 2011.

p. 225 The Polish-American youngster Weiss recalled that Turek deserted at this time, but Turek's court martial records show that he left the line on 28 October 1944. See Turek, Frank J., CM297854, Court Martial File, Office of the Clerk of the Court, US Army Judiciary, 901 North Stuart Street, Suite 1200, Arlington, VA, 22203-1837.

p. 226 'You could never' Steve Weiss, Interview with the author, the Vosges, 30 April 2011.

p. 226 'The longer the' Major Duncan Stewart *et al.*, 'Anvil/Dragoon, Combat & Staff Lessons, Seventh Army, Invasion of Southern France', CSI Battlebook 3-D (AD-A151 685), Combat Studies Institute, Fort Leavenworth, KS, 1984, p. 65. See also Army Ground Forces Board, Report 639, Washington, DC: Government Printing Office, 1945, p. 62.

p. 226 Sixty-three infantrymen from Branch Office of the Judge Advocate General, 'History, Branch Office of the Judge Advocate General with the United States Forces European Theater, 18 July 1942–1 November 1945, Washington, DC, 1946, p. 17, from the files of US Army Legal Services Agency, US Army Court of Criminal Appeals, 901 North Stuart Street, Arlington, VA 22203-1837.

p. 227 'The enemy fired' Lieutenant John D. Porter, 'The Operations of the 442nd Regimental Combat Team in the Vosges Mountains, 29 September–20 November 1944, Rhineland Campaign (Personal Experience of a Platoon Leader)', The Infantry School, General Section, Military History Committee, Fort Benning, GA, Advanced Officers Course, 1946–7, p. 20.

p. 227 'Overseas most combat' Arnold M. Rose, 'The Social Psychology of Desertion from Combat', *American Sociological Review*, Vol. 16, No. 5, October 1951, p. 616.

p. 227 'Most mess sergeants' WD/Second Draft, p. 99.

p. 227 By this time 'High Officer Reveals: 12,000 Yanks AWOL in Europe, Half of Them in Black Market', *Washington Post*, 26 January 1945, p. 1. In 1944, military censors did not approve stories on deserters in France or Italy, and many reporters did not file stories out of self-censorship.

p. 228 'Our venture was' WD/Second Draft, p. 99.

p. 228 Physicians in the European The General Board, European Theater, 'Combat Exhaustion', US Army, Office of the Chief Clerk, Military History, General References Branch, File: R704/11, Study No. 91, 1945, p. 1

p. 229 'My mother and' Steve Weiss, Interview with the author, Paris, 17 July 2010.

p. 229 'Fair play was' WD/Second Draft, p. 100.

p. 229 'If one day' Steve Weiss, Interview with the author, Paris, 17 July 2010.

p. 229 'I was so depressed' *Ibid.*

p. 230 'ordered him to return' Affidavit of First Lieutenant Herman L. Tepp, in Turek, Frank J., CM297854, Court Martial File, Office of the Clerk of the Court, US Army Judiciary, 901 North Stuart Street, Suite 1200, Arlington, VA, 22203-1837.

p. 230 Captain Richard J. Thomson 'Receipt for Deserter and A.W.O.L., Statement of Police Officer or Person Returning Subject to Military Custody', signed by Richard J. Thomson, Captain, Infantry, 67th Military Police Company, 30 October 1944. File: Private Office of the Clerk of the Court, US Army Judiciary, 901 North Stuart Street, Suite 1200, Arlington, VA, 22203-1837.

p. 230 The MPs gave WD/Second Draft, p. 101.

TWENTY-SIX

p. 231 'inaptness or undesirable' *A Manual for Courts-Martial*, US Army, Washington, DC: Government Printing Office, 1 April 1928, p. 63.

p. 232 The 442nd did 'ARMY & NAVY – Medals: Record', *Time*, 21 August 1944. *Time* reported that the 100th Battalion of the 442nd Infantry Regiment had earned 'nine Distinguished Service Crosses, 44 Silver Stars, 31 Bronze Stars, three Legion of Merit Medals ... Of the 100th Battalion's 1,300 men (including 500 reserves), 1,000 had been wounded in action ... Most remarkable record of all: since the 100th had been organized it had had not a single case of desertion or absence without leave.'

p. 232 Ford declared that Major Walter L. Ford, 'N.P. Form No. 5, Psychiatric Report in Disciplinary Cases', 2 November 1944, two pages,

Weiss Court Martial File, Private Office of the Clerk of the Court, US Army Judiciary, 901 North Stuart Street, Suite 1200, Arlington, VA, 22203-1837.

p. 232 **'was suffering from'** Major Walter L. Ford, 'Psychiatric Report in Disciplinary Case', 3 November 1944, Turek, Frank J., CM297854, Court Martial File, Office of the Clerk of the Court, US Army Judiciary, 901 North Stuart Street, Suite 1200, Arlington, VA, 22203-1837.

p. 233 **'In that Private'** Turek, Frank J., CM297854, Court Martial File, Office of the Clerk of the Court, US Army Judiciary, 901 North Stuart Street, Suite 1200, Arlington, VA, 22203-1837.

p. 233 **'Well Sir, we'** Turek Court Martial transcript, p. 9.

p. 234 **'It was so dark'** *Ibid.*

p. 235 **'Major Wilson had'** US Court of Appeals, District of Columbia Circuit, Albert C. Homcy versus Stanley R. Resor, Secretary of the Army, 455 F.2d 1345, opinion by Circuit Judge George MacKinnon. http://cases.justia.com/us-court-of-appeals/F2/455/1345/168414/.

p. 237 **'The accused was'** Article of War 75: 'Misbehavior before the enemy. Any officer or soldier who, before the enemy, misbehaves himself, runs away, or shamefully abandons or delivers up or by any misconduct, disobedience, or neglect endangers the safety of any fort, post, camp, guard, or other command which it is his duty to defend, or speaks words inducing others to do the like, or casts away his arms or ammunition, or quits his post or colors to plunder or pillage, or by any means whatsoever occasions false alarms in camp, garrison, or quarters, shall suffer death or such other punishment as a court-martial may direct.' See William M. Connor, 'The Judgmental Review in General Court-Martial Proceedings' *Virginia Law Review*, Vol. 32, No. 1, December 1945, pp. 39–88, at p. 72: '... a new rule of decision as to desertion was erected in the 1917 Manual thus worded: "Desertion is absence without leave accompanied by the intention not to return." Both elements are essential to the offense. The offense becomes complete when the person absents himself without authority from his place of service with intent not to return thereto. A prompt repentance and return are no defense, nor is it a defense that the deserter at the time of departure intended to report for duty elsewhere.'

p. 237 **'Specification 1'** Weiss Court Martial Transcript File, p. 5. (The court reporter consistently misspelled Brechifosse, a Vosges hamlet, 'Brechitosse'.)

p. 238 **When the trial** Weiss Court Martial Transcript File, p. 10.

p. 239 **'It was night'** *Ibid.*

p. 240 **'Captain Simmons'** Weiss was mistaken at this stage of his testimony, as he was in both drafts of his memoir. He could not have reported to

Captain Simmons on his return from his time with the Resistance and the OSS in October 1944, because Simmons was recuperating from a sniper wound to his neck received on 30 September 1944. He returned to duty when Company C was well into Alsace in January 1945. Weiss must have reported to the acting company commander, Lieutenant Darkes. See Russell Darkes, 'Twenty-five Years in the Military', pp. 40 and 43. (Darkes does not mention Weiss in his memoir.)

p. 244 **The court intervened** Weiss Court Martial Transcript File, p. 15.

p. 245 **Defence counsel had** *Ibid.*, p. 16.

p. 246 **The defence called** *Ibid.*, p. 18.

p. 247 **'How did you get'** *Ibid.*, pp. 19–20.

p. 249 **Major Wilson introduced** Major Walter L. Ford, 'N.P. Form No. 5, Psychiatric Report in Disciplinary Cases', 2 November 1944, two pages, File: Private Office of the Clerk of the Court, US Army Judiciary, 901 North Stuart Street, Suite 1200, Arlington, VA, 22203-1837.

p. 251 **'Upon secret written'** Weiss Court Martial Transcript File, p. 22.

p. 252 **'They didn't kill'** WD/Second Draft, p. 114.

TWENTY-SEVEN

p. 254 **The stockade had** 'History: Disciplinary Training Center Branch, 1 October 1944 to 8 May 1945', p. 1, NARA, RG 498, Box 154, ETO Historical Division, Administrative File, 1942–Jan. 1946.

p. 254 **'However, to be fair'** WD/Second Draft, p. 118.

p. 255 **The commanding officer** Colonel Peck assumed command of the Loire DTC on 3 November 1944. See 'History of the DTC Branch, Theater Provost Marshal's Office, 1 October 1944 to 8 May 1945', NARA, RG 498, Box 154, Records of Headquarters, European Theater of Operations, US Army in World War II, Adm 5670 & D PM to 567E Ramps.

p. 255 **'Sometimes I'd see'** WD/Second Draft, p. 120.

p. 255 **'honorably restoring to'** Robert L. Santos, *The Army Needs Men: An Account of the U.S. Army Rehabilitation Center at Turlock, California, 1942–1945*, Alley-Cass Publications, Denair, CA, 1997, p. 20. http://wwwlibrary.csustan.edu/bsantos/army.html

p. 255 **At the Lichfield** Jack Gieck, *Lichfield: The U.S. Army on Trial*, Akron, OH: University of Akron Press, 1997.

p. 255 **Guidelines set by** Letter, Major General Milton A. Reckord, US Army Theater Provost Marshall, to all provost marshals, 19 February 1945, NARA, RG 498, Box 154, Records of Headquarters, European Theater of Operations, US Army (World War II), Adm 5670 & D PM to 567E Ramps, p. 1.

p. 256 'a large area' 'History: Disciplinary Training Center Branch, 1 October 1944 to 8 May 1945', p. 1, NARA, RG 498, Box 154, ETO Historical Division, Administrative File, 1942–Jan. 1946.

TWENTY-EIGHT

p. 257 **The 38th Regiment** Barkley, *In Death's Dark Shadow*, p. 238. Based on his father's account, Barkley wrote, 'Deeper to the rear, squad huts were constructed and life was relatively comfortable for a fighting front.' See also Wood and Ashbrook, *D + 106: The Story of the 2nd Division*, p. 4. Branch, 1 October 1944 to 8 May 1945', p. 1, NARA, RG 498, Box 154, ETO Historical Division, Administrative File, 1942–Jan. 1946.

p. 257 **'It was also true'** Charles B. MacDonald, *The Siegfried Line Campaign*, US Army in World War II, European Theater of Operations, Center of Military History, US Army, Washington, DC, 1993 (originally published, 1963), p. 613.

p. 258 **'those back home'** Whitehead Diary, p. 142.

p. 258 **'That kind of propaganda'** Whitehead Diary, p. 143.

p. 259 **'To the veterans'** Barkley, *In Death's Dark Shadow*., p. 269.

p. 259 **'When we reached'** Whitehead Diary, p. 145.

p. 259 **'By midnight the'** Charles B. MacDonald, *The Siegfried Line Campaign*, US Army in World War II, European Theater of Operations, Center of Military History, US Army, Washington, DC, 1993 (originally published, 1963), p. 610.

p. 260 **Neither they nor** Brigadier General A. Franklin Kibler, Assistant Chief of Staff, G-3, *et al.*, 'Strategy of the Campaign in Western Europe, 1944–1945', The General Board, European Theater of Operations, File 385/1, Study No. 1, p. 65. The report stated, 'By the night of 15–16 December, the [German] assault divisions had closed into final assembly areas, the bulk of the artillery was in position, and reserve divisions were en route. Existing and forecast weather conditions were now most favorable for attack.'

p. 260 **'Not knowing the'** Whitehead Diary, p. 148.

p. 261 **'No pity was'** *Ibid.*, p. 155.

p. 261 **'outstanding courage, skill'** Robertson, *Combat History of the Second Infantry Division in World War II*, p. 103. See also Second Battalion Staff, 'The Second Battalion, 38th Infantry, in World War II', p. 35. The Citation, later called the Presidential Unit Citation, added, 'Attacking and successfully penetrating the Siegfried Line in the vicinity of the Monschau Forest, the 2nd BATTALION was ordered to move 6 miles to the vicinity of Krinkelt where enemy tanks were driving in force. The last unit to leave the forest, the 2nd BATTALION successfully withdrew and under intense enemy artillery, mortar, and sporadic small arms fire moved to Krinkelt where defensive positions were occupied in the darkness without time for prior reconnaissance. Infiltrating enemy riflemen fired at the men as they moved into position at Rocherath. They fought off an attacking Panzer unit. Three times the enemy armor breached the main line of resistance. On one occasion ten tanks overran the positions, firing point blank range, employing spotlights to reveal their targets as the tank crews raked the area with machine gun and cannon fire. Although heavy casualties were sustained in this bitter engagement, the 2nd BATTALION 38th INFANTRY, successfully repelled the fanatical thrusts, killing or wounding nearly 500 of the attacking enemy.'

p. 261 'a long natural ridge' *Ibid.*, p. 103.

p. 261 **Nor was he in a German** Ethell and Caldwell, *The Thirty-Eighth United States Infantry*, p. 23. Since recovering from wounds suffered in Normandy and returning to combat, battalion sniper Kviatek had killed seventeen more Germans to reach a total of thirty-eight notches on his Springfield. Kviatek survived the prisoner of war camp and returned to the United States at the end of the war.

TWENTY-NINE

p. 264 **'I was not only pleased'** WD/Second Draft, p. 121.

p. 264 **'those having no salvage'** 'History: Disciplinary Training Center Branch, 1 October 1944 to 8 May 1945', p. 3, NARA, RG 498, Box 154, ETO Historical Division, Administrative File, 1942–Jan. 1946.

p. 265 **'Cruelty or unusual'** Letter, Major General Milton A. Reckord, US Army Theater Provost Marshal, to all provost marshals, RG 498, Box 154, Records of Headquarters, European Theater of Operations, US Army (World War II), Adm 5670 & D PM to 567E Ramps.

p. 265 **'I remember running'** Steve Weiss, Interview with the author, Vosges, France, 30 April 2011.

p. 266 **A Texan Weiss** *Ibid.*

p. 266 **'Hanging is considered'** 'EXECUTION OF DEATH SENTENCES', 8 July 1943, sent by Adjutant General A. E. O'Leary to the Commanding General, Services of Supply, p. 1. NARA, RG 498, Box 154, ETO Historical Division, Administrative File, 1942–Jan. 1946.

p. 266 **'expressed doubt that'** Judge Advocate File HWH/var, 14 September 1944, Lieutenant Choffel, NARA, RG 498, Box 154, ETO Historical Division, Administrative File, 1942–Jan. 1946.

p. 267 **Classified confidential survey** 'OUTGOING CLASSIFIED MESSAGE', Dated 16 September 1944 at 0102 Hours from Lee to All

Base Section Commanders, Reference No. EXO47032, NARA, RG 498, Box 154, ETO Historical Division, Administrative File, 1942–Jan. 1946.

p. 267 Corporal Eric Klick 'INCOMING CLASSIFIED MESSAGE', Dated 16 September 1944 at 1733 Hours, from Loire Section, Reference No. LS4093, NARA, RG 498, Box 154, ETO Historical Division, Administrative File, 1942–Jan. 1946.

p. 267 A simple check See 'Oklahoma Executions', Complete List of executions in Oklahoma between 1841 and 1966, http://web.archive. org/web/20080329184835/users.bestweb.net/~rg/execution/ OKLAHOMA.htm. See also Texas Department of Criminal Justice, 'Electrocutions 1923 to 1973', http://www.tdcj.state.tx.us/stat/ prefurman/electrocutions.htm.

p. 267 'G-1 has promised' Letter, Major General Milton A. Reckord, US Army Theater Provost Marshal, to General Lord, 28 September 1944, NARA, RG 498, Box 154, ETO Historical Division, Administrative File, 1942–Jan. 1946. Technician Third Grade was the equivalent pay grade to a staff sergeant.

p. 268 The War Department's War Department Pamphlet 27-4, 'Procedure for Military Executions', War Department, Washington, DC, 12 June 1944.

p. 269 'of black sateen', War Department Pamphlet 27-4, 'Procedure for Military Executions', War Department, Washington, DC, 12 June 1944, p. 9.

p. 269 'the lower portion' Adjutant General A. E. O'Leary to the Commanding General, Services of Supply, ETO, 8 July 1943, p. 3, NARA, RG 498, Box 154, European Theater of Operations, Historical Division, Administrative File, 1942–Jan. 1946.

p. 269 The medical officer Emmett Bailey, a white soldier who had witnessed sixteen military executions, informed author Alice Kaplan he had not recovered from the experience. 'It was the old KKK procedure,' he said. 'It was a legal lynch.' See Alice Kaplan, *The Interpreter*, New York: Free Press, 2005, p. 171.

p. 269 'Every precaution will' Adjutant General A. E. O'Leary to the Commanding General, Services of Supply, ETO, 8 July 1943, p. 3, NARA, RG 498, Box 154, European Theater of Operations, Historical Division, Administrative File, 1942–Jan. 1946.

p. 269 'In the event' Judge Advocate memo, 27 September 1944, 'Subject: Execution of Death Sentences', HWH/Ext 2069, p. 4, NARA, RG 498, Box 19, ETO Judge Advocate Section, Decimal File, 1942–1945, 250.3–250.35.

p. 270 'Whether it was' WD/Second Draft, p. 123.

p. 270 '– all enlisted men' Branch Office of the Judge Advocate General, Judge Advocate General, 'History, Branch Office of the Judge Advocate General with the United States Forces European Theater, 18 July 1942–1 November 1945, Washington, DC, 1946, p. 10, from the files of US Army Legal Services Agency, US Army Court of Criminal Appeals, 901 North Stuart Street, Arlington, VA 22203-1837.

p. 270 **The bodies of** Alice Kaplan, *The Interpreter*, pp. 169–70. Kaplan wrote (p. 156), 'In France, 130 of the 180 men charged with rape and murder were African-Americans; in Europe as a whole, 55 of the 70 men executed for rape and murder were African-Americans ... No one, as yet, was willing to venture the obvious: it was patently absurd that 8.5 percent of the armed forces could be responsible for committing 79 percent of all capital crimes.'

p. 270 'If the next' War Department Pamphlet 27-4, 'Procedure for Military Executions', p. 6.

p. 270 **'Appropriate information will'** 'Procedure for Execution of the Death Sentence on the Continent', Letter from Brigadier General R. B. Lovett, 14 December 1944, NARA, RG 498, Box 19, ETO Judge Advocate Section, Decimal File, 1942–1945, 250.3–250.35.

p. 271 'The sentence is' General Court-Martial, Orders No. 125, 9 November 1944, Private Stephen J. Weiss trial papers, Office of the Clerk of the Court, US Army Judiciary, 901 North Stuart Street, Suite 1200, Arlington, VA, 22203-1837.

p. 271 'I am writing' File, Weiss, Stephen J., CM297441.P101.2, Office of the Clerk of the Court, US Army Judiciary, 901 North Stuart Street, Suite 1200, Arlington, VA, 22203-1837.

p. 273 'The problem of' Letter, Major General John E. Dahlquist to Lieutenant General Ben Lear, 27 February 1945, NARA, RG 498, Box 5, Records of the Office of the Deputy Theater Commander, General Correspondence, 1945, 210.26–293 (File: 220.26. Reduction of Enlisted Men). General Dahlquist added, 'We have about 5,600 veterans of Salerno still in the Division.' This meant that about 10,000 of the original contingent that fought in Italy had either died, been seriously wounded, captured, deserted or otherwise gone missing. This was in addition to the replacements who had been lost.

p. 273 'I do not agree' Letter, Major General E. S. Hughes to Lieutenant General Ben Lear, 9 March 1945, *Ibid*.

p. 274 'I reported to' WD/Second Draft, pp. 124–5.

p. 274 **At this time** Colonel Julien C. Hyer, Chief, Judge Advocate Section, The General Board, United States Forces, European Theater, *et al.*, 'The Military Offender in the Theater of Operations', Center of Military

History, Department of the Army, Washington, DC, 1945, File 250/2, Study No. 84, p. 3.

p. 275 At the Loire *Ibid.*, p. 4.

THIRTY

p. 276 'That was the best' Whitehead Diary, p. 173.

p. 276 Whitehead arrived at 'Information from locator cards', Whitehead Court Martial File.

p. 277 Steve Weiss resented Whitehead's court martial file contradicts his memoir on this point. The file says he told an examining officer at the time of his arrest that 'he was tired of fighting; went to Paris and got drunk'. See 'Data for First Clemency Petition', Whitehead Court Martial File.

p. 278 Corley was promoted Charles B. MacDonald, *The Siegfried Line Campaign*, US Army in World War II, European Theater of Operations, Center of Military History, US Army, Washington, DC, 1993 (originally published, 1963), p. 309.

p. 278 A month before William Marshall, *Baseball's Pivotal Era, 1945–1951*, Lexington: University Press of Kentucky, 1999, p. 14, and H. Allen Smith and Ira L. Smith, *Three Men on Third*, New York: Doubleday, 1951, p. 141.

p. 278 In Paris the Whitehead Diary, p. 177.

p. 279 In the dreams The 1930 US Census stated that Uel was three years younger than Alfred Whitehead.

p. 279 'So we took' Whitehead Diary, pp. 180–1.

p. 280 'Of course, no black' Colonel Julian C. Hyer, Chief, Judge Advocate Section, The General Board, United States Forces, European Theater, *et al.*, 'Legal Phases of Civil Affairs and Military Government', File R/013, Study No. 85, p. 10.

p. 280 Another deserter advised Whitehead Diary, p. 184.

p. 281 'we stole more' *Ibid.*, p. 185.

p. 282 'In the eleven' 'History: Criminal Investigation Branch, 1 October 1944 to 8 May 1945' (Theater Provost Marshal), NARA, RG 498, Box 154, Adm 567C & D to 507E, Ramps, p. 6.

p. 282 'Informal G.I. markets' 'Army & Navy: G.I. Black Market', *Time*, 2 October 1944. See http://www.time.com/time/magazine/article/0,9171,933146,00.html.

p. 282 The Criminal Investigation 'History: Criminal Investigation Branch, 1 October 1944 to 8 May 1945' (Theater Provost Marshal), NARA, RG 498, Box 154, Adm 567C & D to 507E, Ramps, p. 2.

p. 283 Al Whitehead prospered Whitehead Diary, pp. 192–3.

p. 284 **An army telegram** 'War Department Messageform', 13 December 1945, from General Eisenhower to Commanding Officer, 9th Replacement Depot, APO 545, Whitehead Court Martial File.

p. 284 **On 12 and 13 July** Robertson, *Combat History of the Second Infantry Division in World War II*, pp. 156–7.

p. 284 **Whitehead nonetheless wrote** Whitehead Diary, p. 194.

p. 284 **'During his confinement'** 'Informal Routing Slip – HQ 9th Reinforcement Depot', signed A.R.W., Whitehead Court Martial File.

p. 285 **The sentry assigned** Whitehead Diary, p. 196.

p. 285 **'Due to the relative'** 'Informal Routing Slip – HQ 9th Reinforcement Depot', signed A.R.W., Whitehead Court Martial File. Corporal Shumate was not held responsible for 'negligence', as guarding prisoners in different locations was 'obviously more than one man could accomplish'.

p. 285 **'I rolled over'** Whitehead Diary, p. 197.

p. 286 **'A search for'** Letter, First Lieutenant John F. Conley to Commanding Officer, 9th Reinforcement Depot, APO 545, US Army, 'Subject: Escape of Prisoner from Confinement', 24 July 1945, in Whitehead Court Martial File.

p. 286 **Lying camouflaged in** Whitehead Diary, p. 198.

THIRTY-ONE

p. 288 **'All the other'** Scannell, *Kings*, p. 213.

p. 288 **'if I stayed'** Scannell, *Tiger*, p. 9.

p. 288 **'I really loathed'** Michael Parkinson interview.

p. 289 **With at least** 'Political Notes', *The Times*, 22 March 1945, p. 2.

p. 289 **Among the many** 'British Family Fined for Help to AWOL Yanks', *Chicago Daily Tribune*, 11 July 1946, p. 22. See also 'AWOL Tarzan Pair', *Los Angeles Times*, 27 October 1946, p. 4. This was one case among many, in which families who had sheltered deserters, both American and British, received fines. The courts appeared reluctant to impose prison terms.

p. 289 **The seventy-year-old father** 'News in Brief', *The Times*, 18 January 1945, p. 2.

p. 290 **Bain was propelled** Paul Trewhela, 'Vernon Scannell, a Poet in Bohemian London', *Times Literary Supplement*, 5 December 2007. Trewhela added that Cliff Holden was then 'the oldest surviving member of the London Group, which was founded before the First World War and included [David] Bomberg, Walter Sickert, Wyndham Lewis and other celebrated British painters of the last century'.

p. 291 **'Very good fighters'** IWM Interview.

p. 292 **About half of** '20,000 Youths Drafted to British Mines Desert', *Chicago Daily Tribune*, 24 October 1945, p. 2.

p. 292 **'one of the greatest'** 'London in the Grip of Gangsterism', *Baltimore Sun*, 10 December 1945, p. 1.

p. 292 **London's Commissioner of** 'Crime Since the War: Theft and the Shortage of Goods', *The Times*, 23 January 1948, p. 5. *The Times*'s 'Special Correspondent' added, 'The deserter, by reason of his being more or less outlawed, tends to gravitate into a life of crime. Even if he has succeeded in establishing himself in normal society as a law-abiding citizen, which necessitates some degree of deception, he is dogged by the fear of being unmasked.'

p. 292 **A prominent criminal** Duncan Campbell, 'London in the Blitz', *The Observer*, 29 August 2010. See also Harry Mount, 'The Kray of South Ken', *Times* Online, 29 March 2002, www.timesonline.co.uk/tol/incomingFeeds/article759674.ece?print=yes&randnum=1248020486302.

p. 292 **While they cordoned** *Ibid.* [confirm reference]

p. 292 **Of the 15,161 men** 'Question 15,161 in London Drive on Crime Wave: Comb City for 10,000 Army Deserters', *Chicago Daily Tribune*, 16 December 1945, p. 21. See also 'Huge Roundup of Deserters', *Los Angeles Times*, 15 December 1945, p. 1. [See also Jones and Hulten.]

p. 293 **'He told me'** John Scannell, Interview with the author, London, 15 February 2011. Paul Trewhela wrote, 'But how did he acquire his new surname? He does not say. [Cliff] Holden recalls that it was provided by a prostitute, who worked for a brothel-owner friend.' Trewhela, 'Vernon Scannell, a Poet in Bohemian London'.

p. 293 **In the freezing** Vernon Scannell, 'Coming to Life in Leeds'.

p. 293 **'in a sense'** *Ibid.*

p. 293 **'I started to'** Scannell, *Tiger*, p. 37.

p. 294 **'For the first'** Vernon Scannell, 'Coming to Life in Leeds'.

p. 294 **'I was delighted'** Scannell, *Tiger*, p. 41.

p. 294 **The position seems** Letter from Woodrow Wyatt, MP, to Prime Minister Clement Attlee, 20 November 1946, British National Archives, CAB/128/9.

p. 294 **'any mitigating circumstances'** 'House of Commons', *The Times*, 23 January 1947, p. 8.

p. 295 **This fell short** 'Few Deserters Give Up', *New York Times*, 1 April 1947, p. 14.

p. 295 **In a letter** 'Deserters from the Forces', *The Times*, 17 October 1947, p. 7.

p. 295 **At this time** Prime Minister's Private Office Memorandum, 27 November 1947, British National Archives CAB/128/9.

p. 295 **'If sleep should'** Vernon Scannell, 'On the Run', Typescript (original version 1970, rewritten March 1996), Alan Benson Collection of Vernon Scannell, 2008-10-07P, Box 4, Folder: 5.1 Scannell – Correspondence – 2007, January–March, Harry Ransom Center, University of Texas.

p. 295 **One Sunday afternoon** Scannell, *Tiger*, pp. 45–6.

p. 296 **'And they looked'** Michael Parkinson interview.

p. 296 **'Something has gone'** Vernon Scannell, 'Casualty – Mental Ward', *Of Love and War*, p. 34.

p. 297 **'After a short'** Vernon Scannell, 'Coming to Life in Leeds'.

p. 297 **'The shades of'** Scannell, *Tiger*, p. 60.

p. 297 **A former army colleague** John Scannell, Interview with the author, London, 15 February 2011.

THIRTY-TWO

p. 299 **'But,' he wrote** Whitehead Diary, p. 200.

p. 300 **'I questioned the'** 'Summary of Evidence in the Case of Whitehead, Alfred T.', in Whitehead Court Martial File.

p. 300 **'They were still'** Whitehead Diary, p. 200.

p. 301 **'Witnesses requested by'** Headquarters Seine Section Casus 1 Command (Prov) APO 887, 17 December 1945, in Whitehead Court Martial File.

p. 301 **Asked on a form** 'Memorandum to accompany the record of trial in the case of US v. Alfred T. Whitehead', Whitehead Court Martial File.

p. 302 **As in the court** Court Martial Transcript, p. 9, and 'Review of the Staff Judge Advocate', p. 1, Whitehead Court Martial File.

p. 304 **At 10.25 that** Court Martial Transcript, pp. 1–9, Whitehead Court Martial File.

EPILOGUE

p. 305 **When the army remitted** 'Memorandum for: The Secretary of the Army', from S. Harrison, Jr, Acting Chairman, Clemency and Parole Board No. 2, 22 June 1949, Whitehead Court Martial File.

p. 306 **'I find a one-inch'** R. C. Kash, Letter, To Whom It May Concern, 23 March 1949, reproduced in Whitehead Diary, p. 228. This letter is not in the Whitehead Court Martial File, which indicates it was not sent to the Department of Defense as part of his appeal.

p. 306 **In response to Whitehead's** 'Memorandum for the Secretary of the Army', from S. Harrison, Jr, Acting Chairman, Clemency and Parole Board No. 2, 22 June 1949, Whitehead Court Martial File.

p. 306 **'I am writing'** Letter, C. Alex Meacham to the Honorable Jimmy Carter, 14 March 1977, Whitehead Court Martial File.

p. 307 **'The day it arrived'** Whitehead Diary, p. 230.

p. 307 **Division veteran Jesse** 'Friends of US 2nd Division' site (Message 4208), http://groups.yahoo.com/group/Friends_of_US_2nd_Infantry_Division_WWII/message/4208

p. 309 **'I listened to'** Thomas Lindsay, email to the author, 13 October 2009.

p. 309 **'For years Dad'** Whitehead Diary, p. 230.

p. 309 **Jenkins recalled his** Simon Jenkins, 'Created on a Canvas of Needless Pain: A Poet Who Inspired the Underbelly', *The Guardian*, 29 November 2007.

p. 311 **'I was meant'** John Scannell, Interview with the author, London, 15 February 2011.

p. 311 **The ex-deserter received** email from John Scannell to the author, 9 March 2012.

p. 312 **On 11 May 1970** Vernon Scannell, Letter to James Gibson, 11 May 1970, J. Gibson Collection, Recip., Harry Ransom Center, University of Texas.

p. 312 **'And then they came'** Vernon Scannell, 'Walking Wounded', *Of Love and War*, p. 17.

p. 313 **'Would like to know'** www.bydand.com/intch5.htm.

p. 313 **Captain Horton immediately** Darkes, 'Twenty-five Years in the Military', pp.19–20.

BIBLIOGRAPHY

Books

Addison, Paul and Calder, Angus, eds., *Time to Kill: The Soldier's Experience of War in the West, 1939–1945*, London: Pimlico, 1997.

Army Ground Forces Board, *Report 639*, Washington, DC: Government Printing Office, 1945.

Barkley, Cleve C., *In Death's Dark Shadow: A Soldier's Story*, published by the author, 2006.

Barnes, B. S., *Operation Scipio: The 8th Army at the Battle of Wadi Akarit, 6th April 1943, Tunisia*, New York: Sentinel Press, 2007.

Beevor, Antony, *D-Day: The Battle for Normandy*, London: Penguin, 2009.

Bierman, John and Smith, Colin, *Alamein: War without Hate*, London: Penguin, 2003.

Bowlby, Alex, *The Recollections of Rifleman Bowlby*, London: Cassell & Co., 1999 (reprinted 2002) (originally published London: Leo Cooper, 1969).

Brager, Bruce, *The Texas 36th Division: A History*, Austin, TX: Eakin Press, 2002.

Chambers, John Whiteclay, *OSS Training in the National Parks and Service Abroad in World War II*, Washington, DC: US National Park Service, 2008.

Churchill, Winston S., *The Second World War: Vol. VI, Triumph and Tragedy*, Boston: Houghton Mifflin, 1953.

Clark, Mark, *Calculated Risk: The War Memoirs of a Great American General*, London: Harrap, 1951.

Clarke, Jeffrey J. and Smith, Robert Ross, *Riviera to the Rhine, United States Army in World War II: The European Theater of Operations*, Washington, DC: Center of Military History, US Army, 1993.

Committee of the National Research Council with the Collaboration of Science Service as a Contribution to the War Effort, *Psychology for the Fighting Man, Prepared for the Fighting Man Himself*, Washington, DC: The Infantry Journal, (and Penguin Books), 1943.

Cooke, Elliot D., *All But Thee and Me: Psychiatry at the Foxhole Level*, Infantry Journal Press, Washington, DC: 1946.

Cooper, Artemis, *Cairo in the War, 1939–1945*, London: Penguin, 1998.

Corns, Cathryn and Hughes-Wilson, John, *Blindfold and Alone: British Military Executions in the Great War*, London: Cassell, 2001.

Craig, Norman, *The Broken Plume: A Platoon Commander's Story, 1940–1945*, London: Imperial War Museum, 1982.

Crozier, S. F., *The History of the Corps of Royal Military Police*, Aldershot: Gale and Polden Ltd, 1951.

Delaforce, Patrick, *Monty's Highlanders: 51st Highland Division at War, 1939–1945*, Brighton: Tom Donovan, 1991.

Douglas, Keith, *Alamein to Zem Zem*, London: Faber & Faber, 2008 (originally published by Editions Poetry, 1946).

Douglas, Keith, *Complete Poems*, Oxford: Oxford University Press, 1978.

Ducros, Louis-Frédéric, *Montagnes Ardéchoises dans la guerre*, Vol. III: *Combats pour la libération: du 6 juin 1944 au 7 septembre 1944*, Valence, 1981.

Ellis, John, *The Sharp End: The Fighting Man in World War II*, London: Aurum Press, 1990.

Ethell, Edward O. and Caldwell, Paul, *The Thirty-Eighth United States Infantry*, Pilzen: Planografia, Novy Vsetisk and Grafika, June 1945.

Fantina, Robert, *Desertion and the American Soldier, 1776–2006*, New York: Algora Publishing, 2006.

French, David, *Raising Churchill's Army: The British Army and the War against Germany, 1939–1945*, Oxford and New York: Oxford University Press, 2000.

Funk, Arthur Layton, *Hidden Ally: The French Resistance, Special Operations, and the Landings in Southern France, 1944*, London and New York: Greenwood Press, 1992.

Fussell, Paul, *Doing Battle: The Making of a Skeptic*, Boston: Little, Brown, 1996.

Gieck, Jack, *Lichfield: The U.S. Army on Trial*, Akron, OH: University of Akron Press, 1997.

Glass, Albert J. *et al.*, eds., *Overseas Theaters: Neuropsychiatry in World War II*, Vol. II, *Medical Department, U.S. Army in World War II: Clinical Studies*, Washington, DC: Government Printing Office, 1973.

Hanson, Frederick R., ed., *Combat Psychiatry, Special Supplement, Bulletin of the U.S. Army Medical Department*, Vol. 9, November 1949.

Heller, Joseph, *Catch-22*, London: Jonathan Cape, 1962.

Hoyt, Edwin P., *The GI's War: American Soldiers in Europe during World War II*, New York: Da Capo Press, 1991.

Bibliography

Information and Education Division, U.S. Army Service Forces, *What the Soldier Thinks: A Digest of War Department Studies on the Attitude of American Troops, December 1942–September 1945*, Washington, DC: Government Printing Office, 1945.

Kaplan, Alice, *The Interpreter*, New York: Free Press, 2005.

Lewis, Norman, *Naples '44*, London: Eland Books, 1983 (originally published London: William Collins, 1978).

Linderman, Gerald, *The World within War: America's Combat Experience in World War II*, New York: Free Press, 1997.

Lockhart, Vincent, *T-Patch to Victory: The 36th Infantry Division from the Landing in Southern France to the End of World War II*, Texas: Staked Plains Press, 1981.

McLean, Allan Campbell, *The Glasshouse*, London: Calder and Boyars, 1969.

Marshall, William, *Baseball's Pivotal Era, 1945–1951*, Lexington: University Press of Kentucky, 1999.

Matloff, Maurice, *Strategic Planning for Coalition Warfare, 1943–1944*, Washington, DC: Center of Military History, US Army, 1990.

Mead, Gary, *The Doughboys: America and the First World War*, New York: Overlook Press, 2002.

Methuen, Algernon, *Anthology of Modern Verse*, London: Methuen, 1921.

Miles, Wilfrid, *The Life of a Regiment*, Vol. V: *The Gordon Highlanders, 1919–1945*, Aberdeen: The University Press, 1961.

Moorehead, Alan, *Eclipse*, New York: Harper and Row, 1968 (originally published London: Hamish Hamilton, 1945).

Moorehead, Alan, *The African Trilogy: The North African Campaign, 1940–43*, London: Cassell, 1998 (originally published London: Hamish Hamilton, 1944).

Morris, Eric, *Circles of Hell: The War in Italy 1943–1945*, London: Hutchinson, 1993.

Morison, Samuel Eliot, *The Invasion of France and Germany*, Boston: Little, Brown, 1957.

Murphy, Audie, *To Hell and Back*, New York: Picador, 2002 (originally published New York: Henry Holt, 1949).

Packard, Reynolds, *Rome Was My Beat*, Secaucus, NJ: Lyle Stuart, 1975.

Reid, Brian Holden, ed., *Military Power: Land Warfare in Theory and Practice*, London: Frank Cass, 1997.

Reynolds, David, *Rich Relations: The American Occupation of Britain, 1942–1945*, London: HarperCollins, 1995.

Rigby, Ray, *The Hill*, London: W. H. Allen, 1965.

Robertson, Walter M., *Combat History of the Second Infantry Division in World War II*, Baton Rouge, LA: Army and Navy Publishing Co., 1946.

Robichon, Jacques, *The Second D-Day*, London: Arthur Barker, 1969 (originally published in French as *Le Débarquement de Provence: 15 Août 1944*).

Salmond, J. B., *The History of the 51st Highland Division, 1939–1945*, Edinburgh: William Blackwood and Sons, 1953.

Santos, Robert L., *The Army Needs Men: An Account of the U.S. Army Rehabilitation Center at Turlock, California, 1942–1945*, Denair, CA: Alley-Cass Publications, 1997. http://wwwlibrary.csustan.edu/bsantos/army.html

Scannell, Vernon, *Epithets of War*, London: Eyre and Spottiswoode, 1969.

Scannell, Vernon, *The Tiger and the Rose: An Autobiography*, London: Hamish Hamilton, 1971.

Scannell, Vernon, *A Proper Gentleman*, London: Robson Books, 1977.

Scannell, Vernon, *Argument of Kings*, London: Robson Books, 1987.

Scannell, Vernon, *Soldiering On: Poems of Military Life*, London: Robson Books, 1989.

Scannell, Vernon, *Drums of Morning: Growing Up in the Thirties*, London: Robson Books, 1992.

Scannell, Vernon, *Of Love and War: New and Selected Poems*, London: Robson Books, 2002.

Sevareid, Eric, *Not So Wild a Dream*, New York: Alfred A. Knopf, 1946.

Sheean, Vincent, *This House against This House*, New York: Random House, 1945.

Shephard, Ben, *A War of Nerves*, London: Jonathan Cape, 2000.

Slotkin, Richard, *Lost Battalions: The Great War and the Crisis of American Nationality*, New York: Henry Holt, 2005.

Smith, H. Allen and Smith, Ira L., *Three Men on Third*, New York: Doubleday, 1951.

Stouffer, Samuel A. *et al.*, *Studies in Social Psychology in World War II: The American Soldier*, Vol. II: *Combat and Its Aftermath*, Princeton: Princeton University Press, 1949.

Strecker, Samuel A., *Their Mothers' Sons: The Psychiatrist Examines an American Problem*, Philadelphia and New York: J. B. Lippincott, 1946.

Thomas, Donald, *An Underworld at War: Spivs, Deserters, Racketeers and Civilians in the Second World War*, London: John Murray, 2003.

Tobler, Douglas H., *Intelligence in the Desert: The Recollections and Reminiscences of a Brigade Intelligence Officer*, Gold Bridge, BC: self-published, 1978.

Trevelyan, Raleigh, *Rome '44: The Battle for the Eternal City*, New York: Viking Press, 1982.

US Army, *A Manual for Courts-Martial*, Washington, DC: Government Printing Office, 1 April 1928.

Bibliography

Walker, Fred L., *From Texas to Rome*, Dallas, TX: Taylor Publishing, 1969.
Wiltse, Charles M., *The Medical Department: Medical Service in the Mediterranean and Minor Theaters*, Washington, DC: Office of the Chief of Military History, Department of the Army, 1965.
Wood, Edward W. and Ashbrook, Raleigh, *D + 1 to D + 105: The Story of the 2nd Infantry Division*, Czechoslovakia: G-3 Section, 2nd Division Headquarters, 1945.
Zaloga, Steven J., *Operation Dragoon: France's Other D-Day*, Oxford: Osprey Publishing, 2009.

Articles

'27 Paris GIs Held in Paris Black Marketing', Associated Press report, *Washington Post*, 22 September 1944.
'20,000 Youths Drafted to British Mines Desert', *Chicago Daily Tribune*, 24 October 1945.
'2,000,000 Out to See Veterans Pass By', *New York Times*, 7 May 1919.
'A Million Cheer 77th in Final Hike of War Up 5th Av.', *New York Times*, 7 May 1919.
'Appeal to Wilson for Parade of the 77th', *New York Times*, 6 April 1919.
'Army & Navy: G.I. Black Market', *Time*, 2 October 1944.
'Army & Navy – Malefactors Abroad', *Time*, 1 May 1944.
'ARMY & NAVY – Medals: Record', *Time*, 21 August 1944.
'AWOL Tarzan Pair Sentenced', *Los Angeles Times*, 27 October 1946.
'Black Market Deals of US Soldiers Told', Associated Press, *Chicago Daily Tribune*, 26 December 1944.
'British Family Fined for Help to AWOL Yanks', *Chicago Daily Tribune*, 11 July 1946.
'Conservation: Poor Young Men', *Time*, 6 February 1939.
'Crime Since the War: Theft and the Shortage of Goods', *The Times*, 23 January 1948.
'Deserters from the Forces', *The Times*, 17 October 1947.
'Few Deserters Give Up', *New York Times*, 1 April 1947.
'GIs Major Crime in London is AWOL', *New York Times*, 20 April 1944.
'High Officer Reveals: 12,000 Yanks AWOL in Europe, Half of Them in Black Market', *Washington Post*, 26 January 1945.
'History of the 77th', *New York Times*, 4 May 1919.
'House of Commons', *The Times*, 23 January 1947.
'Huge Roundup of Deserters', *Los Angeles Times*, 15 December 1945.
'London AWOL Roundup Traps a One-Star General', *Chicago Daily Tribune*, 18 May 1944.
'London in the Grip of Gangsterism', *Baltimore Sun*, 10 December 1945.

'Medicine: In Uniform and Their Right Minds', *Time*, 1 June 1942.
'MP Killed in Fight as Black Market Gang is Broken Up', Associated Press, *Washington Post*, 8 January 1945.
'News in Brief', *The Times*, 18 January 1945.
'Political Notes', *The Times*, 22 March 1945.
'The Psychiatric Toll of Warfare', *Fortune*, December 1943.
'Punishing the Army Deserter', *New York Times*, 16 June 1918.
'Question 15,161 in London Drive on Crime Wave: Comb City for 10,000 Army Deserters', *Chicago Daily Tribune*, 16 December 1945.
'Storm of Protest May Save Parade', *New York Times*, 6 April 1919.
'Who's Afraid?', *Time*, 22 November 1943.
Bishop, Joseph W., Jr, 'US Army Speech in the European Theater', *American Speech*, Vol. 21, No. 4, December 1946, p. 248. (Full article pp. 241–52.)
Campbell, Duncan, 'London in the Blitz', *The Observer*, 29 August 2010.
Connor, William M., 'The Judgmental Review in General Court-Martial Proceedings', *Virginia Law Review*, Vol. 32, No. 1, December 1945, pp. 39–88.
Ecker, Allan B., 'GI Racketeers in the Paris Black Market', *Yank* magazine, 4 May 1945.
French, David, 'Discipline and the Death Penalty in the British Army in the War against Germany During the Second World War', *Journal of Contemporary History*, Vol. 33, No. 4, October 1998, pp. 531–45.
Hyman, John A., 'From the Riviera to the Rhine', *T-Patch* (36th Division newspaper), First Anniversary Supplement, 1945, republished at texasmilitaryforcesmuseum.org/36division/archives/frame/hymans1.html.
Jenkins, Simon, 'Created on a Canvas of Needless Pain: A Poet Who Inspired the Underbelly', *The Guardian*, 29 November 2007.
Johnson, Douglas, 'Obituary: General François Binoche', *The Independent*, 27 May 1977.
Jones, Edgar and Wesseley, Simon, '"Forward Psychiatry" in the Military: Its Origins and Effectiveness', *Journal of Traumatic Stress*, Vol. 16, August 2003, pp. 411–19.
Marshall, George C., 'Biennial Report of the Chief of Staff of the United States Army, July 1, 1943, to June 30, 1945, to the Secretary of War', *Yank* magazine, 19 October 1945.
Mount, 'The Kray of South Ken', *Times Online*, 29 March 2002.
Pyle, Ernie, 'The Death of Captain Waskow', Scripps Howard News Service, 10 January 1944.
Rose, Arnold M., 'The Social Psychology of Desertion from Combat', *American Sociological Review*, Vol. 16, No. 5, October 1951, pp. 614–29.

Bibliography

Sage, Robert, 'Paris Protests Waste of Gas by Joy Riders', *Chicago Daily Tribune*, 26 October 1944.

Scannell, Vernon, 'Why I Hate the Celebration of D-Day ... and What it Was Like to Be There', *New Reporter*, May 1997.

Trewhela, Paul, 'Vernon Scannell, a Poet in Bohemian London', *Times Literary Supplement*, 5 December 2007.

War Department Pamphlet 27-4, 'Procedure for Military Executions', Washington, DC: War Department, 12 June 1944.

Werner, Wade, 'MPs in France Check U.S. Supply Thefts', *Washington Post*, 20 December 1944.

Recorded Interviews

Scannell, John, Interview with the author, London, 15 February 2011.

Scannell, Vernon, Interview, Imperial War Museum, London, 21 October 1987, Tape No. 10009.

Scannell, Vernon, Interview with Michael Parkinson, *Desert Island Discs*, BBC Radio, 29 November 1987.

Sharland, Timothy (4266), Interview, Second World War Experience Centre, Leeds.

Swales, Wilf (968), Interview, Second World War Experience Centre, Leeds.

Weiss, Steve, Interview with the author, London, 7 October 2009.

Weiss, Steve, Interview with the author, London, 28 June 2010.

Weiss, Steve, Interview with the author, Paris, 17 July 2010.

Weiss, Steve, Interview with the author, Vosges, France, 30 April 2011.

Unpublished manuscripts

Darkes, Russell J., 'Twenty-five Years in the Military', typescript, Lebanon, PA 17042: A. Archery & Printing Place, 1991.

Second Battalion Staff, 'The Second Battalion, 38th Infantry, in World War II, 1945 (edited with permission of Lieutenant Colonel Jack K. Norris by Cleve C. Barkley, 1985).

Weiss, Stephen J., 'War Dance (1943–1946)', second draft, London, 2009. Weiss has written two drafts of his memoir, which are hereafter referred to as WD/First Draft and WD/Second Draft.

Weiss, Steve, personal papers, London.

Whitehead, Alfred T. (contributing material by Selma B. Whitehead), 'Diary of a Soldier', Cape Cod, MA: printed privately by Alfred T. Whitehead and Selma B. Whitehead, 1989.

Vernon Scannell Miscellaneous

Scannell, Vernon, 'Baptism of Fire', Alan Benson Collection of Vernon Scannell, 1948–2007, Box 4, Folder 4.1 Scannell – Correspondence, 2001, January–May, Harry Ransom Center, University of Texas.

Scannell, Vernon, 'Coming to Life in Leeds', *The Listener*, 22 August 1963, galley proof in Vernon Scannell Collection, Box 4, Vernon Works: The Walking Wounded, A, T and TCCMSS Letters Recip, Miscellaneous, Folder: Scannell Letters [Corris, Eric C.], Harry Ransom Center, University of Texas.

Scannell, Vernon, notes for his autobiographical novel *The Big Time*, Scannell papers, University of Reading Archives, Special Collections Service.

Scannell, Vernon, 'On the Run', typescript (original version 1970, rewritten March 1996), Alan Benson Collection of Vernon Scannell, 1948–2007, 2008-10-07P, Box 4, Folder 5.1 Scannell – Correspondence – 2007, January–March, Harry Ransom Center, University of Texas.

Scannell, Vernon, 'The Unknown War Poet', Alan Benson Collection of Vernon Scannell, 1948–2007, 2008-10-07P, Box 4, Folder 5.1, Scannell Correspondence – 2007, January–March, Harry Ransom Center, University of Texas.

Scannell, Vernon, 'War Wounds', original transcript, Alan Benson Collection of Vernon Scannell, 1948–2007, 2008-10-07P, Box 4, Folder 5.1, Scannell – Correspondence – 2007, January–March, Harry Ransom Center, University of Texas.

Archives and Libraries

American Library in Paris, 10 rue du Général Camou, 75007 Paris, France.

Archives Nationales de France, 60 rue des Francs-Bourgeois, 75141 Paris, France.

British Library, 96 Euston Road, London NW1 2DB.

British National Archives, Kew, Richmond, Surrey TW9 4DU.

Harry Ransom Center, University of Texas, 300 West 21st Street, Austin, TX 78712.

Library of Congress, 101 Independence Avenue, Washington, DC 20540.

London Library, 14 Saint James's Square, London SW1Y 4LG.

Musée des Collections Historiques de la Préfecture de Police de Paris, 1 bis, rue des Carmes, 75005, Paris, France.

National Archives and Records Administration, 8601 Adelphi Road, College Park, MD 20740-6001 [NARA].

New York Public Library, 455 Fifth Avenue, New York, NY 10016.

Bibliography

Office of the Clerk of the Court, US Army Judiciary, 901 North Stuart Street, Suite 1200, Arlington, VA 22203-1837.
Staff Department, Advanced Infantry Officers Course, The Infantry School, Fort Benning, GA 31905.
University of Reading Library, Whiteknights, Reading, Berkshire RG6 6AE.
US Army Center of Military History, Department of the Army, Collins Hall, 102 4th Avenue, Building 34, Fort McNair, Washington DC 20319-5060.
US Army Legal Services Agency, US Army Court of Criminal Appeals, 901 North Stuart Street, Arlington, VA 22203-1837.

Films

Bad Boys of the Blitz. Directed by Steve Humphries, Testimony Films, 2005.
The Battle of San Pietro. Directed by John Huston, US Army Pictorial Service, 1945.
The Hill, Directed by Sidney Lumet, MGM, 1965.

INDEX